LEADERSHIP EDUCATION III:

LIFE SKILLS AND CAREER OPPORTUNITIES

Cover photographs courtesy of Corbis, PhotoEdit, AP/Wide World Photos, and Ilene Perlman.
Interior photographs by Ilene Perlman, unless otherwise noted.
Excerpts taken from various sources, which are referenced at the end of the book.

Copyright © 2006 by Pearson Custom Publishing
All rights reserved.

This copyright covers material written expressly for this volume by the editor/s as well as the compilation itself. It does not cover the individual selections herein that first appeared elsewhere. Permission to reprint these has been obtained by Pearson Custom Publishing for this edition only. Further reproduction by any means, electronic or mechanical, including photocopying and recording, or by any information storage or retrieval system, must be arranged with the individual copyright holders noted.

All trademarks, service marks, registered trademarks, and registered service marks are the property of their respective owners and are used herein for identification purposes only.

Excerpts from *Content Knowledge: A Compendium of Standards and Benchmarks for K-12 Education*, reprinted by permission of McREL. Copyright © 2003 McREL: Mid-Continent Research for Education and Learning, 2550 S. Parker Road, Suite 500, Aurora, CO 80014.

Printed in the United States of America

10 9 8 7 6

ISBN 0-536-16810-5

2005420490

RG/JS

Please visit our web site at *www.pearsoncustom.com*

PEARSON CUSTOM PUBLISHING
75 Arlington Street, Suite 300, Boston, MA 02116
A Pearson Education Company

Contents

CHAPTER 6 [illegible]

LESSON 1 [illegible]

[illegible]

LESSON REVIEW [illegible]

LESSON 2 [illegible]

[illegible]

LESSON REVIEW [illegible]

LESSON 3 [illegible]

[illegible]

LESSON REVIEW [illegible]

CHAPTER REVIEW [illegible]

[illegible]

Preface

Leadership Education III: Life Skills and Career Opportunities represents a significant revision, bringing up-to-date concepts into the Air Force Junior Reserve Officer Training Corps (AFJROTC) curriculum. This book focuses on the AFJROTC mission to "develop citizens of character dedicated to serving their nation and community" through providing life skills students will need upon graduation.

"Unit I: Mapping Your Future" covers educational and career opportunities. It is designed to provide you with a big-picture view of the choices you have in preparing for the future before you look at specific options. Chapter 1 reviews types of careers that you can pursue, including careers in government service, in the military, and in aerospace. Chapter 2 explores the different paths you can follow immediately after graduation—further education or vocational employment. The intent in linking the educational and technical career paths is to communicate that both choices are viable options.

"Unit II: Charting Your Financial Course" explains important concepts in building wealth. You will learn how to make a plan for earning money and for saving and spending it. A personal financial plan can be the difference between your ability to do the things you want to do and the feeling that you'll never reach your goals in life. Chapter 3 provides cadets with an overall picture of financial management before the text moves on to examine the specifics of education or technical careers. Chapter 4 explains the positive and negative aspects of using credit, the cost of college, the types of insurance options available to protect your resources, and tips for protecting your personal and financial information.

"Unit III: Aiming Toward a College Degree" focuses on applying for college and charting a course of study. In Chapter 5, you'll learn about the *criteria*, or standards, you should think about when choosing a college. You'll learn a strategy for applying to the colleges you've selected. This chapter also covers college entrance exams and college placement tests; how to write your application essay; how to prepare for an admissions interview; and what to look for during a campus visit. Chapter 6 examines aspects of preparing to go to college. It prepares you for adjusting to a more independent lifestyle, in which you'll need to manage your own time and make important choices.

"Unit IV: Pursuing a Career" examines one of the most important parts of your life. In Chapter 7, you'll learn the importance of the job-search process, the purpose of a résumé, and appropriate steps in building interviewing skills. Chapter 8 includes lessons on how to plan your professional development, the communication process in an organization, and how to seek feedback and promotions in the workplace.

This book has been prepared especially for you, the cadet—to increase your knowledge and success as an American citizen and a member of the AFJROTC.

Acknowledgements

The subject matter in *Leadership Education III: Life Skills and Career Opportunities* was based on suggestions received from Air Force Junior Reserve Officer Training Corps (AFJROTC) instructors from around the world. The Air Force Officer Accession and Training Schools (AFOATS) Curriculum Division team involved in the production effort was under the direction of Dr. Charles Nath III, Director of Curriculum, and his deputy, Major Chris Senkbeil, at Maxwell Air Force Base, Alabama. The Chief of Junior ROTC Curriculum, Lieutenant Colonel John Kiecana, and all of the AFJROTC Curriculum Area Managers, especially Naomi L. Mitchell, completed an exceptional leadership team, resulting in an outstanding product for the AFJROTC program. Special thanks go to the curriculum's primary editor DeShana Chisolm. We commend DeShana for her persistent efforts to produce the best academic materials possible for our units worldwide.

We would like to express our gratitude to the Pearson Custom Publishing team for all its hard work in publishing this new book. That team consisted of subcontractors at High Stakes Writing, LLC—Lawrence J. Goodrich, W. Dees Stallings, John G. Birdsong, Linda Harteker, and Keith S. Collins; from Perspectives, Inc.—Philip G. Graham, Catherine Boone, Emily G. Haney, Erika Harvey, and Suzanne M. Perry; Ilene Perlman (photography), Mia Saunders (graphic design and page layout), and numerous Pearson Custom Publishing personnel, including David Gehan, Ed Perlmutter, Christopher Will, Ruth Moore, Jennifer Sczerbinski, Erika Hayden, and Christopher O'Brien.

We would also like to thank the following AFJROTC units for their support in allowing Pearson Custom Publishing photographers to take photos of their facilities, cadets, staff, and activities for publication in this text: VA-091, Randolph-Macon Academy, Front Royal, Virginia; and MA-061, Quincy High School, Quincy, Massachusetts. These units' participation significantly helped us make this new text more appealing to our high school audience and instructors.

The AFJROTC mission is to develop citizens of character dedicated to serving their nation and community. Our goal is to create materials that provide a solid foundation for producing contributing members of society able to productively fulfill their citizenship roles. We believe this course continues the precedent set with the previous curriculum materials. All the people identified above came together on this project—to form one great team providing "world-class" materials to all of our schools.

UNIT 1

Mapping Your Future

Unit Chapters

In Your Home and Community

LEARNING FROM OTHERS' EXPERIENCE

Talk to three adults whom you know. Ask them when they decided which career to follow, what training or education they pursued to qualify for it, and how satisfied they are with their career choices. Also find out if any of them has changed careers, and if so, why. Compare your findings with those of other cadets.

AIR FORCE
JUNIOR
ROTC

CHAPTER

1

Career Opportunities

Chapter Outline

The main thing I tell the kids is to study hard, do their best, and stay in school. I also tell them not to ever give up on their dream if it is something that they really want to do in life. Rejection and failure [are] likely, but persistence can pay off in the end.

—Astronaut Don Thomas

LESSON

1

Researching and Choosing Careers

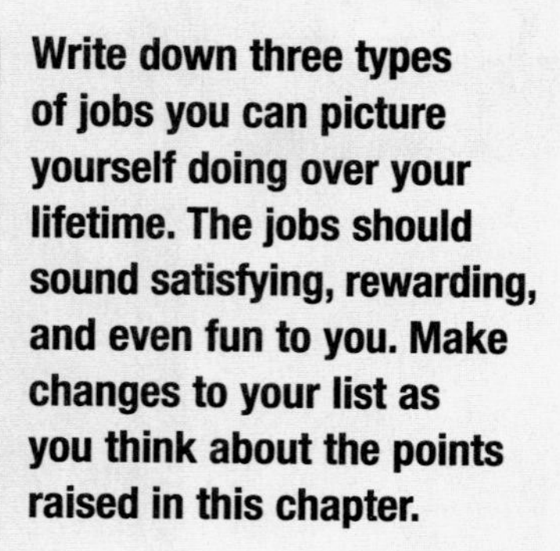

Quick Write

Write down three types of jobs you can picture yourself doing over your lifetime. The jobs should sound satisfying, rewarding, and even fun to you. Make changes to your list as you think about the points raised in this chapter.

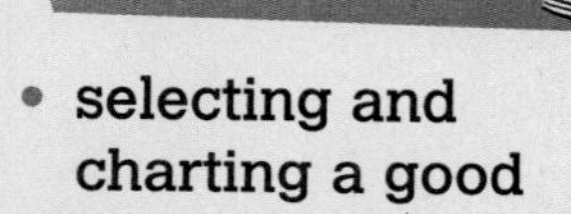

Learn About...

- selecting and charting a good career path
- careers versus jobs
- career direction—getting to know yourself

Selecting and Charting a Good Career Path

You want to have a career that is fulfilling and rewarding, as well as enjoyable. Everyone does. After all, you will probably spend 8 to 10 hours a day or more on the job. That's two-thirds of your waking hours!

Finding the right career isn't easy. The world is getting more competitive and more technical every day. Because of this, most occupations will require a greater understanding of science and math. It will be to your advantage to learn these subjects well.

Good grades are also important. For example, if you want to be a doctor, you will need to go to college and to medical school. Medical schools accept only students who finish college with a very high grade point average. Working hard in all your classes is essential.

College graduation and a job probably seem a long way off right now. But this is the time to figure out the direction you want to take and how to get there. This doesn't mean that you'll be stuck forever with the decision you make now. Most people change their life goals several times as they get older. The average person undergoes several career changes in a lifetime.

Decisions you make now are still very important—if you have a tentative idea of the direction you want your life to take, it will help you focus. This will improve your ability to succeed in school and in life.

Careers Versus Jobs

Though often used interchangeably, the words *career* and *job* have different meanings. The difference is one of attitude and lifestyle. A **job** *is work that a person does to make a living*. A career does much more. A **career** *is activity that defines a person's working life. It provides opportunities for continuous advancement and learning*. The words **profession** and **occupation** have the same meaning as career. If you have a career, you are willing to put in some extra effort to get ahead—go back to school, take training programs offered by your employer, or work extra hours so you can do your job better. Having a career means having a plan to get more skilled at your job as time goes on.

Careers offer opportunities for advancement. A career often involves five or six positions, perhaps in several industries. Each position has a different level of responsibility and difficulty, as well as salary. In each step, you'll have an opportunity to apply your increased experience.

Jobs, by contrast, are positions in which employees perform specific duties within designated hours for specific pay. Generally, these duties are similar from one day to the next. A job generally provides a basic living. It pays for food and shelter. It may not give you a chance to improve your lifestyle or afford many luxuries.

With respect to jobs and careers, what counts is not where you start but what you do once you've started. As an example, at age 16 you might get a job bussing tables at a local restaurant. If you like it, you may decide to make your career in the food industry. Over your working life, you could move on to a succession of positions as a short-order cook, assistant chef, head chef, and manager. You might one day own your own restaurant. These positions all fit the definition of a career. They do not have to be within the same company. They do not always require a college degree. Each does, however, require more training and a higher level of performance. The experience gained in one job helps prepare you for the succeeding position. At some point, you can say that you have a career.

You may also enter the job market bussing tables and not turn that job into a career step. You may move on to a position as a gas station attendant, then a cashier, then something else. Over 40 years of working life, you may hold jobs as a driver, shipping clerk, store salesperson, and maintenance worker. None of these jobs would prepare you directly for your next job. Each position is unrelated to the next. At the end of 40 years, you would have held a series of jobs, but you would not have had a career.

Learn About...

- career options
- what employers are looking for
- career factors
- career planning and information sources

Vocabulary

- job
- career
- profession
- occupation
- aptitudes
- abilities
- interests
- values
- attitude
- Student Educational Employment Program
- networking

Because they require more and more experience, most careers offer better salaries than jobs do. This isn't always the case. While money is an important factor in selecting a job or career, it is not the only consideration.

Career or job: The choice is up to you. If you choose a career, your only limits will be how much you are willing and able to learn, how much authority and responsibility you want, and what lifestyle changes you wish to strive for.

If you choose to have a series of jobs, you will provide for your daily needs, but your ability to advance will be more limited.

It's also important to find something that you enjoy. Work doesn't have to be boring! And if you find something you like to do, you'll probably do it well. That's a good recipe for success in the workplace.

Career Direction—Getting to Know Yourself

The most important thing you can do when choosing a career path is to know yourself. Ask two simple questions:

- What do I want to do?
- What am I suited to do?

A career choice involves your feelings, your personal needs, and your insights into yourself. You must be aware of your aptitudes and abilities, interests, values, attitudes, and physical abilities. In other words, you have to know yourself well.

What Are Your Aptitudes and Abilities?

Aptitudes *are talents or skills you possess or that you believe you can develop with practice or training.* What do you like to do in your spare time? What subjects do you like most at school? The answers to these questions are clues as to where your aptitudes lie. Physical **abilities,** *the powers you were born with,* such as good eyesight and a strong back, come into play as well.

For example, have you always enjoyed taking things apart and putting them back together? This is a sign of a mechanical ability that would be useful in a job as an auto mechanic or a career as an aeronautics engineer. Perhaps you enjoy solving crossword puzzles. This is an indication of an aptitude for problem solving. It would be useful as a program analyst or an accountant. Maybe an English teacher told you that you write well. Positions throughout the business world require this skill.

Think about any part-time jobs you've held. You'll probably realize that you could do some things more easily than you could do others. These, too, are good indicators of aptitudes and abilities. You may realize that you really liked sales—you enjoyed talking to people, and they enjoyed talking to you. You were good at persuading them to do something. Your experience at a plant store may have shown you that horticulture is a field you would like to explore.

What Are Your Interests?

Your *likes, dislikes, hopes, or wishes* are part of your **interests.** Interest tests (called inventories) can tell you how your interests compare with those of people already in the occupations you are considering. Make sure, however, that your interests are matched by an aptitude for the work. An interest in being a graphic artist is just wishful thinking, for example, unless you have the artistic aptitude required.

What Are Your Values?

Values *are what give your life meaning. They are the inner goals you strive for in an effort to be a better person.* People often describe values in terms of moral, religious, or political beliefs.

It's important to consider your values when choosing a career. For example, if you value service to others, you may want to enter a career where you can help others. Such careers include social service, health care, or teaching.

What Are Your Attitudes?

Certain temperaments fit some jobs and careers better than others do. If you are usually calm and not easily disturbed, you would make a better police officer than someone who is quick-tempered.

If you want a reliable indicator of your temperament, ask a guidance counselor to administer an **attitude** inventory. It will tell you about *your typical mood and activity levels.*

But remember that inventories are only a snapshot of one point in your life. They may give you an idea of what traits you want to develop or overcome, but they are not a life sentence. History is full of examples of people who overcame personal limitations to do great things.

Career Options

Several possible career paths lie in front of you. The path you take will influence the amount of education you will need and the experience you must gain to prepare for your chosen career. Among your options are working in the private sector; working for the federal, state, or local government (including as a teacher); or serving in the military. Each option provides employment in a fascinating variety of fields. Some will require a high school diploma; others might demand years of postgraduate university study.

Making informed decisions about a career requires information about opportunities available, especially ones that will be open to you in the future. Figure 1.1 lists what the US Bureau of Labor Statistics (BLS) expects to be the fastest-growing occupations in the United States through the year 2014. Note that health-care occupations make up 10 of the 20 fastest-growing occupations. Computer occupations account for five out of the 20.

Figure 1.2 lists occupations that the BLS expects to show the largest increase in terms of overall numbers of people employed. The 20 occupations listed in this figure will account for more than one-third of all new jobs until the year 2014. Health occupations will account for some of these increases. Other growth areas are education, sales, transportation, office support, and food service.

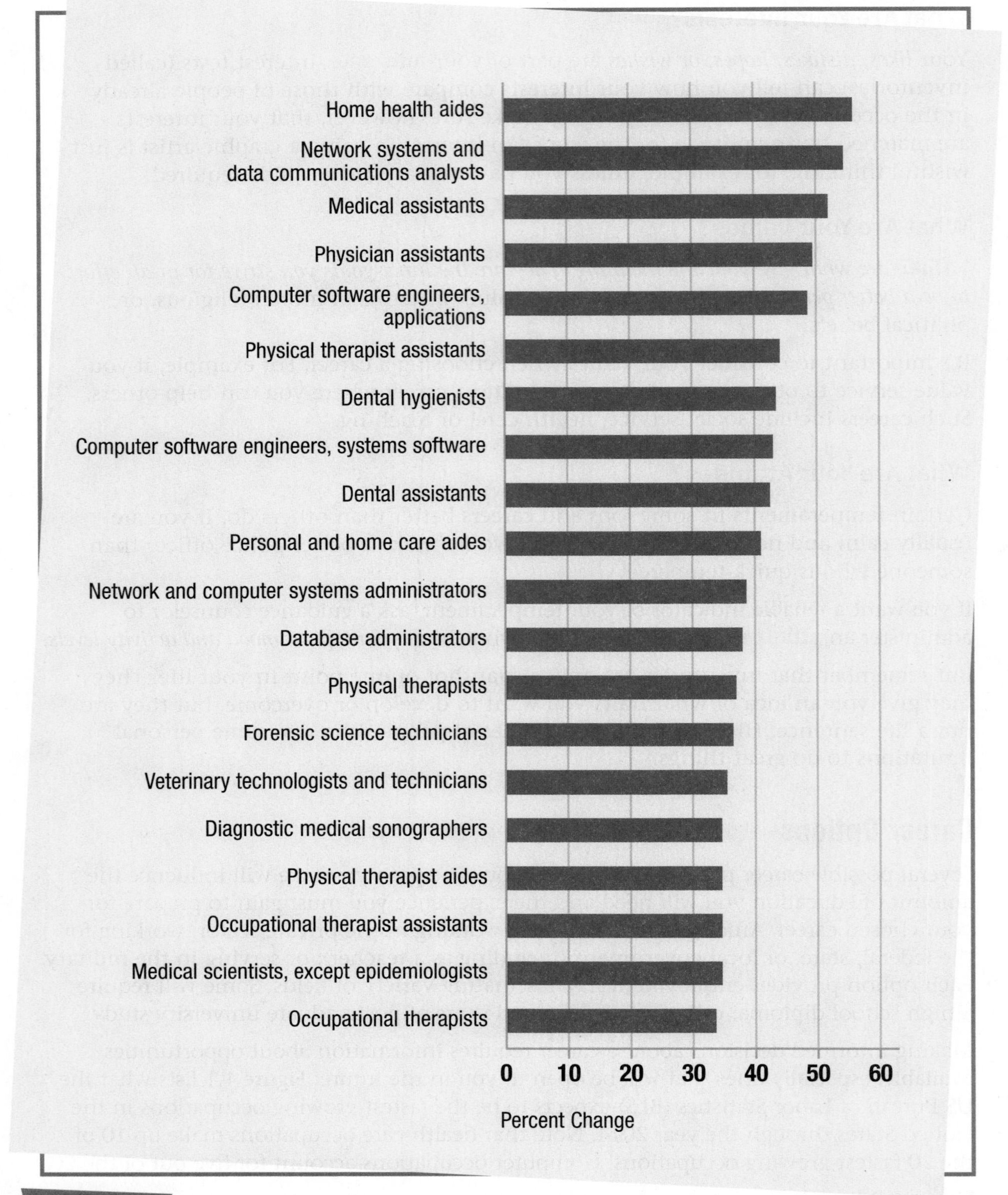

FIGURE 1.1

Fastest Growing Occupations in the United States through 2014

Taken from *www.bls.gov*

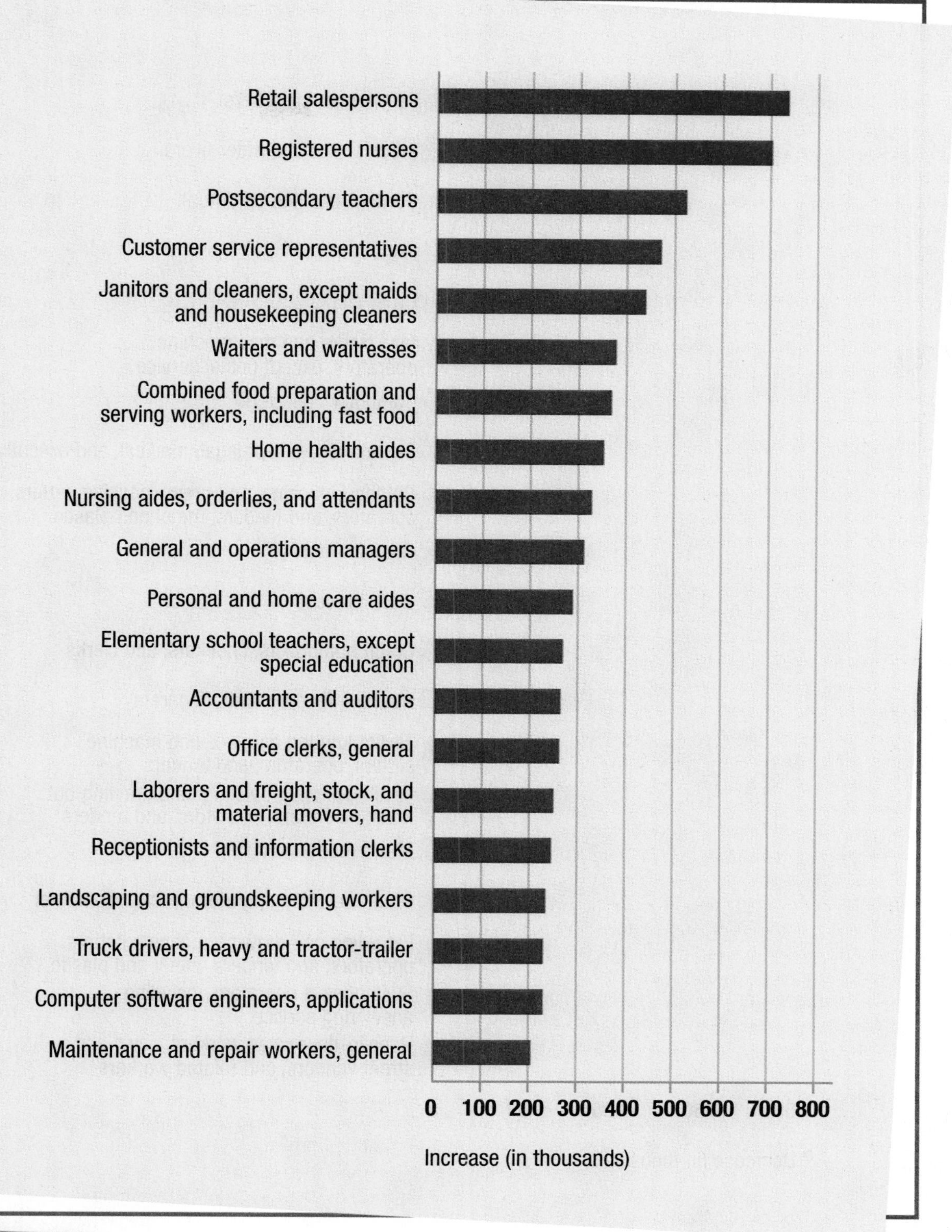

FIGURE 1.2

Occupations with the Largest Numerical Increase in Employment through 2014
Taken from *www.bls.gov*

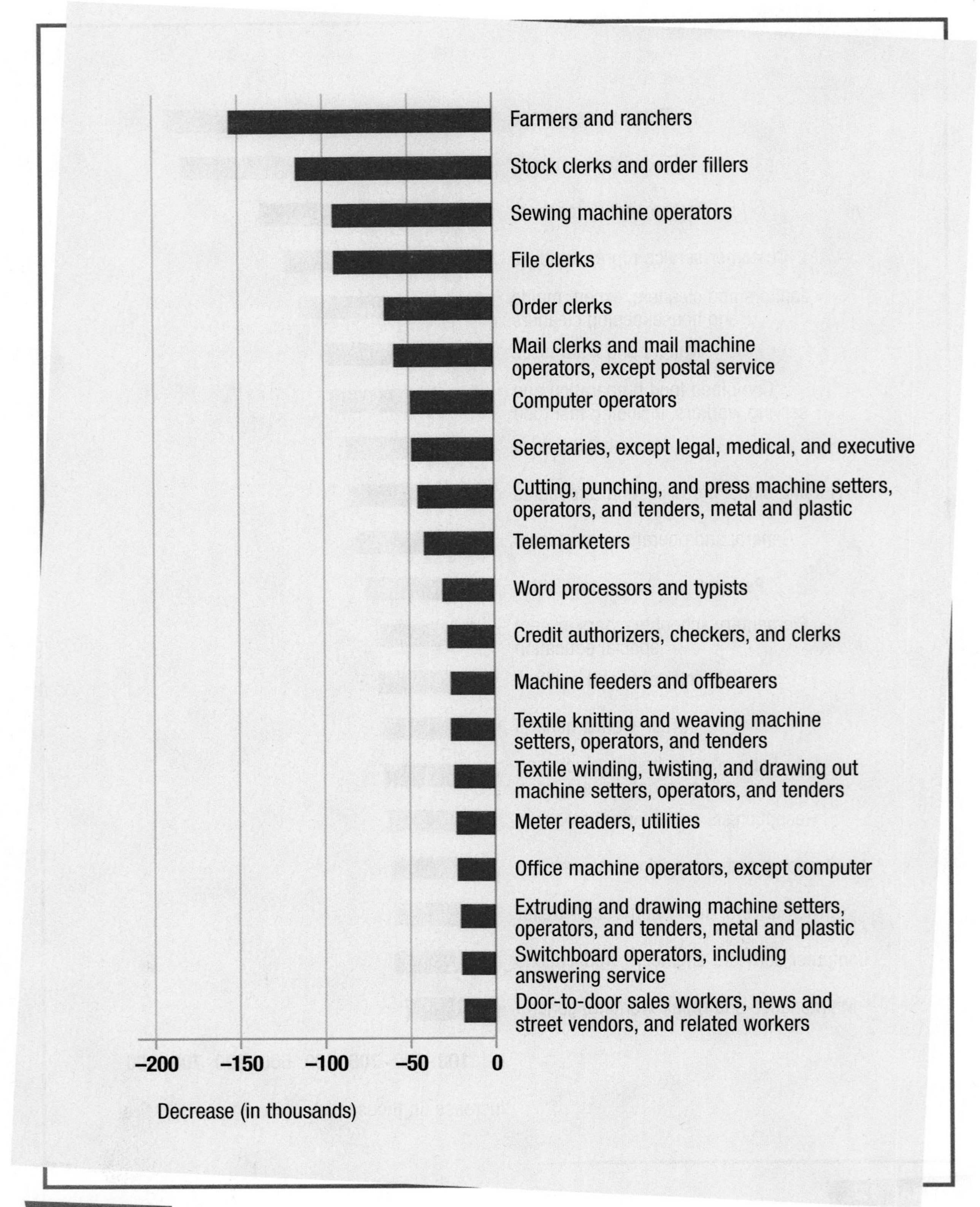

FIGURE 1.3

Occupations with the Largest Numerical Decrease in Employment through 2014
Taken from *www.bls.gov*

All these high-growth occupations are in service-producing industries as opposed to goods-producing industries. This reflects a long-term trend of the US economy.

Some fields are expected to lose jobs, and you'll want to know which they are. Figure 1.3 shows some of these. Economic sectors lose jobs because of technological advances or changes in business practices, among other factors. For example, machines now enable farmers to produce more food with fewer people. At the same time, larger farms are constantly absorbing smaller ones. As a result, there are fewer and fewer jobs for farmers and ranchers.

Most of the 20 occupations with the largest expected decreases are office and administrative support and production occupations. Increased use of technology will largely cause these job decreases as well. For example, employment of typists is expected to decline because of the wider use of personal computers.

So, if you have always wanted to be a farmer or a travel agent (another one of the occupations likely to lose jobs), you may want to think about other ways to work in the agriculture or travel fields than in those particular positions.

In the end, however, statistics are just statistics. Be aware of them, but don't give them too much weight. Consider all the types of positions that interest you, regardless of overall employment prospects in that field. Try to understand what draws you to these particular jobs. If you are drawn to a career that seems to have a bleak future, maybe you'll be the one who changes that future for the better!

Career Examples

Now it's time to look at some specific careers. Here are some examples of careers that interest many people. Even if none of them sounds interesting to you, reviewing them will help you learn how to analyze other careers that are more appealing.

Computer Animator

The Payoff: Movie and television studios, as well as advertising, Internet, and multimedia firms, pay top dollar for technology-versed animators. Most animators start their projects by drawing sketches by hand. Then they re-create the images on a computer program and add movement and sometimes sound. There is work in both two-dimensional (cartoons, for example) and three-dimensional animation.

What You Can Do Now: You will need a solid knowledge of painting and drawing techniques.

Next Step: A bachelor's degree in art, computer animation, or graphics is ideal.

Computer animators draw sketches by hand, transfer the images to a computer, and add movement.
Courtesy of Kim Kulish/Corbis Images

Customer Service Representative

The Payoff: Customer service representatives answer customers' questions about products or services and handle and resolve complaints. They communicate with customers by telephone; by e-mail, fax, or US mail; or in person. Some customer service representatives handle general questions and complaints, whereas others specialize in a particular area.

What You Can Do Now: High school courses in computers, English, or business can help you prepare for a job in customer service. Your state employment service offices can provide information about job opportunities for customer service representatives.

Next Step: Most customer service representative jobs require only a high school diploma. Because employers are demanding a more skilled workforce, however, many customer service jobs now require an associate or a bachelor's degree. Basic-to-intermediate computer knowledge and good interpersonal skills are also important.

Dental Assistant

The Payoff: Dental assistants work side-by-side with dentists as the latter examine and treat patients. They make patients as comfortable as possible in the dental chair, prepare them for treatment, and obtain their dental records. Assistants also sterilize and disinfect instruments and equipment, prepare trays of instruments for dental procedures, and instruct patients on postoperative and general oral health care.

What You Can Do Now: High school students interested in a career as a dental assistant should take courses in biology, chemistry, health, and office practices. The American Dental Association offers information on dental assistant careers at *http://www.ada.org/public/education/careers/assistant_bro.asp*.

Next Step: Most assistants learn their skills on the job, although an increasing number of assistants enroll in dental-assisting programs offered by community and junior colleges, trade schools, technical institutes, or the armed forces.

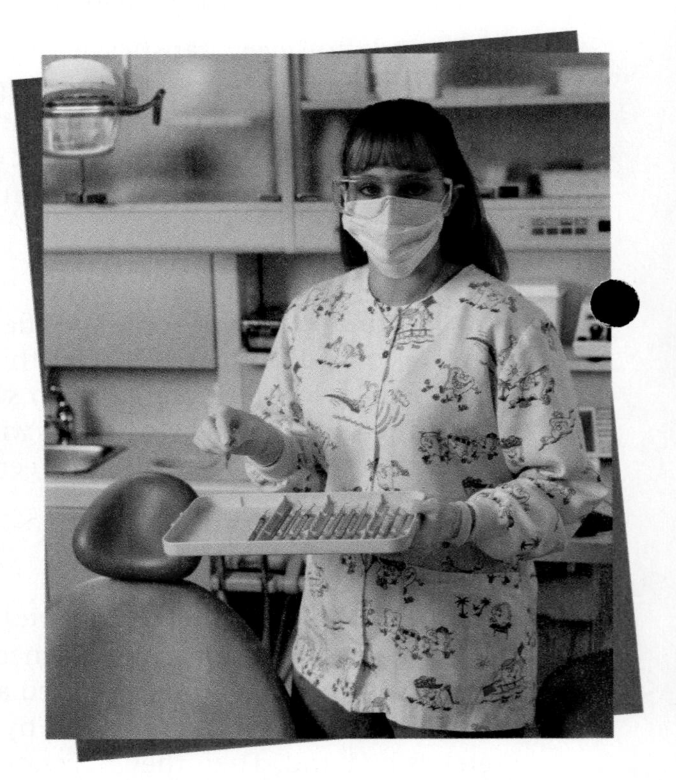

Dental assistants sterilize and disinfect instruments and equipment. They also prepare trays of instruments for dental procedures.
Courtesy of Corbis Images

Environmental Scientist/Engineer

The Payoff: Saving the world is possible, and this career offers one way to do it. Environmental technicians collect and test samples of water, soil, and air. They design ways to prevent and combat pollution.

What You Can Do Now: You can find information and links at the Environmental Career Organization's website at *www.eco.org.*

Next Step: Most technicians have two-year degrees in environmental technologies. Scientists need a four-year degree in environmental or chemical engineering.

Food-Preparation and Serving Workers

The Payoff: Food-preparation workers peel and cut vegetables, trim meat, prepare poultry, and perform other duties, such as keeping work areas clean and monitoring temperatures of ovens and stovetops. Food-and-beverage-serving workers are the frontline of customer service in restaurants, coffee shops, and other food-service establishments. These workers greet customers, escort them to seats and hand them menus, take food-and-drink orders, and serve food and beverages.

What You Can Do Now: High school or vocational school programs may offer courses in basic food safety and handling procedures and general business and computer classes for those who want to manage or open their own business. Almost 19 percent of cooks and food-preparation workers were 16 to 19 years old in 2004 and almost 11 percent had variable schedules. Most serving jobs are part-time, so many opportunities exist for young people; in fact, about one-fourth of part-time workers in these jobs in 2004 were 16 to 19 years old. You can find information about restaurant careers on the National Restaurant Association's website, *www.restaurant.org/careers/advice.cfm.*

Next Step: Most positions as fast-food or short-order cooks and food-preparation workers require little education or training. These workers learn most of their skills on the job. You won't need a high school diploma for beginning jobs, but you should have one if you're planning a career as a cook or chef. Most food-and-beverage-serving workers pick up their skills on the job by observing and working with more-experienced workers. Some full-service restaurants provide new dining room employees with some form of classroom-type training.

Geneticist

The Payoff: Studies say you can blame genes for everything: your health, your weight, even how happy you are. Genetics is one of the leading fields of biomedical research. Researchers are needed to use our knowledge of genetics to find treatments for disease and to study the genetic makeup of plants and animals.

What You Can Do Now: Try for an internship at a hospital, university lab, biotechnology firm, or pharmaceutical company. You can read the pamphlet Careers in Genetics at the Genetics Society of America website, *genetics.faseb.org/genetics/g-gsa/genetics_careers.shtml.*

Next Step: You will need a bachelor's degree in biology or chemistry. Advanced degrees in genetics are helpful.

Health Care Information Specialist

The Payoff: Maybe you are interested in medicine but can't stand the sight of blood. This position combines knowledge about health with computer skills—but no needles. Specialists are in charge of patients' files in hospitals and clinics. They might ponder security or legal issues when computerizing files or create databases to analyze medical data.

What You Can Do Now: Volunteer at a hospital or in a doctor's office. Knowledge of spreadsheet programs, as well as courses in business, computers, and life sciences, are a key. You can learn more online from the American Health Information Management Association at *www.ahima.org/careers/career_counseling.asp.*

Next Step: In the health care information field, an entry-level job—the first job in a series of jobs that eventually defines a career—might require only a high school education. But if you want to move up in this field, you'll need to go to college and study computer science or a similar technical subject. You'll also need to take courses in biology, chemistry, and the medical field.

Intellectual Property Lawyer

The Payoff: Protecting the ideas of inventors and creators—from musicians and artists to scientists—is big business. These lawyers deal with issues such as who owns what online and who has the right to make a certain product.

What You Can Do Now: Communication skills are essential, so join the debate team, and focus on writing or even acting classes. Look for internships in the legal departments of companies and at law firms.

Next Step: Get ready for at least seven more years of school! You'll need a college degree as well as a law school diploma.

Medical Assistant

The Payoff: Medical assistants help doctors and other health-care practitioners keep their offices running smoothly. They perform many administrative duties, including answering telephones, greeting patients, updating and filing patients' medical records, filling out insurance forms, handling correspondence, scheduling appointments, arranging for hospital admissions and laboratory services, and handling billing and bookkeeping.

What You Can Do Now: Volunteer experience in the health-care field is helpful. The American Association of Medical Assistants offers career information on the Web at *http://www.aama-ntl.org/medassisting/ma_career.aspx.*

Next Step: You'll probably need at least a high school diploma or the equivalent. Many medical assistants also get a certificate or an associate's degree. Recommended high school courses include mathematics, health, biology, typing or keyboarding, bookkeeping, computers, and office skills.

Online Content Developer

The Payoff: Don't be fooled by the technical title. Creative people with computer skills are wanted on the Internet to write, edit, and design.

What You Can Do Now. Here's your excuse to surf the Web all the time! Get familiar with what's new and out there.

Next Step: There are no strict requirements. A degree in journalism, English, or the arts is helpful.

Physical Therapist

The Payoff: Therapists use exercise and endurance training to treat people with muscular problems. Their patients include victims of strokes and even athletes.

What You Can Do Now: A hospital is the best place to volunteer. But opportunities are everywhere, including health centers, sports facilities, and nursing homes. A career guide, *A Career in Physical Therapy,* is available from the American Physical Therapy Association at *www.apta.org/Content/NavigationMenu/Consumers/ACareerinPhysicalTherapy/Default1756.htm*

Next Step: Almost 150 colleges offer a four-year degree in physical therapy. To practice, you must pass a state examination.

Telecommunications Technician

The Payoff: Demand is on the rise for technicians who can install software, configure modems, and set up cables and networks.

What You Can Do Now: You will need basic know-how regarding computers and electrical currents. Try to get some experience in computer and Internet services companies as well as at firms such as financial brokerage houses, which need constantly updated information.

Next Step: No degree or license is needed to become a technician. Telecommunications courses are helpful.

Webmaster

The Payoff: Every company wants a website, and every website needs someone to maintain it. A webmaster's duties may include computer programming, marketing, updating content, and generating concepts.

What You Can Do Now: Hypertext Markup Language (html) is the basic programming language, and it is not too hard to learn. Eventually, you will need to learn Internet applications and graphics programs.

Next Step: A bachelor's degree in computer science is useful, but many webmasters have backgrounds in marketing or communications. What's important are your computer and programming skills.

Working for the Federal Government

The federal government is the largest employer in the United States. It employs more than 2,715,000 people. It hires hundreds of thousands of people each year. Federal jobs are found in every state and every large city, as well as in 200 countries around the world.

Working for the federal government can be very fulfilling. The Office of Personnel Management (OPM), with headquarters in Washington, D.C., is the employment agency for the United States Government. OPM maintains a website (*www.usajobs.opm.gov*) that lists all federal jobs.

When a federal department or agency has a position available, it issues a vacancy announcement. The information is posted to the USAJobs website listed in the paragraph above. The announcement provides information on the duties and requirements of the position and instructions on how and where to apply.

Two workers with the US Department of Agriculture inspect a row of plants at a government research facility.
Courtesy of Richard T. Nowitz/Corbis Images

Once the deadline for applications is reached, the agency looking for employees asks the OPM to prepare a list of the qualified persons who applied for the vacancy. The agency reviews the applications and contacts the most promising candidates.

Besides OPM's USAJobs website listed above, you can visit *federaljobs.net/employme.htm* for a listing of federal jobs and other helpful information on federal employment.

Student Educational Employment Program

The purpose of the **Student Educational Employment Program** is to attract students into the government jobs sector. These programs *offer on-the-job experience that could lead to a full-time career with the government after you finish your schooling*. Industry and government use these programs to identify prospects for future hiring. The Student Education Employment Program is open to students pursuing a diploma, academic or vocational certificate, or degree. You may be hired under this program if you are working at least half-time for:

- a high school diploma or general equivalency diploma (GED)
- a vocational or technical school certificate
- a degree (associate, baccalaureate, graduate or professional).

The Student Educational Employment Program has two components. The first component, the Student Temporary Employment Program, introduces students to the work environment and teaches basic workplace skills. The second component, the Student Career Experience Program, provides experience that is related to the student's academic and career goals. You can find complete information on federal student employment opportunities at *http://www.opm.gov/employ/students/intro.asp*

What Employers Are Looking For

What qualities do employers want their employees to have? Besides skills associated with the particular occupation, here are a few more:

- ability to work with others
- problem-solving and creative-thinking skills
- technical aptitude (for example, computer literacy)
- good communication skills
- willingness and ability to learn and accept responsibility
- versatility and flexibility
- dependability and honesty
- good reading, writing, and math skills
- personal financial literacy (ability to handle the money you earn as well as to exercise appropriate responsibility regarding the organization's property).

Employers also want people who have developed personal responsibility toward their work. This means getting to work on time, getting your work done, and working as a team player to accomplish company goals.

Career Factors

You'll need to consider many factors as you decide on a career path or specific job. Table 1.1 lists some of the primary career factors that will influence your choice.

TABLE 1.1

Primary Career Factors

EDUCATION	Your level of formal knowledge and training. Education greatly increases your career potential.
EXPERIENCE	Your combined knowledge, skills, and self-confidence gained through events and activities. Experience adds to your earning potential and can come from jobs, internships, and volunteer work.
SKILLS AND TALENTS	Abilities you possess. Education and training enhance your abilities.
INTERESTS AND TEMPERAMENT	Aspects of your personality that affect the kinds of work you prefer and the settings in which you can work effectively.
JOB AVAILABILITY	Positions available at a given time and place that match your skills, experience, and education. Some jobs are available only in specific locations, such as large cities or company headquarters.
EARNING POTENTIAL	Certain professions or careers have higher earning potential than others do.
PERSONAL NEEDS	Fringe benefits and other factors that influence job satisfaction, such as insurance, vacation, on-site child care, and sick leave.

Career Planning and Information Sources

What is right for you? A job or a career? Will you enter the work force right out of high school, or will you pursue a higher education? Will you join the military? Make the choice with a lot of thought. But also be willing to change if a particular direction doesn't seem right. Eventually, you'll find a path that's good for you. Go for it!

Good career planning includes four tasks:

1. discovering your attitudes, interests, abilities, and preferences
2. gathering information on different career options
3. matching your interests with possible occupations
4. taking the steps necessary to reach your career goal.

Later chapters in this book will discuss the job-search process in detail, including writing a résumé, applying for a job, and job interviewing. The remainder of this lesson will discuss how to gather the information you'll need for good decision-making.

In the Internet age, you have more information available to you than high school students have ever had. But many more-traditional information sources can still give you valuable information you might not find anywhere else.

Online Job Information Sources

The following sites are good resources. Both may also be available as books in your school career center or library:

- *The Occupational Outlook Handbook,* a career-information resource produced by the US Department of Labor that provides information on approximately 250 civilian and military occupations. You can find it at *www.bls.gov/oco/.*
- *The Dictionary of Occupational Titles* gives titles for thousands of jobs. It might be a good source of ideas if you are having a hard time imagining what you could do for a career. You can find it at *www.wave.net/upg/immigration/dot_index.html.*

Several other websites provide information to help people assess their potential in the job market. Some offer free assessments, and others offer the assessment for a fee. The following websites are two examples:

- *www.assessment.com* provides a free online career assessment test and appraisal through MAPP, also known as the Motivational Appraisal of Personal Potential.
- *www.Careerexplorer.net* offers aptitude and assessment testing to help you find a satisfying career.

Other Sources of Information

Books

A quick visit to your local library or bookstore will reveal dozens of books that give career and job-seeking advice. Check out or buy a couple that look interesting, read them, and compare the differences.

Local Resources and Services

You can get career and job information at many places in your local community. Visit your state or local job services office. Read newspaper or online job ads to get an idea of what kinds of skills employers are looking for. Glance through the business section of your local newspaper to see what kinds of new businesses might be opening. Visit the local chamber of commerce. Attend trade shows if there are any in your area. Visit the local branch of a union if the members work in an area that interests you.

Networking

You will hear the word **networking** a lot throughout your career. It means *meeting people and making contacts*. It is one of the best ways to learn about job or career openings.

Begin by consulting your friends. They know you best. Interacting with fellow cadets to discuss career paths and preferences can be a valuable way to explore new ideas and see whether yours make sense.

Ask relatives or neighbors about possible careers. People who are working often hear about job openings before businesses make them public, and those people may be able to give you a good lead.

Finally, talk with professionals and the people who visit your school during career days. If possible, attend the career days at other schools, including colleges and universities in your areas. Use these events to learn about the requirements for entering various occupations.

CHECKPOINTS

Lesson 1 Review

Using complete sentences, answer the following questions on a sheet of paper.

1. Why is it important to select the right career?
2. What is the difference between a job and a career?
3. What aptitudes and abilities, interests, values, and attitudes make you the person you are?
4. What careers sound most appealing to you? How could you learn more about them?
5. What qualities do you have that employers will appreciate?
6. What qualities do you think you need to develop to make yourself more valuable to employers?

Applying Career-Choosing Skills

7. Take the list of three types of jobs you wrote for the Quick Write. Look up each job in the **Occupational Outlook Handbook** and write down the educational qualifications and salary information. Then write a list of the advantages and disadvantages of each position and rank them in your order of preference. Which factors helped you decide the rankings?

LESSON 2

Military Careers

Quick Write

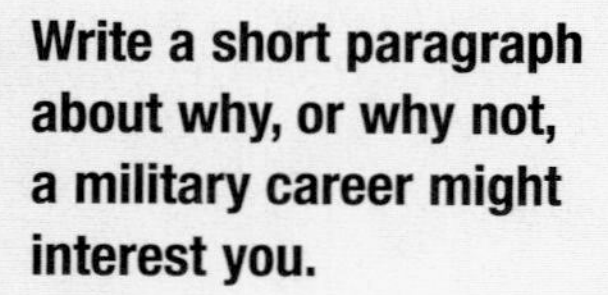

Write a short paragraph about why, or why not, a military career might interest you.

Learn About...

- military service as a career option
- the Air and Space Expeditionary Force
- entering the Air Force as a member of the enlisted corps
- entering the Air Force as a member of the officer corps

Military Service as a Career Option

When you're starting to make plans for your career, the options are endless. Service in the armed forces is one of those options. The armed forces include four branches: the Air Force, Army, Navy, and Marine Corps. Each branch has its own mission and purpose.

The armed forces are America's largest employer. More than 1.4 million people are part of the armed forces today. These men and women have varied skills, knowledge, and talents. The armed forces have more than 4,100 career specialties. With such a wide range of career options, military service offers something for almost everyone.

As a branch of the armed services, the United States Air Force (USAF) consists of approximately 325,000 men and women. The USAF is the primary air and space arm of our nation's armed forces. The men and women of the Air Force fly, maintain, and support the world's most technically advanced air and space vehicles. These vehicles include long-range bombers, supersonic fighters, reconnaissance aircraft, and many others. The Air Force uses them to protect the interests of the United States and its allies.

If you want to join the armed forces, you have two basic options. You may enter military service after high school. During military training, you'll gain job skills and work experience. Or you may go to college first. This will be the first step in preparation for a career as an Air Force officer.

This lesson contains basic information about careers in the military. It explains career options and entry requirements and describes the benefits of a military career.

Why Choose a Military Career?

Military careers are challenging. They require hard work and intelligence. The work offers great responsibility. It requires you to be strong—in mind, body, and spirit. Military careers appeal to people who are adventurous. In return for your dedication, the military will give you a chance to learn job skills and gain work experience. You may choose to make the military your career. You may apply the skills gained in the military to a job as a civilian. A **civilian** *is a person who is not on active duty in the armed forces.*

Families often find military service to be a calling—a family tradition that is passed from one generation to the next. But in today's military, families are creating traditions of their own. Take brothers Greg and Matthew Arnig. Each is an Air Force captain and pilot. Their father, a retired Air Force senior master sergeant, used to take them to air shows at Hanscom Air Force Base, Massachusetts, when they were young. Those trips sparked their desire to attend the US Air Force Academy and become Air Force pilots.

Vocabulary

- civilian
- civilian equivalents
- enlisted personnel
- Airman
- noncommissioned officer
- senior noncommissioned officer
- security investigation
- term of enlistment
- basic training
- commissioned officers
- cadet

Military work requires you to be strong in mind, body, and spirit.

(Clockwise from top left) Courtesy of: Ed Kashi/Corbis Images; Steve Kaufman/Corbis Images; Adrin Snyder/AP/The Daily Press

On Thanksgiving Day 2005, Greg, flying a KC-135 Stratotanker, refueled Matthew's E-8 JSTARS at 25,000 feet. "When I was attempting the [air refueling] that night, I knew [Matthew] was in the plane. So I told myself 'Oh man, you can't fall off tonight' because I'd never hear the end of it," he said. "I knew that night I had to be on top of my game."

What Military Life Is Like

To make a smart decision about a military career, you need to know some basic facts. For example:

Earnings. Pay starts fairly low in the military. But it increases quickly as you are promoted and you receive raises for time served. People serving in some positions receive extra pay for hazardous duty or foreign duty. In addition to salary, you'll have an allowance for clothing and housing. These benefits make earnings from a military career comparable to those offered by many civilian careers.

Working conditions. Military personnel do much of their work outdoors. So be prepared for plenty of exercise. They are deployed in many locations around the United States and the world, in climates ranging from extreme winter to the tropics.

Hours. The hours vary, depending on your job. The mission comes first. You may have to work more than eight hours a day.

Age. You must be at least 18 years old (or 17 if a parent or guardian consents) to join the military.

Physical Requirements. You must be in good physical shape.

By serving in the military, you'll be serving your country. That's probably the most important attraction for most people who choose this career.

But there are many other advantages. The job security is great. While you are in the service, the military will meet most of your basic needs. Other benefits include health care for you, your spouse, and children. You'll get 30 days of vacation with pay each year and low-cost life insurance. You'll be able to shop on the base, where prices are lower than in the civilian sector. Military bases also offer a variety of recreational facilities. Plus, you get to travel abroad and see different countries.

Finally, you can retire with full benefits after only 20 years of service. So if you're 18 when you enter, you could retire and begin a brand-new career at age 38. Your military service will provide training and experience that future civilian employers will value highly. They will also appreciate your discipline and leadership skills.

How Military Training and Experience Can Be Used in Civilian Jobs

Each branch of the military offers the opportunity to gain different types of skills. Once you've gained them, you'll be prepared for many career options—both in the military and in civilian life. Many positions in the military have **civilian equivalents,** *jobs that are the same or similar to those in civilian life.* These offer the opportunity to take your skills beyond the military into a successful career elsewhere. In fact, 80 percent of armed services career specialties have similar job functions in the civilian world.

In the Air Force, these options include jobs as pilots and positions that involve operating and maintaining aircraft. But they also include managers, engineers, mechanics, and computer specialists.

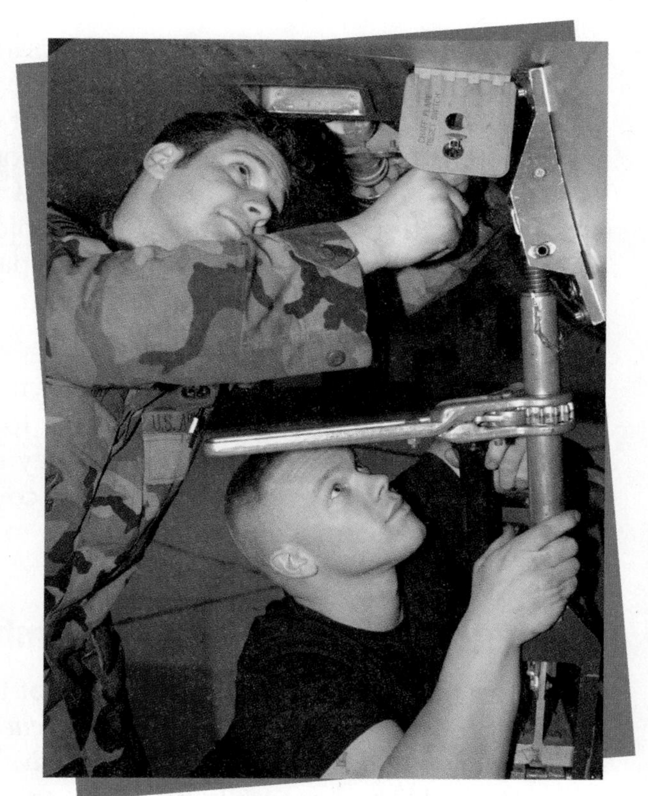

Air Force job options include maintaining and repairing aircraft.
Courtesy of the US Air Force

So, when you're considering a career, you might think of the military as a training ground for your future. Do you want to go to college right after you graduate? Or do you want to enter the workforce right away? Or maybe work now and get more training later? Whatever your choice, the military offers many exciting possibilities.

The Air and Space Expeditionary Force

As the world and the United States change, new threats to the United States emerge. These affect the shape of the Air Force. During the cold war with the Soviet Union, Air Force units served for several years in specified locations from which they rarely deployed overseas.

Since the end of the cold war in the early 1990s, however, that has changed. Beginning with the first Gulf War, the Air Force, along with the other military services, has found itself deployed on missions around the world—some short, many longer. With the Global War on Terrorism, which government officials believe will last for a long time, US military personnel must expect to be deployed overseas far more often than before. In fact, they must count on being deployed and away from their families on a regular basis. Whether you are in the regular Air Force, the Air Force Reserve, or the Air National Guard, deployment will no longer be the exception—it will be the rule.

The Air Force's new concept of organization is called the *Air and Space Expeditionary Force (AEF)*. The Air Force is organized into 10 AEFs and five *Mobility Leadership Wings*. Each AEF will have about 150 aircraft of different types and between 10,000 and 25,000 Airmen. At any given time, two of the 10 AEFs will be deployed overseas. Units will serve in 20-month cycles—14 months of "normal" duty, two months of preparation, and four months of deployment. During the 14 months at their permanent stations, units will train, repair their equipment, and get new equipment. Airmen will be able to spend time with their families, schedule leave, take training classes, and further their education.

About two months before their deployment, Air Force units will enter a preparation period. They will use this to get ready for their deployment, learning about the area they will be deployed to and what they may expect to experience there. The purpose of this 20-month cycle is to meet the country's national security needs while allowing Air Force personnel and their families to plan their personal lives.

Entering the Air Force as a Member of the Enlisted Corps

The majority of the military consists of two kinds of personnel: enlisted personnel and officers. **Enlisted personnel** *are generally young men and women who enter the armed forces with a high school diploma or equivalent.* They make up 85 percent of military personnel. They generally fill office, transportation, mechanical, human services, and combat jobs.

Since 1973, when the draft was eliminated, all four armed forces have relied on volunteers to fill thousands of enlisted job openings each year. In the Air Force, the enlisted force consists of the following levels:

- **Airman,** *an individual who enters at the beginning level and who focuses exclusively on learning skills (note that when used generically,* Airman *can refer to any member of the Air Force)*
- **Noncommissioned officer (NCO),** *a person who has developed advanced technical skills and is qualified to serve in some leadership positions*
- **Senior NCO,** *a person who is highly skilled and serves among the top enlisted leaders and managers.*

If you enlist, you will move up the ranks as you develop new technical and leadership skills. Enlisted personnel carry out the fundamental operations of the military. For example, they work as carpenters, mechanics, air traffic controllers, and electronics technicians.

Requirements for Entering the Air Force as an Enlisted Member

To be eligible to enter the Air Force as an enlisted member, you must be in good health and have at least a high school diploma or equivalent. You'll also have to take a test, and your new job may require a security clearance.

Armed Services Vocational Aptitude Battery

To make sure that candidates will be able to do the work, the Air Force requires that perspective Airmen score at least 36 on the Armed Services Vocational Aptitude Battery (ASVAB) if you graduated from high school, and 64 if you have a general equivalency diploma (GED). Most high school students take this test during their junior year. This test assesses your aptitude for training in the mechanical, administrative, general, and electronic areas. The Air Force uses the results to determine your job classification and training needs.

All four branches of the armed forces use the ASVAB. If you have taken the test for another branch of the service, the Air Force can convert your score to its requirements.

Some enlistees also take an *interest inventory* as part of the ASVAB process. On the interest inventory, you indicate your preferences for the various activities, education, training, and occupations presented to you. Based on your answers to the questions, the inventory determines your resemblance to one of six interest types. This helps you decide which types of work you are best suited for.

Security Investigations

All prospective enlisted members of the Air Force undergo a preliminary security investigation. A **security investigation** *involves providing information on any past arrests or questioning by law enforcement officers.* Air Force members have to maintain high standards of behavior. They also handle secret national-security information and equipment. This preliminary security clearance will be the basis of a complete security clearance, which will be performed if you enter a job that requires it.

Occupational Groups for Enlisted Personnel

Air Force enlistees may choose from the following occupational groups:

- administrative
- combat specialty occupations
- construction
- electronic and electrical equipment repair
- engineering, science, and technical
- health care
- human resource development
- machine operator and production
- media and public affairs
- protective service
- support service occupations
- transportation and material handling
- vehicle and machinery mechanic.

For information on the types of careers possible under each group, see Table 1.2.

TABLE 1.2

Air Force Enlisted Occupations

Administrative	• Administrative Support Specialists • Finance and Accounting Specialists • Flight Operations Specialists • Legal Specialists and Court Reporters • Preventive Maintenance Analysts • Sales and Stock Specialists
Combat Specialty Occupations	• Special Forces
Construction	• Building Electricians • Construction Equipment Operators • Construction Specialists
Electronic and Electrical Equipment Repair	• Avionics Technicians • Electrical Products Repairers • Electronic Instrument and Equipment Repairers • Power Plant Electricians • Precision Instrument and Equipment Repairers • Weapons Maintenance Technicians
Engineering, Science, and Technical	• Communications Equipment Operators • Computer Systems Specialists • Environmental Health and Safety Specialists • Intelligence Specialists • Meteorological Specialists • Non-Destructive Testers • Ordnance Specialists • Radar and Sonar Operators • Space Operations Specialists • Surveying, Mapping, and Drafting Technicians • Unmanned Vehicle Operations Specialists
Health Care	• Cardiopulmonary and EEG Technicians • Dental and Optical Laboratory Technicians • Dental Specialists • Medical Care Technicians • Medical Laboratory Technicians • Medical Record Technicians • Medical Service Technicians • Optometric Technicians • Pharmacy Technician • Physical & Occupational Therapy Specialist • Radiologic (X-Ray) Technicians

TABLE 1.2 *continued*

Human Resource Development	• Personnel Specialists • Recruiting Specialists • Training Specialists and Instructors
Machine Operator and Production	• Machinists • Survival Equipment Specialists • Water and Sewage Treatment Plant Operators • Welders and Metal Workers
Media and Public Affairs	• Audiovisual and Broadcast Technicians • Broadcast Journalists and Newswriters • Graphic Designers and Illustrators • Interpreters and Translators • Musicians • Photographic Specialists
Protective Service	• Emergency Management Specialists • Firefighters • Law Enforcement and Security Specialists
Support Service Occupations	• Caseworkers and Counselors • Food Service Specialists • Religious Program Specialists
Transportation and Material Handling	• Air Crew Members • Air Traffic Controllers • Cargo Specialists • Flight Engineers • Petroleum Supply Specialists • Transportation Specialists • Vehicle Drivers • Warehousing and Distribution Specialists
Vehicle and Machinery Mechanic	• Aircraft Mechanic • Automotive and Heavy Equipment Mechanics • Heating and Cooling Mechanics • Powerhouse Mechanics

The job to which you are assigned when you enlist in the Air Force is based on four factors:

1. the needs of the Air Force
2. your experience
3. your qualifications (aptitude scores, citizenship, health, physical strength, vision, and others)
4. your personal preference.

The Air Force does its best to put enlistees in the jobs they prefer. But the needs of the Air Force are the major consideration. Every job is important to the Air Force mission. Good performance will provide a vital service to both the Air Force and the country.

Educational Opportunities for Enlisted Members of the Air Force

The Air Force offers enlistees many educational opportunities. These include job training, technical education, and opportunities for college-level work. Most Air Force bases offer off-duty programs for enlisted personnel. These programs lead to professional certificates or to an associate, bachelor's, or master's degree.

If you're serious about your studies, you should be able to complete at least an associate degree during your first term of enlistment. The **term of enlistment** *is number of years you agree to remain in the military before having the option to leave or sign up for another term.* If you remain in the Air Force, you could earn a bachelor's or master's degree.

Testing Programs

Enlistees may also earn college credits by passing certain tests. Testing is a fast and inexpensive method of obtaining college credit. Air Force enlisted personnel may take the College-Level Examination Program (CLEP). CLEP consists of a series of examinations that test a person's college-level knowledge. You can gain this knowledge through courses or through independent study, cultural pursuits, travel, or other avenues. The tests cover five topics:

1. English composition
2. social science, history
3. natural sciences
4. humanities
5. mathematics.

Each college and university has its own CLEP evaluation system, which it uses to determine how much credit to give you for your knowledge. Some colleges offer up to 30 hours of credit to enlistees who pass the tests.

The Air Force offers enlisted personnel many educational opportunities.
Courtesy of the US Air Force

Community College of the Air Force

The Community College of the Air Force (CCAF) is the largest multicampus, two-year college in the world. It has more than 355,000 students. CCAF offers an associate of applied science degree in Air Force specialties. It combines credit for off-duty formal education with training in Air Force specialties. All active-duty Air Force enlisted personnel are eligible for admission to CCAF after they pass the ASVAB and complete basic military training. **Basic training** *is the period during which an enlistee enters the service and learns basic military skills.*

Airman Education and Commissioning Program

The Airman Education and Commissioning Program allows Airmen on active duty to earn degrees in technical fields that the Air Force needs. These include meteorology, nursing, foreign languages, foreign area studies, mathematics, physics, computer science, and engineering. The Airmen attend a civilian college or university full time and earn their second lieutenant's commission through the Officer Training School (OTS).

Delayed Entry Program

If you want to enter the Air Force but wish to delay your entry until a more convenient time, you may often do so. Under the Delayed Entry Program, you can enlist in the Air Force before you graduate from high school and report for training after you graduate. After you enlist, you can put off starting your training for up to 365 days. You will not be required to participate in any active duty military activities or receive pay or benefits during the waiting period. You agree to enter active duty on a certain date, and the Air Force agrees to accept you (if you're still qualified) and provide training and initial assignment in the aptitude area or job specified.

TABLE 1.3

General Officer Qualifications

AGE	Each service sets its own qualification requirements for officers. Generally, ROTC candidates must be at least 17 years old; a person appointed as a commissioned officer must be able to complete 20 years of active service by age 62.
CITIZENSHIP STATUS	Must be US citizen.
PHYSICAL CONDITION	Must meet minimum physical standards listed below. Some occupations have additional physical standards.

Height—		*Maximum*	*Minimum*
	For males	6′5″/190.5 cm	5′0″/152.4 cm
	For females	6′5″/190.5 cm	4′10″/147.3 cm

Weight— There are minimum and maximum weights for the various services according to height, wrist size, and/or percentage body fat.

		Maximum	*Minimum*
	For males	243 lb/110.4 kg	100 lb/45.35 kg
	For females	203 lb/93.18 kg	90 lb/40.82 kg

Vision—	The requirements are specific for each service and are determined by job specialty. In general, service members must have at least 20/400 or 20/200 vision that can be corrected to 20/20 with eyeglasses or contact lenses. The vision requirements are also based on depth perception as well as color blindness.
Overall Health—	Must be in good health and pass a medical exam. Certain diseases or conditions may exclude persons from enlistment, such as diabetes, severe allergies, epilepsy, alcoholism, and drug addiction.
EDUCATION	Must have a four-year college degree from an accredited institution. Some occupations require advanced degrees or four-year degrees in a particular field.
APTITUDE	Must achieve the minimum entry score on an officer qualification test. Each service uses its own qualification test.
MORAL CHARACTER	Must meet standards designed to screen out persons unlikely to become successful officers. Standards cover court convictions, juvenile delinquency, arrests, and drug use.
MARITAL STATUS AND DEPENDENTS	May be either single or married for ROTC, OCS/OTS, and direct-appointment pathways. Must be single to enter and graduate from service academies.
WAIVERS	On a case-by-case basis, exceptions (waivers) are granted by individual services for some of the above qualification requirements.

Entering the Air Force as a Member of the Officer Corps

Commissioned officers *are personnel who enter the armed forces with a four-year college degree or better, who compete to enter and earn a commission from the president after confirmation by Congress.* They fill managerial, professional, and technical jobs. They include doctors, nurses, lawyers, engineers, and pilots.

Commissioned officers make up 15 percent of armed forces personnel. Air Force commissioned officers are those with the rank of second lieutenant and above. Air Force officers with the rank of second lieutenant, first lieutenant, and captain are called *company-grade officers.* Majors, lieutenant colonels, and colonels are called *field-grade officers.* An officer who ranks above colonel is a *general officer.*

The general qualifications for commissioned officers in the US armed forces are presented in Table 1.3.

The Air Force has some 70,000 commissioned officers. Air Force officers receive the same benefits as enlisted personnel, but their pay and housing allowances are higher, given their higher rank and responsibility.

To be a commissioned officer, you must be a US citizen and have at least a bachelor's degree from an accredited college. To earn a commission as an officer you must successfully complete an officer-commissioning program through the Air Force Academy, Air Force ROTC, or OTS. Some positions require a graduate degree or specific courses. You must also achieve the required minimum scores in each of five areas (pilot, navigator, verbal, quantitative, and academic aptitude) on the Air Force Officer Qualifying Test (AFOQT). This standardized test is similar to the ACT or SAT. In addition, you must be physically fit and of high moral character.

Air Force Officer Occupations

Air Force officers fill the following general occupations:

- combat specialty
- engineering, science, and technical
- executive, administrative, and managerial
- health care
- human resources development
- media and public affairs
- protective services
- support services
- transportation.

The Air Force needs flight, science, engineering, and missile officers. Young officers are needed to fly aircraft, operate computers, work in research and development, and specialize in such fields as law and medicine. The Air Force especially needs engineers and scientists with training in aviation, space technology, and communications. Also, officers are needed in nontechnical areas such as general management. In all fields, the Air Force assigns young officers to responsible positions early in their careers.

Table 1.4 gives more information on career options for officers.

TABLE 1.4

Air Force Officer Occupations

Combat Specialty	• Missile Officers • Combat Mission Support Officers • Special Forces Officers
Engineering, Science, and Technical	• Aerospace Engineers • Civil Engineers • Communications Managers • Computer Systems Officers • Electrical and Electronic Systems Engineers • Environmental Health and Safety Officers • Industrial Engineers • Intelligence Officers • Lawyers and Judges • Life Scientists • Ordnance Officers • Physical Scientists • Space Operations Officers
Executive, Administrative, and Managerial	• Administrative Officers • Finance and Accounting Managers • Health Services Administrators • International Relations Officers • Logisticians • Management Analysts and Planners • Purchasing and Contracting Managers • Store Manager • Supply and Warehousing Managers

TABLE 1.4 *continued*

Health Care	• Dentists • Dieticians • Optometrists • Pharmacists • Physical and Occupational Therapists • Physician Assistants • Physicians and Surgeons • Psychologists • Registered Nurses • Speech Therapists
Human Resource Development	• Personnel Managers • Recruiting Managers • Teachers and Instructors • Training and Education Directors
Media and Public Affairs	• Audiovisual and Broadcast Directors • Music Directors • Public Information Officers
Protective Service	• Emergency-Management Officers • Law Enforcement and Security Officers
Support Service	• Chaplains • Food Service Manager • Social Workers
Transportation	• Air Traffic Control Managers • Aircraft Navigators • Aircraft Pilots • Helicopter Pilots • Transportation Maintenance Managers • Transportation Managers

How to Become a Commissioned Officer

There are four main paths to becoming a commissioned officer: The Reserve Officer Training Corps (ROTC), the service academies, Officer Training School (OTS), and direct appointment.

Reserve Officer Training Corps

Undergraduate students may receive training to become officers under the Reserve Officer Training Corps (ROTC) Program. ROTC programs for the Army, Navy, Air Force, and Marine Corps are available in more than 1,400 colleges and universities nationwide.

Depending on the service and option they select, ROTC students train for two, three, or four years. Many receive scholarships for tuition, books, fees, and uniforms. They also get a monthly allowance, or stipend.

In addition to their military and college course work, ROTC candidates perform leadership-building activities and drills for a number of hours each week. At some point, they take part in military training exercises for several weeks during the summer. Graduating ROTC candidates receive commissions as military officers. They then go on active duty or become members of Reserve or National Guard units.

Air Force ROTC

The Air Force Reserve Officer Training Corps (AFROTC) is the largest and oldest source of commissioned officers for the Air Force. Its mission is to "develop quality leaders for the Air Force." AFROTC headquarters is at Maxwell Air Force Base in Montgomery, Alabama. AFROTC offers a four-year and two-year educational program.

The AFROTC program recruits, educates, and commissions officer candidates through college campus programs. A **cadet** *is an ROTC candidate.*

Cadets normally enroll in the first two years of ROTC classes at the same time and in the same manner as they enroll in other college courses. ROTC instructors are normally active-duty Air Force officers (although there are some Reserve instructors, depending on the university). Most have a master's degree and usually hold the academic rank of assistant professor.

Four-Year Program. The first two years of this program are the General Military Course. Cadets learn the history, mission, and structure of the Air Force. They receive an introduction to military life. They study air and space power—from hot-air balloons to spacecraft and their respective missions.

The Air Force offers many exciting career possibilities for both enlisted personnel and officers.
Courtesy of Jeff Greenberg/PhotoEdit

After successfully completing this two-year program, a cadet must compete for entry into the last two years of the program, the Professional Officer Course. Before entering this course, cadets who have been selected based on competition must complete a four-week field-training course at an Air Force base. The field training is demanding and rigorous—it focuses on leadership principles, physical conditioning, weapons practice, drill, problem solving, and evaluations.

After field training, cadets enter the Professional Officer Course. These last two years focus on advanced training in leadership, management, communicative skills, national security issues, regional studies, and preparation for active duty (real-life Air Force situations).

Once enrolled in the Professional Officer Course, all cadets are enlisted in the Air Force Reserve. They receive a small monthly allowance during the academic year.

Two-Year Program. The two-year program is the same as the last two years of the four-year program. It involves enrolling in and completing the Professional Officer Course. Candidates for both programs are selected based on a competition. Two-year applicants, however, must successfully complete a one-week academic session prior to the four-week field-training program. The additional week of preparation prior to field training prepares them for entry into the Professional Officer Course.

AFROTC Scholarships

AFROTC high school scholarships are available on a competitive basis to high school students. Scholarship recipients are chosen based on several factors, including a physical-fitness assessment, ACT/SAT scores, grade point average, leadership, and an interview.

Air Force ROTC provides three- and four-year scholarships in three basic types:

- *Type 1* pays full college tuition, most fees, a $250 monthly stipend, and $600 per year for books.
- *Type 2* pays college tuition and most fees up to $15,000, a $250 monthly stipend, and $600 per year for books. If a student attends an institution where the tuition exceeds $15,000 per year, then he or she pays the difference. All three-year scholarships are Type 2.
- *Type 7* pays full college tuition, fees, a $250 monthly stipend, and $600 per year for books, but the student must attend a college or university where the tuition is less than $9,000 per year—*or* a public college or university at which the student qualifies for the in-state tuition rate. However, if tuition is more than $9,000 per year, the scholarship must be converted to a three-year Type 2 scholarship. The recipient pays tuition the first year and receives up to $15,000 per year beginning with the sophomore year. Likewise, there is no book allowance or stipend the first year.

All scholarship cadets are required to meet certain academic, military, and physical-fitness standards to maintain their scholarship benefits. Four-year scholarship recipients agree to:

- enroll in the academic area in which the scholarship is offered
- enlist in the Air Force Reserve and enroll in Air Force ROTC, beginning with the fall term
- satisfactorily complete a four-week summer field-training course at an Air Force base (normally between the sophomore and junior years)
- complete the Air Force ROTC Professional Officer Course
- accept a commission as an Air Force officer
- serve at least four years on active duty.

ROTC cadets climb ropes on an obstacle course at Oregon State University, Corvallis, Oregon.
Courtesy of Bohemian Nomad Picturemakers/Corbis Images

All scholarship cadets receive a nontaxable monthly allowance during the academic year.

AFROTC has detachments at more than 1,000 schools. If the college you choose has no AFROTC program, you may still be able to participate at a "crosstown" school. In this arrangement, you attend regular classes at your school while attending AFROTC classes at a nearby host university.

The Service Academies

The United States has three service academies:

- United States Military Academy at West Point, New York. (Army)
- United States Naval Academy at Annapolis, Maryland. (Navy and Marine Corps)
- United States Air Force Academy at Colorado Springs, Colorado. (Air Force)

Competition for entry into the academies is keen. Only the highest-qualified candidates are accepted. To be eligible for admission to any of the academies, you must be at least 17 years old, a citizen of the United States, of good moral character, and academically and physically qualified.

In addition, candidates for the Army, Navy, and Air Force Academies must be nominated—usually by a US senator or representative, but sometimes by the vice president or the president. The process for obtaining a congressional nomination is not political, and candidates do not have to know their senator or representative personally to secure a nomination. To request a nomination, you can call or write a senator or representative's office (from your state or territory) to ask for information.

Each member of Congress and the vice president can nominate up to five nominees attending a service academy at any time. Additional nomination slots are available for children of career military personnel, children of disabled veterans or veterans who were killed in action, or children of Medal of Honor recipients.

The academies offer four-year programs of study leading to a bachelor of science degree. Students receive free tuition, room, board, medical and dental care, and a monthly allowance. Graduates receive a commission as a military officer. After graduation, they must serve on active duty for at least five years.

United States Air Force Academy

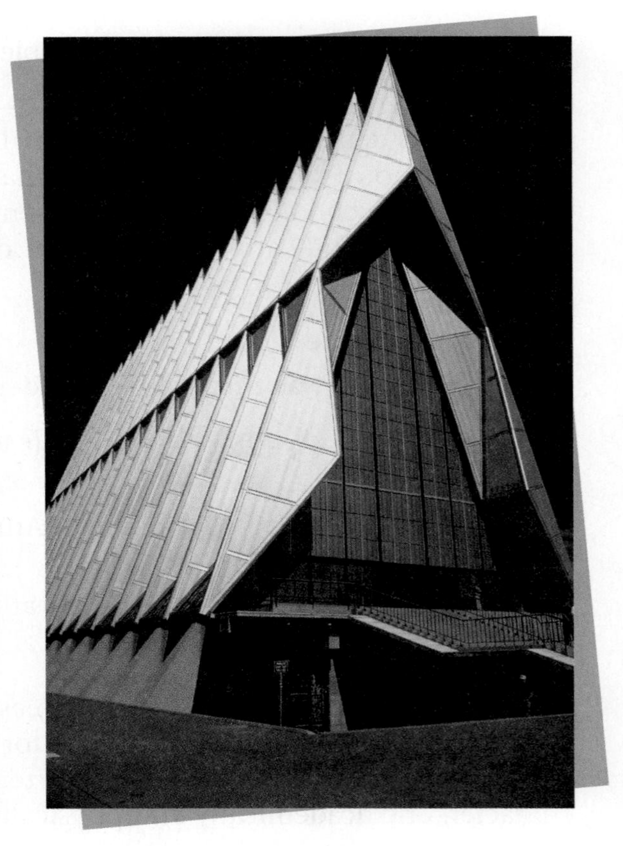

The US Air Force Academy chapel in Colorado Springs, Colorado
Courtesy of Tim Thompson/Corbis Images

Established in 1954, the United States Air Force Academy prepares cadets for careers as Air Force officers. The academy stresses character development, military training, and physical fitness as well as academics. Cadets receive a broad education in the basic sciences, engineering, humanities, and the social sciences.

The composition of the student body mirrors that of the Air Force officer corps. It includes about 12 percent women and 16 percent minorities. Students come from all 50 states, Central and South America, Europe and Africa, Puerto Rico and the Virgin Islands, and the South Pacific.

Graduates receive a bachelor of science degree in one of 30 majors. They also receive a commission as a second lieutenant in the Air Force. Cadets maintain a vigorous daily schedule, conform to discipline, and live by an honor code.

To enter the academy upon graduation from high school, students should apply as soon as possible after January 31 of their junior year. Once nominated, they must take a physical fitness test, a medical exam, and either the SAT I exam of the College Board or the ACT exam.

Officer Training School

The *Officer Training School* (OTS) also trains and commissions officers for the Air Force. (Other branches of the military call this *Officer Candidate School.*) OTS candidates go through Basic Officer Training (BOT). The program operates in partnership with the Air Force Academy, Air Force ROTC, and others. BOT is open to college graduates. It consists of 12 weeks of military instruction.

The goal of OTS is to instill high standards of conduct and provide officer candidates with the military knowledge and skills needed for effective performance. Once trainees complete all OTS requirements, they are commissioned as second lieutenants in the US Air Force.

Direct Appointments

Professionals in medicine, law, biomedical engineering, and religion who are fully qualified in their fields may apply to receive direct appointments as military officers. After entering military service, they can begin practicing their professions with a minimum of military training. Their appointments last two years, although some are longer. Some scholarship programs are available to assist students in these fields in return for several years of service.

Other Entry Points to a Commission

In addition to the four main paths described above, all five services have programs that enable qualified enlisted personnel to earn commissions as officers. Once selected for an enlisted-commissioning program, enlisted personnel must follow one of the four major pathways in order to receive a commission.

Assignments

Air Force officer assignments are based on the needs of the Air Force. All officers, including those with dependents, are eligible for and subject to assignments anywhere in the world where the Air Force maintains a presence. Officers may volunteer for service in certain areas, but there is no guarantee they will be stationed there. If an officer is married to another officer, the two may apply for a joint-spouse assignment, but the Air Force cannot guarantee approval. The Air Force does the best it can, however, to avoid separating spouses.

Most young lieutenants are assigned to small units. As they gain experience and progress in rank, they are assigned to larger units.

Air Force Educational Leave of Absence Program

Under the Air Force Educational Leave of Absence (AFELA) program, enlisted or officers are temporarily released from military duty to attend a college or university. To be eligible, service personnel must be working toward a bachelor's or higher degree. They must attend college full time. They receive their basic military pay (but no allowances) while attending school but must pay all education expenses, including tuition, books, and travel.

Upon graduation, AFELA enrollees return to their previous duty. The Air Force extends their service commitment to cover twice the length of time that they've spent at college. So, if you went to college for nine months under the AFELA program, you would have to spend 18 months in the Air Force beyond your original commitment.

CHECKPOINTS

Lesson 2 Review

Using complete sentences, answer the following questions on a sheet of paper.

1. What is the primary air and space arm of our nation's armed forces?
2. What factors determine the level of pay and allowances an Air Force member receives?
3. Explain the Air and Space Expeditionary Force concept.
4. Describe the differences between an enlisted person and an officer.
5. What is the name of the test administered by the armed forces to decide eligibility for enlistment and show aptitude for training?
6. List six occupational groups available to enlisted personnel.
7. List four types of training you can receive in the military.
8. Name and describe the four main pathways to becoming a commissioned officer.
9. List the three service academies.
10. What do you need to receive an appointment to the Air Force Academy?
11. What is the purpose of the Air Force Educational Leave of Absence program?

Applying Career Skills

12. Assume that you decide to enlist in the Air Force after you graduate from high school or college. Write a letter to a relative that explains why you chose to take this step. Make your letter at least four paragraphs long.

LESSON

3

Careers in Aerospace

Aerospace as a Career Option

Careers in aerospace are challenging and rewarding. The aerospace field needs engineers, scientists, technologists, and technicians. If you decide to enter one of these careers, you can be a tremendous help to the United States and the world.

What Does "Aerospace" Mean?

Aerospace *combines "aero," from aeronautics, describing flight within earth's atmosphere, and "space," describing flight beyond the atmosphere.*

It's sometimes hard to make a distinction between these two types of flight. One reason is that scientists haven't agreed on where the earth's atmosphere ends and space begins. That's why the word *aerospace* is a handy way to refer to either type of flight. It refers to general, commercial, and military aircraft. It also covers spacecraft, satellites, and space probes.

If you pursue a career in aerospace, you will need a full range of skills, training, and education. But the time invested in your education will be worth it. If you enter this field, you can design, build, pilot, or maintain aerospace vehicles. Aeronautical and astronautical engineers, machinists, managers, pilots, and flight attendants are among the people employed in the hundreds of careers available in aerospace. So are aircraft maintenance and technicians, air traffic controllers, and astronauts.

How Do You Know If You Want an Aerospace Career?

One way to decide if a career in aerospace is right for you is to examine your abilities and interests. Think about your favorite courses as well as your hobbies. Consider even your daydreams. When you gaze into the night sky, do you wonder about the stars and the planets? Do you wonder about extraterrestrial life? Have you ever wondered what makes an airplane fly? Or what could make it fly more quietly or safely?

Quick Write

Pick three careers in aerospace that you might like to pursue. Write a short paragraph describing what you know about each one. Review your paragraphs after you read this chapter. See how your current ideas of careers in this field match the reality.

Learn About...

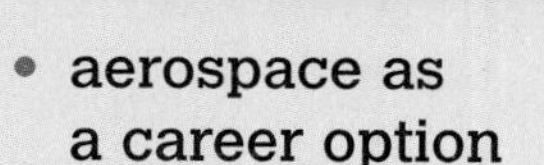

- aerospace as a career option
- major agencies in the aerospace sector
- education required for aerospace careers
- types of careers available in the aerospace industry
- preparing for a career in aerospace

Vocabulary

- aerospace
- engineer
- scientist
- technician
- technologist
- National Aeronautics and Space Administration
- Federal Aviation Administration
- education
- training

Other questions to ask yourself include the following:

- Do you like to solve problems and puzzles?
- Do you like to create and build things?
- Do you enjoy working with computers?
- Do you enjoy math and science?
- Do you get good grades?
- Do you have an inquiring mind?
- Are you prepared to study hard?

If you answered "yes" to most of the questions, you may want to consider an aerospace career.

Engineers

Engineers *are people who design products, systems, and structures*. Engineers have designed skyscrapers, race cars, jumbo jets, and space vehicles. Computers, television, and satellites depend on engineers. If some terrific new machine is invented in the 21st century, it will no doubt come from the mind of an engineer.

Engineering is the second-largest profession in the United States. Among the professions, only teaching employs more people. The total number of engineers in this country is greater than the number of lawyers, doctors, dentists, and pharmacists combined.

Engineers are practical thinkers. They change ideas and theories into realities. They use science and math to solve problems. They take the results of scientists' research to make products that people use every day. Engineering is the link between scientific discovery and practical use.

Scientists

Scientists *are knowledge seekers*. They try to discover why things happen the way they do. They are always questioning. They are fascinated by nature, earth, and the universe. Scientists seek answers and expand our knowledge.

While engineers deal with objects and systems, scientists focus on theories and concepts. They deal with abstractions, which are the inner qualities or properties of things. Scientists do this in a process called research.

There are three major kinds of research: *basic research, applied research,* and a combination of the two approaches. Scientists who conduct *basic*, or pure, research have no particular goals in mind at the start. They are trying to develop theories that explain events. They base their theories on the discoveries of other scientists and their own findings. *Applied* research is more focused; these scientists use their findings to solve a particular problem or to develop a product. Scientists advance knowledge by sharing their findings with other scientists.

Most scientists do their research in schools or universities. Many teach as well. They also work in industry and for the government.

Technicians and Technologists

A **technician** *is someone who translates the technical plans created by engineers into useful products and services.* Technicians are experts in detail. They work closely with scientists and engineers. On the aerospace team, technicians use their skills to operate wind tunnels, construct test equipment, build models, and support many types of research. To prepare for their work, technicians must complete either a two-year technical training program or on-the-job training programs.

A **technologist** *does work similar to that of a technician, but at a higher level. Technologists are graduates of four-year engineering-technology programs.*

Both technicians and technologists play a supporting role in all areas of science and engineering. They work in all phases of the aerospace industry, from theory through construction, testing, and operations. Thousands of career opportunities today require technical training.

Salaries in Aerospace

The aerospace industry needs top-notch people. To get them, it offers competitive salaries. Table 1.5 lists salaries of some typical careers in the industry. These figures were current as of 2005.

TABLE 1.5

Aviation Jobs and Salary Ranges

Career/Industry Group	Minimum Salary	Average Salary	Maximum Salary
Airport	$25,000.00	**$41,494.61**	$ 79,200.00
AP Mechanic	$14,137.20	**$50,978.16**	$120,000.00
Avionics	$18,000.00	**$53,059.06**	$150,000.00
Computer	$49,938.00	**$56,093.00**	$ 62,248.00
Dispatch	$25,000.00	**$31,166.67**	$ 55,000.00
Engineering and Aerospace	$20,000.00	**$68,426.33**	$115,000.00
Executive	$60,000.00	**$72,500.00**	$ 80,000.00
Flight Attendant	$25,940.00	**$53,740.00**	$100,620.00
Ground-Ramp	$38,000.00	**$47,875.00**	$ 65,000.00
Management	$16,476.00	**$62,652.67**	$120,000.00
Office and Administrative	$14,137.20	**$36,422.83**	$ 64,728.00
Other	$20,000.00	**$47,057.14**	$ 75,000.00
Pilot	$14,137.10	**$52,962.11**	$130,000.00
Sales/Marketing	$28,000.00	**$56,000.00**	$120,000.00

2006 aviation salary data provided by Avjobs, Inc. *www.avjobs.com*

Major Agencies in the Aerospace Sector

Two main agencies in the US government oversee developments and operations relating to the aerospace industry: the National Aeronautics and Space Administration and the Federal Aviation Administration.

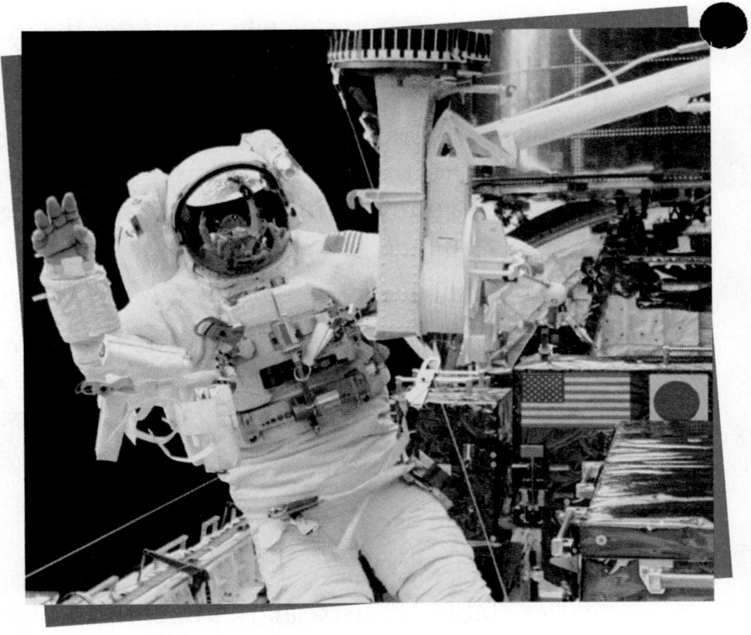

An astronaut working in the cargo bay of a NASA space shuttle in orbit around Earth
Courtesy of Stock Trek/Getty Images

National Aeronautics and Space Administration

The **National Aeronautics and Space Administration,** or **NASA,** *is the government agency responsible for the US space program and general aerospace research.* It conducts research into both civilian and military aerospace systems. NASA is headquartered in Washington, D.C., but has activities around the world. NASA has supported research that has led to many improvements in our everyday lives.

Since time began, humans have been fascinated by space. But it wasn't until the 1950s that scientists and engineers were able to tackle some basic questions about space exploration. What's out there? How do we get there? What will we find? What can we learn from exploring space that will make life better here on earth?

In the late 1950s, the Soviet Union launched *Sputnik*, the first space satellite. This was the beginning of space exploration. Hoping to help the United States gain the lead in the "space race," President Dwight D. Eisenhower established NASA in 1958. Through the Mercury and Gemini projects, NASA developed the technology and skills for further explorations. On 20 July 1969, US astronauts Neil Armstrong and Buzz Aldrin became the first men to walk on the moon.

In the 1970s, NASA focused on developing a way to give the United States ready access to space. The outcome of this work was the space shuttle. NASA launched its first space shuttle in 1981. By 2005, NASA had recorded more than 112 successful manned flights. Two crews, however—aboard the shuttles *Challenger* and *Columbia*—have been lost. In 2000, the United States and Russia established a permanent human presence in space aboard the international space station.

Meanwhile, NASA's planetary research program continues. In 1997, Mars Pathfinder became the first in a fleet of spacecraft that will explore Mars. NASA also launched Terra and Aqua, satellites that orbit Earth. The data sent back from these satellites help us understand life on planet Earth. NASA's aeronautics teams are also focused on improving aircraft travel. Two goals are to make it safer and less polluting.

NASA Mission Directorates

NASA conducts its work in four main organizations, called mission directorates:

- *Aeronautics*—pioneering and proving new flight technologies. These technologies improve our ability to explore space. They also have practical applications on earth.
- *Exploration systems*—creating ways to have exploration that is affordable and sustainable, or able to be maintained, even when funding is low.
- *Science*—exploring the Earth, moon, Mars, and beyond and reaping the benefits of exploration for society.
- *Space operations*—providing technologies needed for other NASA operations. This includes the space shuttle, the international space station, and flight support.

Working for NASA

NASA offers career opportunities for scientists, engineers, computer programmers, personnel specialists, accountants, writers, maintenance workers, and many others. At its website, *www.nasajobs.nasa.gov*, you can review employment opportunities with NASA. You can also find opportunities for student internships and summer employment.

For many young people interested in NASA, the ultimate goal is to be an astronaut. Former astronaut Dr. Sally K. Ride, the first American woman in space, has these suggestions:

> The most important steps that I followed were studying math and science in school. I was always interested in physics and astronomy and chemistry, and I continued to study those subjects through high school and college and into graduate school. That's what prepared me for being an astronaut. It actually gave me the qualifications to be selected to be an astronaut. I think the advice that I would give to any kids who want to be astronauts is to make sure that they realize that NASA is looking for people with a whole variety of backgrounds. They are looking for medical doctors, microbiologists, geologists, physicists, and electrical engineers. So find something that you really like and then pursue it as far as you can, and NASA is apt to be interested in that profession.

Federal Aviation Administration

The **Federal Aviation Administration,** or **FAA,** *is the government agency responsible for the safety of civil aviation.* The FAA was formed in 1958. Its major roles include:

- regulating civil aviation, or the design, development, production, and operation of nongovernment and nonmilitary aircraft
- encouraging and developing civil aeronautics, including new aviation technology
- developing and operating air traffic control and navigation systems for civil and military aircraft
- researching and developing the National Airspace System and civil aeronautics
- developing and carrying out programs to control noise and other environmental effects of civil aviation
- regulating US commercial space transportation.

The FAA conducts work in many areas, including the following:

Safety Regulation

- enforcing regulations and minimum standards in manufacturing, operating, and maintaining aircraft
- certifying civilian airmen and airports that serve air carriers.

The nation's air traffic controllers work for the Federal Aviation Administration.
Courtesy of Chad Slattery/Getty Images

Airspace and Air Traffic Management

- operating a network of airport towers, air traffic control centers, and flight service stations
- developing air traffic rules, assigning the use of airspace, and controlling air traffic.

Air Navigation Facilities

- maintaining, operating, and ensuring the quality of air navigation facilities.

Civil Aviation Abroad

- promoting aviation safety and encouraging civil aviation abroad
- exchanging aeronautical information with foreign governments
- taking part in international conferences.

Commercial Space Transportation

- regulating and encouraging the US commercial space transportation industry.

Research, Engineering, and Development

- developing better aircraft, engines, and equipment
- conducting aeromedical research, or medical research that deals specifically with the aerospace field.

Other Programs

- registering aircraft and recording ownership documents
- administering an aviation insurance program
- publishing information on airways, airport services, and other technical subjects.

Education Required for Aerospace Careers

Several careers in aerospace require graduate degrees, such as doctorates in engineering or physics. Managers need to have college degrees. But many people work in aerospace with only a high school diploma. They have received training to learn specific skills. The choice depends upon your particular career goals.

Training Versus Education

As you prepare for a career in aerospace, you'll need both education and training. Although people use these two words interchangeably, they have different meanings.

Education *involves broad-based learning.* When you earn a college degree, you sample many fields of knowledge, and then concentrate on one specific field. Because of its broad basis, education prepares you for a variety of career possibilities.

Training *has a narrower focus. It prepares you to perform a function that requires a specific set of skills.* Training can prepare you, for example, to work on jet engines or aircraft radios.

Different careers need people with different mixes of education and training. But it's not an "either/or" situation. Even the most highly educated people need training, and even entry-level trainees need some education.

General Educational Requirements for Careers in Aerospace

Engineers, Scientists, and Mathematicians

A career in aerospace as a scientist or an engineer requires from four to seven years of college study. A four-year bachelor's degree is essential. After that may come a master's degree, which usually takes about two years. You need an additional two to four years to earn a doctorate.

A starting position as an engineer, a mathematician, and a scientist requires a bachelor's degree. (A master's or doctoral degree is highly desirable in life sciences.) Areas of study for engineering students who are preparing for careers in aerospace include electrical and mechanical engineering, as well as aerospace engineers. Bachelor's degrees that provide a foundation for aerospace careers include physics, chemistry, geology, meteorology, mathematics, psychology, and biology.

Technicians

Engineering technicians typically hold a two-year associate of science degree. Some may continue for two years and obtain a bachelor's degree in engineering technology. Others may earn a bachelor's degree in engineering or a physical science. A few complete a five-year apprenticeship program offered at some NASA field centers.

Other Careers

Some careers require a high school diploma plus on-the-job training. No matter which career you choose and how well educated you are when you start out, a career in aerospace demands lifelong learning. The field is competitive and constantly changing. You'll need to update your skills and knowledge throughout your career—by going back to school or through on-the-job training.

Types of Careers Available in the Aerospace Industry

The aerospace industry needs people with a wide range of knowledge and skills. For example, it must have pilots, aircraft maintenance technicians, and air traffic controllers. It must have flight dispatchers, reservationists, technicians, and safety inspectors.

You may be surprised to learn, however, that the industry also needs medical doctors, lawyers, analysts, accountants, and marketing personnel. It needs machinists, sheet-metal workers, welders, and carpenters. Nonskilled employees such as typists, drivers, receptionists, and building maintenance workers are needed as well. Regardless of your education or training, you can find a place among the many positions in aerospace.

Table 1.6 lists the titles of some of the major aerospace careers.

TABLE 1.6

Aerospace Career Titles

Pilots or Crew Members	• pilot astronaut • mission specialist • payload specialist
Physical Scientists	• astronomer • chemist • geologist • meteorologist • physicist • oceanographer
Life Scientists	• biologist • medical doctor • physiologist • nutritionist • psychologist
Social Scientists	• economist • sociologist
Mathematicians	• computer scientist • mathematician • systems analyst • statistician
Engineers (specialties)	• aerospace/astronautics • chemical • civil • biomedical • computer • electrical • industrial • environmental • materials • mechanical • nuclear • petroleum • plastics • safety • systems

continued on next page

TABLE 1.6 *continued*

Aerospace Career Titles

Technicians (specialties)	• electrical/electronics • engineering • aerospace model • aircraft • avionics • fabrication • materials • pattern making and molding
Technical Communicators	• writer • artist • editor • education specialist • public relations specialist • audiovisual specialist • photographer
Other Fields	• quality control inspector • ground radio operator

Examples of Specific Careers in the Aerospace Field

Aerospace Engineer

Aerospace engineers develop new technologies for use in aviation, defense systems, and space exploration. They design, develop, and test aircraft, spacecraft, and missiles. They also supervise manufacturing of these products.

Aerospace engineers specialize in areas such as design, guidance, navigation and control, instrumentation and communication, or production methods. They may also specialize in a particular type of vehicle, such as fighter jets, helicopters, or missiles and rockets.

Aerospace engineers are involved in the analysis, design, and operation of aircraft that operate within the Earth's atmosphere as well as in space. For this reason, the terms *aerospace* and *aeronautics* are interchangeable. Aerospace engineers who work with aircraft are considered *aeronautical engineers*. Those working specifically with spacecraft are *astronautical engineers*.

Working Conditions

Most aerospace engineers work a standard, 40-hour week. At times, deadlines or design standards may bring extra demands. When this happens, engineers may work long hours and experience considerable stress.

Most aerospace engineers work in offices. Some outdoors work may be required. For example, an engineer may travel to a test site to perform product tests such as firing a rocket engine.

Other Engineering Specialties

Aerospace engineering may not appeal to you. Still, you may want to work in the aerospace industry. In that case, consider *electrical engineering*. Many of the people who work in aerospace have an electrical engineering background. That's because electronic components are essential parts of satellites and aircraft.

Another option is *mechanical engineering*. This will lead to you working on mechanical components, such as the landing gear of airplanes or shuttles.

Aviation Safety Inspector

Aviation safety inspectors develop and enforce regulations concerning civil aviation safety. They are concerned about how well aircraft fly and the competence of pilots, mechanics, and other personnel. They are also responsible for the safety of aviation facilities and equipment. These positions require knowledge and skill in the operation, maintenance, or manufacture of aircraft and aircraft systems.

Working Conditions

These jobs require considerable travel. This is because inspections, consultations, and investigations must be done at various facilities and locations or at the scenes of accidents.

Requirements and Experience

Because safety inspectors need a broad range of knowledge, they often come to this career after working in other areas of aerospace. Some are former pilots or crew members. They can also be experienced air traffic controllers, mechanics, machinists, or electronics technicians. You need a four-year college degree for this position.

Air Traffic Control Specialist

Air traffic controllers separate landing and departing aircraft. They give pilots instructions for taxiing and takeoff as well as weather advice.

Controllers use radar or manual procedures to keep track of flights. They use computers, radio, radar, telephones, and other electronic communication devices. They must be able to quickly recall registration numbers of aircraft under their control, aircraft types and speeds, positions in the air, and the location of navigational aids or landmarks.

Working Conditions

Because they work with radar equipment, air traffic controllers often work in semidarkness. They never see the aircraft they control except as "blips" on the radar scope.

Requirements and Experience

To be an air traffic controller, you must have experience in administrative, technical, or other work. You may be able to substitute a four-year college degree, however, for the general-experience requirement.

Aircraft Manufacturing Scientist

Scientists in the aircraft manufacturing industry specialize in many fields. They include aerodynamics, chemistry, physiology, metallurgy, and meteorology. They also include cryogenics, which is a branch of physics that deals with the production and effects of very low temperatures, such as those in space, and avionics, or aviation electronics.

Aircraft manufacturing scientists' chief concern is basic and applied research. That is, they focus on the search for scientific knowledge. This includes developing concepts and testing theories, as well as applying this knowledge and theory.

Requirements and Experience

Aircraft manufacturing scientists are team players. They must be able to collaborate with other scientists, engineers, and technicians. Other requirements include self-discipline, a willingness to accept responsibility, and a sound foundation in technology. A college degree in one of the sciences is the minimum requirement. An advanced degree is often necessary.

Aircraft Manufacturing Technician

Technicians include all persons engaged in work that requires knowledge of how to apply information in the physical, life, engineering, and mathematical sciences. Examples of technician position titles include senior documentation analyst, software programmer, contracts administrator, and technical illustrator.

Working Conditions

Technicians work in research departments, labs, or engineering departments. Some outdoor work may be necessary.

Requirements and Experience

You will need at least a two-year associate degree in science or engineering. You may want to get a diploma from a college or university, junior or community college, technical institute, or technical or vocational school. You may qualify for some technician jobs by completing an on-the-job training program. Or you may just get experience through other jobs or outside courses. You can get such training and experience while on active duty with the military.

Aircraft Mechanic

Aviation maintenance mechanics keep airplanes and their equipment working safely and efficiently.

An aircraft mechanic may be licensed or unlicensed. The licensed mechanic may receive a mechanic or repairman certificate from the FAA. A person with a mechanic certificate can work on only the specific parts of the aircraft for which he or she is rated. Similarly, a mechanic with a repairman certificate can work on only on those parts of the aircraft that the certificate specifically allows, such as radio or instruments or propellers.

Licensed aircraft mechanics receive certification from the FAA.
Courtesy of Peter Kneffel/epa/Corbis Images

If you have an interest in electronics, you may choose to specialize in avionics. This includes aircraft navigation and communication radios, weather radar systems, autopilots, and other electronic devices. This field is becoming more interesting and challenging as the technology expands.

Working Conditions

Depending on the type of work they do, aircraft mechanics and repairmen work in hangars, on the flight line, or in repair shops. They use hand and power tools along with test equipment. They often work under pressure to maintain flight schedules.

Requirements and Experience

An aircraft mechanic should have an above-average mechanical ability and a desire to do hands-on work with equipment and systems. He or she should also have an interest in aviation, appreciation of the importance of doing a job carefully and thoroughly, and a desire to learn throughout a career.

A high school diploma is not required to become an apprentice aircraft mechanic. Employers give preference, however, to applicants who are high school or vocational school graduates. Mathematics, physics, computer science, chemistry, English, and aerospace education courses are suitable subjects to pursue while in high school.

Aviation Specialist

Aviation specialists promote aviation education and safety. They inspect airports and flight schools to make sure they comply with federal and state regulations. They confer with airport and local governmental officials relative to compliance with state and federal laws and regulations relating to approach maintenance, approach clearing, runway marking, use of donated airport property, and other airport-related matters.

Working Conditions

Some positions require travel to visit the airports and flight schools you are inspecting or to meet with local, state, and federal government officials.

Requirements and Experience

To work as an aviation specialist, you'll need a bachelor's degree from a four-year college, a pilot's license, and two years of professional experience as a pilot, air traffic controller, certified flight instructor, or a similar position.

Avionics Technician

Avionics technicians repair and maintain components used for aircraft navigation and radio communications, weather radar systems, and other instruments and computers that control flight, engine, and other primary functions. Because of the increasing use of technology aboard aircraft, technicians spend more time repairing electronic systems, such as computerized controls. Technicians also may be required to analyze and develop solutions to complex electronic problems.

Working Conditions

Avionics technicians usually work in aircraft factories, hangars, or other indoor areas. When hangars are full or repairs must be done quickly, however, they may have to work outdoors, sometimes in unpleasant weather. They often work under time pressure to maintain flight schedules.

Requirements and Education

Although a few people become aviation mechanics and technicians through on-the-job training, most learn their job in one of about 170 trade schools certified by the FAA. About one-third of these schools award two-year and four-year degrees in avionics, aviation technology, or aviation maintenance management. Avionics duties may require additional licenses, such as a radiotelephone license issued by the US Federal Communications Commission (FCC).

Jobs at Airports

As noted earlier, you don't need to be able to fly or fix an airplane to work in the aerospace industry. Many different jobs are available at commercial airports. These range from airline ticket agents to customer service agents to baggage handlers to security officers to inspectors for the federal Transportation Security Administration. Airports also employ a variety of building maintenance and repair workers. Many airport jobs require only a high school education, while others will require a two- or four-year college degree.

The best way to select your program is to decide which area of aerospace most interests you. Are you a research-and-development person, or would you be more suited to design and manufacture? Apply to the programs that most closely match your dreams.

Jobs at airports include airline ticket agents and customer service agents.
Courtesy of Corbis Images

A career as a pilot begins with good grades in high school and college.
Courtesy of Jonathan Nourok/PhotoEdit

Preparing for a Career in Aerospace

It's never too early to begin preparing for your career. Take as many courses as you can that will teach you the skills and knowledge you need. Use every opportunity to practice those skills.

A grade point average of 3.0 or better (on a 4.0 scale) increases your chances of getting a job with NASA or the private aerospace industry. Your studies should focus on science, mathematics, and English. Some recommended courses are algebra, geometry, trigonometry, calculus, computer math, biology, chemistry, physics, English composition, and literature.

Extracurricular activities and healthy life experiences should also be part of your career plan. Get involved in after-school sports and clubs. Look for opportunities to explore career choices through co-op or internship programs, summer jobs, career days, or volunteer work.

Finally, learn as much as you can about the field. Public libraries are good sources of information. Read books about key events in the history of aerospace. Include science fiction, such as stories about interplanetary travel, living and working in space, or the colonization of the moon and Mars. Then use critical thinking to decide whether these books are "good science" or "bad science." Read magazines about the latest developments in airplanes and the most recent discoveries in the solar system.

CHECKPOINTS

Lesson 3 Review

Using complete sentences, answer the following questions on a sheet of paper:

1. What are the roles of engineers, scientists, and technicians in the aerospace field? Define each role and show how it differs from the other two.
2. Explain the roles of NASA and the FAA and why each was created.
3. What is the difference between education and training?
4. What education will you need beyond high school if you are interested in a career as an aerospace scientist or engineer?
5. What are three areas that you might want to major in if you decide to pursue a career in aerospace?
6. List some aerospace careers that require no college but do require specialized training.

Applying Career Skills

7. Pick one of the careers in aerospace that you wrote down under "Quick Write" at the beginning of this lesson. Imagine that you'd spent many years in that career and are ready to retire. Write a story, no longer than one page, that describes your experience in that field. What will your life have been like?

AIR FORCE
JUNIOR
ROTC

CHAPTER

2

Educational and Career Paths

Chapter Outline

Despite what many people believe, the job search does not begin with a résumé—rather it begins with discovering who you really are, what you want, and where you wish to go.

—Carolyn R. Robbins, career development consultant and author

LESSON 1

Aptitudes and Orientations

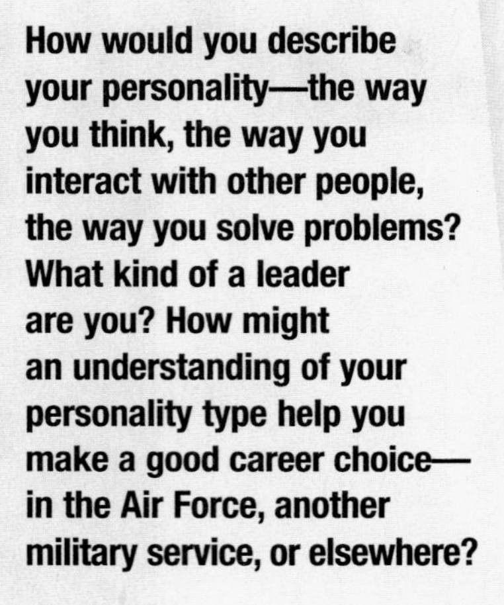

How would you describe your personality—the way you think, the way you interact with other people, the way you solve problems? What kind of a leader are you? How might an understanding of your personality type help you make a good career choice—in the Air Force, another military service, or elsewhere?

- personality types of the Myers-Briggs Type Indicator® (MBTI®)
- what the MBTI says about leadership styles and work environments
- career paths based on your MBTI personality type

Personality Types of the Myers-Briggs Type Indicator

Personality is one of the things that make each person unique. Have you ever wanted to learn more about your personality and better understand how it affects your life?

Many educators and professionals use a well-tested tool for this purpose. It's called the Myers-Briggs Type Indicator®, or MBTI®. The MBTI was developed in the 1940s. It is based on the work of a famous Swiss psychologist, Carl Jung.

Although the MBTI is sometimes called a "test," it has no right or wrong answers. All answers are equally acceptable. The purpose of the MBTI is simply to help people identify their personality preferences. As its name suggests, the MBTI can *indicate* what type of person you are. Millions of people have taken the MBTI, and many have used the results to make smart career choices.

In this lesson, you'll learn about the MBTI, how to use it to determine your own personality preferences, and the connection between your personality type and good career choices.

What Are Personality Preferences?

Personality preferences *are the ways you like to think and behave.* They define what makes you unique. You might compare them to handedness. You have two hands. You use them both. But most people are either right-handed or left-handed. That is, they have a natural inclination, or preference, to use one hand. They feel more comfortable using that hand. In a similar way, you have many facets to your personality. You use them all. You have a natural inclination, however, for certain ways of thinking and behaving. They're part of what makes you "you."

Advantages of Knowing Your Personality Type

Knowing your personality type is helpful in many ways. For example, it can help you understand how you learn best. Some people like a lot of structure in the classroom; others learn best in a looser environment. Again, it's not a matter of "right or wrong"—it's just a matter of different learning styles.

The MBTI can help you understand what kind of leader you are. For example, do you like to lead by example or by force? Or do you not prefer to lead at all? Finally, as noted above, knowledge of your personality preferences can help you make good career choices.

Vocabulary

- personality preferences
- extraverted
- introverted
- complementary
- instinctive
- sensing
- intuition
- conceptual
- thinking
- feeling
- judgment
- perception
- hierarchy

The MBTI—Step by Step

The MBTI is based on four questions, or *dimensions*. For each question, you choose one of two options. To determine your personality preferences, you then combine those choices.

Ready to learn more about the MBTI? Start with the four questions. As you read on, try to think which of the options best describes you.

1. **Where do you prefer to direct your energy? Is your energy flow outward or inward?**

If you are **extraverted** (E), *you prefer to direct your energy to people, things, activities, or the "outer world."*

If you are **introverted** (I), *you prefer to direct your energy to ideas, information, explanations, and imagination, or the "inner world."*

The words *extraverted* and *introverted* describe two different aspects of human nature. These two aspects are **complementary;** in other words, *they support each other and round each other out.* Every person has a mix of these two energy "faces." But at the same time, most people have a preference for either the outer or the inner world. That preference is innate, or inborn. In every human being, one of these faces takes the lead in personality development. It has a bigger role in behavior than the other face does. This preferred behavior is called **instinctive;** in other words, *it is unconscious and happens naturally.*

Knowing your personality preferences can help you understand how you learn best and the kind of careers you would prefer.

A person with mainly *extraverted* characteristics might tend to:

- act first and think later
- feel deprived if cut off from interaction with the outside world
- be open to and motivated by people and things
- have a wide variety of friends from different backgrounds.

Extraverted people are motivated by people and things. Introverted people are motivated by internal factors.

A person with *introverted* characteristics would usually:

- think before acting
- periodically need some "private time" to think things through
- be motivated by internal, rather than external, factors
- prefer one-to-one communication and relationships.

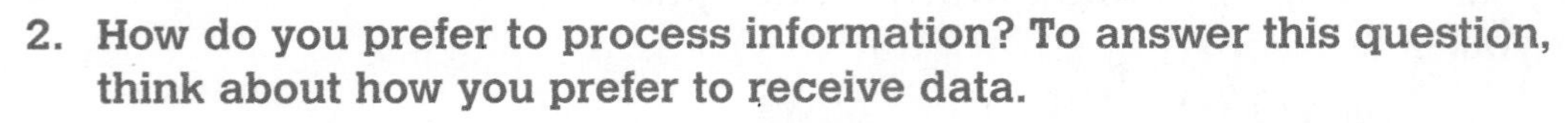

2. How do you prefer to process information? To answer this question, think about how you prefer to receive data.

You prefer **sensing** **(S)** *if you like dealing with facts, certainty, and clarity.* You notice sights, sounds, smells, and other sensory details. You like to categorize, organize, record, and store details. Your thinking and behavior are reality based.

You have a preference for **intuition** **(N)** *if you prefer to deal with ideas, look into the unknown, generate possibilities, or anticipate what isn't obvious.* (The letter *N* is used for "intuition" because the letter *I* has already been used for "introverted."). You seek to understand, interpret, and form patterns of information. You concentrate on the big picture rather than on details. You tend to be imaginative and you like being **conceptual,** *or focused on concepts and ideas rather than things. You trust your insights.*

Every person needs and uses both kinds of perceiving. But each person also instinctively favors one kind over the other.

A person with *sensing* characteristics might, for example:

- pay more attention to the present than to the future
- use common sense to create practical solutions
- be able to recall facts and events in detail
- make decisions on the basis of experience
- like clear and concrete information; dislike having to guess.

By contrast, a person with *intuitive* characteristics might:

- spend more time than most people thinking about the future
- be imaginative and like to create new possibilities
- find it easy to see patterns and connections
- make decisions on the basis of theoretical understanding
- be comfortable with uncertainty and with having to guess.

3. How do you prefer to make decisions?

You decide things on the basis of **thinking** (T) *if you prefer to make decisions on the basis of logic, using an analytic and detached approach.* You tend to see things in terms of black and white, or true and false. You usually rely on rules and accepted procedures.

You decide things on the basis of **feeling** (F) *if you prefer to make decisions on the basis of values and your own personal beliefs.* You might see the world in shades of gray rather than black and white. You rely on your own ideas, rather than someone else's standards, to make decisions.

People who make decisions on the basis of *thinking* might:

- search for facts and use logic when they must make a decision
- notice tasks and work to be accomplished
- find it easy to provide an objective analysis
- accept conflict as a natural part of life.

People who make decisions on the basis of *feeling* might:

- rely on personal feelings rather than on rules
- be sensitive to people's needs and reactions
- be consensus builders; try to find common ground
- be upset by conflict.

4. How do you prefer to organize your life?

You have **judgment** (J) characteristics *if you prefer your life to be planned, stable, and organized.* You prefer to approach the world with a plan. You try to organize your surroundings and be prepared. You like to make decisions and reach closure.

You have **perception** (P) characteristics *if you prefer to be flexible and to take the outside world as it comes.* You tend to "go with the flow"; you're open-minded. You welcome new challenges, and changing plans doesn't bother you.

People who prefer *judgment* might:

- plan as many details as possible before acting
- be task oriented; prefer to complete one part of a project before moving on
- use targets, dates, and routines to manage their lives.

People who prefer *perception* might:

- be comfortable acting without a plan or planning "on the go"
- like to do many things at once; to mix work and play
- work best when deadlines are close
- avoid making commitments that interfere with flexibility, freedom, and variety.

What the MBTI Says About Leadership Styles and Work Environments

When you put together the eight personality types just described in various combinations, you get 16 MBTI codes. These 16 combinations are often presented in the form of the following list:

MBTI Personality Types

ISTJ	ISFJ	INFJ	INTJ
ISTP	ISFP	INFP	INTP
ESTP	ESFP	ENFP	ENTP
ESTJ	ESFJ	ENFJ	ENTJ

For example, *INTJ* indicates that you prefer Introversion, iNtuition, Thinking, and Judging. Remember, this indicates *preferences* only. An INTJ also uses Extraversion, Sensing, Feeling, and Perception. Those functions are less instinctive, however, than the preferred functions are.

Now it's time to connect the MBTI to reality. Table 2.1 contains some general descriptions of the leadership styles and work environments that each of the 16 personality types favors. Which combination describes you best? Which describes you least?

The best way to learn your four-letter type is to take the 93-question MBTI test from a certified administrator. Many counselors and psychologists are certified to administer and evaluate the test.

TABLE 2.1

Personality Types, Leadership Styles, and Preferred Work Environments

PERSONALITY TYPE	LEADERSHIP STYLE	PREFERRED WORK ENVIRONMENT
ISTJ	• uses experience and knowledge of the facts to make decisions • reliable, stable, and consistent • respects tradition and **hierarchy,** *or established levels of authority* • rewards workers who follow the rules • pays attention to the immediate and practical needs of the organization.	• contains hard-working people focused on facts and results • provides security • rewards those who work at a steady pace • structured, orderly • task-oriented • allows privacy and few interruptions.
ISTP	• leads through actions and example • prefers a team approach • responds quickly to problems • manages loosely; offers minimal supervision • acts on the basis of principles rather than details.	• contains action-oriented people focused on the immediate situation • flexible; not governed by rules • provides many new and urgent problems to solve • provides hands-on experience • action-oriented • fosters independence.
ESTP	• takes charge in crises • persuasive • direct and assertive • chooses the most convenient route • seeks action and immediate results.	• contains lively, results-oriented people who value firsthand experience • not bureaucratic, or rigidly devoted to the details of administrative procedure • allows times for fun • provides flexibility • technically oriented • physically attractive.
ESTJ	• seeks leadership directly and takes charge quickly • applies and adapts past experiences to solve problems • able to quickly analyze an issue and get to the core of a situation • makes decisions quickly • respects tradition and hierarchy.	• contains hard-working people focused on getting a task done correctly • task oriented • organized and structured • stable and predictable • focused on efficiency • rewards those who meet goals.

continued on next page

TABLE 2.1 *continued*

Personality Types, Leadership Styles, and Preferred Work Environments

PERSONALITY TYPE	LEADERSHIP STYLE	PREFERRED WORK ENVIRONMENT
ISFJ	• may be reluctant to accept leadership, but will step in when asked • expects everyone to comply with organizational needs, structure, and hierarchy • uses personal influence behind the scenes • follows procedures and manages conscientiously • thinks things through; strives for practical results.	• contains conscientious people working on well-structured tasks • secure • calm, quiet, efficient • allows for privacy • service-oriented.
ISFP	• prefers a team approach • uses personal loyalty to motivate others • more apt to praise than to criticize • adapts to change • persuades by tapping into others' good intentions.	• contains cooperative, courteous people • allows for private space • flexible • aesthetically appealing • people-oriented.
ESFP	• leads by promoting goodwill and teamwork • manages crises well • eases tense situations by bringing together conflicting factions • focuses on immediate problems • facilitates interactions among people.	• contains adaptable, easygoing people focused on present realities • lively, action-oriented • harmonious • attractive.
ESFJ	• leads through personal attention to others • gains people's trust through relationship-building • keeps people well informed • sets an example of hard work and follow-through • upholds organizational traditions.	• contains conscientious, cooperative, sensitive people • focused on helping others • goal-oriented people and systems • organized • friendly • operates on the basis of facts.

TABLE 2.1 *continued*

PERSONALITY TYPE	LEADERSHIP STYLE	PREFERRED WORK ENVIRONMENT
INFJ	• leads through a vision of what is best for others and the organization • earns cooperation rather than demands it • chooses a quiet yet persistent course of action • inspires others with their ideals.	• contains people focused on ideals that make a difference to human welfare • provides opportunities for creativity • harmonious, quiet • has a personal feel • allows time and space for reflection • well organized.
INFP	• tries to make things easier for everyone • tends to lead in nontraditional ways • works independently toward a vision • more likely to praise than to critique others • encourages others to act on their ideals.	• contains pleasant, committed people focused on values of importance to others • cooperative atmosphere • allows privacy and flexibility • unbureaucratic • allows time and space for reflection.
ENFP	• leads with energy and enthusiasm • likes to be in charge of the start-up phase • communicates and often becomes a spokesperson for values relating to people • works to include and support others • pays attention to what motivates others.	• contains imaginative people • focused on human possibilities • colorful, unconstrained, lively • thinks that participation is important • offers variety and challenge • idea-oriented.
ENFJ	• leads through personal enthusiasm • takes a direct role in managing people and tasks • responsive to followersí needs • challenges the organization to make actions consistent with its values • inspires change.	• contains individuals focused on changing things for the betterment of others • people-oriented • supportive and social • has a spirit of harmony • encourages self-expression • settled, orderly.

continued on next page

TABLE 2.1 *continued*

Personality Types, Leadership Styles, and Preferred Work Environments

PERSONALITY TYPE	LEADERSHIP STYLE	PREFERRED WORK ENVIRONMENT
INTJ	• drives self and others to attain organizational goals • acts strongly and forcefully in the field of ideas • can be tough-minded • conceptualizes, designs, and builds new models • willing to reorganize a whole system when necessary.	• contains decisive, intellectually challenging people focused on implementing long-range visions • allows privacy for reflection • efficient • includes effective and productive people • encourages autonomy • provides opportunities for creativity • task-focused.
INTP	• leads through conceptual analysis of problems • applies logical thinking to tasks • seeks personal independence • likes to lead people who are independent • relates to others on the basis of expertise rather than position • interacts at an intellectual rather than an emotional level.	• contains independent thinkers focused on solving complex problems • allows privacy • fosters independence • flexible • quiet • rewards self-determination.
ENTP	• plans theoretical systems to address organizational needs • encourages independence in others • applies systems thinking • uses compelling reasons to support a chosen course of action • acts as catalyst between people and systems.	• contains competent, independent people working on models to solve complex problems • flexible and challenging • change-oriented • rewards risk-taking • encourages autonomy • not unbureaucratic.
ENTJ	• takes an action-oriented approach • provides a long-range vision to the organization • manages directly; tough when necessary • enjoys complex problems • takes on as much responsibility as possible.	• contains results-oriented, independent people focused on solving problems • efficient systems and people • challenging • rewards decisiveness • includes tough-minded people • structured.

Career Paths Based on Your MBTI Personality Type

Each of the 16 personality types tends to be attracted to certain careers. Think about which of the personality types just described is closest to yours. Then consult the lists below to see what kinds of careers may be closest to your natural preferences.

The career lists in Table 2.2 are a starting point. They are far from complete. Use them to help you begin to think about career choices. Many people have found such lists helpful. You can take the information about leadership styles and working environments found in Table 2.1 and combine it with the careers listed in Table 2.2 to create a more complete picture of the types of career and work environment you are most likely to prefer. For example, if you are an ESTJ and prefer a work environment that is task oriented, organized and structured, and stable and predictable (Table 2.1), you can look up ESTJ on Table 2.2. There you will find that jobs in the military or the aerospace industry that you might like include auditor, business administrator or manager, computer analyst, electrical engineer, financial officer, judge, military leader, police officer, and detective.

But remember: There's no guarantee that any of these careers will be appropriate for you or that your best career match is among those listed. That's because, more than anything else, you need to understand yourself and the personality traits that will have an impact on your career. You need to know what is really important to you. The MBTI is one tool that can help you do that. Once you understand your strengths and weaknesses and are aware of what you truly value, you'll be in an excellent position to pick a rewarding career.

Another thing to keep in mind: Once you choose a career, you may face lots of pressure from family, friends, and others to go in a different direction. For example, on the basis of your aptitudes, personality preferences and interests, you may decide on a career as an actor, but your family may want you to be a doctor. Or you may want to be an Air Force officer, and your friends think you should stay in the private sector and become a business executive.

It's not always easy to resolve conflicts such as these. It might help to realize that most people pursue several careers over their lifetimes, and there may be a way to do both. For example, a doctor may be able to act in plays in his or her spare time, and then pursue acting as a full-time career later in life. Or an Air Force officer may retire in 20 years and become an executive for an airplane manufacturer.

See whether any of these careers match your interests. Careers that you can pursue in the military or in aerospace appear in bold italics. Note that word *aerospace* includes both careers in the military, particularly the Air Force, and positions with employers in the civilian sector, such as NASA, the airlines, or airplane manufacturers.

The lessons that follow this will help you explore your options in career and educational paths. Later you'll learn about how to apply for college, how to find and apply for a job, and how to develop your career skills.

TABLE 2.2

Personality Types and Careers

ISFJ

- ***administrative assistant***
- ***administrator, manager***
- ***bookkeeper***
- child-care worker/early childhood development specialist
- ***member of the clergy, religious worker***
- ***designer***
- interior designer
- ***librarian***
- ***nurse***
- ***office manager***
- ***paralegal***
- real estate agent
- shopkeeper
- ***social worker, counselor.***

ESTP

- ***aircraft mechanic***
- ***computer technical support***
- ***emergency medical technician, paramedic***
- ***entrepreneur***
- ***flight attendant***
- ***marketer***
- ***computer technician network cabler***
- ***police officer, detective***
- real estate broker
- ***sales representative.***

ISTJ

- ***accountant***
- ***financial officer***
- ***business executive, administrator, manager***
- ***computer programmer, systems analyst, computer specialist***
- ***dentist***
- ***electrician***
- ***engineer***
- ***geologist***
- ***judge***
- ***lawyer***
- ***medical doctor***
- ***military leader***
- ***police officer, detective***
- stockbroker.

ESFP

- artist, performer, actor
- athletic coach
- child-care worker
- ***consultant***
- fashion designer
- ***flight attendant***
- interior designer
- ***photographer***
- ***public relations specialist***
- ***sales representative***
- ***social worker, counselor***
- veterinarian.

A career as an artist might be attractive to some people of the ESFP and the INFJ personality types.
Courtesy of Tom Stewart/Corbis Images

TABLE 2.2 *continued*

INFJ	• alternative health-care practitioner (for example, a chiropractor or reflexologist) • artist • child-care worker, early childhood development specialist • ***member of the clergy, religious worker*** • ***dentist*** • ***medical doctor*** • ***marketer*** • ***musician, artist*** • ***photographer*** • ***psychiatrist*** • ***psychologist*** • ***social worker, counselor*** • teacher.	**ENFP**	• actor • ***computer programmer, systems analyst, computer specialist*** • ***conference planner*** • ***consultant*** • ***counselor*** • ***engineer*** • ***entrepreneur*** • massage therapist • politician, diplomat • ***psychologist*** • ***scientist*** • teacher • ***television reporter*** • ***writer, journalist.***
INTJ	• ***business administrator, manager*** • ***computer programmer, systems analyst, computer specialist*** • ***corporate strategist, organization-builder*** • ***engineer*** • ***judge*** • ***lawyer*** • ***management consultant*** • ***mathematician*** • ***medical doctor*** • ***dentist*** • ***military leader*** • professor, teacher • ***scientist.***	**ENTP**	• actor • ***computer programmer, systems analyst, computer specialist*** • ***consultant*** • ***engineer*** • ***entrepreneur*** • ***lawyer*** • literary agent • ***marketer*** • ***photographer*** • ***psychologist*** • ***sales representative*** • ***scientist*** • ***systems designer.***

continued on next page

TABLE 2.2 *continued*

Personality Types and Careers

ISTP	• athlete • carpenter • ***computer programmer, system analyst, computer specialist*** • ***engineer*** • ***entrepreneur*** • firefighter • forensic pathologist • ***mechanic*** • ***medical technician*** • ***pilot, driver*** • ***police officer, detective*** • race car driver.	**ESTJ**	• ***auditor*** • ***business administrator, manager*** • ***computer analyst*** • ***electrical engineer*** • ***financial officer*** • funeral director • ***judge*** • ***military leader*** • ***police officer, detective*** • teacher • ***sales representative.***
ISFP	• artist • ***chef*** • child-care worker, early childhood development specialist • ***designer*** • forest ranger • ***mechanic*** • ***musician, composer*** • pediatrician • ***psychologist*** • ***social worker, counselor*** • teacher • veterinarian.	**ESFJ**	• ***administrator*** • ***administrative assistant*** • ***bookkeeper, accounting*** • childcare worker • ***member of the clergy, religious worker*** • family practice physician • insurance agent • ***nurse*** • ***office manager*** • retail owner • ***social worker, counselor*** • teacher.

A career as a pilot might be attractive to some people of the ISTP type, although people of other personality types may also want a flying career.
Courtesy of Roger Tully/Getty Images

TABLE 2.2 *continued*

INFP

- ***member of the clergy, religious worker***
- ***graphic designer***
- ***journalist***
- ***musician***
- ***psychiatrist***
- ***psychologist***
- ***social worker, counselor***
- teacher, professor
- ***writer.***

ENFJ

- ***member of the clergy, religious worker***
- ***consultant***
- ***event coordinator***
- facilitator
- ***human resources representative***
- ***manager***
- politician, diplomat
- ***psychologist***
- ***recruiter***
- ***social worker, counselor***
- ***sales representative***
- teacher
- ***travel agent***
- ***writer.***

INTP

- ***computer programmer, systems analyst, computer animation, computer specialist***
- ***engineer***
- forensic researcher
- park ranger
- ***judge***
- ***lawyer***
- ***mathematician***
- ***photographer***
- ***scientist***
- ***strategic planner***
- ***technical writer***
- professor.

ENTJ

- ***business administrator, manager***
- ***chemical engineer***
- ***computer consultant***
- ***corporate executive officer, organization builder***
- entrepreneur
- ***human resources manager***
- ***judge***
- ***lawyer***
- mortgage broker
- ***sales manager***
- university professor or administrator.

Computer-related jobs are attractive to people of many different personality types. Why do you suppose that is?

CHECKPOINTS

Lesson 1 Review

Using complete sentences, answer the following questions on a sheet of paper.

1. Based on your answers to the four questions in the first section of this lesson, which of the 16 MBTI personality types do you think is closest to yours? In other words, what combination of extraverted and introverted, sensing and intuition, thinking and feeling, and judgment and perception fits you best?
2. Reread the characteristics of the relevant leadership style that seems closest to yours and describe what kind of leader you probably are.
3. On the basis of what you've learned about your personality, describe the work environment in which you might do best.
4. Name three careers that fit your personality type, and explain why each might be a good option for you.
5. Think of two famous people who might fit into your personality category. Choose one person from history and one person who is living today. Write a short paragraph about each person, explaining why you think his or her personality and leadership traits are similar to yours.
6. In the workplace, some of the greatest challenges and accomplishments come when people with opposite personalities interact. What personality traits would be most different from yours? Why? How would you learn to get along with someone with a personality that is very different from yours?
7. Are there any aspects of your personality that you don't like? If so, what can you do about it? (If you answer "nothing," you're wrong!)

Applying Personality Skills

8. Talk with a friend about the MBTI personality types. Compare your personality characteristics with those of your friend. Does your friend see you in the same way that you see yourself? If you and your friend worked for the same organization, do you think you'd get along well? Why or why not?
9. Consider your leadership style and that of your friend. How does your style differ from your friend's? How is it the same? What types of careers would be suitable for each leadership style?

LESSON

2

Career Paths

The Advantages of a Technically Oriented Career Path

Some people follow career paths that require a college or university education. Lesson 3 will cover these kinds of careers and the education you would need to be successful in them. But what if you don't think that college is right for you, at least at this point in your life? You have many other options, as you're about to learn. You can choose a **technically oriented career path,** *or a career path focused on mastering technical skills that do not require a college or university education.*

A technically oriented career path has at least three important advantages:

- It provides a way to earn a good living without spending time and money pursuing a college education
- It gives you an opportunity to learn a trade that can benefit both you and society
- It can enable you to develop your knowledge of science and technology, which are so important in today's world.

Many people who follow a technically oriented career path achieve success. Those who do best have thought about their choice, defined their goals, and then worked hard to achieve them. You might be one of them.

Quick Write

Based on what you've read in previous lessons, which factors do you think a person should consider in deciding whether to choose a technically oriented career or one that involves getting a college degree first?

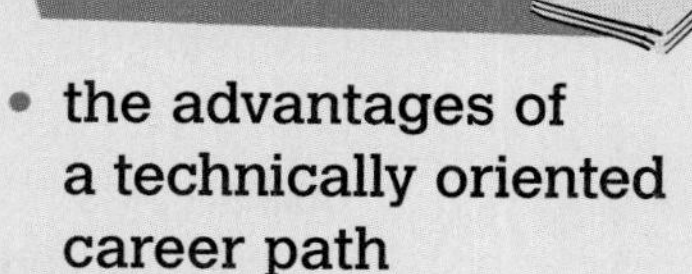

- the advantages of a technically oriented career path
- job classifications associated with technically oriented career paths
- earning potential of a technically oriented career path
- four ways to pursue a technically oriented career path

Vocabulary 

- technically oriented career path
- technical training program
- cooperative education
- vocational school
- internship
- volunteer
- reference
- mentor
- apprenticeship

Job Classifications Associated with Technically Oriented Career Paths

If you decide to enter a technically oriented career, you'll have many job classifications from which to choose. Table 2.3 lists some of the technically oriented career paths, or career fields, and it's just the beginning. That's because each of the fields in Table 2.3 has dozens of possible careers within it. As an example, Table 2.4 shows a few of the types of jobs you can pursue in just five of the career paths listed in Table 2.3.

TABLE 2.3

Examples of Technically Oriented Job Classifications

Agriculture	Health
Auto Body Repair	Horticulture and Landscape Design
Automotive Service Technology	Hospitality, Recreation, and Tourism
Aviation and Aerospace	Heating, Ventilation, and Air Conditioner Repair
Broadcast Media	Journalism
Business	Machining
Carpentry and Construction	Manufacturing
Child Care and Education	Masonry
Computer Information	Military Service
Cosmetology	Painting and Repair
Criminal and Legal	Performing Arts
Culinary Arts	Photography and Film
Electrical Occupations	Plumbing
Electronics	Printing
Energy and Power	Protection and Investigation
Engine Technology	Security and Risk Management
Engineering	Telecommunications
Entrepreneur	Transportation
Environment	Visual Arts
Food Science	Welding and Metal Arts
Graphic Arts	

TABLE 2.4

Examples of Jobs within Five Different Technically Oriented Career Paths

Automotive Service Technology

- Alternative Fuels Vehicle Technician
- Diesel Mechanic
- Dispatcher
- Truck Driver

Culinary Arts

- Baker
- Butcher
- Waiter or Waitress
- Wedding Cake Designer

Health

- Dental Hygienist
- Home Care Aide
- Massage Therapist
- Medical Laboratory Technician

Hospitality, Recreation, and Tourism

- Aerobics Instructor
- Bus Driver
- Hotel Detective
- Public Relations Specialist

Telecommunications

- Frame Wirer
- Line Installer or Repairer
- Radio Mechanic
- Telecommunications Equipment Technician

A technically oriented career path can allow you to make a good living without going to college, as well as pursue a trade that can benefit both you and society.
Courtesy of Don Mason/Corbis Images

To find more-detailed information about these career paths and jobs, or about job classifications in other fields, you can check the *Occupational Outlook Handbook* at *www.bls.gov/oco* or visit the following websites:

- Vocational Information Center at *www.khake.com*
- America's Career Resource Network at *www.acrnetwork.org/students.aspx*
- Career Voyages at *www.careervoyages.gov/*.

TABLE 2.5

Earnings Potential for Six Technically Oriented Career Paths

Position	Earning
Butcher	$15,800–$42,400/year
Bus Driver	$8.66–$23.53/hour
Disc Jockey	$6.14–$24.92/hour
Flight Attendant	$23,450–$95,850/year
Pipe Fitter	$23,800–$69,200/year
Small Engine Mechanic	$15,300–$38,200/year

Earning Potential of a Technically Oriented Career Path

If you decide on a technically oriented career path, you probably won't get rich, but you can earn a decent living. If you continue to gain new skills and advance in your work, your earnings can be even higher.

How much can you earn? Table 2.5 shows the earning potential for six technically oriented career paths. These figures are based on earnings from 2004 and 2005. They won't be current by the time you enter the field, but they still provide good estimates of relative earnings in these six areas. Also, these are salary ranges. Some people earn more than the highest figure, and others earn less. How much you'll earn depends on many factors, such as where the job is, how much experience you have, and how hard you are willing to work.

You'll notice that some of the earnings in Table 2.5 are yearly salaries and some are hourly wages. You can employ your math skills to compare them. For example, a typical workweek is 40 hours, and a year has 52 weeks. If you multiply the hourly earnings of the highest-paid bus driver—$23.53—by 40 and then by 52, you'll get $48,942. So you can see that a well-paid bus driver who works full time for a year will probably make more than the best-paid butcher will.

Four Ways to Pursue a Technically Oriented Career Path

If you plan to follow a technically oriented career path, there are several types of training programs you can take advantage of—some while you are still in high school:

- technical training programs
- internship programs
- apprenticeship programs
- pre-apprenticeship programs.

Technical Training Programs

A **technical training program** *is a learning experience that will give you the knowledge and skills you need to start a technically oriented career.*

Technical training programs most commonly cover these career areas:

- agriculture (careers related to food and fiber production, and agricultural business)
- business (office administration and entrepreneurship)
- family and consumer sciences (culinary arts, family management, and life skills)
- health occupations (nurse, dental assistant, and medical technician)
- retail sales
- trade and industrial (skilled trades such as automotive technician, carpenter, and computer technician)
- technology (transportation, manufacturing, electronics, communications, aviation, computer graphics, and construction).

The Association for Career and Technical Education estimates that there are about 11 million technical-education students in the United States. These students are enrolled in a variety of programs. Some high schools offer technical-education and **cooperative education** (co-op) programs. In a "co-op" program *you can work part-time in a career field you are interested in, while taking job-related courses at school.* You receive school credit for both your work-related class work and your real-world work experience. Two-year community colleges also provide technical education.

Another option is a **vocational school,** *a school that offers courses to prepare students for a technically oriented career.* Most of these schools offer technical programs together with work-based experiences such as internships or apprenticeships (see below).

Most high school technical-education programs last at least two years. They are usually designed for high school juniors and seniors, although some programs accept high school sophomores and other programs begin in the ninth grade. Sometimes high school technical courses are linked to community college programs. In such cases, students can earn college credit while they're still in high school. Community and technical college programs also generally last two years. These programs can be shorter for students who earn college credits while still in high school.

Many private organizations also offer technical training. Courses can last anywhere from two weeks to several years. For example, one company in California trains workers for the construction industry. At locations around the state, it offers courses for carpenters, painters, plumbers, electricians, and other workers. These courses include everything from job skills to safety rules. Another company, with locations in Arizona, Texas, California, and Illinois, gives courses for people aiming for careers in the automotive industry. Courses cover such topics as automotive and diesel technology. Before you enroll in a school run by a private company, check its background with your state board of education.

Community colleges, vocational schools, and programs offered by private organizations usually charge fees for trainees. To find out more about costs or other information about technical training programs, see your high school guidance counselor or go to the website of the Association for Career and Technical Education at *www.acteonline.org*. If you have a specific career path in mind, such as construction or auto repair, you can also contact a company or an industry association in your area to ask about where to get training.

Internship Programs

Once you've narrowed your decision about which technically oriented career to pursue after high school, think about an internship. An **internship** *is a low-paying or volunteer job in a field that interests you.*

For example, if you think you might want to be a plumber, contact a local plumbing company and see if you can arrange a part-time internship with the company while you're in school. The company may pay you a small wage. Or you might be a **volunteer,** *or unpaid worker.* Although making money may seem important, a volunteer internship could be very beneficial in the long run.

Whether you're a paid worker or volunteer, an internship gives you real-life experience that can help you decide whether a career is right for you. If you are in school while you are an intern, a teacher may supervise your experience, and you may be required to submit a paper after the internship is over.

An internship can:

- give you work experience
- boost your self-esteem and make you more responsible
- give you references—a **reference** *is a person whom future employers can contact to ask about what kind of worker you are*
- give you the chance to meet a **mentor,** *or a life coach who guides, advises, and advocates for you in your individual life path*
- help you grow and learn your true interests and talents.

To see if you qualify for an internship, contact the company, organization, or government agency you're interested in. Many of these maintain websites where you can learn how to apply for an internship.

A high school internship can give you the chance to meet a mentor.
Courtesy of Peter Mason/Getty Images

Apprenticeship Programs

An **apprenticeship** *is an opportunity to learn a trade on the job while also learning in class.* Apprenticeship programs vary in length from one to six years. Throughout that time, apprentices work and learn as employees.

Apprenticeships are available in the United States for more than 850 occupations. Construction and manufacturing apprenticeships are most common, but apprenticeships are available in many other fields as well, including computers. Possibilities include anything from telecommunications, environmental protection, and pastry making to health care, child care, and the arts. Table 2.6 lists the 25 apprenticeships that attracted the most workers in the United States in 2005, according to the US Department of Labor. Table 2.7 shows apprenticeship occupations with the highest earnings in 2000. Table 2.8 shows apprenticeships that will have the most openings between 2000 and 2010.

Although most apprenticeships are in the civilian sector, the military also offers apprenticeships. People who enlist in certain occupations, such as cook or engine mechanic, can complete registered apprenticeships during their military training. That experience may have a civilian equivalent, which means that you can carry the skills and experience you've gained in the military into a successful career elsewhere.

TABLE 2.6

The 25 Most Popular Apprenticeships in 2005

Rank	Occupation	Total Active Enrolled	Number of Active Programs	Average Enrollment/ Program
1	Electrician	38,706	3,280	11.8
2	Carpenter	22,434	481	46.6
3	Plumber	15,787	2,353	6.7
4	Pipe fitter (construction)	8,460	794	10.7
5	Sheet metal worker	7,629	582	13.1
6	Structural-steel worker	4,724	131	36.1
7	Elevator constructor	4,475	55	81.4
8	Roofer	4,397	140	31.4
9	Sprinkler fitter	4,271	85	50.2
10	Bricklayer (construction)	4,148	217	19.1
11	Construction craft laborer	4,136	71	58.3
12	Painter (construction)	3,937	245	16.1
13	Operating engineer	3,370	126	26.7
14	Child care development specialist	2,953	1,017	2.9
15	Boilermaker	2,556	31	82.5
16	Heating/air-conditioner installer	2,442	622	3.9
17	Power-line maintainer	2,418	268	9.0
18	Power-line installer and repairer	2,289	78	29.3
19	Correction officer	2,269	55	41.3
20	Millwright	2,261	438	5.2
21	Cook (hotel and restaurant)	1,837	404	4.5
22	Electrician (maintenance)	1,828	915	2.0
23	Machinist	1,739	1,346	1.3
24	Tool and die maker	1,733	1,486	1.2
25	Insulation worker	1,732	104	16.7

Taken from *www.doleta.gov*

TABLE 2.7

Apprenticed Occupations with the Highest Earnings in 2000*

Occupation	Median Annual Earnings 2000
Power distributor and dispatcher	$48,570
Electrical and electronics repairer, powerhouse, substation, and relay	$48,540
Ship engineer	$47,530
Elevator installer and repairer	$47,380
Power plant operator	$46,090
Electrical power-line installer and repairer	$45,780
Petroleum pump system operator, refinery operator, and gauger	$45,180
Gas plant operator	$44,730
Telecommunications equipment installer and repairer, except line installer	$44,030
Avionics technician	$41,300
Tool and die maker	$41,110
Aircraft structure, surfaces, rigging, and systems assembler	$40,850
Chemical plant and system operator	$40,750
Aircraft mechanic and service technician	$40,550
Stationary engineer and boiler operator	$40,420

*Includes apprenticeable occupations for which long-term on-the-job training or a postsecondary vocational award is the most common form of training, according to the Bureau of Labor Statistics.

Taken from *www.pueblo.gsa.gov*

TABLE 2.8

Apprenticed Occupations Expected to Have the Most Openings, 2000–2010*

Occupation	Total Job Openings for Workers New to the Occupation Projected 2000–2010
Cook, restaurant and cafeteria	502,435
Automotive service technician and mechanic	349,049
Licensed practical and licensed vocational nurse	321,841
Carpenter	301,791
Police and sheriff's patrol officer	268,745
Electrician	251,152
Hairdresser, hairstylist, and cosmetologist	237,720
Maintenance and repair worker, general	221,172
Welder, cutter, solderer, and brazer	211,365
Plumber, pipe fitter, and steam fitter	134,007
Machinist	127,139
Bus and truck mechanic and diesel engine specialist	113,581
Emergency medical technician and paramedic	97,499
Firefighter	89,574
Computer-controlled machine tool operator, metal and plastic	89,390
Heating, air-conditioning, and refrigeration mechanic and installer	79,485
Telecommunications line installer and repairer	76,170
Automotive body and related repairer	69,430
Cabinetmaker and bench carpenter	66,263

*Includes apprenticeable occupations for which long-term on-the-job training or a postsecondary vocational award is the most common form of training, according to the Bureau of Labor Statistics.

Taken from *www.pueblo.gsa.gov*

What Apprentices Do

Apprentices start by learning simple, repetitive tasks, then gradually progress to duties that are more complex. Electrician apprentices, for example, might begin by learning to cut and install wire. Eventually, they learn to plan projects; set up, wire, and test entire construction sites; and diagnose and fix electrical problems.

In addition to learning by doing, apprentices take classes to learn the basics in their field. The first class might teach the names and uses of the equipment a student will see on a job site. Later, students learn skills such as drafting, estimating costs, or reading blueprints.

A beginning apprentice generally earns about one-third to one-half of what an experienced, fully trained worker in that field earns. For example, the average electrician earns about $20.33 per hour. Depending on experience, apprentices usually start at around $6.09 to $10.16 per hour.

Apprenticeship programs give you an opportunity to learn a trade on the job and in the classroom.
Courtesy of Ken Chernus/Getty Images

Finding an Apprenticeship Program

Apprenticeship programs are popular. Finding a program that has openings can be a challenge, especially in occupations that don't employ large numbers of workers.

To locate an apprenticeship program, check several sources. For information on any type of apprenticeship, visit career-counseling offices. Many apprenticeship sponsors publicize openings at career centers and local high schools, and career counselors usually know about the programs in their community. You can also find information on apprenticeships in newspapers and on job boards.

You might also contact the Bureau of Apprenticeship or the office of the US Department of Labor in your state. These agencies keep lists of current programs. You might also want to consult the US Department of Labor's apprenticeship website at *http://www.doleta.gov/atels_bat/.*

Trade unions and industry associations have information on apprenticeships, too. These organizations often recruit apprentices once or twice a year. You can get information about applying for such an apprenticeship from a local union office, the national union headquarters, or the national industry association headquarters.

If you are interested in an apprenticeship in the armed forces, contact your local recruitment office or check out the military branch's website. Each branch of the military has its own rules about apprenticeships.

For general information on apprenticeships, check the *Encyclopedia of Associations* or the *Occupational Outlook Handbook*. Both are available at libraries and career centers. If you can't find an apprenticeship program that fits you, consider studying at a community college or vocational school. Later, you might be able to transfer credits you've earned in one of these schools to an apprenticeship program.

Applying for an Apprenticeship Program

Once you find a good apprentice program, you have to apply for entrance. Request an application from the organization conducting the apprenticeship and follow the instructions.

Qualifications

Most apprenticeship programs require that applicants be at least 18 years old and have a high school diploma or a passing score on the high school equivalency exam. Some programs require applicants to complete specific classes related to the occupation.

Interview

If you meet the basic qualifications, you may be invited for an interview. At that time, you'll probably meet with the head of the organization sponsoring the apprenticeship as well as a few other people.

During the interview, they will ask you about your work and school experience. They may ask why you want to be an apprentice. The interviewers will also probably ask questions that will reveal your personality traits. Interviewers want to hire people who have determination and commitment to the occupation. Curiosity is also important. Interviewers might ask questions such as:

- Why do you think you would be good at this job?
- Have you ever worked as part of a team?
- Do you know what the work is like?
- What do you think you'll be doing in five or 10 years?
- How dependable and resourceful are you?
  For example, how would you get to work if your car broke down?

Tour of the Work Site

Before deciding to join a program, you'll want to see what life will be like on the job. Tour the worksite for clues about the quality of training and the work environment. Is the equipment modern? Is the work site comfortable and safe? Do workers seem willing to demonstrate and teach skills? What would the work schedule be like? How would you get to the work site? If you don't have a car, is public transportation available?

A tour is an excellent opportunity to ask employees about their jobs. By asking questions, you can learn a lot about the occupation and the program sponsor.

Dress neatly and behave professionally when visiting potential employers. Each conversation you have during a tour of the work site is like an interview.

Pre-apprenticeship Programs

Many nonprofit organizations, schools, and government agencies help people qualify for apprenticeships by offering pre-apprenticeship programs. The goal of these programs is to help young people get jobs and stay employed. The programs focus on specific groups, including high school students, disadvantaged youth, veterans, and women.

One of the fastest-growing of these initiatives is the school-to-apprenticeship program. School-to-apprenticeships allow high school students to begin their apprenticeships as juniors and seniors. These students take occupational classes in addition to their regular high school courses. They concentrate on math, science, or other classes important to the occupation they are considering.

In a pre-apprenticeship program, students take occupational classes in addition to their regular high school courses.
Courtesy of Spencer Grant/PhotoEdit

Students in school-to-apprenticeship programs work part-time, often earning school credit for on-the-job training. After graduation, they become full-time apprentices, with the advantage of having already completed many of the requirements.

To learn more about school-to-apprenticeship programs, ask your high school guidance counselor or call your school district office.

The following organizations can provide more information on work-experience options for high school students. Some of them have local high school chapters you can join.

- National Mentoring Center at: *www.nwrel.org/mentoring*
- Job Shadowing at: *www.jobshadow.org*
- National Service-Learning Clearinghouse at: *www.servicelearning.org/*
- Junior Achievement at: *www.ja.org*
- Future Business Leaders of America (FBLA) at: *www.fbla-pbl.org/*
- Future Farmers of America (FFA) at: *www.ffa.org/*
- Distributive Education Clubs of America (DECA) at: *www.deca.org/*

CHECKPOINTS

Lesson 2 Review

Using complete sentences, answer the following questions on a sheet of paper.

1. What are three main advantages of a technically oriented career path?
2. What are three fields in which you can have a technically oriented career?
3. Which two federal government departments are good sources of information about technically oriented careers?
4. What is the earning potential for some technically oriented careers?
5. What are the three types of programs that can prepare you for a technically oriented career? How are they similar and different?
6. Pick a technically oriented career path that you are interested in. Then find out what you could earn at the beginning of your career and what you might earn when you reach the top of your profession. You might need to do some research on the Web to find the answers.

Applying Career Skills

7. Choose a technically oriented career that is available in your community. Collect as much information as you can about it: What are the advantages of a job in this field? What organizations in your area offer jobs in this field? What are some of those jobs, and what do people who hold them do? What might you earn in such a job, both as a beginner and an experienced worker? How would you train for such a job? When you finish your research, you'll have a good idea of what following a technically oriented career path means.

LESSON

3

Educational Paths

Advantages of Pursuing a Higher Education

Should you continue your education after high school? If your goal is to become a more informed citizen, a critical thinker, and a well-rounded person, or if you just want to earn a better living, a college education can help you achieve your goal.

Maybe you've always dreamed of going into a particular career. Perhaps you want to work in sports or in the entertainment industry. Maybe you're interested in law, marketing, or medicine. Or is being a military officer your goal? Whatever your dream job, one thing is certain: Pursuing a **higher education,** *or study at a college or university—perhaps starting at a community or junior college—* can help make your dream a reality. In fact, it will open more possibilities and choices than you ever imagined possible. If that's not enough, you will probably also have a wonderful time while you're there. You'll meet people and make friends for a lifetime.

Pursuing a college education can help make your career dream a reality.
Courtesy of Digital Vision/Getty Images

Quick Write

Why do you think it makes a difference whether you get a college education?

Learn About...

- advantages of pursuing a higher education
- jobs associated with educational tracks
- earning potential of college-educated professionals
- how to pursue an education-oriented career

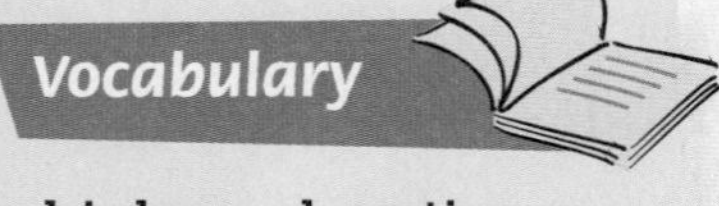

Vocabulary

- higher education
- white-collar job
- blue-collar job
- junior and community colleges
- open-admissions policy
- continuing and adult education
- graduate school
- undergraduate education
- major

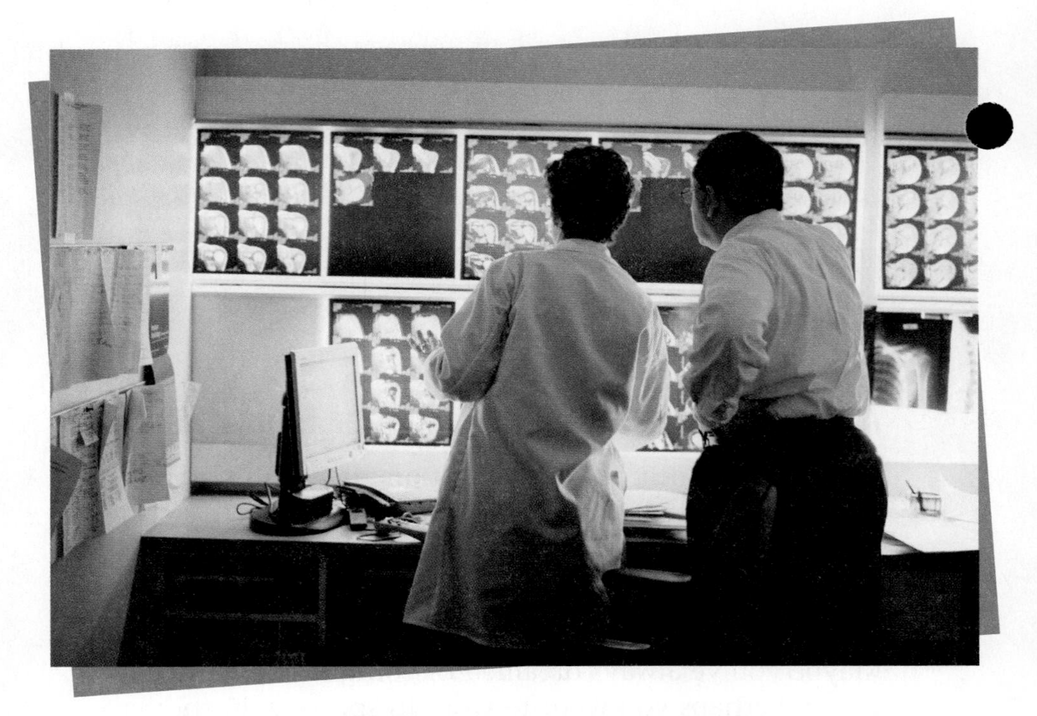

Your career opportunities will be greater if you get a college degree.
Courtesy of Reza Estakhrian/Getty Images

This lesson uses the words *college, university,* and *higher education* interchangeably. Although universities are generally larger than colleges, they both offer higher education and cover roughly the same subjects. A degree from a four-year college is the same as a university degree. A degree from a two-year community or junior college, however, is not the same as a college or university degree, as you will see later. Here are some good reasons for beginning and completing a course of study in higher education:

- The difference between what you can earn with a college degree and what you can earn with just a high school diploma is substantial. If you don't complete high school, your earning potential is even less.
- Whatever you do in life, your career opportunities will be greater if you get a college degree. A person who has attended college usually works in a **white-collar job,** *or a job that does not involve manual labor and for which people generally do not have to wear uniforms or protective clothing*. This differs from a **blue-collar job,** *or a job that often involves manual labor and for which people may need to wear a uniform or protective clothing*. The term *white collar* originally referred to a suit, shirt, and tie, but dress is often less formal today. The term *blue collar* originally referred to a blue work shirt or worker's coverall. White-collar workers tend to work in offices or other facilities with air conditioning and heating. They have conveniences (ranging from computers, to on-site childcare, to consistent work hours) that make the work environment more appealing. White-collar jobs also tend to offer more benefits, such as retirement and pension plans and paid vacations, than other jobs do.

Blue-collar jobs are more likely to be outdoors (construction jobs, for example), in dangerous locations (mining jobs), in factories and warehouses, or in vehicles (commercial driving jobs).

- Colleges and universities are exciting places to be. They have social and cultural centers with much to offer students of any age, nationality, or social background.

Four-Year Colleges and Universities

The degree that will enable you to call yourself a college graduate comes from a four-year college or university. These institutions provide courses in a wide variety of subjects. The courses are both theoretical and practical. Colleges and universities offer their students the knowledge and background necessary to be successful in many fields. They also can help place you in internships, where you will gain work-related experience that will help you get a better job.

For more information on colleges and universities, visit your local library, talk with your high school guidance counselor, or contact individual colleges. A good place to start is by visiting college websites. Information on how to find a college that's right for you is available online from the US Department of Education at *www.ed.gov/students/landing.jhtml?src=pn* and from the College Board (which administers the SAT exam) at *apps.collegeboard.com/search/index.jsp*.

Junior and Community Colleges

Junior and community colleges *offer courses and programs that lead to associate's degrees and training certificates*. Community colleges are usually less expensive than four-year colleges and universities. They are often more willing to accommodate part-time students. They often tailor their programs to the needs of local employers. Many have an **open-admissions policy,** *or a policy that permits enrollment of a student who has a high school diploma or equivalent, or in some cases, regardless of academic qualifications.* They arrange their schedules to accommodate people who are employed.

Students who aren't able to enroll in a college or university because of their academic record, limited finances, or distance from such an institution, can enroll at a junior or community colleges and earn credits that they can apply toward a degree at a four-year college. Junior and community colleges also have important roles in **continuing and adult education,** *that is, evening or weekend courses designed for working adults who are not able to enroll in college full-time.* (Many four-year schools also offer weekend, evening, and online classes—sometimes off-campus—for working adults. Some four-year schools cater specifically to people who are working.)

Jobs Associated with Educational Tracks

A degree from a four-year college or university or from a junior or community college opens many more career paths than a high school education does.

Four-Year College or University

To enter careers such as those listed below, you'll need a degree from a four-year college or university. In some cases, you'll need education beyond a four-year college to progress to higher levels in the career. This education will come from **graduate school,** *or formal education after you graduate from college, which will give you in-depth knowledge about your specific career area.*

- accountant
- business executive
- doctor or dentist
- computer systems analyst
- engineer
- environmental or natural sciences manager
- financial manager
- lawyer
- military officer
- rehabilitation counselor
- scientist
- sales manager
- social worker
- teacher

Junior or Community College

If you earn a certificate or two-year degree, careers such as the following will probably be open to you:

- auto mechanic
- barber
- broadcast technician
- computer support specialist
- cosmetologist
- dental hygienist
- electrician
- medical records and health information technician
- plumber
- registered nurse
- veterinary technologist or technician
- welder

The Occupational Outlook Handbook

The federal government publishes a book that offers information about many jobs. It's called the *Occupational Outlook Handbook,* and you can find it online at *http://www.bls.gov/oco/*. The government updates it every two years.

In the handbook, you can learn about careers in such areas as management, service, sales, administration, agriculture, construction, production, and transportation. The handbook also provides information about careers in the armed forces. It will give you information such as:

- the training and education you need for a specific job
- earning potential
- job prospects
- typical job activities and responsibilities
- working conditions.

The handbook also contains job-search tips, links to information about the job market in each state, and more.

Earning Potential of College-Educated Professionals

A hundred years ago, a college education was not necessary, even for high-level jobs. Many people could find good, well-paying jobs, regardless of their education and training. In those days, many people saw a college education as a luxury.

Today, however, higher education is often a necessity if you want to earn a better living. By the year 2020, experts say, there will be 15 million new jobs requiring college preparation. As the skill requirements of jobs continue to rise, more and more young people will need to go to college.

Table 2.9 shows how the amount men and women can earn increases as they get more education. For example, in 2004, the median salary for a working woman with a high school diploma was $488 per week. The median salary for the average woman with a bachelor's degree was $792 per week. The median salary for a working man was $645 a week in 2004 if he had a high school diploma, while the median salary was $1,044 if he had a bachelor's degree. A *median* means that half the salaries are above the amount stated, while half are below.

What can you expect to earn when you start out as a college graduate? Table 2.10 presents average annual salaries of college graduates a year after they got their degrees.

What can you earn in a specific career when you have a college degree? Salaries vary, depending on many things, including location. Salaries tend to be higher near big cities and in many areas along the coasts. The cost of living, however, also tends to be higher there. As an example, Table 2.11 gives the earning possibilities in one state—Colorado—for several careers.

Finally, although it may seem a long way off, it's important to think of salary in terms of your lifetime earning potential. According to the US Census Bureau, over their entire working lives, high school graduates earn an average of $1.2 million; associate degree holders earn about $1.6 million; and bachelor's degree holders earn about $2.1 million.

TABLE 2.9

Median Earnings by Educational Attainment and Sex*

Education	Men	Women
Less than high school	$446	$334
High school, no college	$645	$488
Associate's Degree	$788	$608
Bachelor's Degree	$1,044	$792

**Workers over 25 years of age*

Taken from *www.bls.gov*

TABLE 2.10

Average Annual Salary of Bachelor's Degree Holders One Year after Graduation

	Men	Women	Earnings Ratio
All graduates	$39,400	$32,600	83%
Business	$42,300	$39,000	92%
Education	$29,600	$28,100	95%
Engineering, Math, and Science	$45,200	$34,200	76%
Health Vocation, Technical, and Professional	$38,100	$34,300	90%
Humanities and Social Science	$34,600	$29,400	85%

Source: Peter, Katharin & Laura Horn. (2005). *Gender Differences in Participation and Completion of Undergraduate Education and How They Have Changed Over Time* (NCES 2005-169).

Taken from "Public Perceptions of the Pay Gap," American Association of Women Educational Foundation, *www.aauw.org*

TABLE 2.11

Jobs in Colorado Requiring Higher Education

GROWING OCCUPATIONS	Average Entry-Level Wage	Average Annual Wage	Average Experience Wage
Manicurists and Pedicurists *Postsecondary vocational training*	$13,500	$21,410	$21,850
Skin Care Specialists *Postsecondary vocational training*	$11,750	$22,180	$23,800
Preschool Teachers, Except Special Education *Postsecondary vocational training*	$16,260	$22,640	$24,150
Recreation Workers *Bachelor's degree*	$13,470	$22,670	$27,150
Hairdressers, Hairstylists, and Cosmetologists *Postsecondary vocational training*	$15,350	$23,880	$26,850
Barbers *Postsecondary vocational training*	$19,160	$23,980	$27,100
Veterinary Technologists and Technicians *Associate degree*	$19,020	$24,680	$27,780
Slot Key Persons *Postsecondary vocational training*	$18,030	$26,050	$28,780
Substance Abuse and Behavioral Disorder Counselors *Master's degree*	$19,570	$28,560	$33,650
Medical Records and Health Information Technicians *Associate degree*	$19,880	$29,530	$34,690
Medical Secretaries *Postsecondary vocational training*	$20,100	$30,430	$34,760
Rehabilitation Counselors *Master's degree*	$16,960	$30,560	$35,390
Broadcast Technicians *Associate degree*	$14,550	$30,630	$39,030
Emergency Medical Technicians and Paramedics *Postsecondary vocational training*	$19,660	$30,770	$37,130

continued on next page

Taken from "Jobs in Colorado Requiring Higher Education: Looking Ahead to 2012," by the Colorado Workforce Center and the Colorado Department of Labor and Employment, *www.coworkforce.com*

TABLE 2.11 *continued*

Jobs in Colorado Requiring Higher Education

DECLINING OCCUPATIONS	Average Entry-Level Wage	Average Annual Wage	Average Experience Wage
Travel Agents	$17,030	$27,050	$32,940
Radio Mechanics	$17,900	$47,110	$62,100
Aerospace Engineers	$50,090	$71,300	$86,240
Mathematicians	$46,330	$80,710	$94,260
Embalmers	$19,830	$26,570	$31,040
Electrical and Electronics Repairers, Powerhouse, Substation, and Relay	$34,800	$50,570	$58,980
Architects, Surveyors, and Cartographers, All Other	$24,180	$37,540	$44,860
Gaming and Sports Book Writers and Runners	$13,100	$16,590	$17,900
Economists	$51,680	$72,960	$84,910
Agricultural and Food Science Technicians	$18,180	$31,480	$34,790
Agricultural Engineers	$40,010	$62,340	$72,910
Anthropologists and Archaeologists	$23,720	$42,320	$54,870
Foresters	$38,310	$53,880	$62,410
Law Clerks	$25,080	$37,110	$42,300
Forest and Conservation Technicians	$20,250	$27,780	$30,430

TABLE 2.11 *continued*

TOP GROWTH OCCUPATIONS	Average Entry-Level Wage	Average Annual Wage	Average Experience Wage
Registered Nurses *Associate degree*	$36,010	$50,160	$ 57,390
General and Operations Managers *Work experience plus bachelor's or higher degree*	$39,420	$97,010	$123,950
Business Operations Specialists, All Other *Bachelor's degree*	$31,270	$56,730	$ 70,360
Computer Software Engineers, Applications *Bachelor's degree*	$43,100	$77,240	$ 89,770
Elementary School Teachers Except Special Education *Bachelor's degree*	$27,210	$40,010	$ 48,460
Computer Systems Analysts *Bachelor's degree*	$45,080	$68,780	$ 82,900
Accountants and Auditors *Bachelor's degree*	$33,770	$58,780	$ 65,730
Computer Software Engineers, Systems Software *Bachelor's degree*	$52,390	$78,620	$ 92,390
Teachers, Primary, Secondary, and Adult, All Other *Bachelor's degree*	$23,850	$39,610	$ 48,400
Secondary School Teachers, Except Special and Vocational Education *Bachelor's degree*	$29,220	$43,870	$ 54,090
Management Analysts *Work experience plus bachelor's or higher degree*	$31,090	$81,150	$ 98,960
Computer Support Specialists *Associate degree*	$28,500	$47,540	$ 55,580
Automotive Service Technicians and Mechanics *Postsecondary vocational training*	$20,310	$38,060	$ 46,460
Network Systems and Data Communications Analysts *Bachelor's degree*	$41,460	$64,690	$ 78,240

continued on next page

TABLE 2.11 *continued*

Jobs in Colorado Requiring Higher Education

GROWING OCCUPATIONS—HIGHEST PAYING	Average Entry-Level Wage	Average Annual Wage	Average Experience Wage
Dentists *First professional degree*	$90,650	$167,860	NA
Chief Executives *Work experience plus bachelor's or higher degree*	$78,140	$159,110	NA
Engineering Managers *Work experience plus bachelor's or higher degree*	$66,340	$105,320	$122,740
Computer and Information Systems Managers *Work experience plus bachelor's or higher degree*	$58,070	$ 99,580	$118,610
General and Operations Managers *Work experience plus bachelor's or higher degree*	$39,420	$ 97,010	$123,950
Lawyers *First professional degree*	$47,690	$ 95,520	$114,670
Materials Scientists *Bachelor's degree*	$55,320	$ 89,120	$110,940
Sales Managers *Work experience plus bachelor's or higher degree*	$41,570	$ 89,100	$111,120
Health Diagnosing and Treating Practitioners, All Other *Bachelor's degree*	$31,870	$ 88,750	$121,040
Natural Sciences Managers *Work experience plus bachelor's or higher degree*	$50,700	$ 88,370	$107,780
Petroleum Engineers *Bachelor's degree*	$50,720	$ 88,350	$113,710
Financial Managers *Work experience plus bachelor's or higher degree*	$48,060	$ 87,740	$104,160
Marketing Managers *Work experience plus bachelor's or higher degree*	$45,340	$ 86,290	$108,710
Computer Hardware Engineers *Bachelor's degree*	$56,400	$ 86,190	$103,510

How to Pursue an Education-Oriented Career

If you decide to pursue a higher education, you will first have to choose a college for your **undergraduate education,** *or basic college education.* This is a big decision. You'll find more information on choosing colleges in Chapter 5, Lesson 1.

If you've already settled on two or three possible career choices, you should also explore whether the colleges that you are considering have strong programs in those areas. That's because when you enroll in college, you will need to select a **major,** *or subject area on which you want to focus.* The courses you complete in your major will give you the knowledge you need to start your career in your chosen field. Table 2.12 shows all the majors (more than 170!) at The Ohio State University, a large state university. The college or university you eventually choose may have many of these majors, or even more.

Summer Internship Programs

One good way to get work experience while attending college is to do a summer internship. In internships, students learn details about a job and get practice doing it. They also make valuable contacts that can lead to a permanent position. Many internships offer college credit.

During an internship, you will do work that is useful for the organization. The person who oversees your internship may give you assignments relevant to your college studies. When your internship ends, the organization usually submits a brief report about your experience to your college.

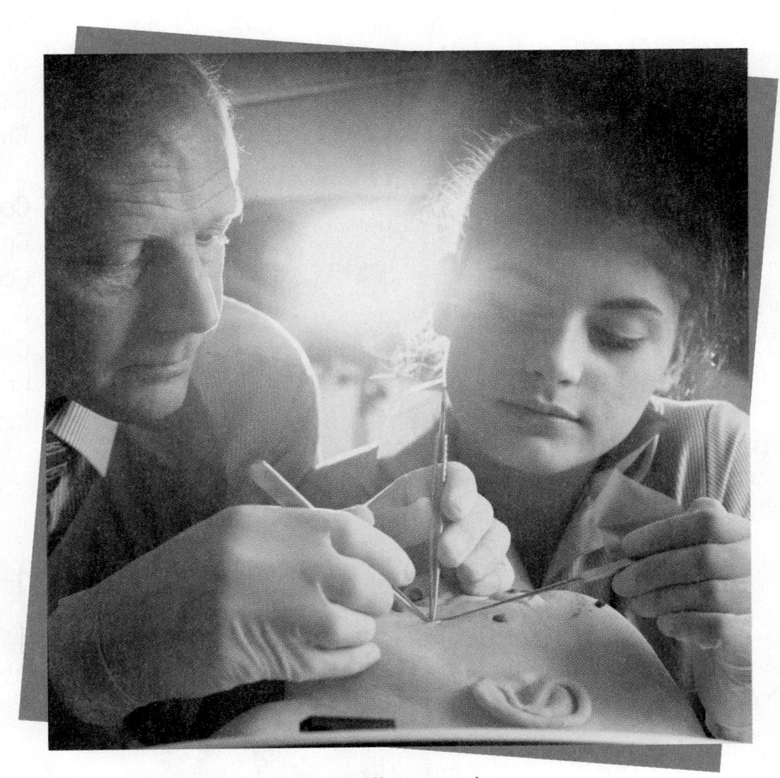

Summer internships allow college students to learn the details about a job and get practice doing it.
Courtesy of Spencer Rowell/Getty Images

TABLE 2.12

Undergraduate Majors at The Ohio State University

A

Accounting
Actuarial Science
Aeronautical and Astronautical Engineering
African-American and African Studies
Agribusiness and Applied Economics
Agricultural Communication
Agricultural Education
Agricultural Systems Management
Allied Medical Professions General Information
Animal Sciences
Anthropology
Arabic
Architecture
Art
Art Education
Astronomy
Athletic Training
Aviation

B

Biochemistry
Biology
Business Administration General Information

C

Chemical Engineering
Chemistry
Chinese
Circulation Technology
Civil and Environmental Engineering
Classics
Communication
Comparative Studies
Computer and Information Science
Computer Science and Engineering
Construction Systems Management
Criminology
Crop Science

Taken from *www-afa.adm.ohio-state.edu*

The Wexner Center for the Arts at The Ohio State University
Courtesy of Eisenman Architects

TABLE 2.12 *continued*

D

Dance
Dental Hygiene
Dietetics (Medical Dietetics)

E

Early and Middle Childhood Pre-Education
Economics
Electrical and Computer Engineering
Engineering, Undecided
Engineering Physics
English
Entomology
Environmental Science
Evolution and Ecology
Exercise Science Education
Exploration

F

Family and Consumer Sciences Education
Family Resource Management
Finance
Food, Agricultural and Biological Engineering
Food Business Management
Food Science and Nutrition
Forestry, Fisheries, and Wildlife
French

G

Geography
Geological Science
Geomatics Engineering
German

H

Health Information Management and Systems
Health Sciences
Hebrew
History
History of Art
Hospitality Management
Human Development and Family Science
Human Dimensions in Natural Resources
Human Nutrition
Human Resources

I

Industrial Design
Industrial and Systems Engineering
Information Systems
Interior Design
International Business Administration
International Studies
Islamic Studies
Italian

J

Japanese
Jazz Studies (Music Performance)
Jewish Studies
Journalism

L

Landscape Architecture
Landscape Horticulture
Linguistics

continued on next page

TABLE 2.12 *continued*

Undergraduate Majors at the Ohio State University

M

Mapping and Land Information Science
Marketing
Materials Science and Engineering
Mathematics
Mechanical Engineering
Medical Dietetics
Medical Technology
Medieval and Renaissance Studies
Microbiology
Middle Childhood Education (pre-licensure)
Modern Greek
Molecular Genetics
Music Composition
Music Education
Music History
Music Performance—Jazz Studies
Music Performance—Orchestral Instruments
Music Performance—Piano
Music Performance—Voice
Music Theory

N

Nursing
Nutrition

O

Operations Management
Orchestral Instruments (Music Performance)

P

Pharmaceutical Sciences
Philosophy
Physics
Piano (Music Performance)
Plant Cellular and Molecular Biology
Plant Health Management
Political Science
Portuguese
Psychology

R

Radiologic Technology
Real Estate and Urban Analysis
Respiratory Therapy
Risk Management and Insurance
Russian

S

Social Work
Sociology
Spanish
Special Education
Speech and Hearing Science
Sport and Leisure Studies

T

Technical Education and Training
Technology Education
Textiles and Clothing
Theatre
Transportation and Logistics
Turfgrass Science

U

Undecided (Exploration)

V

Visual Communication Design
Voice (Music Performance)

W

Welding Engineering
Women's Studies

Z

Zoology

CHECKPOINTS

Lesson 3 Review

Using complete sentences, answer the following questions on a sheet of paper.

1. Why does it make sense to pursue a higher education if you want a satisfying career?
2. What is the difference between a college and a university? Between a university and a junior or community college?
3. What are five types of jobs that typically require a four-year college education?
4. What are five types of jobs that will be open to you with the proper certificate or two-year associate's degree from a junior or community college?

Applying Education Skills

5. Have you ever thought about which college you might want to attend? Contact that college by mail or through its website. Find out what undergraduate majors it offers. Pick three majors that you can see yourself studying. Then make a list of careers you could enter with that educational background.

KAMEL
ORLOVA

UNIT 2

Charting Your Financial Course

Unit Chapters

In Your Home and Community

COMPARING RATES AND PRICES

Visit at least three branch banks in your community or county and compare their rates for savings and checking accounts. Then visit three grocery or convenience stores and compare their prices for a half-gallon of milk and the same-size box of Rice Krispies breakfast cereal. What differences did you find?

4.85
WILSON

CHAPTER

3

Planning Your Finances

Chapter Outline

Priorities lead to prosperity.

—Michelle Singletary, personal-finance columnist and author

LESSON

1 Creating a Budget

Quick Write

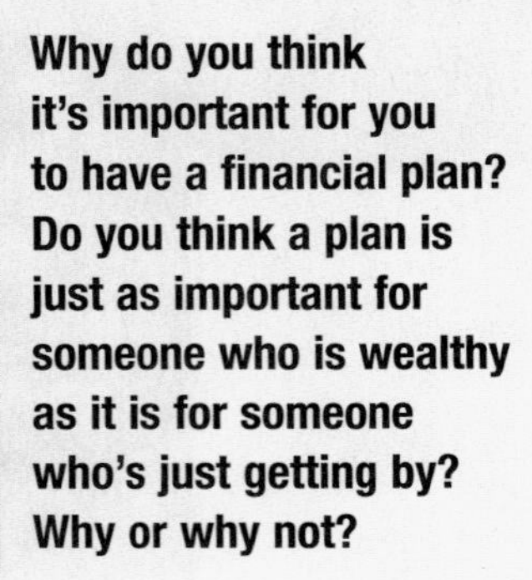

Why do you think it's important for you to have a financial plan? Do you think a plan is just as important for someone who is wealthy as it is for someone who's just getting by? Why or why not?

Learn About...

- the components of a personal financial plan
- the steps for developing a financial plan
- the elements of a budget

The Components of a Personal Financial Plan

Would you put on a big party without planning? Not likely! First, you'd probably decide on the date and time. Then you'd figure out where to have it: at your house? At a restaurant? You would decide on the food, decorations, and music. Of course, you'd have to make a list of guests and send out invitations. Before the plans went too far, you'd have to make sure you could afford everything.

Planning for your financial future is much more important than planning a party. But it, too, involves answering a series of questions. What are your goals? Do you want to go to college? Buy a car? Buy a home? Build up a savings account? Start a family and then help your children become financially secure? Take an early retirement? All these things require money. And if you want to have money, you have to make a plan for how you're going to get it and how you're going to save and spend it.

Planning for your financial future involves answering a series of questions about your goals.

The word *finance* refers to money, and the term **personal finance** *refers to how you manage your money and other things of financial value.* A personal financial plan can make the difference between being able to do the things you want to do and feeling that you'll never reach your goals in life.

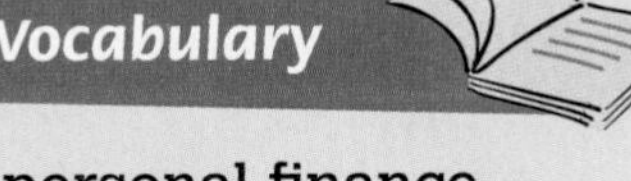

- personal finance
- financial plan
- budget
- liquidity
- financing
- interest
- asset
- insurance
- investment
- retirement
- risk
- income
- expense
- spending limits

Advantages of Understanding Personal Finance

An understanding of personal finance helps you:

- make good financial decisions. Good financial decisions will increase the wealth you accumulate over time and make it more likely that you'll be able to purchase the products and services you want.
- evaluate the opinions of financial advisers. Financial advisers are experts in financial planning. When you're older, you may want to get advice from such a professional. But it will be up to you to determine whether you're getting good advice. You'll also need to know the right questions to ask to feel more secure. No one can predict the future. The firm you've worked with for years may go out of business. You may become seriously ill and not be able to work. An investment may turn sour. The more you know about financial planning, the better you'll be able to adapt to unexpected circumstances.

And who knows? If you decided, after studying an earlier lesson in this book, that you wanted to pursue a career path in personal finance, you might want to become a financial adviser yourself.

Creating a Personal Financial Plan

The first step in mastering your personal finance is to create a **financial plan,** *or a document that outlines your financial goals and how you plan to reach them.* A financial plan sets forth your decisions in six areas:

A budget helps you plan for and control your spending.

1. Managing Your Budget

A **budget** *is a detailed summary of expected expenses and income for a given period.* A budget helps you plan for and control your spending.

Think again about the decisions you'd make when planning the party mentioned above. Many of them involve money. As you began to plan, you would want to draw up a budget. The budget would show your estimated expenses, or how much you think you'd need to spend for invitations, decorations, food, and other items. To make those estimates as accurate as possible, you'd have to do research. For example, if this were a birthday party, you could visit several bakeries to see where you could get the best deal on a cake.

Once you'd estimated the expenses, you'd need to look at your financial resources. You'd need to know whether you had enough money to pay for your party. If you did not, you'd either have to find a way to get more money or plan a less expensive party.

To create a budget as part of a long-term financial plan, rather than for a specific event such as a party, you list your expected expenses and income over a certain period. (You'll learn more about budgets later in this lesson.) This could be the next year, the next 10 years, or even a lifetime.

Based on the information in your long-term budget, you can decide if your income will be adequate to enable you to have the standard of living that you want to have. Your goal should be for your income to be greater than, not just equal to, your expenses. If this is the case, you will be able to save, and saving is essential for creating wealth and building a good future.

2. Managing Your Liquidity

A financial plan must take into account your liquidity. **Liquidity** *is access to funds to cover a short-term cash need.* Even though they've made good plans, people often need money for an unexpected expense. They might own valuable items, such as land, a house, or a car, but those items will be useless if they need cash quickly. In that case, they will need liquidity.

If liquidity is a problem, some people borrow money. Borrowing is usually necessary to finance a major expense, such as a college education, a house, or a new car. But borrowing has risks, as you'll learn later in this lesson.

3. Financing Large Purchases

Financing *is obtaining or providing money for a specific purpose.* The person obtaining the money is the borrower, and the other party (usually a company) is the lender. Financing generally comes in the form of loans.

For example, if you plan to go to college, your parents or guardian may be able to pay part of the cost from their savings. You may be able to contribute something from your earnings. But college can be expensive, and you and your family may not have enough to pay for everything. In this case, you may want to take out a student loan. This loan will cover the difference between what you and your family can give and the total cost of your education.

Most people need to take out loans at one point or another. But you should never get dependent on loans, because you must pay all those loans back. And when you repay them, you'll have to pay **interest,** *which is a charge on borrowed money.* Interest charges seem small, but they add up.

For example, say you borrowed $10,000 to pay for part of your college tuition. The interest rate on the loan was 5 percent per year. If you didn't make any payments in the year after you got your loan, you would have to add 5 percent, or $500, to the $10,000 that you borrowed. If you made no payments on your loan for 10 years, your interest would total a whopping $6,289. Of that sum, $5,000 would be interest on the $10,000 you had borrowed. The remaining $1,289 would be interest on the unpaid interest, which is called *compound interest.*

Most people pay back their loans gradually. Their interest payments go down, rather than up, over the years. Still, interest payments add up, and you need to be aware of and keep track of them.

4. Protecting Your Assets

An **asset** *is something of value that you own.* Maybe you have a car. Or you might own stock in a company. Perhaps your collection of baseball cards is valuable. Or you may have inherited a gold ring from your grandmother or a piece of equipment from your grandfather's wood shop. These are tangible assets. *Tangible* means a physical item that you can touch.

In making a financial plan, you will want to protect your assets. You can do this by buying insurance. **Insurance** *is an agreement between two parties under which one party—usually an insurance company—guarantees the other that if an asset is lost or destroyed, the insurance company will pay for it.* To insure an asset of any kind, you must pay a monthly fee, or *premium,* to the insurance company.

Insurance also covers *intangible* assets—assets that are not tangible. For example, you can insure your health or your life. Health insurance covers medical benefits. Life insurance pays a certain amount of money, or benefit, should you die.

You will want to insure your most important assets. For example, if you buy a car you will need to buy insurance. Then, if you have an accident and the car is damaged, your insurance policy will pay for the repairs.

5. Investing

Investments are an important part of a financial plan because they are one of the best ways to increase your wealth. An **investment** *is something you own that you expect to increase in value over time.* For example, you might purchase *stock,* or a share of ownership in a company. You expect that stock to increase in value. That's an investment. At some point you may buy a house and expect it to increase in value. That is also an investment. *Bonds,* or certificates issued by companies or the government in order to raise funds, are also a possibility. Some people buy art or jewelry because of its investment value. A car, however, is generally not an investment. Cars usually decrease in value as they get older.

6. Planning Your Retirement

Because a financial plan is a long-term document, it should include your retirement. **Retirement** *is the period of life during which you no longer work at a job.* A lot of people retire at age 65, but many retire earlier and some retire later. If you entered the military, for example, you could retire with benefits after just 20 years of service (although you may also want to get a civilian job at the same time).

During retirement you won't be getting a paycheck, but you'll still need money to live. So making sure you have enough money for retirement is important. And the better you plan for your future, the more likely you can choose when to retire. If you love your job and want to go on working into your 70s, that's fine. But if you'd rather retire and move on to something else, you'll need a steady source of income.

You probably think that retirement seems so far away that it's not worth thinking about. But just ask a grandparent or another older adult. Retirement age comes a lot quicker than most people think it will. If you start planning for retirement now, you'll be glad you did. The longer you save money, the more it will earn for you over the years between the time you save and the time you retire.

The Steps for Developing a Financial Plan

Now that you know the basic ingredients of a financial plan, you can build your own. Ready to start? Here are the six steps involving in creating a financial plan:

1. Establish Your Financial Goals

The first question might sound obvious, but it's important: How important is money to you? Some people get along well with just the basics. Others want a more luxurious lifestyle.

Next, consider what you need money for. Do you want to buy a new car every year? Pay for college, or even graduate school? Help your family? Make a down payment on a home? Contribute to a worthy cause? To make your plan work, you must have goals. After all, as the saying goes, if you don't know where you're headed, any path will take you there.

When you set those goals, be realistic. For example, a financial plan that requires you to save more than half your income is probably not realistic, no matter how much you earn. A plan that requires you to accumulate $1 million within one year is certainly not realistic (unless you beat enormous odds and win a state lottery).

Timing is important. A financial plan usually covers three time segments:

- A short-term plan, usually covering the next year—the goal of a short-term plan might be to buy a car within six months
- An intermediate-term plan, covering one to five years—for someone your age, the goal of an intermediate-term plan might be to save enough money for college tuition
- A long-term plan, which covers more than five years—a long-term goal might be to save enough to retire by age 55.

2. Consider Your Current Financial Position

Look at your present financial situation. Any future decisions about what you want to buy, how much money to save or borrow, and where to invest your money, depend on it. If you're lucky enough to have plenty of money, your financial decisions will be very different from those of someone who is struggling to make ends meet.

Chances are that your current financial position is limited. But that will change, and you need to know what to do with your finances when it does. The career path you choose and the amount of money you earn will greatly influence your financial position. So if your goals require a lot of money, you will want to choose a well-paying career.

But don't choose a career just for the money. If you don't love your work, you'll be miserable, no matter how much money you've got in the bank. Try to find a good balance.

3. Identify and Evaluate Alternative Ways to Achieve Your Goals

If one of your goals is to save $200,000 within 10 years, you could try to do it by putting a big portion of your income each month into a savings account. Or you could put your earnings into an investment. Of these two alternatives, the first choice is safer. The US government insures the money in most bank and credit union savings accounts up to $100,000.

Savings accounts have another advantage. They pay you interest. While you *pay* interest on a loan, you *earn* interest on a savings account. The interest on your savings account will be a small percentage, paid monthly, of the amount that you have saved. For example, say you deposited $1,000 into a savings account at 3 percent interest. One year later, your balance would be $1,030. Although it's not likely, let's assume that the interest rate stayed the same for the next nine years. Even if you made no additional deposits to your account, you would have a balance of $1,349 by the end of that time—thanks to compound interest.

A second way to reach your goal is to buy stocks or another investment. If you do, you'll face a certain degree of **risk**, or *uncertainty as to the outcome of an investment.* The government does not insure stocks. You might make a lot of money buying stock from a company—more than you ever could through savings. But if the company has problems, you could lose some, or even all, of the money you invested.

You can also buy bonds. Bonds have much less risk than stocks, but the amount of money you earn from them is less, too. Both bonds and stocks are long-term investments.

Many people have both savings accounts and investments in stocks and bonds. The portion of their income that they invest in each depends on how much risk they're willing to take. Never take on more risk than you are comfortable with. Most important, never invest more money than you can afford to lose.

The US government insures the money in most bank and credit union savings accounts up to $100,000.

4. Select the Best Plan for Achieving Your Goals

Choose the plan that you think will best help you reach your goals. It should be a plan that you can stick with. It should also have an acceptable level of risk.

5. Evaluate Your Financial Plan

Don't put your plan in a drawer and forget about it. Review it regularly to see how you're doing. You may have decided that you want to save $100 a month, but after a year you find that this is impossible. If that's the case, it's time to go back to the drawing board.

6. Revise Your Financial Plan

Look over each item on your plan. Note where it's worked and where it hasn't. Then think about how your financial situation and goals have changed since you drew up your plan. Perhaps you've gotten a new job, with a 15 percent increase in pay. Or maybe you've just gotten married or had a baby. Major life changes will require changes in your financial plan.

No one can predict the future. You can only make an educated guess. When reality says you need to change, don't be afraid to do so. Flexibility is a sign of strength, not of weakness. You'll get better at planning with each plan you make. Financial planning will become a part of your life.

The Elements of a Budget

Knowing how to draw up budget is a valuable skill. You don't need to be a math wizard. Here are the basics.

Every budget has two main elements: income and expenses. **Income** *is money that you receive regularly.* Income falls into many categories. The main categories for most people are:

- salary or wages
- savings
- investments
- other (gifts from relatives, income from things you've sold).

An **expense** *is money you spend.* Major categories of expenses for someone your age include:

- clothing
- entertainment
- travel
- books and CDs
- food
- car (payments, insurance, fuel, repair).

The point of having a budget is to compare your income versus your expenses. It helps you see what you are spending money on, and where you need to lower your spending—so you will have enough for expenses and still have money left over for savings. It allows you to set **spending limits,** or *the amount above which you should not spend if you are to meet your financial goals.*

Table 3.1 shows a sample monthly budget for Steven Johnston. Steve is 20 years old. He's an electrician apprentice. He's living on his own for the first time, and finances are tight. Steve earns $24,000 a year after taxes and withholding, and wants to save at least $200 per month. His budget is in balance. In other words, the total income and total expenses are the same.

That doesn't mean that Steve is spending all the money he gets. Look closely and you'll see that Steve has set a spending limit of $200 less than his income. In keeping with his financial plan, he's putting $200 a month into a savings account.

The next lessons will discuss how to save and invest your money, and how to make good buying decisions.

TABLE 3.1

Sample Monthly Budget for Steven Johnston

INCOME	
Salary	$2,000
Savings interest	10
Investment income	50
Total Income	**$2,060**
EXPENSES	
Rent	$ 500
Electricity and water	50
Telephone (home and cell)	80
Cable TV	60
Food	250
Entertainment and recreation	150
Health care insurance and expenses	300
Clothing	170
Car expenses	300
Savings	200
Total Expenses	**$2,060**

CHECKPOINTS

Lesson 1 Review

Using complete sentences, answer the following questions on a sheet of paper.

1. Why is a personal financial plan important?
2. What are the six parts of a personal financial plan?
3. What are the six steps involved in creating a personal financial plan?
4. What is a budget, and why is it important?

Applying Budgeting Skills

5. Create a budget for yourself for the next three months. List your expenses and income. Is your budget in balance? Is your budget realistic? If not, work on the budget until it is.
6. List your three financial goals for the next year. For the next five years. For the next 35 years.

LESSON 2

Savings and Bank Accounts

Quick Write

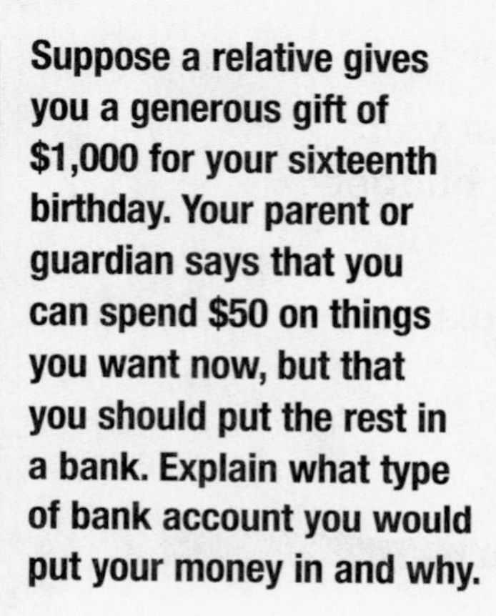

Suppose a relative gives you a generous gift of $1,000 for your sixteenth birthday. Your parent or guardian says that you can spend $50 on things you want now, but that you should put the rest in a bank. Explain what type of bank account you would put your money in and why.

Learn About...

- the advantages of bank services
- types of bank services
- how to choose a bank
- how to conduct banking transactions

The Advantages of Bank Services

After you graduate from high school, you might get a job and move into your own apartment. Or, if you go to college, you'll probably live in a dormitory or an off-campus apartment.

Most high school graduates are excited about setting out on their own. But they sometimes don't take time to think enough about the responsibilities that go along with independence. Knowing how to manage your money is one of these responsibilities.

You may already have some savings. You may have a part-time job and receive a regular paycheck. Or perhaps you've saved some of the money that your parents, a guardian, or a relative may have given you on birthdays or other occasions.

No matter where your money comes from, you'll need a safe place to keep your extra cash. That's where banks come in. Banks help keep the flow of money safe and orderly in society. Without banks, our economy couldn't function.

To keep your money safe and to conduct financial transactions such as check writing, you'll need to open a bank account.

To keep your money safe and to conduct financial transactions such as check writing, you will need to open a bank account. A **bank account** *is a formal relationship between you and a bank, where the bank keeps your money for you until you need it.*

Owning a bank account has several advantages:

- You know your money is safe—if someone breaks into your home, or if you lose your wallet, you won't lose all your money
- The US government protects the customers of licensed banks—if something happens to the bank, the government will pay you the amount you had deposited in the bank, up to $100,000
- You can get your money if you need it
- You can keep track of how much money you've used and how much you still have
- You can cash checks, get loans, buy travelers' checks, and perform many other financial transactions more easily than people without bank accounts can
- You will receive *interest* on the money you have in certain accounts. As you remember from Chapter 3 Lesson 1, interest is money that the bank pays you each month—the interest is a small percentage of the amount you have in your account
- You will be able to show that you are responsible with your money. This is important, for example, if you want to get a credit card or take out a loan.

Vocabulary

- bank account
- savings account
- checking account
- check
- checkbook register
- account statement
- debit card
- certificates of deposit
- credit card
- credit
- credit union

Types of Bank Services

Banks offer two main types of accounts: *savings* accounts and *checking* accounts. Banks also offer a number of other financial services, as described below.

Savings Accounts

Even before they reach adulthood and financial independence, many people establish savings accounts. A **savings account** *is an account for depositing money that you want to keep.* Perhaps your parent or guardian has already created a savings account for you. If you received cash as a gift, someone probably encouraged you to put some of that money into your savings. Or you may have established a savings account so that you could deposit part of your earnings from a part-time job. A big advantage of a savings account is that your bank will pay you interest on the money you deposit. It will even pay interest on the interest, which is called *compound* interest. The money grows by itself!

Once you have a savings account, your bank will send you statements every month or quarter. The statements will list the deposits and withdrawals you've made and the interest your account has earned. Many banks also enable you to access your account information online.

Many banks enable you to access your account information online.

Checking Accounts

A **checking account** *is a bank account into which you deposit money and from which you can withdraw money by writing checks.* A **check** *is a written order that directs a bank to pay money.* A checking account provides a means of storing your money safely and using it to pay bills or buy things.

To open a checking account, bring to the bank some cash or a check that's made out to you. The bank employee who opens your account will explain the requirements and benefits of the account. Some checking accounts pay interest; others don't. If the checking account offers interest, you may have to keep a certain minimum amount in your account. The bank may also charge a monthly fee, which it will deduct from the amount in your account. This may also depend on how much money you keep in the account. The bank employee will ask you to sign a signature card so that the bank knows what your signature looks like.

When you open your account, the bank will give you some temporary checks. You can use these checks as soon as you've established your account. Within a week or so, you'll receive your own checks. These checks will have your name and address on them. They will be numbered in sequence.

Included with the checks will be a **checkbook register,** *which is a form on which you keep track of the money you deposit or withdraw.* You will write the amount of your first deposit in your checkbook register so that you know how much money you are starting with. That amount will be your beginning *balance*. From that point on, you'll either add to or subtract from that number to get a new balance. If you make a deposit, you'll add to the balance. If you write a check, you'll subtract from it.

The best time to make an entry in your checkbook register is when you make your deposit or write a check. Don't wait until later—you might forget!

As you make each additional deposit and write each check, you will make an entry in the checkbook register. You'll include the date of the transaction, the person or company to which the check was written, the check number (if applicable), and the amount involved. Using the current balance as the basis, you'll add or subtract to get your new balance.

A checkbook register is useful only if you make accurate entries. If you keep it up to date, it can help prevent you from writing checks when you don't have enough money in your account to cover them. You don't want a check to "bounce," or be returned for insufficient funds. The bank will charge you a fee for these checks, and the store or payee may refuse to accept any more checks from you.

Once a month, your bank will send you an **account statement,** or *a list of transactions in your checking account over the month.* Through your checkbook register and your statement, you can keep track of how much you deposit in your account and how much you spend. The checkbook register and statement should agree. You'll find more information on how to balance your account later in this lesson.

If you need to know your balance and your statement isn't due to arrive for a while, you may be able to check your balance online. Many banks offer this service. It lets you know instantly how much money the bank says you have in your account. But if you have written checks that haven't been cashed, you have less money in your account than the bank's record shows. Be careful! The only way to know for sure how much money you have in your account is to keep an accurate, up-to-date record in your checkbook register.

Many banks offer debit cards to their checking account customers. When you use a **debit card,** *the bank automatically withdraws the amount of your request from your checking account.* Debit cards are a convenient way to get cash or to pay for things from your checking account. Think of a debit card as a plastic check that you don't have to write. If your checking account doesn't have enough to cover the transaction, however, the debit card won't work. This is another reason you must keep an accurate record in your checkbook register of how much money you have in your account.

Debit cards are a convenient way to get cash or pay for things from your checking account.

If you need cash when your bank isn't open, or you just want to save time, you can use your debit card to withdraw cash from your account at an automatic teller machine, or ATM. You will need your debit card and a personal identification number, or PIN, to access your account from an ATM.

You can access your account from nearly anywhere in the world through ATMs. They are very convenient. But if you use a card at a bank where you don't have an account, you may be charged a fee of up to several dollars.

Other Bank Services

Banks offer many additional services, including certificates of deposit, safe deposit boxes, and credit cards.

Most banks offer other services besides checking and savings accounts. For example, you can rent a safe deposit box, where you can store valuable documents or other items. You can purchase **certificates of deposit,** which are like savings accounts. They *pay higher rates of interest than savings accounts, but you have to agree not to withdraw your money for a certain amount of time.*

Some banks offer a *direct deposit* service. With it, your employer can deposit your paycheck directly into your account. That way, you don't have to worry about making a special trip to the bank—or spending your check before you get home!

Loans are one of the most important services that banks offer. Banks loan people money to buy cars, homes, and other things. To get a loan, you have to prove that you can handle your money responsibly. You must have a good credit history, which means that you repay on time the money you owe.

Banks also offer **credit cards,** *which represent a promise that the bank will give you credit to buy things.* A bank that gives you **credit** *is offering to loan you money.* Banks limit the amount of credit that they will offer their customers—you can't continue to borrow more and more money. But if you pay your bills on time, the bank may raise your credit limit.

Because they make lots of money on interest from these cards, banks advertise them heavily. After you turn 18, you may receive offers for credit cards in the mail. Be careful about applying for and using these cards. When you use a debit card, you're using money you already have. The bank deducts the amount of your purchase from your checking account. But using a credit card is like taking out a loan. You are borrowing money from the bank that issued the card. If you don't pay what you owe right away, you'll be charged interest. Credit card interest rates can be quite high. If you let your debt grow and can't repay the loan, you can run into big trouble quickly.

Credit cards can give you a false sense of financial security. Get a credit card only if you are sure you can handle the responsibility.

Credit cards often allow you to make a minimum monthly payment. Many people wrongly believe that if they make this minimum payment they are paying down their loan. But this is not so—often the minimum payment is less than the interest on the loan for that month. This means that if you pay only the minimum payment, the amount you owe the bank actually goes up! The best way to use a credit card is to pay off the full amount you owe at the end of every billing period.

How to Choose a Bank

When you choose a bank, you should consider several things:

- How convenient is it? You may need to go to your bank a lot, so it should be easy to get to.
- How friendly is the staff? The staff should be willing to explain anything that you don't understand.
- What are the hours? Banks are famous for having short hours (Monday through Friday, 9 a.m. until 3 p.m. used to be common). But today banks are extending their hours. They are often open in the evenings and on weekends. Make sure the bank is open at times when you'll be able to visit.
- What are the fees? If the bank wants to charge you a monthly fee for maintaining your account, make sure you understand why. Are you comfortable with the reason? If not, shop around for another bank. You may end up back at this bank, but at least you'll know your options.
- What kinds of accounts does the bank offer? Some banks pay interest on checking accounts as well as on savings accounts. This is a good option for some people. But if you have such an account, the bank may charge a fee if you don't keep a certain amount of money in it at all times. If you don't have a lot of money to spare, an interest-bearing checking account may not be a good option.
- Does the bank offer online services? If you want to access your account information from your home computer, make sure the bank has such a service. Some banking services, especially savings services, are available only online. They pay a higher rate of interest than most banks.
- What is the interest rate? Banks pay different rates of interest on savings and other accounts. Shop around to make sure that your money is earning as much as it can. For example, if a bank pays 3 percent interest and you deposit $1,000, you will have $1,030 in the account at the end of the year. If a bank pays 4 percent, you will have 10 dollars more, $1,040.
- Finally, make sure the bank has a good reputation. This is especially true for newer banks, such as those that offer only online savings services. Make sure the bank you chose is insured by the US government's Federal Deposit Insurance Corporation (FDIC).

You may also be eligible to join a **credit union.** A credit union *is a not-for-profit cooperative that is owned by its members.* It provides members with many, but not all, of the same services that banks do—such as savings and checking accounts, credit cards, and some types of loans. Often the credit union charges lower fees and pays higher interest than a bank does. Check to make sure the credit union you want to join is insured by the US government's National Credit Union Administration (NCUA).

How to Conduct Banking Transactions

Writing a Check

Here's how you write a check:

- Check your balance in your checkbook register. Make sure you have enough in your account to cover the check you're about to write.
- On the line in the upper-right corner, fill in the date.
- On the line starting "Pay to the order of," fill in the name of the person or company (called the "payee") who will receive your money.
- To the right of the payee line, write the amount of the check in numbers. Include both dollars and cents, such as $12.92. Make sure the dot between the dollars and cents is clear, so someone doesn't think it says $1,292!
- On the line under the payee, write the amount of the check in words. Write the cents as a fraction. You would write $12.92 as "Twelve and 92/100." Then draw a line all the way to the right, where "dollars" is printed on the check. The bank will compare the number you've written on the previous line and the words you write on this line to make sure it pays the amount that you request.
- On the "For" line at the bottom left, write the reason for the check (for your own information) or the account number that the company to which you're making the payment has assigned you (this is optional).
- At the bottom right, sign the check in the same way you did when you signed the signature card at the bank.

Figure 3.1 is an example of a written check.

Always write checks in ink. If you make a mistake, don't erase or write over the error. You could initial your mistake and write it correctly, but it's better to tear up the check and start over. (If you do this, be sure and make a note in your checkbook register.) Always make sure you write clearly.

Always write your checks in ink. If you make a mistake, tear up the check and start over.
Courtesy of Bill Aron/PhotoEdit

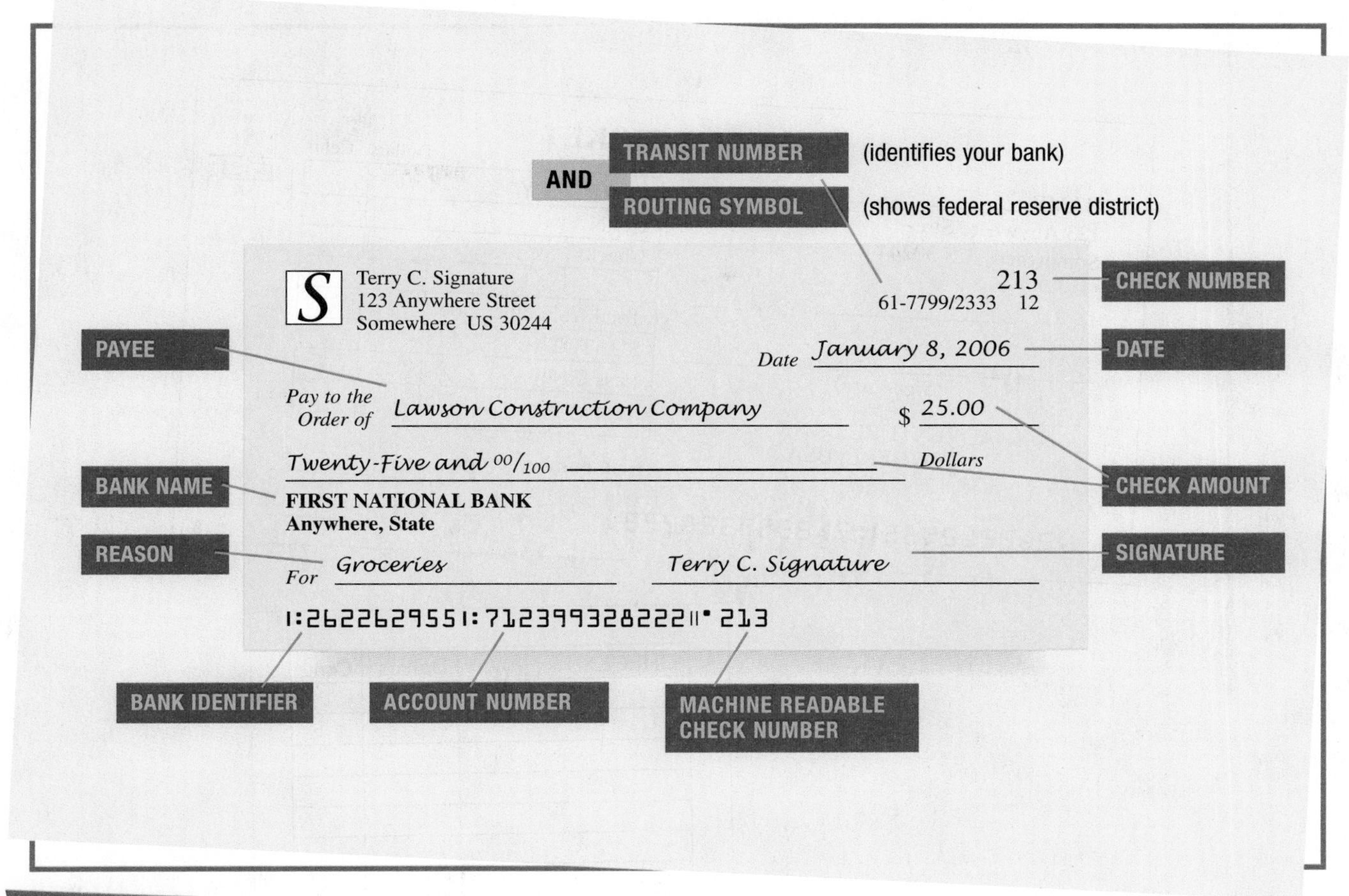

FIGURE 3.1

Example of a Written Check

From Mitchell, N.L. (1999). *Leadership Education III: Life Skills.* Maxwell Air Force Base, AL: Air Force Reserve Officer Training Corps.

Other Information on the Check

If you've never looked at a check closely, you may be surprised to see that it has other information printed on it. The bank uses this information to process your check.

Look again at Figure 3.1. Your check number appears at the top right of the check. The number underneath this identifies the routing number the bank will use when it processes the check. The bank's name will appear somewhere on the check. At the bottom of the check are a bank-identifying number and your account number. The number on the check that appears to the right of your account number is the check number. The strange-looking numbers at the bottom of the check are designed so a scanner can read them.

DEPOSIT TICKET

NAME ____________________
123 Anywhere Street
Somewhere US 30244

DATE ______________ 20 ___

____
(Signature)

ADVENTURE BANK
ANYWHERE, USA

	Dollars	Cents
CURRENCY		
COIN		
Checks		
Total from other side		
SUBTOTAL		
Less Cash		
TOTAL		

07-123
456

Total number items

1:262262955 1:712399328222

CHECKS	Dollars	Cents
TOTAL		

ENTER TOTAL ON THE FRONT

FIGURE 3.2

Sample Deposit Slip

From Mitchell, N.L. (1999). *Leadership Education III: Life Skills.* Maxwell Air Force Base, AL: Air Force Reserve Officer Training Corps.

Filling Out a Deposit Slip

You'll have to fill out a deposit slip each time you add money to your checking or savings account (except for direct deposits). The bank usually includes a supply of deposit slips in the back of your checkbook. If you don't have your own slip, you can use the bank's slips, which are available for checking and savings accounts on a counter in the bank. Fill in the form with your account number, and hand it to the teller with the money you are depositing. The teller may ask for identification when you make a deposit.

The bank does not immediately credit money that you deposit to your account. It usually takes one working day for the bank to process your transaction. So if you plan to write a big check right after you've made a deposit, be sure to wait at least a day.

Balancing a Checkbook

Each month, the bank will send you a statement. The statement will show your deposits, withdrawals, bank charges, debit transactions, and canceled checks (or pictures of them). Check right away to see if the bank's records and your records agree.

Comparing the bank statement to your checkbook register is called *balancing,* or *reconciling,* your checkbook. The purpose of balancing is to make sure the deposits and withdrawals, the checks you wrote and payees cashed, and the debit transactions you made are the same on the statement and on the register. In short, it's a way to ensure that you and the bank agree on how much money is in your account.

You may find an error as you reconcile the account. Common problems are:

- addition or subtraction errors
- failing to record a deposit or withdrawal
- failing to record the amount of a check or debit transaction.

When you receive your monthly statement:

- Sort the canceled checks (checks that have been cashed) by number. (You won't be able to do this if your bank sends photocopies or just lists the checks.) Match the checks against your checkbook register and against your bank's list of checks cashed.
- Match the deposits you have recorded in your register with the deposits the bank says you made. Do you and your bank agree? If not, figure out why. Did you forget to record a deposit? Did the bank make a mistake? (Not likely, but it can happen.)

- Go through the same matching process for any withdrawals and debit card transactions you made during the month.
- Make sure the bank has charged you the appropriate fees, if any, and that you have recorded them in your register. If your checking account pays interest, add it to your checkbook register.

Once you have confirmed that all transactions on the statement and all transactions in your register match, you can balance your checkbook.

- Start with the "New Balance" shown on your statement—this is the amount that the bank says you had on the date it prepared your statement
- Subtract any checks that you've written but that have not been cashed or recorded by the bank as of the date of the statement
- Subtract any withdrawals or debit card transactions that the bank had not recorded as of the date of your statement
- Add any deposits you made after the statement was prepared.

The resulting number should be the same as the current balance that appears in your checkbook register. If it isn't, you need to find the source of the mistake. Try again. If you still can't find the mistake, visit your bank and see if someone there can help you.

Keep your statements and canceled checks in a safe place. They are a financial record—your receipts for purchases made. You may also need them for tax purposes.

CHECKPOINTS

Lesson 2 Review

Using complete sentences, answer the following questions on a sheet of paper.

1. What are three advantages of opening a bank account?
2. Why should you have a savings account?
3. Why should you have a checking account?
4. What is the procedure for setting up a checking account?
5. What happens in your checking account when you use a debit card to pay for something or when you withdraw money from an ATM?
6. What's the difference between a debit card and a credit card? Why can credit cards give you a false sense of financial security?
7. What questions should you always ask yourself when choosing a bank? Give at least four.

Applying Banking Skills

8. Find the blank check form in your student workbook. Pretend that you are paying a bill to the Acme Telephone Company for $43.29. Fill the check out correctly.
9. Suppose you deposited $275 in your savings account on December 31. Your bank pays 3 percent annual interest on savings accounts. If you didn't deposit any more money in the account, what would be the balance on December 31 of the following year?

LESSON 3

Real-Life Issues in Buying and Selling

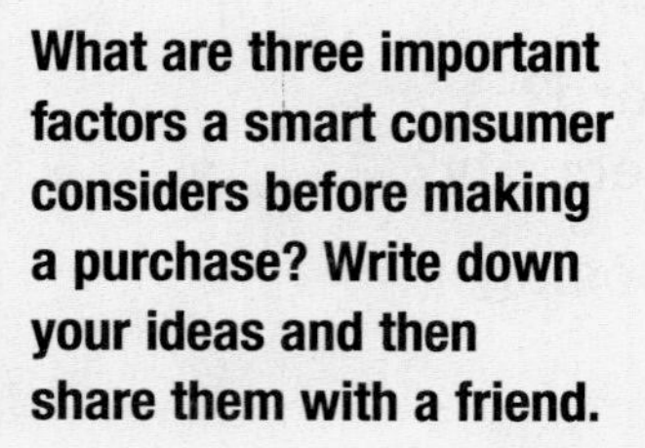

Quick Write

What are three important factors a smart consumer considers before making a purchase? Write down your ideas and then share them with a friend.

Learn About...

- shopping issues in daily life
- renting an apartment
- buying or leasing a car

Shopping Issues in Daily Life

In the last lesson, you learned about bank accounts. You've also learned how to make a budget. This lesson focuses on the decisions you'll have to make about buying everyday items such as groceries and clothing. You'll also learn about making big decisions that don't come up every day—decisions about such things as renting an apartment or buying or leasing a car. This lesson, in short, is about learning how to be a smart consumer. The smarter you are, the more money you'll save.

Shopping for Groceries

Studies show that the average person uses at least 15 products every morning before he or she even goes out the door. These products include toothpaste, soap, shampoo, and other bathroom products. They also include food—cereal, bread, eggs, juice, and milk, for example. All these products are available on the shelves of your favorite grocery store. Although none of them is expensive by itself, their costs add up. So it's important to shop intelligently. Being a smart shopper takes a lot of thinking, as you'll find out below.

Starting Off Right: Some Basic Tips

You'll be a smarter shopper if you prepare beforehand and follow these basic rules:

- Plan your meals, and make a shopping list. Write down items when you think of them. Don't wait until you're ready to head out for the store.
- Watch for sales. Check the current ads in your newspaper or the flyers at the store for special deals. Compare weekly ads of stores in your community, and find the best bargains.

- Buy store brands rather than nationally known manufacturers' brands whenever you can. There's often little or no difference in quality, but a big difference in price.
- Have a grocery budget and stick to it.
- Don't go to the store hungry. If you do, you may buy too much.
- Don't buy on impulse. The spur-of-the moment items you throw into the cart can be budget breakers.
- Minimize purchases of processed foods, such as instant potatoes. Instead, buy raw foods, such as real potatoes. Raw foods often cost less than processed foods. They also tend to be more nutritious.
- If you have a freezer and the prices are right, buy more than you need. Store the extra items in your freezer. For example, if the store is offering a "buy one, get one free" sale on bread, buy two loaves and stick one in the freezer.
- Clip coupons from newspapers and magazines. They are great money savers. Sort the coupons by type (for example, cleaning supplies, canned foods, or pet food). Then place a "C" beside each item on your list for which you have a coupon. This will help you remember the coupon at the checkout counter. Finally, make sure to look at the expiration dates on the coupons. If you have two coupons for the same item, use the coupon with the shortest expiration date first.

Vocabulary

- comparison shopping
- unit price
- product expiration date
- brand
- produce
- tenant
- landlord
- gross income
- real estate agent
- lease
- security deposit
- utilities
- net income
- down payment
- equity

Comparison Shopping

Smart shoppers don't buy the first thing they see. Instead, they make it a habit to do **comparison shopping**, which means *comparing the prices and quality of different items to see which one is a better deal.*

Consider how Sara handles her grocery shopping. With her shopping list in hand, Sara heads to the frozen-food section to find the first item on the list: corn. She sees that a 16-ounce bag of Brand A corn costs $1.36. A 24-ounce bag of Brand B corn sells for $2.20. Which brand is the better buy?

If you answered Brand A, you are right. But how did you know? The bags are different sizes, so you can't tell which one is cheaper by comparing the prices. To know which brand is the better buy, you must know the cost of one ounce of each brand of corn. To calculate the cost per ounce, you divide the cost of the item by the total number of ounces.

For Brand A, divide $1.36 by 16 ounces, and you get $0.85 per ounce. For Brand B, divide $2.20 by 24 ounces, and you get $0.91 per ounce. Since Brand A costs less per ounce than Brand B, Brand A is the better buy, at least in terms of price.

You don't necessarily need to bring a calculator to the store to determine the cost of an ounce of most foods today. Beneath each stack of items on many supermarket shelves is a label that provides the **unit price,** *or cost per serving.* The grocer has divided the price of each item by the number of servings, or units, in each package. (Unit pricing also works for nonfood items. The unit price for facial tissues, for example, is the cost of a single tissue.)

Unit pricing is very helpful when you're comparing two sizes of a product. You'd expect that the larger size would be a better deal, and it often is. But not always: The only way to be sure is to look at the unit price.

Even if you've decided that the larger size is a better deal, don't drop it in your cart too fast. Look at the product expiration date. The **product expiration date** *is the date after which the item will be stale or no longer be at its finest quality.* You'll usually see it stamped on the bottom or side of the package. If you think you won't use the product by the expiration date, it's probably better to buy the smaller quantity. Otherwise, you may have to throw away the remaining food and you won't have saved any money.

Price isn't the only thing to consider when comparison shopping. Quality is important. You may trust one **brand,** *or distinctive name identifying a product or manufacturer,* more than another. So, if you knew, on the basis of experience, that the more expensive brand tasted a lot better or that it was more nutritious, you might buy it, despite the higher cost.

Tips for Buying Particular Food Items

Fruits and Vegetables

Produce, *or fresh fruits and vegetables,* is an excellent source of vitamins. The rule of thumb is, "The darker the green or brighter the orange, the more the vitamins." In other words, vegetables such as broccoli and carrots have many times more vitamins than pale vegetables such as celery.

Fresh produce costs less when it's in season.
Courtesy of Michael Krasowitz/Getty Images

Eating a variety of fresh fruits and vegetables may be expensive, however, unless you are careful to purchase produce when it's in season in your area. In other words, buying a watermelon in July is cheaper than buying it in December. It's usually less expensive to buy canned or frozen fruits and vegetables in the winter months, when prices of fresh produce increase. Dried fruits are also an option.

Other ideas for saving money on produce include:

- Buy certain items in bulk. For example, buy potatoes in five- or 10-pound bags, not by the piece or by the pound. But when you buy in bulk, don't overdo it. Potatoes, for example, may spoil if you keep them more than two weeks.
- If you buy produce in bulk, keep it refrigerated. Store items in plastic bags so they won't dry out.
- Don't be put off by appearance. For example, did you ever notice the dark-brown bananas that the grocer puts in bags and sells half-price? They may not look great, but they taste fine. Buy them and store the extras in the refrigerator. Although the cold will darken the skin, the fruit is not affected.
- Test green beans for freshness by snapping one in half. It should break easily.
- Buy oranges not by their color (most oranges are dyed) but by their firm skin.
- Lemons are best when they're slightly green on the ends and with a smooth skin. Store lemons in a sealed container of water to keep them juicy. If you need just a few drops of juice, puncture the lemon and squeeze them out; don't slice the whole lemon.
- Wash and drain salad greens, then refrigerate them in a plastic container or bag. Tear the greens; don't cut them. They'll stay fresh longer. A bag of salad greens will remain fresh in the refrigerator for several days. But don't try to save time by making a whole salad in advance. If you add tomatoes or cucumbers to the bag, the salad will become soggy. Add these extras just before serving.
- Store strawberries in the refrigerator in the plastic basket the grocer provided. This allows air to circulate around them and keep them firm. To make sure that strawberries keep their sweetness, don't wash them until just before serving.

Meat

The US Department of Agriculture (USDA) oversees the safety of America's meat. Federal laws require regular inspection of facilities where meat is prepared.

Meats are sold fresh and frozen. Both require cooking before you can eat them. It is important to cook meats to the appropriate temperature. You can find information on these temperatures on the package or in a good cookbook.

Processed meats, such as cold cuts, do not require cooking. They contain several added ingredients, such as salt and preservatives. They also have a high fat content. You can store processed meats in the refrigerator up to a week or in the freezer for up to a month. Always check the product expiration date and read the label when you buy processed meats. If you're watching your salt or fat intake, you might want to avoid them.

The most popular types of meat sold in the United States are beef, pork, and lamb. Here are some details on each of these types of meat.

Beef

After inspection, beef is cut and graded. The best grade is *prime.* A prime cut of beef has the greatest degree of marbling, or flecks of fat, that help make meat tender, juicy, and flavorful. It is the most expensive cut of beef. You can find prime beef in restaurants and better grocery stores. *Choice* and *Select* grades are less expensive and have less fat.

Beef cuts from the *round* of the animal have little fat, so they often require tenderizing. Beef cuts from the *loin* and *rib* are more tender. They are excellent for broiling. Beef cuts labeled *chuck* are lowest in price. You must cook them longer than you do rib or loin cuts.

Pork

The most popular cuts of pork are *ribs, roasts,* and *chops.* All these cuts come from the *loin,* the meat that runs along either size of the backbone. The *tenderloin* is a strip of choice meat that is cut from the center of the loin. Pork chops come from the rib. The *shoulder* is cut from the front leg. The lower section of a shoulder cut is often labeled a *picnic cut.* The upper section of the shoulder is *pork butt* or *Boston butt.* The *ham* is cut from the back leg. Shoulder cuts and hams are sold both fresh and smoked. *Bacon* and *spare ribs* come from the underside of the animal.

Lamb

The most popular cuts of lamb are *leg, chops, rack,* and *loin. Leg of lamb,* a choice cut, comes from the hind leg of the animal. Lamb *chops* come from the rib. The *rack* is the rib section of the lamb. Lamb *loins* run along either side of the backbone.

Poultry

The word *poultry* refers to a farm-raised bird, as opposed to one that a hunter shoots in the wild. The main types of poultry are chicken and turkey. Most chicken is sold fresh; turkeys are sold both fresh and frozen. The USDA oversees the safety of poultry. Poultry is a nutritious, economical food. It is generally less expensive than meat.

You can buy a chicken whole and roast it in the oven or cook it on the grill. You can also buy chicken parts, such as *breast, legs (drumsticks), thighs,* and *wings.* Breast meat is white and is the most expensive cut. Chicken wings, which have little meat, have become a popular snack item. Turkeys are usually sold whole, although you can buy turkey breast, legs, and frozen ground turkey.

Fish

The National Oceanic and Atmospheric Administration (NOAA) oversees the management of fisheries in the United States. It also maintains a voluntary seafood-inspection program. Fish that has passed NOAA inspection bears a special mark that may read "US Grade A," "processed under federal inspection (PUFI)," or "lot inspection." But the sale of seafood, unlike that of poultry and meat, is not regulated by the US government.

The two main types of fish are *fin* fish and *shellfish*. Fin fish include salmon, cod, halibut, flounder, tuna, trout, and many others. The two main cuts of fish are *steaks* and *fillets*. A steak is cut crosswise. A fillet is cut down the length of the body of the fish. Popular shellfish include shrimp, lobster, crabs, clams, scallops, and oysters.

Most fish is sold both fresh and frozen. Both are equally nutritious and tasty, provided they have been properly stored and handled. Beware of fish that smells "fishy." Fish should have a fresh, natural aroma. Some fish, such as salmon and tuna, are also sold canned.

Canned and Packaged Goods

Canned goods have a long shelf life. The product expiration dates may be two years from the date of purchase. This means that you can stock up when these items are on sale. But again, buying food in quantity will not save you money if you never eat it.

When buying canned or packaged goods, read the labels. Federal law requires that every package of food display the name of the product, the name and address of the manufacturer, net amount of contents by weight (or by weight and volume if it's a liquid), a Nutrition Facts label, and a list of ingredients.

The *Nutrition Facts label* is full of valuable information. If you check out this label before you make a purchase, you can make better decisions about healthy eating. At the top, the label shows serving size (for example, one cup for dry cereal) and the amount of servings per container (a 15-ounce box of dry cereal has around 14 servings). The label then lists the calories, as well as total amount of fat, carbohydrates, and protein, in a serving. Finally, the label has information on the product's vitamin and mineral content. It tells you what percentages of your daily requirements of these nutrients are in one serving. For example, a cup of oat cereal provides 3 percent of your daily recommended fat content, 7 percent of your daily recommended carbohydrate intake, and no protein. It contains 45 percent of your daily requirement of iron and 10 percent of your daily requirement for vitamin C, as well as other vitamins and minerals. Add milk to the cereal, and those percentages go up considerably, as the label for cereal also shows.

The ingredients list may be eye-opening. By law, it must begin with the main ingredient and then move on, item by item, to the ingredient used least. For example, suppose you're comparing two bottles of pasta sauce. Both contain 28 ounces of sauce, and both cost $2.99. The first ingredient on one label is water. The first ingredient on the label of the other bottle is tomato puree. Which do you think is the better deal? The ingredients list also tells you what chemical additives and dyes are in the food.

Dairy Products

Milk is a low-cost source of calcium. But some types of milk have more fat than others. If you're concerned about keeping trim, check out the fat content. Milk with the highest fat content is labeled "4 percent butterfat." Skim milk, at the other extreme, has no fat.

You can also find eggs, butter, sour cream, and other products in the dairy case. Eggs come in several sizes. Check the price of each size. If the price difference between two sizes of eggs, say medium and large, is less than five cents per dozen, buy the larger size. Always check the expiration date before buying eggs.

You can buy cheese in several forms; for example, in blocks, sliced, and grated. Sliced or grated cheese has a higher unit price than block cheese does. Save money by buying cheese in blocks and slicing or grating it yourself. Hard cheeses may turn green as they age. This is a natural process. Just cut off the mold before eating. Store extra cheese, butter, or margarine in the freezer to reduce spoilage.

Frozen Foods

Americans today have less time to cook than ever before, and sales of frozen foods have increased dramatically. The frozen-foods section in the grocery store has fruits, vegetables, breads, and desserts, as well as main dishes and low-calorie meals. Although frozen meals, or entrees, are usually more expensive than home-prepared meals, people depend on them because they are so convenient—particularly when you have a microwave oven.

You can save money buying these foods by comparing ads from various stores. Since frozen foods are so popular, many grocers regularly put them on sale to increase business. You can also use manufacturers' coupons to reduce the cost of these items.

Other Foods

You can buy breads fresh off the shelf, frozen, or partially baked. Many supermarkets have in-store bakeries. These bakery products vary in cost, depending on their quality and other factors. Compare costs by reading labels and determining the cost per serving.

Cereals appeal to kids, and they're heavily advertised. You can save money by clipping coupons. You can also buy store brands rather than name brands. The packaging of the store brand may not be as glitzy, but the product is often just as good as the name brand is.

Baking needs such as flour, sugar, spices, and oils usually are in the same aisle of the grocery store. Again, look for store brands, which vary little from national brands in quality. When selecting flour, consider the unbleached variety, even though it costs a bit more. The nutritional content is higher.

Rice and pasta are good sources of carbohydrates. They supply quick energy. Some people call them "meat extenders" because they satisfy hunger but cost less than meat. Pasta comes in various forms, both fresh and dried. The labels provide excellent cooking ideas. Rice and pasta store well: Buying them in large quantities can save money.

Condiments include pickles, sauces, and spreads. These items add zest to meals, but they are usually expensive. Again, compare the national and the store brands for quality and price. Consider mixing your own salad dressings. It doesn't take long, and the result is often more flavorful and less expensive per serving.

Many shoppers spend a large percentage of their grocery budget on snack foods and soft drinks. These items provide little or no nutritional value, but they may have lots of calories. If you include these on your grocery list, look for specials and volume discounts. Since they are popular items, grocers offer competitive prices.

Nonfood Items

Supermarkets are "super" because they offer more than just food. You may rent movies, buy cosmetics, or even buy furniture, tires, and appliances in a supermarket. Buying nonfood items while grocery shopping may save you a trip to a discount store. But remember, impulse purchases are tough on the budget. Avoid browsing and stick to your list.

Over a lifetime, most people will make thousands of trips to the supermarket. It will pay off in the long run to learn to shop efficiently.

Shopping for Clothing

When you have your own money, you may be tempted to spend a lot on clothing. Dressing well is important: It makes a big difference in how you feel. You also need to dress well to get a good job. But clothing can be expensive. When shopping for clothing, keep these tips in mind:

- Don't overspend—think about the gaps in your wardrobe and buy only what you need
- Buy pieces you can mix and match—a shirt or blouse that you can wear with several outfits is more economical than one you can wear only with a certain skirt or pair of pants

You shop more efficiently when you plan your purchases rather than buying on impulse.

- Shop at discount stores rather than at malls whenever possible—they often have good clothes at bargain prices
- Don't buy something just because it's the latest fashion—the best bargain is what looks good on you, not what's trendy
- Even if you find a good sale, be careful. You don't want to fill your closet with things you can't use—sale items also may be of lower quality than nonsale items
- Don't shop just for shopping's sake. Some people shop just to feel good—that's an expensive way to calm your nerves
- Try to buy clothing at the end of a season—for example, the best time to find a winter coat at a bargain price is in February, not November.

Spending on Entertainment

A lot of teenagers spend a good deal of their money on entertainment, such as movies, CDs, and video games. The key issue here is budget: Decide how much you can afford to spend each month on entertainment, and then stick to it. Don't get distracted by what's in the mall, what your friends have, or what you see on TV.

Renting an Apartment

Renting an apartment is often less expensive, at least over the short term, than buying a house. Renting is often necessary for young people who are just starting out and don't have enough money for a down payment on a house. Renting is also a good idea if you're not sure whether you'll be staying in an area for more than a year or two.

Apartments are often clustered in complexes on a large piece of property. Fancy apartments offer amenities such as tennis courts, pools, clubhouses, and laundry facilities for their tenants. A **tenant** *is a person who rents an apartment.* Tenants pay a monthly fee to the **landlord,** *or apartment owner.* Tenants are responsible for keeping their units safe and clean, but they are not responsible for the maintenance of the apartment. If something goes wrong, they call the landlord, who arranges for the repair.

If you've decided to rent an apartment, the next thing to do is to choose where you want to live. Explore various neighborhoods. Think about such factors as neighborhood safety, as well as access to public transportation, shopping, libraries, and other community services.

Determine what size apartment you want. The smallest apartment is called a *studio* or an *efficiency*. It has one large room, a bathroom, and a kitchen. Landlords refer to larger apartments based on how many bedrooms, and in some cases bathrooms, they have.

Some apartment complexes have professionals on the property who can show and rent apartments.
Courtesy of Corbis Images

Rental fees of apartments vary widely. They can range from a few hundred dollars a month to thousands, depending on where you live and how fancy the building is. So one important thing to think about before you even start looking is how much you can afford to spend on rent. Experts recommend that you pay no more than 30 percent of your **gross income,** *or income before taxes and other deductions,* on rent, gas, heat, and electricity. This will allow you to have enough extra money for other living needs.

To find an apartment, look at newspaper ads. These are usually the best sources of information on apartments currently available. Some large apartments also provide information online. Some apartment complexes have professionals on the property who can rent apartments. Another option is to call a real estate agent. A **real estate agent** *is a professional who helps people buy, sell, or rent homes and apartments.* Many real estate agents prefer to deal with people who are buying rather than renting. If you are interested in using a real estate agent, ask which type is his or her primary focus. If the agent doesn't usually help renters, you may want to find another agent who does. If you use a real estate agent, he or she may charge a fee.

If you are interested in a particular apartment building, try to find out information about the landlord from the previous tenant or other people in the building. For example, does the landlord fix things promptly? Does the landlord have a habit of showing up unannounced to inspect the apartment? If so, living there could be difficult.

When you agree to rent an apartment, you will sign a **lease,** *or an agreement to pay rent and fulfill other obligations for a certain length of time.* A lease is usually for one year, but it can be for more. Some apartments have monthly leases, but this is relatively rare.

A lease is a legal document. When you sign it, you are legally bound to its terms. Read it carefully. It will spell out your responsibilities and those of your landlord. If you break the lease and move out early, don't pay your rent, or don't follow the terms of the lease in any other way, the landlord has grounds for taking legal action against you.

Items covered in a lease may include the amount of the rent, the security deposit and utilities (see below), the number of people who may live in the unit, where you can park your car, responsibilities for maintenance of the apartment, a policy on pets, and similar items.

One of the terms of the lease may be that you leave the apartment in good shape when you move out. If you have not kept the apartment in good shape (for example, if there are spills on the carpet, holes in the walls, or structural damage), the landlord may withhold some or all of your security deposit A **security deposit** *is a payment to make sure you meet your obligations as a tenant.* Deposits vary widely. Some landlords require a first and last month's rent; some require only one month's rent. The landlord will refund your security deposit at the end of the lease if you have met the terms of the lease.

Young people often share an apartment with one or more roommates. This helps cut the cost of living. If you and a friend want to rent an apartment together, ask yourself, and each other, two big questions:

1. Who will sign the lease? If you both sign, you are *both* legally responsible for fulfilling *all* its terms. If everything goes as planned, you'll both save money. But if your roommate decides to move out early or breaks one of the requirements of the lease, you will be responsible for the rent and other obligations. If one of you expects to leave earlier than the other, it might be best for the one who intends to stay longer to sign the lease alone. The bottom line is to have a roommate you can trust.
2. Do you have similar living habits? For example, if you like to have loud parties on weekends and your roommate values privacy, you may have problems. If dirty dishes in the sink, a messy bedroom, and dust and grime don't bother your roommate and you're a "neat freak," watch out.

Discuss both questions in advance. If you can't agree, you'd better decide to live alone or find another roommate. Saving money is important, but it's not your only consideration. You don't want to risk losing a friend or getting into the legal problems that a broken lease might create.

Tips for Apartment Shopping

Shopping for an apartment is a big deal. Here are some tips to help you succeed.

- Don't rush into anything. Spend enough time searching for an apartment to be sure you will be happy.
- Know whether utilities are included in your rental rate. **Utilities** *are electricity, heat, gas, and water.* They can be expensive. If they are not included in your rent, you will need to pay for them separately (Try to find out from the landlord or the previous tenant how much utilities will cost.) You will always have to pay separately for things such as your telephone and cable TV. You may also have to pay a deposit to the telephone company or another utility company. You'll get your deposit back when you move out, as long as you have paid your bills, but you need to count it in when you are planning your budget.
- Before you sign the lease, figure out your monthly rent and utilities expenses. Make sure they total no more than 30 percent of your gross income. For example, if you're earning $24,000 a year, your rent and utilities should total no more than $8,000. A rent of $650 a month ($7,800 per year) is too high.
- Apartments usually have basic kitchen appliances, such as a refrigerator and oven. Many, however, do not include a microwave or laundry facilities.
- Most apartments are unfurnished. If you need to buy your own furniture, figure that into your budget. Rental fees for furnished apartments are usually higher than fees for unfurnished apartments.
- Calculate the costs associated with moving. If you have some furniture, you will probably want to rent a truck, get some friends, and move it yourself. Moving companies can be expensive. Check their rates, and do comparison shopping. Also, be sure to see if the building has specified move-in times.
- Bring someone with you to look at apartments you are thinking of renting. Sometimes a second party can point out things you may not have noticed.
- If you are concerned about safety, you might want to rent an apartment on the second floor or above. Make sure the locks are strong and that they work well. Better yet, install a new lock. This is because the previous tenant might have given out keys to other people. If being in the neighborhood makes you nervous, no matter how good a deal the apartment is, you should probably rent somewhere else. You want to be able to walk around outside without fear and sleep peacefully.

Pets

Many apartment buildings don't allow their tenants to have pets. Ask about this when you visit the apartment. If you have a pet, don't lie about it. Instead, find an apartment with a "pet-friendly" policy. Some landlords require a pet deposit or an extra security deposit to cover damage that your pet could cause.

When you're hunting for a car, think about what kind of car you need, how much you can afford to pay, and whether you should get a new car or a used one.
Courtesy of David Young-Wolff/Getty Images

Buying or Leasing a Car

Getting a car is a major goal for many young people. When you're ready to take this step, you'll need to decide what kind of car to get, how much you can afford to pay, and whether to buy or lease.

Selecting a Car

When you're ready to choose a car, think about the following questions:

- What kind do you *need*? The car you need may be different from the car you *want*. Be realistic. Do you need a small car that is easy to park and gets good mileage? Do you need an SUV that holds lots of people and equipment? The SUV will use much more gas, but if you really need a big car, then you'll have to be willing to pay for fuel. As gas prices climb, that becomes an even more serious consideration.
- How much can you afford? Stay within your budget. Don't buy or lease a car that will require you to get a second job or borrow more money than you can afford. Remember, if you borrow money to buy the car, you will probably be making monthly payments for the next several years. A good rule of thumb is to spend no more than 20 percent of your **net income,** *or income after taxes and other deductions,* on monthly car payments.
- Should you get a new car or a used one? New cars require less maintenance, but they're much more expensive than used ones. A compromise may be a "gently used" car that is a few years old.

- If you've decided on a used car, what kind of condition is it in? Check the outside: Is the paint worn or chipped? Is it rusty? Is there body damage? Are the tires in good shape? Then check the inside: Is the upholstery worn? Do the electronic devices work? Finally, look under the hood: Does everything work, particularly the engine? If you don't have the knowledge to inspect the engine, hire a mechanic to do it for you. This will cost you some money, but if it prevents you from buying a car that needs lots of repair, it will be worth it.
- What kind of insurance will you need? Insurance rates for some cars, usually more-expensive ones, sports cars, or models that are popular targets of car thieves, are higher than rates for other cars. Get an insurance estimate before buying a car.
- What kind of resale value will the car have? You cannot perfectly predict the resale value of a car, but you can get a rough idea from various websites, such as the Kelly Blue Book site at *www.kbb.com*. Compare cars and choose the one that has a good resale value.
- How much will repairs cost? Some cars cost more than others to fix. Generally, the more expensive the car when it is new, the more expensive it is to repair. It usually costs more to fix a Mercedes, for example, than a Chevy.
- What is the financing rate? If you'll need a loan to pay for your car, visit several dealers and banks and see which one will give you the best interest rate. You may have to make trade-offs: For example, one dealer may charge a lower price for the car but charge a higher interest rate.

Should You Lease or Buy?

For some drivers, leasing is an attractive option. An advantage of leasing is that you may not need a **down payment,** or *partial payment that you make when purchasing something*. Your monthly payment may be less than a loan payment would be. Another advantage is that you return the car to the dealer at the end of the lease period, so you don't need to worry about finding a buyer.

But leasing a car also has serious disadvantages. Since you do not own the car, you do not have **equity,** or *ownership value,* in it. You will, however, be responsible for maintenance costs. You will have to pay for repairing any damage to the car over the lease period. You will have to pay an extra fee if you drive more than the maximum number of miles specified in the lease. You may have to pay a fee if you return the car before the end of the lease. And you may be charged very large "lease acquisition fees" or "lease disposal fees" of several hundred dollars each. One authoritative source, the nonprofit magazine *Consumer Reports,* says that for many reasons it usually costs more to lease than to buy a car.

Let's say Stephanie is considering whether to buy or lease a car. The model she wants costs $18,000. As you see in Figure 3.3, if she purchased the car, she would make a down payment of $1,000. If she had no other money to put down on the car at that time, she'd need to take out a $17,000 loan. To pay off that loan, she would make payments of $412 per month for 48 months. Considering these expenses, and the fact that she would not be able to collect the $160 in interest that she would earn if that $1,000 remained in her savings account, the car would cost her $20,936.

Cost of Purchasing the Car	Cost
1. Down payment	$1,000
2. Down payment of $1,000 results in forgone interest income: Forgone Interest: Income per Year = Down Payment × Annual Interest Rate = 41,000 × .04 = $40 Forgone Interest over Four Years = $40 × 4 = $160	160
3. Total monthly payments are: Total Monthly Payments = Monthly Payment × Number of Months = $412 × 48 = $19,776	19,776
Total	$20,936
Minus: Expected amount to be received when car is sold in four years	−10,000
Total cost	**$10,936**

Cost of Leasing the Car for Four Years	Cost
1. Security deposit of $800 results in forgone interest income (although she will receive her deposit back in four years): Forgone Interest: Income per Year = Down Payment × Annual Interest Rate = $800 × .04 = $32 Forgone Interest over Four Years = $32 × 4 = $128	$128
2. Total monthly payments are: Total Monthly Payments = Monthly Payment × Number of Months = $300 × 48 = $14,400	14,400
Total cost	**$14,528**

FIGURE 3.3

Comparison of the Cost of Purchasing versus Leasing a Car

From Madura, Jeff. (2006). *Personal Finance*, Second Edition. Boston, MA: Addison Wesley, p. 239.

In this example, if she leased the car, Stephanie would not have to make a down payment. She would give the dealer a security deposit of $800, which she would receive back at the end of the lease period. She would not collect $128 in interest on that $800. She would make monthly payments of $300 for the 48 months. Her cost would be $14,528.

But the story isn't complete. At the end of the lease period, Stephanie would have to return the car to the dealer. She would not be able to sell it. If Stephanie had bought the car and could sell it for $10,000, her total cost for purchasing would be $10,936. In this case, buying would be a better deal. It would save Stephanie more than $3,500.

CHECKPOINTS

Lesson 3 Review

Using complete sentences, answer the following questions on a sheet of paper.

1. What are four things you can do to make sure you are a smart food shopper?
2. What is comparison shopping?
3. What are three tips for buying produce or keeping it fresh at home?
4. What are three ways you can make sure you are spending wisely on clothing?
5. What are three of the most important things to consider when renting an apartment?
6. What are the advantages of buying a car? What are the advantages of leasing a car?

Applying Buying and Selling Skills

7. Look in the classified section of your local newspaper and find two apartments that sound like great places to live. On the basis of the ads, compare the apartments. Consider their prices and features (such as air conditioning, size, parking), plus what you know about their location. Which one sounds better to you?

CHAPTER

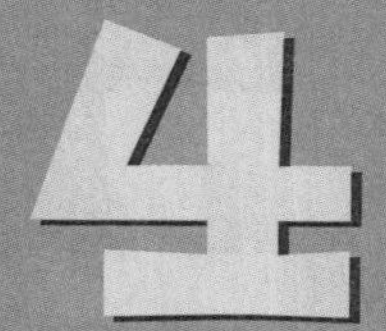

Managing Your Resources

Chapter Outline

There is no dignity quite so impressive, and no independence quite so important, as living within your means.

—Calvin Coolidge,
30th President
of the United States

LESSON

1 Avoiding the Credit Trap

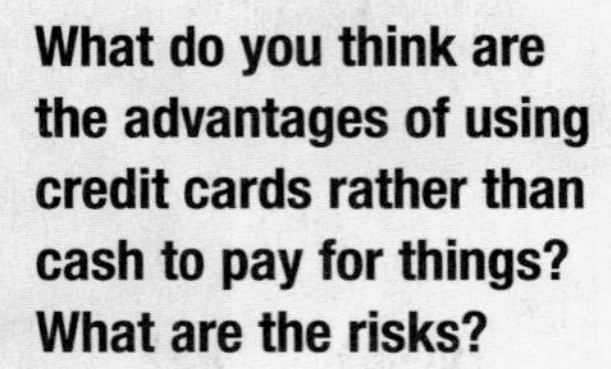

What do you think are the advantages of using credit cards rather than cash to pay for things? What are the risks?

- what credit is
- using credit responsibly
- credit and credit card options
- the consequences of deficit spending

What Is Credit?

The American economy is built on credit. Americans have $1.7 trillion in consumer credit. If people didn't use credit, they'd have to give up a lot of the things they now take for granted—a car, a home, a college education, a great vacation. Few people have $20,000 or so on hand to buy a new car. But they can't get along without one. So they have to use credit to get the money.

Credit is providing or loaning money with the expectation of future repayment. Credit enables you to postpone payment for something you buy. The **creditor,** usually *a bank or a financing company that loans money,* makes the payment for you. You promise to pay the creditor back what you've borrowed within a certain time period, with interest. (As you remember from an earlier lesson, *interest* is a charge on borrowed money.) An **annual percentage rate,** or **APR,** *is the yearly interest rate.* **Finance charge** *is another term for interest and APR.*

Credit may come through a direct loan; for example, the bank may loan you money to buy a car. Credit may also come through a credit card that you use to purchase goods and services.

Suppose you need a loan of $15,000 to buy a new car. *The money you borrow is called the* **principal.** A direct loan will have a **maturity date,** which is *the date by which you must repay the money you borrowed.* You cannot wait until the maturity date to make payments on your loan. You must make monthly payments, which include both the principal and interest. Credit card loans have no maturity date. You simply pay a minimum amount each month on your credit card bill. If you don't pay the remaining balance of your bill each month, you'll also pay interest.

Using a credit card wisely will help you establish a good credit rating.
Courtesy of Tony Hopewell/Getty Images

Vocabulary

- creditor
- annual percentage rate (APR)
- finance charge
- principal
- maturity date
- credit rating
- minimum payment
- bankruptcy
- installment
- cash advance
- annual fee
- collateral

(continued on next page)

Some people think that it's never a good idea to buy things on credit. They don't like the idea of being in debt. But virtually no one today can get along without borrowing money at some point. In addition, if you never borrow, you won't establish a **credit rating,** or *an assessment of how trustworthy you are in paying your bills.*

It's actually a good idea to get one or two credit cards—as long as you have an income from steady employment. But don't overspend, and do make your payments regularly. In that way, you will establish a good credit rating. Then creditors will be more likely to give you a loan when you need one for a big purchase, such as a car or a house.

Good credit can help you reach your goals. In this lesson, you'll learn how using credit wisely can be an important part of managing your finances.

Vocabulary

(cont.)

- credit history
- periodic rate
- variable rate
- grace period
- default
- unsecured loan
- cosigner
- credit bureau
- delinquent

Important Credit Terms

Credit is a complex subject. If you know the meanings of some basic terms, you'll find it easier to understand. The "Credit Dictionary" defines some of the words that come up most in discussions of credit. Perhaps you've heard some of them before. Others will probably be new.

Most of the words on this list appear in bold text in this lesson. Check back to this list if necessary as you go through the lesson. Then keep the list handy and refer to it when you need it. Soon these words will come rolling off your tongue.

A Credit Dictionary

Account statement: a summary of the activity in your credit card or other account. It includes how much you charged, borrowed, and paid during the past month, as well as updated information on the overall status of your account

Annual percentage rate (APR): the yearly interest rate you must pay for the use of the money loaned to you. If you have a $10,000 loan and the APR is 5 percent, you'll pay $500 a year in interest

Annual fee: a yearly fee that some credit card companies charge in addition to the interest charge

Bankruptcy: a situation in which a court rules that a person is not able to pay his or her bills

Collateral: possessions such as a home or car that a borrower pledges in return for a loan. If a borrower does not repay a loan, the lender has the right to take possession of an item used for collateral. You can also use the money in a savings account as collateral

Cosigner: a person with a good credit rating who signs a loan note along with a borrower—the cosigner agrees to be responsible for repaying the loan if the borrower defaults

Credit bureau: a public or private agency that gathers credit information on people—the information includes where, when, and how much you have borrowed and whether you made your payments on time

Credit history: the record of a person's use of credit, often compiled by a credit bureau

The Positive and Negative Aspects of Using Credit

Credit has one big advantage: You can buy something you need, even if you don't have the money right now. There are also other advantages to using credit. For example, using a credit card makes day-to-day purchases more convenient. You don't have to carry a lot of cash with you. Credit can be useful in emergencies, too.

Using credit has many disadvantages, however. If you borrow too much money, you may have difficulty making your payments. Having credit can tempt you to make impulse purchases that you cannot afford.

According to MSN Money, the total credit card debt held by the average American in 2002 was $8,940. Young adults, especially those who have borrowed to finance a college education, may be in worse shape. Many young people accumulate considerable debt by the time they graduate from college. The average new college graduate today has more than $20,000 in debts, including credit cards, student loans, and other debts, such as car loans.

Credit rating: a rating that a credit bureau gives you based on your history of borrowing and repaying money, your character, and your assets

Default: failure to make a loan payment as scheduled

Delinquent: an account for which payment is overdue

Down payment: an initial cash sum that a buyer must pay in order to make a credit purchase or get a loan, usually a small percentage of the total amount of the purchase

Finance charge: a charge for using credit—another term for APR or interest

Grace period: the time during which you can pay a credit card bill on new purchases without being charged interest

Installment: a partial payment of a loan, usually paid monthly

Interest: the cost of borrowing money, expressed as a percentage—you **earn** interest when you invest your money in a savings account; you **pay** interest when you borrow money

Maturity date: the date by which you must repay your loan

Minimum payment: the smallest amount you must pay in any given month in order to keep your credit account in good standing—usually a great deal less than the total amount you have charged on your account

Periodic rate: The monthly interest rate on a credit card—for example, the periodic rate on a credit card with an 18 percent APR is 18 divided by 12, for a periodic rate of 1.5 percent

Principal: the amount of the money borrowed—payment of the principal is usually spread out over the term of the loan

Variable rate: An interest rate that changes over time

Because they have big debts and are always struggling to get by financially, many people make only the **minimum payment**—*the smallest amount due to keep your credit in good standing*—on their credit cards each month. They're always hoping that they'll be able to pay off their balance when they get more money. This frequently doesn't work—the accumulating interest fees catch many people by surprise. Their debt grows each month instead of decreasing and can quickly become difficult to manage.

More than 1 million people in the United States file for **bankruptcy** each year. Bankruptcy is *a situation in which a court rules that a person is not able to pay his or her bills.* A primary reason for these bankruptcies is that the individuals obtain more credit than they can repay.

Sources of Credit

Credit is available from a variety of sources. Some of the most common sources are charge accounts, credit cards, charge cards, installment loans, and layaway plans.

Charge Account or Retail Account

These accounts let you buy goods or services at a specific store on credit. For example, a charge account from Sears allows you to charge things at Sears, but nowhere else. In return for your promise to pay in full by a later date, the store lets you pay in monthly payments. This *monthly payment* is an **installment.** The store will charge interest on the amount that you have not yet paid. If you fail to pay on time, the store may charge you a late fee.

Credit Card

You can use a credit card to pay for goods or services at any business establishment that accepts the card. The credit card has a code number that tells the issuing company who you are and where to send your bill. If you pay your entire bill at the end of the month, you will not have to pay interest. If you pay your bill in monthly installments, you will be charged interest.

With credit cards, you may be able to get a **cash advance,** or *borrowed cash,* through the card. If you get a cash advance, you will usually have to pay a higher interest rate than if you bought something with your credit card. So it's a good idea to avoid taking cash advances. In addition to interest, the credit card company may charge you an **annual fee,** *a yearly fee that some companies charge in addition to the interest charge.*

Charge Card

A charge card looks like a credit card, but it is quite different. If you buy something with a charge card, you must pay the entire balance very quickly, usually within 30 days or less.

Installment Loan

People usually use installment loans when they need to make a single expensive purchase, such as a car or a home. You may use the item, but the lender holds ownership until you repay the loan. Installment loans may require you to make a down payment or pledge **collateral,** *possessions such as a home, car, or savings that a borrower pledges in return for a loan.* (Often the collateral will be the item you are taking out the loan to buy.) You will make fixed payments over a set period. The interest rate may be lower than that of other kinds of credit.

Layaway Plan

When you buy something on layaway, the store holds it until you have paid for it in full. You must usually make a down payment and then make regular payments according to a contract. The store may add a service charge. If you fail to pay on time, the store may no longer hold the item for you.

How Credit Works

How does all this work? Say you have a credit card with an APR of 18 percent. You want to buy a $250 stereo. When you make the purchase, you hand your credit card to the store clerk. The clerk contacts the credit card company (usually by swiping your card into a computer reader) to make sure you have sufficient credit to cover the purchase. He or she then checks your signature and the card expiration date, and sells you the item. The store charges $250, plus any sales tax, to your account.

When you receive your credit card account statement the following month, you make the minimum monthly payment. Suppose that minimum is 10 percent of the balance. In that case, you'd pay $25 within the specified time. This would leave you with a balance of $225.

So far, so good. But it's at this point that many people get into trouble. That's because for each month that you do not pay your entire balance, the company adds interest to the remaining balance. Thus, once you'd made your initial $25 minimum monthly payment, you would be charged an APR of 18 percent on your remaining balance. As long as you didn't pay off your total debt, your interest would continue to accumulate. If you continued to charge additional items on your card and pay only the minimum amount required, your interest and principal would continue to grow each month. If you have several credit cards and pay only the minimum monthly balance on each, your interest will really add up, overwhelming your ability to pay.

Simple Interest Rate	Simple Interest Payment per Year	Total Simple Interest Payments over Four Years
6%	$600	$2,400
8%	$800	$3,200
10%	$1,000	$4,000
12%	$1,200	$4,800
14%	$1,400	$5,600
16%	$1,600	$6,400
18%	$1,800	$7,200
20%	$2,000	$8,000

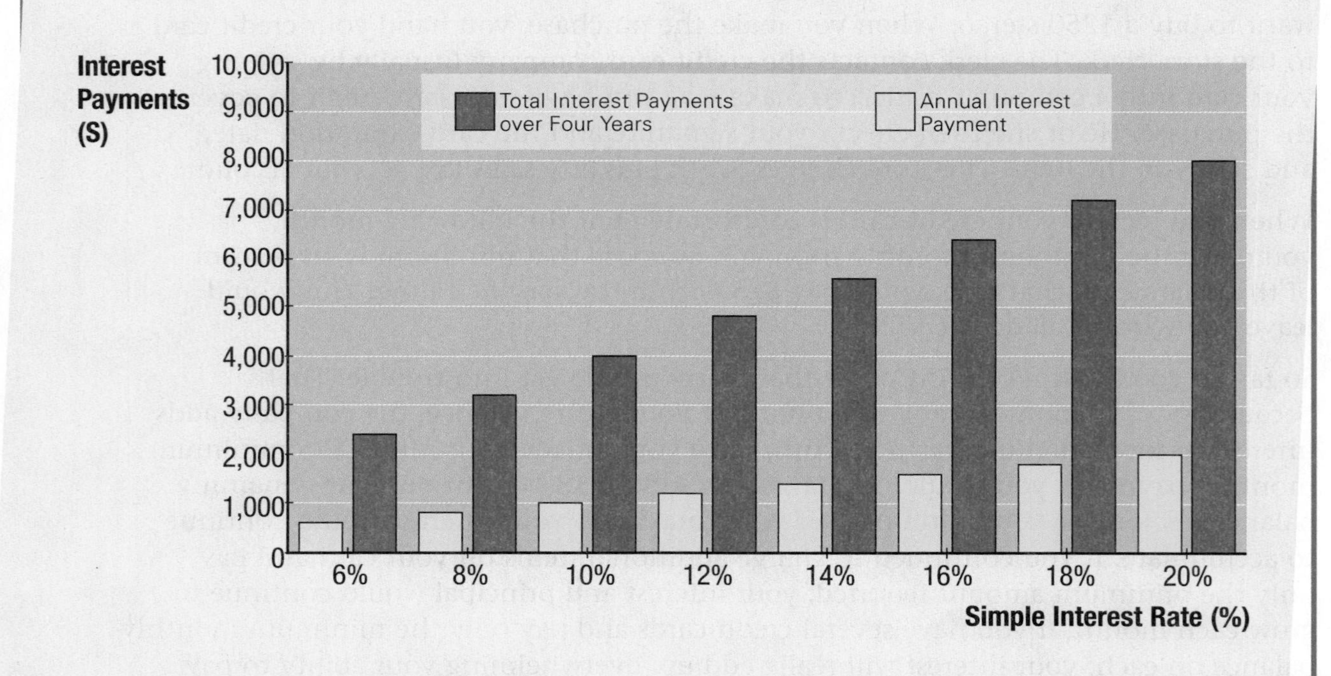

FIGURE 4.1

How Interest Payments Are Influenced by Interest Rates

From Madura, Jeff. (2006). *Personal Finance*, Second Edition. Boston, MA: Addison Wesley, p. 189.

To see what effect interest can have on your financial situation and what difference the interest rate can make, look at Figure 4.1. It shows what happens with a $10,000 loan at various interest rates. If you borrow money at an 8 percent rate, your interest, or finance charge, will be $800 during a year. But if you borrow at an 18 percent APR—the standard interest rate for credit cards today—the charge will be $1,800. If you don't make any payments for four years, you will owe $7,200 just in interest.

Most people are responsible, and they make monthly payments. But again, they often make only the minimum monthly payments. That means that their debt will quickly grow.

Using Credit Responsibly

Using credit wisely is an essential part of managing your finances. You should use it within the limits of your resources and your overall financial plan. Here are some tips for managing your credit:

- Pay all your bills on time. Remember that you will be able to get credit only as long as your **credit history,** *or record of paying your bills,* is good.
- Don't think of a credit card as extra cash. When you use your card, think of it as borrowing money. Before charging a purchase, ask yourself, "If I had to pay cash, would I still buy it?"
- Never borrow more than your budget shows you can pay back. A good rule of thumb is never to borrow more than 20 percent of your net income.
- Never get into the position of having to borrow money to pay credit debts.
- Always pay your other regular monthly bills, such as rent, utility, and telephone on time. And try to pay more than your monthly minimum on your credit card bills. Whenever possible, avoid paying high finance charges by paying off your balance each month.
- Limit yourself to no more than two credit cards. Make sure that one card has the lowest interest rate available. Use this card for purchases or services that you plan to pay for over a period of time, if that's really necessary. If the other card has a higher interest rate, pay the full balance on it each month.

Credit and Credit Card Options

When you're looking for credit, you need to be a smart shopper, just as when you buy groceries, clothing, or anything else. You need to comparison shop.

Say you're like most people and don't pay the balance of your credit card bill each month. If so, you should look at either the annual interest rate or the **periodic rate,** or *monthly rate,* the card issuer uses to calculate your finance charge. That rate is fixed. Some credit card companies offer a **variable rate,** *an interest rate that changes over time.* It starts low, but the company can then raise it after you've had the card for a while. Variable rates can also go down, although this does not happen often with credit cards.

Are you a person who pays off your bills each month? Then the credit card that has no annual fee and offers a **grace period,** *the time during which you can pay a credit card bill on new purchases without being charged interest,* is good for you.

Other questions to ask when shopping for credit include the following:

- Which kind of credit is appropriate for your purchase? Should you put the item on a credit card or take out a loan, which would usually have a lower interest rate?
- What kind of maturity period do you want? A longer maturity means smaller monthly bills. A shorter period costs less interest. Which plan best fits your budget? Is there a penalty if you pay off the loan before the maturity date?
- Do you have to pledge collateral? What collateral do you have?
- Does one credit card have a higher annual fee than another?

Applying for a Credit Card

You must be 18 years old to get a credit card. In most cases, in order to get credit, you must also have the following:

- steady employment
- a checking or savings account
- a history of paying your bills on time
- an income that exceeds your budgeted expenses
- a permanent residence.

You must fill out an application from the store or bank offering the card. Be honest on the application. The company has its requirements for a reason. If you are tempted not to be fully honest about your income or expenses, you probably can't afford credit at this time.

Once you've applied, the company has 30 days to respond to your application.

When it comes time to apply for a credit card for the first time, ask yourself these 10 questions:

1. Do I really need to establish this account? What will I use it for?
2. Can I qualify for credit?
3. What is the interest rate?
4. Are there additional fees?
5. What percentage is the monthly minimum payment, and when is it due?
6. Can I afford to make the monthly payments?
7. What will happen if I don't make the payments on time?
8. Are there any nontangible costs if I use credit? That is, can I sleep at night, or will I worry about my debts?
9. Given my current earnings and other regular expenses, what is the maximum credit card debt that I can handle?
10. All things considered, is using a credit card worth it?

If the company does not approve your application, it must tell you why.

If your application is accepted, the company will ask you to sign a credit agreement. Read this very carefully. The Truth in Lending Act, a federal law, requires that a company issuing the credit card disclose the following information to you:

- the annual percentage rate that you will be charged
- how the annual percentage rate will be determined, if it is variable
- the method for computing your balance at the end of each month
- the annual fee that the company will charge.

Don't sign the agreement until you fully understand it. If you need help, ask the lending officer to explain what you want to know. Ask that person to confirm how much is due each payment, how long the grace period is, and what happens if you **default**, *or fail to pay your bill on time*. In short, know what you are getting into. If the creditor has not filled out all the blanks on the form, don't sign until the company has filled out all the information.

How the Creditor Evaluates Your Application

Credit institutions use various guidelines to determine who qualifies for credit. Most lenders look at three things. These are sometimes referred to as the "three Cs of credit."

- **Character:** Are you reliable? Do you pay your bills on time? The application form may ask you for references or the names of other creditors.
- **Capacity:** Is your income enough to pay the debt? Do you have a job? Do you have other debts? Is it likely you can continue to earn your present salary, or even more, in the future? If you don't hold a job and have no regular income, you'll probably have a hard time obtaining credit.
- **Collateral:** Do you have enough assets? What do you own that has value and that you could use to repay the debt? A car? A savings account? Another word for collateral is *security*. *A loan that does not require collateral* is called an **unsecured loan**.

Building Your Credit History

The "three Cs" sound good, but what if you're just starting out? What if you don't have collateral or sufficient capacity? There are many ways to start building good credit. Most banks are willing to work with small loans. A good practice is to borrow a small amount of money from a bank and pay it back quickly.

The best collateral you could probably use for your first loan is your savings account. For example, if you had $450 saved, you could borrow $375 for a sofa and pledge your $450 savings against the loan as collateral. Be sure to make regular payments on your loan and be on time. When you pay off the loan, you have started a good credit history.

Most banks are willing to make small loans. Paying off such a loan on time helps you build a good credit history.
Courtesy of Mary Kate Denny/PhotoEdit

Another way to establish credit is to apply for a credit card or charge account at a local business or bank. Charge a few items that you would normally buy with cash, and pay the bill in full when it is due.

A third alternative is to have someone cosign your loan. The **cosigner,** *a person with a good credit rating who signs a loan note along with a borrower,* should be a relative or other responsible adult who has a good credit history and the ability to pay. If you are unable to make payments on the loan, the person who cosigned is responsible for paying the debt.

Still another way to start credit would be to purchase something on the installment plan. Many stores, such as furniture companies, encourage first-time credit for such purchases.

Once you borrow money and pay it back on time, the **credit bureau,** *a public or private agency that gathers credit information on people,* will have a record of your credit history. That's a good beginning, because other companies will then be more likely to give you credit.

Using a Credit Bureau

If a company turns you down for a loan or a credit card, you will want to find out why. Under the Fair Credit Reporting Act, you have the right to get a copy of your credit report. Write to the credit bureau and request it. You may have to pay a small fee for this service.

If you find errors on your credit report, write the credit bureau giving proof of the error. The credit bureau will then correct your report. It will send the corrected information to any company that requested your credit report in the previous six months.

There are three main credit bureaus in the United States: TransUnion, Experian, and Equifax. Each bureau covers a different region of the country, but since credit card and other companies have offices nationwide, you will likely deal with all three at some point in your life. You can find out more at the companies' websites. It's good practice to check your credit rating every year or so, even if you don't have any problems.

Credit Bureaus

TransUnion:
www.tuc.com

Experian:
www.experian.com

Equifax:
www.equifax.com

Avoiding Credit Card Fraud

Credit card fraud is a growing problem. It's all too easy for dishonest people to find ways to use your credit for their own purchases. They can do this by stealing your card, of course. But people who engage in fraud have more tricks up their sleeves.

Preventing Misuse of Your Credit Card

Follow these steps to reduce your risk of credit card fraud:

- Always sign a new credit card as soon as you receive it—when you buy something, the salesperson will compare the signature on back of the card with your signature at the bottom of the receipt for your purchase
- Save your receipts from credit card purchases—compare them with the charge amounts on each month's account statement
- Never give out a credit card number to someone who has called you on the phone—give out your number only if you have made the call and you're sure you're dealing with a reputable company
- If you're purchasing on the Internet, make sure you're using a secure site (look for the little lock on your browser's status bar)
- Destroy any preapproved credit offers you receive in the mail—a dishonest person might pull the blank application from your trash and apply for the card in your name
- Destroy any old or canceled credit cards.

If Your Card Is Stolen

What if your card or card number is stolen and a thief runs up charges? Federal law protects you. It states that credit card holders who are victims of theft or fraud are not responsible for more than $50 *if* they report the theft promptly.

Keep a record of all your account numbers and the phone numbers for any credit card or charge card companies you deal with. If you lose your card, if someone steals it, or if someone uses your credit card number fraudulently, contact the company immediately.

Identity Theft

Thieves may steal not only your credit card but also your identity. They do this by getting access to your personal information. You may have given this information on a job application, a credit card application, or an online transaction. The thief steals this information. He or she then uses your name, address, date of birth, and Social Security number to apply for a credit card in your name. Any purchases charged to the account appear under your name. When the thief uses a credit card and doesn't pay the bills, the **delinquent** or *overdue* account is posted on your credit report. Meanwhile, you are not even aware that this account exists.

Many states use your Social Security number as your driver's license number. But they are supposed to provide you the option to use a different number. People often demand to see your driver's license as proof of your identity. By using a different number on your driver's license, you protect your Social Security number from people who have no business seeing it. So when you apply for a driver's license, ask if the state can issue you a different number instead of using your Social Security number.

The best way to discourage identity theft is to regularly check your account statements and credit report. Never give out your Social Security number unless you are sure the person or company requesting it is reputable. Before you reveal any personal identifying information, find out how it will be used.

Most accounts involve the use of a password. When you create yours, make it something that an identity thief could not easily guess. For example, don't use your initials, your date of birth, or part of your Social Security number. Use something unique. But then be sure to record it in a secure place, in case you have a memory lapse.

For more information on how to protect yourself from identity theft, visit the government website *www.consumer.gov/idtheft.*

Another way to avoid identity theft problems is to contact creditors if your monthly bills don't arrive on time. A missing credit card bill could mean an identity thief has changed your billing address to cover his or her tracks.

The Consequences of Deficit Spending

If you make a habit of deficit spending, or spending more than you earn, sooner or later you'll wind up in a credit crunch. This inability to make all your payments can strain more than your wallet. Money worries can bring stress and low morale, hurt family and social life, and cause poor performance at your job or in school.

The minute you think you're getting into trouble, take the following steps:

- Stop borrowing. Leave your credit cards at home. Carry only enough money to get through the day.
- Cut expenses both big and small. Limit trips to the snack machines. Clip coupons for shopping, but only for items you really need. Borrow CDs or books at the library instead of buying them. Make do with what you have instead of replacing it with something new.
- Talk to creditors. Explain your problem. They may be willing to work out an easier payment schedule for you.
- Learn from your mistakes. Did an emergency throw you off course? Was your budget unrealistic? In both cases, you probably need to revise your budget, as discussed in the previous lesson. But if your problems result from spending money irresponsibly, you need to get serious about your financial future.

To help protect yourself from identity theft, contact the credit card company if your bill doesn't arrive on time.

Bankruptcy

Some people who get into serious debt decide to file in court for personal bankruptcy. They see no other way out of their financial difficulties. If a bankruptcy court approves this request, the person's debts are eliminated or severely reduced.

While filing for bankruptcy does release you from heavy debt burdens, it has serious long-term disadvantages. The court may seize most of your property to pay your bills. A history of bankruptcy will stay on your credit report for up to 10 years. This means you may have trouble getting credit, because creditors do not like to extend credit to someone who has filed for bankruptcy.

In 2004, 1.1 million credit card holders filed for bankruptcy. Some of these people, of course, have legitimate reasons to file for bankruptcy. For example, they may suddenly incur a huge medical bill that they can't pay. If someone you know has filed for bankruptcy, it doesn't automatically mean that he or she is irresponsible.

Still, bankruptcy is not a good solution to debt problems. It could have a long-term, even permanent effect on your financial future. It almost always involves a lot of pain and suffering for many people. Keep your credit situation under control, and you won't have to deal with the difficult problem of bankruptcy.

The Importance of a Financial Plan

It's up to you to make sure your credit decisions fit your financial plan. The key question to ask yourself is: How will buying something through credit affect my future?

By making proper decisions, you can keep a lid on your credit. This will increase the amount of money you have available now and enable you to buy the things you need.

Figure 4.2 shows a good example of how to manage credit. Stephanie Spratt has had to make the same decisions regarding credit that you will have to make soon. Note how she first set out in words her goals for managing credit. Then she figured out how much money ($1,100) she had left each month after paying basic bills. She explained to herself why this $1,100 could be used for credit card purchases, if necessary. Finally, she decided to make a real effort to reduce her debt. She decided that any extra money she gets will go first to paying back credit card bills. She wants to reduce her debt. This is because credit cards charge a higher rate of interest than she would earn by putting that money into savings account.

Goals for Managing Credit

1. *Set my own limit on credit card purchases to ensure that I will always be able to pay off the credit balance in the same month.*
2. *Set a policy to avoid incurring high interest expenses on credit cards.*

Analysis

Monthly Cash Inflows	$2,500
− Typical Monthly Expenses (paid by checks)	−1,400
= Amount of Funds Available	1,100

Liquid Assets	Balance	Annualized Interest Rate (%)
Cash	$100	0
Checking account balance	800	0
Money market fund	400	3.0
One-month CD	1,200	4.3
Credit card balance	600	20.0

Decisions

Decision on Credit Limit:
Given that I have $1,100 each month left from my salary after paying typical expenses (by check), I have $1,100 remaining that can be used for credit card purchases if necessary. I will impose a maximum limit of $1,100 on my credit card spending. As my income rises over time, I may consider increasing my credit limit, but only up to some level that I can afford to pay off immediately when I receive the bill.

Decision on Paying Off Credit Balances:
Given the interest rates that I can earn on deposit accounts versus the interest rate I would pay on a credit card balance, I will always pay off my credit card balance, even if I must withdraw funds from my savings account to do so.

FIGURE 4.2

How Credit Management Fits Within Stephanie Spratt's Financial Plan
From Madura, Jeff. (2006). *Personal Finance*, Second Edition. Boston, MA: Addison Wesley, p. 206.

Annual percentage rate (APR) for purchases	2.9% until 11/1/06 after that, **14.9%**
Other APRs	Cash-advance APR: 15.9% Balance-Transfer APR: 15.9% Penalty rate: 23.9% See explanation below.*
Variable-rate information	Your APR for purchase transactions may vary. The rate is determined monthly by adding 5.9% to the Prime Rate.**
Grace period for repayment of balances for purchases	25 days on average
Method of computing the balance for purchases	Average daily balance (excluding new purchases)
Annual fees	None
Minimum finance charge	$0.50
Transaction fee for cash advances: 3% of the amount advanced Balance-transfer fee: 3% of the amount transferred Late-payment fee: $25 Over-the-credit-limit fee: $25	

*Explanation of penalty. If your payment arrives more than ten days late two times within a six-month period, the penalty rate will apply.

**The Prime Rate used to determine your APR is the rate published in the *Wall Street Journal* on the 10th day of the prior month.

FIGURE 4.3

Sample Credit Card Disclosure Box

Taken from *www.federalreserve.gov*

CHECKPOINTS

Lesson 1 Review

Using complete sentences, answer the following questions on a sheet of paper.

1. What is the definition of credit?
2. What are the main advantages and disadvantages of credit?
3. Name three sources of credit and describe key features of each.
4. How can you use a credit card responsibly?
5. How can you start building a good credit history right now?
6. What are three of the ways in which a dishonest person could use your credit card or steal your identity? How can you protect yourself from credit card fraud and identity theft?
7. What are the consequences of deficit spending?

Applying Credit Skills

8. Study the sample credit card disclosure box in Figure 4.3. Read it and analyze its terms. What is the interest rate? Are there other fees? Is there a grace period? What is the penalty rate? Get used to reading and understanding such information in credit card agreements. You will read many over your lifetime.

LESSON 2

Financing for College

Quick Write

How much do you think it costs to go to college? Make a short list of ways you can get the money you need to attend the college of your choice.

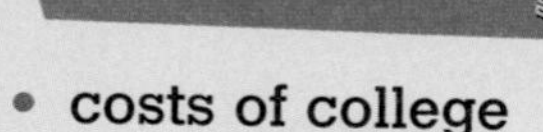

Learn About...

- costs of college
- sources of college funds
- planning to finance a college education

Costs of College

A college degree can lead to a great future. As you know, it can open the door to hundreds of careers—as a doctor, a lawyer, an engineer, or an Air Force Officer, for example.

But you've probably heard that college can cost a lot. In some cases, that's true. At an expensive college, **tuition,** or *the fee for instruction,* can cost more than $30,000 a year. Most colleges, however, cost far less. In fact, only 2 percent of US students attend colleges where the annual tuition is $33,000 or higher. Sixty percent of students pay less than $6,000 for tuition per year.

Tuition is not the only cost of college. If you're no longer living at home, you will also have to pay **room,** or *the cost of a place to live,* and **board,** or *the cost of food.* You'll have other expenses as well. In college, unlike high school, you'll have to pay for books. You will pay laboratory fees, library fees, and medical fees. And then there's the cost of transportation. Some students have cars on campus. That means fuel, repair, and insurance costs. If you don't have a car and your college is a good distance from your home, you'll have long-distance travel expenses whenever you go home for vacation.

But if you want to go to college, don't be discouraged by all those costs. The College Board, a nonprofit organization, reports that $129 billion in financial aid is available to help students pay for college. This financial aid is available from a variety of sources. In this lesson, you'll learn about the costs of college and on how to get financial aid to cover those costs.

Two-Year Colleges

Vocabulary

- tuition
- room
- board
- in-state resident
- out-of-state student
- public university
- private university
- scholarship
- grant
- need based
- subsidized
- unsubsidized
- capitalizing

The least expensive option for higher education is usually a two-year college. This can be a community college, junior college, or a technical college. Technical colleges are often more expensive than community colleges.

If you attend a two-year college, you can earn an associate's degree after two years of study. A two-year degree does not prepare you for as many careers as a four-year degree does. But if you are not sure whether a four-year college is right for you, this option is worth considering. Attending a two-year college, then transferring to a four-year school, can help you keep your costs down. Forty-four percent of college students attend two-year colleges.

A year of tuition at a community college in the United States cost an average of $2,191 in 2005. This was the average fee for an **in-state resident,** or *a resident of the state in which the college is located.* **Out-of-state students,** or *students who do not live in the state in which the college is located,* pay on average an additional $4,160 for tuition at community colleges. So, for example, if you live in Illinois and go to a community college in Illinois, you will pay one rate. But if you live in Indiana and go to a school in Illinois, you will pay a much higher rate.

Since most students at community colleges live at home, they save a lot on room and board. If you make that choice, you may be able to use the money you save to complete the last two years of your education at a four-year school.

Four-Year Colleges and Universities

Four-year colleges and universities are more expensive than two-year schools. For the 2005–2006 school year, average tuition at a **public university,** or *an institution of higher learning that is operated and funded by the state in which it is located,* was $5,491. This was for in-state residents. Out-of-state residents paid an average of $7,673 more. Average annual tuition at a **private university,** or *an institution of higher learning that is operated by a private organization,* was $21,235.

Attending a two-year college, then transferring to a four-year school, can help you keep your costs down.
Courtesy of David Butow/Corbis SABA

Private universities have to charge higher tuition costs than public schools because they receive no money from the state. Because these schools do not receive state funds, they charge all students the same rate, regardless of where they are from.

So the amount you'll have to pay depends on which college you attend. It's a good idea to start thinking about your preferences now. Will it be a two-year or a four-year school? Public or private? In state or out of state? Start to put together a list of possibilities, and then get cost information from the website of each college you're thinking about. And don't forget: Tuition is the biggest cost, but it's not the only one.

Good grades are important, but you don't need a 4.0 grade point average to get a college scholarship.
Courtesy of Rudy Sulgan/Corbis Images

Sources of College Funds

You or your family may already have saved enough money to pay for your college. If so, you have a lot to be grateful for.

Most young people, however, have to find the money to finance their college educations. Fortunately, once they start looking, they find many sources of financial aid—so many, in fact, that it takes time and patience to sort through them. If you are planning to go to college, start your financial preparation early—at least by the spring of your junior year. This section describes the major sources of financial assistance for college students. They include scholarships, grants, and loans.

Scholarships and Grants

Scholarships and **grants** *are types of student financial aid that you do not have to repay. Scholarship* recipients are usually selected based on academic, athletic, or artistic merit. *Grant* recipients are usually selected based on their financial need. College students receive thousands of scholarships and grants each year.

Most scholarships go to students with special qualifications, such as academic, athletic, or artistic talent. Scholarships are also available for students who want to pursue a particular field of study, such as the sciences. Members of particular groups, such as ethnic or religious groups, may also be eligible for certain scholarships. Scholarships are available for students who live in certain areas of the country or who demonstrate financial need. Good grades are important, but you don't have to have a 4.0 grade point average (GPA) to get a scholarship.

Finding Information on Scholarships

To find out which scholarships you might qualify for, talk to your high school guidance counselor or go to your school or public library. They will have lists of scholarships, including application requirements.

If you have already decided which colleges you will apply to, contact each school's financial aid office for lists of its scholarship programs. Many schools have their own financial aid programs.

Scholarship information is free, and there's lots of it out there. Three good places to start are:

- ***www.fastweb.com*—this website, affiliated with Monster.com, matches students to scholarships at no charge**
- ***http://apps.collegeboard.com/cbsearch_ss/welcome.jsp*—this College Board website also helps you search for financial aid**
- ***http://www.srnexpress.com*—this website contains a database of more than 8,000 programs.**

To find more sources of scholarship information online, just type "scholarships" into your favorite search engine and go from there.

Many small local scholarships sometimes aren't listed in books or databases. To learn about these opportunities, look for notices on bulletin boards at your school's guidance office, in a public library, or outside the financial aid office at nearby colleges and universities.

Applying for a Scholarship

Once you've identified scholarships for which you think you are eligible,request the application forms. Look carefully at the application requirements. Do you meet all of them? If not, is there a way you can? For example, if an application calls for a 3.7 GPA and you have a 3.6, can you raise your GPA before the deadline?

Many scholarships are very competitive. The most competitive ones give one award for every 400 applicants, and even the least competitive ones give only one award for every 10 applicants. Do everything you can to make yourself look good to the people who will evaluate your application. Answer all the questions completely.

Some scholarships have unusual eligibility requirements. For example, you can find scholarships for left-handed students, people of short stature, and people who are obese! Get information on these and other unusual scholarships at *www.finaid.org/scholarships/unusual.phtml*

Don't give up if you are rejected. Apply for other scholarships. One thing is for sure: If you never apply for a scholarship, you'll never get one.

But be careful. Every year, scholarship scams defraud several hundred thousand students and parents. The victims of these scams lose more than $100 million annually. Scam operations often imitate legitimate government agencies, grant-giving foundations, education lenders, and scholarship matching services. They use official-sounding names containing words such as National, Federal, Foundation, or Administration. In general, be wary of scholarships with an application fee, scholarship services that guarantee success, scholarship-search services that charge a fee, advance-fee loan offers, and sales pitches disguised as "financial aid seminars."

Remember, when it comes to scholarships, if you have to pay money, it's probably a scam.

To apply for a Pell grant or any other federal government student loan, you must complete the Free Application for Federal Student Aid (FAFSA).
Courtesy of David Young-Wolff/PhotoEdit

US Government Grants

Pell Grants

If you need money to finance your education, a federal *Pell grant* might be one of your best options. Pell grants are **need based,** or *given to students who have a serious financial need.*

To apply for a Pell grant, you must complete the Free Application for Federal Student Aid (FAFSA) form. It is available online at *www.fafsa.ed.gov.* Fill out the FAFSA form as soon as you can after January 1 of the year you will start college. To complete the form, you'll need your most recent tax forms along with those of your parents or guardian, as well as your Social Security number.

Once you submit your application, the US Department of Education will determine whether you are eligible. In reviewing your application, it will look at the amount that your family can afford to contribute to your education. It will take into account your family's income during the past year, current assets, and expenses. The maximum Pell grant for the 2005–2006 school year was $4,050. This maximum can change from year to year.

Federal Supplemental Educational Opportunity Grants

Another US government grant is the *Federal Supplemental Educational Opportunity Grant* (FSEOG). The FSEOG is for students with exceptional financial need. It gives priority to students who receive Pell grants.

You can receive between $100 and $4,000 a year for a FSEOG, depending on when you apply, your need, and the policies of your school's financial aid office. But you have no guarantee of a FSEOG, even if you qualify. Each school receives enough money from the government to pay for all its Pell grantees, but the government does not guarantee money for every FSEOG applicant.

US Government Loans

Scholarships and grants often don't cover all college expenses. Many students rely on federal government loans to finance their educations. These loans have low interest rates and do not require credit checks or collateral. They have a variety of repayment terms.

Such loans are very popular—in fact, two-thirds of undergraduate students graduate with some debt. The average federal student loan debt among graduating seniors in a recent year was $19,202, according to the 2003–2004 National Postsecondary Student Aid Study. The following describes federal loans available for students and students' families.

Stafford Loans

The most common federal loan for students is the Stafford loan. Through a Stafford loan you can borrow up to $2,625 your first year, and a little more each year after that, to a maximum of $23,000 for four years. Stafford loans have variable interest rates, with a maximum of 8.25 percent.

A Stafford loan has two variations:

- *Federal Family Education Loan Program* (FFELP) loans are provided by private lenders, such as banks
- *Federal Direct Student Loan Program* (FDSLP) loans are provided by the US government directly to students or their parents.

A Stafford loan may either be **subsidized,** meaning *the government pays the interest while you're in school,* or **unsubsidized,** meaning *you pay all the interest.* Unsubsidized Stafford loans are available to all students. To receive a subsidized Stafford Loan, you must demonstrate financial need. Many students combine subsidized loans with unsubsidized loans to borrow the maximum amount permitted each year.

You can defer payments on an unsubsidized Stafford loan until after graduation by capitalizing the interest. **Capitalizing** means *adding the interest payments to the loan balance.* Capitalizing will relieve you from repaying your debt while you are still in college, but it will increase the overall amount of your debt.

Perkins Loans

Perkins loans are awarded to students with exceptional financial need. Although funded through the federal government, they are offered through a college. Perkins loans are subsidized—the federal government pays the interest while you are in school. In 2006 the interest rate is 5 percent, and the repayment term is 10 years, with a minimum payment of $40 a month.

The student financial aid office at your college or university will determine the amount of a Perkins loan you receive. The maximum is $4,000 per year for undergraduate students.

Parent Loans for Undergraduate Students

Your parents or a stepparent can also take out loans to help with your education. They can do this through the Parent Loan for Undergraduate Students (PLUS) program. Like Stafford loans, PLUS loans can come through private lenders, such as banks, or directly from the government.

PLUS loans have variable interest rates, with a maximum of 9 percent. Repaying them is the parent's financial responsibility, not the student's.

Applying for US Government Loans

To apply for a Stafford, Perkins, PLUS, or any other federal government loan, you must submit the FAFSA, the same form that you fill out for the Pell grant. The form is online at *www.fafsa.ed.gov*. You only have to fill out the FAFSA once, even if you are applying for several loans and grants.

Private Loans

Government loans are the best deal for students because of their lower interest rates. If you've taken maximum advantage of these loans and still need money, however, you may consider a private lender.

Private lenders such as banks and private companies sometimes charge fees when they make loans. These fees can substantially increase the cost of the loan. If you can get a loan with a low interest rate but high fees, you might end up paying more for the loan than if you had a higher interest rate with no fees. A good rule of thumb is that if you have to pay fees equal to 3 percent of the money you are borrowing, this is about the same as a 1 percent higher interest rate.

Just how much are those lending fees? The Student Loan Marketing Association, a major source of student loans, says that if a student wants to borrow $6,500, he or she will have to pay a fee ranging from $130 (2 percent of the sum borrowed) to $585 (9 percent of the sum borrowed). The difference depends on the student's credit rating or the rating of his or her parents, guardian, or cosigner.

In an effort to do business with students, lenders sometimes advertise a low interest rate during the in-school and grace period. After you graduate, however, they raise the rate. Be sure to read the loan agreement carefully.

For more information about student loans, contact:

- Sallie Mae, the nation's No. 1 paying-for-college company, at *www.salliemae.com*
- The US Department of Education at *www.studentaid.ed.gov*

You can learn about the military's loan-repayment benefits at

- *www.todaysmilitary.com/app/tm/get/collegehelp/support#repayment*

Other Sources of Financial Aid

Other sources of financial aid include the following:

Many colleges offer their own scholarships, tuition-payment plans, and other forms of aid.
Courtesy of Rachel Epstein/PhotoEdit

- *Federal aid.* The US government offers a number of student aid programs in addition to those described above. To find out about any federally supported student grant or loan program, contact the Federal Student Aid Information Center. The center's phone number is 1-800-4-FED-AID (1-800-433-3243). Its website is *www.studentaid.ed.gov.*
- *State aid.* Your state may offer scholarship or grant money for education. When you complete the FAFSA, the federal government will automatically forward your information to the appropriate agency in your state.
- *Federal Work-Study Program.* This program provides part-time jobs for college students with financial need, which allows them to earn money to help pay their education expenses. You'll earn at least the current federal minimum wage or more, depending on the type of work you do and the skills required. You can apply for a work-study program through the FAFSA.
- *Military benefits.* ROTC scholarships can be a great advantage for someone who wants to enter the armed forces after college. Military service members are also eligible for several tuition-support programs.
- *College-controlled aid.* Many colleges offer their own scholarships, tuition-payment plans, and other forms of aid. Contact the financial aid office of the colleges you intend to apply to for information.
- *Scholarship lotteries.* A number of websites give money away to students for their educations. Your chances of winning are small because so many people participate. You can access these sites free of charge, but if you do, they will probably sell your e-mail address and you may receive unsolicited messages.

Planning to Finance a College Education

Now that you have the basic information on college costs and sources of funds, how should you start planning?

As mentioned above, the best place to start out is your high school guidance counselor. Your public library will also have information. Surfing the Web will yield lots of good information as well.

Once you've completed this background research, decide what kind of college you want to attend. If it's a community college and you intend to live at home, your costs will be relatively low. If it's a public college in another state or a private college, your costs will be much higher. If you're not sure which college is best for you, choose your highest-cost option, and start planning for that. Then if it turns out you need less money than you thought, you'll be in great shape.

Next, talk to people in the financial aid offices of the schools you intend to apply to. Ask them what kinds of aid they offer. Once you are accepted at a college, they should work closely with you to make sure you have the funds you need. In most cases, the college wouldn't accept you for admission if it weren't willing to help you find the money to pay for your education.

At the same time, start collecting information on specific scholarships, grants, loans, and other sources of money. Note the requirements and application dates of each source. Talk to your high school counselor about aid sources available in your community. Start applying.

Complete the FAFSA shortly after January 1 of your senior year. This form opens the door to many sources of financial aid. The government will forward your information to the schools you are applying to as well as to several sources of funding. When completing the form, be honest. You may use student loans for educational purposes only. Giving false information is a criminal offense. Be sure to keep copies of all the application forms that you submit.

Finally, borrow only what you need. Remember, you or your family must repay any loans you take out. And when you begin repaying, keep your payments up to date—failing to do so will affect your credit rating.

As part of your planning, you should talk to people in the financial aid offices of the schools you intend to apply to.
Courtesy of Davis Barber/PhotoEdit

CHECKPOINTS

Lesson 2 Review

Using complete sentences, answer the following questions on a sheet of paper.

1. What do the basic costs of college include?
2. What is the difference between a public university and a private university?
3. What is the main advantage of a scholarship over a loan?
4. What is the difference between a subsidized and an unsubsidized loan?
5. What are three financial aid programs you can apply for through the FAFSA?
6. What are three sources of aid other than scholarships, grants, and loans?

Applying Financial-Aid Skills

7. Say you need a $10,000-a-year loan to cover costs at the college you've decided to attend. Do research to identify scholarships that you might qualify for that would enable you to obtain the funds you need.

LESSON

3 Insurance for Protecting Your Resources

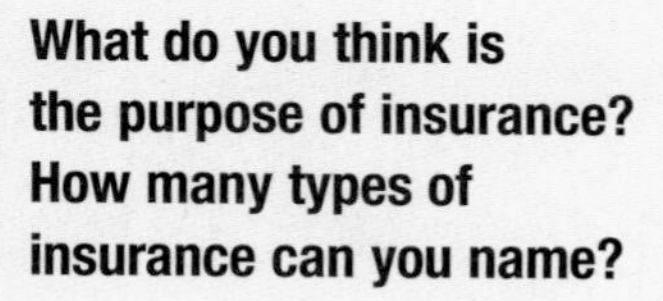

What do you think is the purpose of insurance? How many types of insurance can you name?

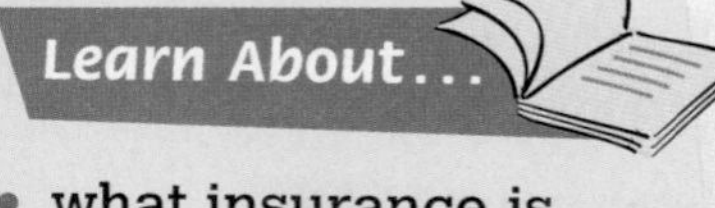

- what insurance is and why it is necessary
- major types of insurance
- how to protect your personal and financial information

What Insurance Is and Why It Is Necessary

As you grow older, you will take on more responsibilities. These responsibilities will probably include having a full-time job and owning a car, a home, and other valuable property.

But what would happen if you were injured and couldn't work? Who would pay your medical bills? What would you live on? What if your house and its contents were damaged by a fire or a flood? How would you repair or replace your car if it were damaged or stolen?

Bad as these situations are, you might find yourself in even bigger problems. What if you accidentally injured someone and a court determined that you had **liability,** or *legal responsibility,* for causing the injury? The injured person could sue you, and you could lose a lot of money.

Accidents happen. You have to expect the unexpected. This is where insurance comes in. Insurance is the means by which people protect themselves financially against losses or liability incurred as a result of unexpected events.

Insurance works on the principle of shared risk. For example, suppose that 100 people buy auto insurance. Each person pays a **premium,** or *fee for being protected by the insurance,* of $50 per month. In exchange for these monthly premiums, the insurance company provides each person with a **policy,** *or contract that promises to pay for any losses.*

Along with those other 99 policyholders, you share the risk of damaging your car. Some of those car owners probably will have accidents, but the insurance company doesn't know which ones will be the unlucky few. So the company collects premiums from everyone.

If all 100 people are paying the same premiums, in just one month, the company will create a reserve of $5,000 (100 × $50). It will then draw on that reserve to cover car repairs that policyholders might need if their vehicles are damaged. When a policy owner has an accident that is covered by insurance, he or she will make a **claim,** or *demand for payment in accordance with the policy.* The insurance company will then pay for the repairs.

You may never damage your car and may never have to file a claim. And you certainly hope that you won't. No one wants to be in an accident. But an investment in insurance is still a good one. It's not money wasted. This is because insurance gives you financial security and peace of mind. You can drive (or live in your home, go to work, or do just about anything else in life) without worrying about the financial loss that may result from an unexpected event.

One more thing: Although the insurance company will reimburse you for a major part of your claim, an insurance policy doesn't usually cover the entire loss. Most policies have a **deductible,** or *amount that you must pay before the insurance company pays anything.*

Deductibles vary. If you choose a low deductible, you'll probably have higher premiums. If your deductible is higher, your premiums will be lower. This is the company's way of rewarding you for accepting a greater share of the up-front financial responsibility for loss. It makes sense to choose a deductible that is large enough to reduce premiums. But the deductible needs to be small enough to prevent financial hardship if you suffer a loss.

Vocabulary

- liability
- premium
- policy
- claim
- deductible
- insurance agent
- inventory
- dependent
- indemnity plan
- managed care plan
- copayment
- beneficiary
- term life insurance
- whole life insurance
- universal life insurance
- phishing

Auto insurance allows you to drive without worrying about the financial loss that might result from an accident.
Courtesy of Ted Horowitz/Corbis Images

TABLE 4.1

Common Events That Could Cause a Financial Loss

Event that could cause a financial loss:	Your financial loss is due to:	You can protect against this financial loss by having:
You have a car accident and damage your car	Car repairs	Auto insurance
You have a car accident in which another person in your car is injured	Medical bills and liability	Auto insurance
You have a car accident in which another person in the other driver's car is injured	Medical bills and liability	Auto insurance
Your home or condo is damaged by a fire	Home or condo repairs	Homeowner's insurance
Your neighbor is injured while in your home or condo	Medical bills and liability	Homeowner's insurance
You become ill and need medical attention	Medical bills	Health insurance
You develop an illness that requires long-term care	Medical bills	Long-term care insurance
You become disabled	Loss of income	Disability insurance
You die while family members rely on your income	Loss of income	Life insurance

From Madura, Jeff. (2006). *Personal Finance*, Second Edition. Boston, MA: Addison Wesley, p. 293.

Major Types of Insurance

People face many kinds of risks that they can share through insurance. As Table 4.1 shows, the major types of insurance are:

- automobile
- property (for homeowners and renters)
- liability
- health
- disability
- life.

Automobile Insurance

Automobile insurance protects car owners from financial loss. This loss may be caused by damage to their cars or the cars of other drivers. The loss may also result from medical expenses related to an accident.

For example, suppose you are in a two-car accident. If a court decides that you are liable, you will have to pay for any damages to the other car. If people in the other car are injured, the court may also require you to pay for their medical bills, lost income, and any related pain and suffering. These damages could amount to millions of dollars. The right type of auto insurance will protect you from most of those expenses.

To protect its residents from heavy losses, almost every state requires that car owners have some type of auto insurance before they can register a car.

Types of Automobile Insurance

The major types of auto insurance are as follows:

- *Collision* insurance pays for repair costs of your car if it rolls over or collides with something
- *Comprehensive* insurance pays for repairing damage to your car that is caused by something other than collision or rolling over—these damages might be caused by a fire, a falling object, or vandalism, for example
- *Liability* insurance helps pay the expenses of other people involved in an accident. It also protects you from lawsuits resulting from an accident. The two major types of liability coverage are:
  1. *Property damage* insurance, which helps pay the cost of repairing damage to other people's property
  2. *Bodily injury* insurance, which helps cover medical expenses for injuries to other people
- *Uninsured motorist protection* insurance protects you if your car is damaged by a driver who has no auto insurance
- *Emergency road service* insurance covers the cost of towing your car to a repair shop in an emergency.

Some states have *no-fault* insurance laws. If you live in a state with such laws, your insurance company will pay your expenses and the other driver's insurance company will pay his or her expenses. The issue of liability does not come up. But in most states, the court determines liability. If you get into an accident and the court says that you're liable, your insurance company will have to pay.

Automobile Insurance Rates

The cost of insurance premiums varies. Each insurance company sets its own rates based on a number of factors. One of the most important factors is your driving record and the driving record of people with characteristics similar to yours. You can help keep your premiums low by driving carefully and not getting traffic tickets. Teenagers as a group, however, are poorer drivers because they're inexperienced and take more risks than people who've been driving for a while. In fact, statistics show that 16-year-olds have 10 times as many accidents as people between the ages of 30 and 59 do. So younger drivers usually have to pay higher premiums than other drivers do, no matter how good their individual driving records.

In setting your premium, the insurance company also looks at where you live. Accident rates are higher in cities than in rural areas, so people who live in the country often have lower premiums than people who live in urban areas.

In addition, the company takes into account what type of car you drive. One reason is that some cars cost more to repair than others do. Another reason is that some car models are the specific targets of thieves.

The company will want to know if you are a good student, because records show that good students are more careful drivers. They will even consider your gender, because girls between 16 and 25 tend to be better drivers than boys of the same age are. (Sorry, guys!)

Once you have insurance, the company will keep a record of your driving habits and any claims you file. If the company sees that you drive recklessly, it will raise your premiums. If you have too many accidents, it might refuse to renew your policy.

Buying Auto Insurance

When you're ready to buy insurance, you must choose a reputable company. Ask friends or relatives if they can recommend one. You want to be sure it will stand behind you if you have an accident.

The next step is to find out what type of coverage your state requires. In many states, collision and liability insurance are mandatory. Then decide which additional insurance, if any, you want to purchase. Keep in mind that car repairs are expensive. Although the cost of the premiums might seem high, it will be much less expensive than repair costs if you do have a serious accident. For this reason, comprehensive insurance is usually a good idea, especially if you have a fairly new car.

Also think about deductibles. If you want to keep your premiums low, get a high deductible. But don't forget that this means you will have to pay more if you do have an accident.

Then narrow your search to a couple of companies and compare their rates. Ask whether they offer lower rates to good students and people with safe driving records. You might get a lower fee if you've taken a driver's training course. Companies also offer discounts for people who insure more than one car.

At some point you may want to find an **insurance agent,** or *a person who sells insurance.* You will need an agent if you don't buy insurance directly from an insurance company. Many agents sell policies for several companies. Ask friends or relatives if they can recommend an agent. A good agent may know about the benefits offered by several companies. Remember, however, that the agent's fee is a percentage of your policy's cost. Don't be talked into more than you need. Find the level that makes you feel secure and that fits your budget.

Property Insurance

Property insurance covers valuable items you own, such as clothing and furniture. It also covers real estate, such as a house or condominium. You protect your property and real estate with homeowner's or renter's insurance.

How do you decide how much property insurance to purchase? The basic rule of thumb is simple: Have enough insurance to cover the replacement value of your goods. You might think that your property doesn't have much value, but things add up. In addition, it may cost you more to replace something than it did when you originally bought it. That's why it's a good idea to keep an **inventory,** or *list of your property and its value,* and update it yearly.

Note

Most homeowner's policies don't cover damage from floods caused by heavy rains, melting snow, inadequate drainage systems, failed levees and dams, tropical storms, or hurricanes. To protect your buildings against flood damage, you must purchase special flood insurance.

Homeowners need to insure both their buildings (for example, house and garage) and their contents against damage. Renters do not own the buildings in which they live, so they don't need to insure them. But they still may want to insure their furniture, clothing, and other contents of their apartments.

You protect your valuable items and real estate with property insurance.
Courtesy of Corbis Images

Liability Insurance

Liability insurance is a good idea for homeowners and renters, as well as auto owners. It covers the costs associated with injuries resulting from slips, falls, or other accidents that might happen when someone is on your property.

Liability insurance premiums are based on the company's assessment of the degree to which your home poses a risk to others. For example, if your home has a swimming pool, your rates will be higher than they would be otherwise. Even having a pet can increase your liability premiums.

Renters don't need to insure the building they live in, but may still want to insure their furniture, clothing, and other personal property.
Courtesy of Grace/zefa/Corbis Images

Health Insurance

Most young people are healthy, and they don't have to worry about medical bills. That's fortunate, because even a few days' stay in a hospital can cost thousands of dollars. If you have surgery, the bill will be higher. You'll have to pay medical and surgical bills, as well as the hospitalization costs. That's why health insurance is essential.

Most people in the United States obtain their health insurance through their employers. Workers whose employers provide health insurance benefits can get coverage for themselves and each **dependent,** or *member of their immediate family who relies on them for financial support.* Such policies generally cover children until they reach age 21.

Once you're on your own, you will need your own health insurance. The alternative is to go without, which can be risky. You can buy health insurance yourself, but since it's so expensive, it's better if you can get it through your employer. Always inquire about health insurance when interviewing for a job—it's an important benefit. Some companies pay the entire cost of their employees' health insurance, while others pay part of the premium and deduct the rest from the employee's wages.

If your employer provides your health insurance, you may or may not have a choice of plans. If you pay for your own health insurance, you'll have more choices, but your premiums will cost more than they would if you got your insurance through your employer. If you have any choices about your health insurance, you'll need to do some comparison shopping.

First, you'll need to know that there are two basic types of health insurance plans: indemnity plans and managed care plans.

- An **indemnity plan** *enables you to go to any health provider to receive care.* You can visit a primary-care physician, who handles basic medical needs, or go directly to a specialist. You pay the doctor and send the receipt to your insurance company. The company then sends you a check to you, minus any deductibles.
- A **managed care plan** *requires that you consult a primary physician when you need medical care.* That doctor will examine you and refer you to a specialist if you need one. One of his or her roles is to reduce the number of unnecessary visits to specialists. That saves money and makes better use of resources. Under a managed care plan, the doctor bills the insurance company directly.

  Some managed care plans pay only for visits to certain doctors or medical facilities. These plans are called *health maintenance organizations,* or HMOs. Other plans, called *preferred provider organizations,* or PPOs, offer you greater flexibility in choosing a doctor. Both HMOs and PPOs publish the lists of their providers. You choose your doctor from this list.

The cost of health insurance varies. Indemnity plans are generally more expensive than managed care plans, and HMOs are less expensive than PPOs. Most plans offer reduced prices for prescription drugs. Some include dental or optical care.

TABLE 4.2

Comparison of Private Health Insurance Plans

Type of Private Health Plan	Premium	Selection of Physician
Indemnity Plan	High	Flexibility to select physician or specialist
Managed Care: HMOs	Relatively low	Primary care physician refers patients to specialist
Managed Care: PPOs	Low, but usually higher than HMOs	There is a greater number of physicians to choose from in PPOs than HMOs.

From Madura, Jeff. (2006). *Personal Finance*, Second Edition. Boston, MA: Addison Wesley, p. 326.

Some types of health insurance have deductibles, as auto insurance does. For example, in some plans you have to pay the first $100 of medical bills out of your pocket. Then the insurance company starts paying. In addition, a health insurance policy generally requires that you make copayments. A **copayment** *is money you must pay for a doctor's visit or other health service.* The copayment is a percentage of the total cost of the visit. For example, if your primary care physician charges $60 for a visit, you may have to make a copayment of $10. Your insurance company will pay the remaining $50. Many plans also require copayments on prescription medications.

Disability Insurance

The purpose of disability insurance is to replace part of your income if you cannot work because of injury or illness. The amount of coverage is usually limited to one-half to two-thirds of your earnings at the time of the disability. Coverage is limited in order to encourage you to return to work as soon as you are able. Some employers offer this insurance to their workers. You can also purchase it on your own.

Short-term disability insurance usually covers illness or injuries that last up to one year. Long-term disability insurance covers from one year to retirement, which is usually age 65.

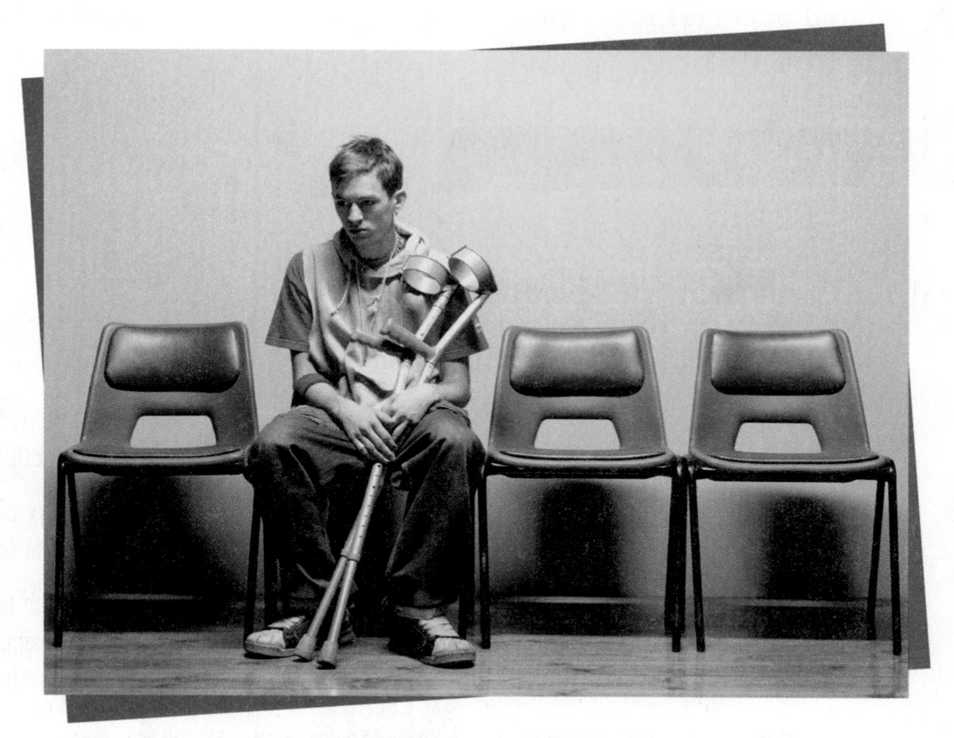

Health insurance policies generally require you to make a copayment, or a percentage of the total cost of a visit to the doctor's office.
Courtesy of Peter Dazeley/zefa/Corbis Images

Most states require that companies provide *workers' compensation insurance* for their employees. This type of disability insurance covers medical expenses and part or all of any income that an employee loses if injured at the workplace. This program covers most workers in the United States; however, the size of payments varies widely from state to state.

The US government is another source of disability coverage. If you have contributed to Social Security and you have an injury that lasts for more than a year, you may be eligible for payments through the Federal Insurance Contributions Act (FICA) program. These payments are not likely to be enough income for you to maintain your standard of living.

Long-term care insurance protects you from financial loss in the case of a disabling long-term illness. You may get this insurance from your employer or buy it from an agent.

Sometimes people are not sure about the difference between long-term care insurance and long-term disability insurance. Long-term care insurance covers the costs of health care services in your home, a nursing home, or some other facility. Long-term disability insurance replaces lost wages.

Government Health Care Plans

Medicare, a federal government program, provides health insurance to people who are aged 65 and older and qualify for Social Security benefits, or who are disabled. There is no fee for Part A coverage (hospitalization insurance) because that's paid for by the Medicare tax deducted from everybody's paycheck. Part B is optional medical insurance for which participants pay a monthly premium.

Medicaid provides health insurance for people with low incomes and those in need of public assistance. It is administered on a state-by-state basis under federal guidelines. People who receive Medicare may also receive Medicaid if they need public assistance.

Life Insurance

Life insurance provides a way to protect your family and loved ones from losses if you should die. No one wants to think about dying, but having the right type and amount of life insurance is an important part of your financial plan.

Life insurance transfers to your insurer the risk associated with your loss. When you purchase a life insurance policy, you transfer to your insurance company the risk that you may die at a younger age than most people do, causing your family to lose your income. Your family can use the proceeds from your life insurance policy to pay bills such as home mortgages and taxes, as well as to meet day-to-day living expenses.

When you get a life insurance policy, you will need to specify your beneficiaries. A **beneficiary** *is a person who will receive your life insurance benefits when you die.* If you name more than one beneficiary, you will also need to decide what percentage of the money each person will get.

If you have a full-time job, your employer may offer life insurance as a benefit. If you decide to buy a policy on your own, find a good agent who can discuss all types of life insurance and help you choose the best.

Types of Life Insurance

There are three main types of life insurance: *term, whole life,* and *universal life.*

- **Term life insurance** *is a policy that you buy for a certain period.* Term insurance is the least expensive kind of life insurance.

  If you buy a term insurance policy for $100,000 for 20 years and you die within that time, your beneficiaries will receive $100,000. If you do not die in that time, you won't receive anything. Term insurance premiums are low for people under 40, since most people do not die before that age. Premiums get higher as you get older.

  If you get a term life insurance policy on your own you will probably have to undergo a physical examination to make sure you are healthy. If you get such a policy through your employer, you probably will not have an exam, since the employer buys insurance for all its employees at once.

- **Whole life insurance** *provides coverage for your entire lifetime.* A whole life insurance policy is more valuable than a term policy because it does not expire, as long as you keep paying the premiums on time. A whole life insurance policy accumulates a cash value as it gets older; a term policy does not.

  Whole life insurance, however, has much higher premiums than term insurance does. The premium and the value of the policy remain the same, unless you use the cash value to buy more insurance. You can cash in your policy and collect the money it has accumulated or borrow against its value.

- **Universal life insurance** *is insurance for a specific period that accumulates savings for policyholders during this period.* It's a combination of term insurance and a savings plan. Because it allows the policyholder to accumulate savings, it's considered a cash-value life insurance policy. Universal life insurance allows you to alter your payments over time. You have a choice of investments that the company administers, and you can decide how to invest the savings plan funds. If you skip premium payments, the company will withdraw the amount needed to cover the term insurance portions from the savings plan.

How much life insurance do you need? If you are single and have no dependents, you might be able to do without it. When you have financial obligations and a family, you will want to make sure you have enough insurance to provide your family a few years' income if you die unexpectedly.

How to Protect Your Personal and Financial Information

In the lesson "Avoiding the Credit Trap," you learned some strategies for preventing identity theft. An identity thief is someone who uses your personal information without your permission to commit fraud or other crimes. Identity thieves are on the lookout for information such as your name, credit card number, Social Security number, and driver's license number. In the year 2002 alone, more than 10 million people were victims of identity theft. Their total loss exceeded $53 billion.

What can an identify thief do with your personal information? He or she can use your name to:

- apply for telephone service
- apply for a credit card or loan
- buy merchandise
- lease a car or an apartment
- obtain medical care.

A crafty identity thief may even work and live under your name!

Preventing Identity Theft

You can do several things to protect yourself against identity theft:

- Keep track of your financial statements—when you get your monthly bank or credit card statement, check it immediately to make sure it matches your receipts
- Check your credit report at least once a year and make sure it is accurate
- Never give account numbers or personal information to someone you don't know—if someone telephones you and asks for such information, hang up
- Destroy all financial documents with personal information on them, including credit card offers you receive in the mail—don't just throw them in the trash, where identity thieves can find and steal them
- Don't give out your Social Security number or other sensitive information over a cordless or a cell phone
- Get a locking mailbox so people can't steal your mail and get access to your financial information.

Reporting Identify Theft

If you think you're a victim of identity theft, take the following steps immediately:

- Report the identity theft to your bank
- Report the identity theft to each of your credit card companies—cancel all your credit cards and ask for new ones with new numbers
- File a report with the local police
- Call the Federal Trade Commission at 877-438-4338 to report the crime
- Contact one of the major credit bureaus (Equifax, Experian, or TransUnion) and ask them to place a fraud alert on all your accounts—you only need to contact one bureau, because each company is required to share its information with the other two
- Visit the Identity Theft Resource Center website at *www.idtheftcenter.org* for assistance in how to clear your name if you become a victim of identity theft.

A Word About Phishing

Electronic communications have created new possibilities for identity theft. One of them is phishing. **Phishing** *is creating a replica of a Web page in order to trick a user into submitting personal, financial, or password data online.*

A phishing expedition is a two-pronged attack. First, the phisher creates and sends a fake e-mail message. Posing as a legitimate source, such as a bank, the phisher tries to lure you into clicking on a hyperlink that will take you to a bogus website. This website will appear legitimate; for example, it may have the same logo and other information that an authentic site would have.

When you log on to the website, the phisher will try to get you to enter your Social Security number, credit card information, passwords, or other personal data. It may do this, for example, by telling you that you need to update your information for the company's files in order to maintain an open account. The reasoning can sound very persuasive.

How can you know if you are dealing with a phisher? Keep these points in mind:

- Look for clues that the message is fake—if the message has no phone number or return e-mail address, be suspicious. Grammar, spelling, or punctuation mistakes are another good clue that it's not legitimate
- Don't be hasty—even if the e-mail appears to come from a source you trust, think before you click on a hyperlink
- Use common sense and trust your instincts—if you suspect something's amiss, chances are you're right.

CHECKPOINTS

Lesson 3 Review

Using complete sentences, answer the following questions on a sheet of paper.

1. Why should insurance be an important part of your financial plan?
2. Explain how insurance works.
3. Why is liability insurance a particularly important type of car insurance?
4. What are three ways to reduce your car insurance premiums?
5. What is a health maintenance organization? Why does it usually cost less to get your health insurance through an HMO than through another type of health plan? What are some disadvantages of an HMO?
6. What are the three basic types of life insurance? How do they differ?
7. List three things you can do to protect yourself from identity theft.
8. What is phishing? What two things can you do to avoid becoming a victim of phishing?

Applying Insurance Skills

9. Think of something you own that has financial value. Do you think it might be a good idea to insure it? How much would insurance cost? What are the advantages and disadvantages to getting insurance to cover that item? Use the Web to research this question.

IBM
AIR FORCE
JUNIOR
ROTC

UNIT 3

Aiming Toward a College Degree

Unit Chapters

In Your Home and Community

RESEARCH A COLLEGE

Go to the website of a college or university near your home. Read about its history: Who founded it and why. Learn how many students attend it, where the students come from, and which majors and degrees it offers. Read the press releases to find out some of the faculty's recent significant achievements. Make a list of ways you believe the college contributes to the life and well-being of your community or your state.

ZHU
AIR
JUNIOR
ROTC

CHAPTER

5

Applying for College

Chapter Outline

All adventures, especially into new territory, are scary.

—Sally Ride, first American female astronaut

LESSON

1 Selecting a College

Quick Write

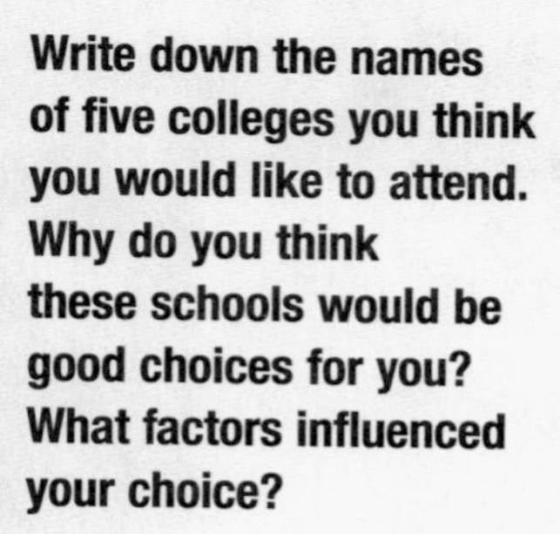

Write down the names of five colleges you think you would like to attend. Why do you think these schools would be good choices for you? What factors influenced your choice?

Learn About . . .

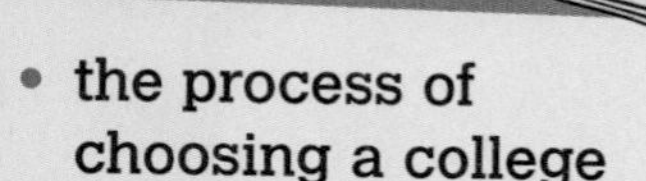

- the process of choosing a college
- criteria for selecting a college
- college admission standards
- identifying the colleges that will best meet your needs

The Process of Choosing a College

Selecting a college isn't easy. It takes a lot of thought and hard work. If you think you already know where you'd like to go to school, stop and reconsider. Don't make the decision quickly. Students too often look for a single, perfect school, when in fact they could get a great education at any of a number of schools. Just because your dad, an older friend, or a famous athlete went to a certain school doesn't necessarily mean that it's the best place for you. And even if the local community college sounds appealing because it's close to home, you should think about more than convenience. You need to find the place where you'll get the best education possible.

Regardless of where other people went to college, you must find the place that is best for you.
Courtesy of Corbis Images

Your choices are many: In 2003, there were more than 4,000 colleges in the United States. It's likely that more than one of these schools will meet your educational needs. So begin the search for a college by casting a wide net. You might end up deciding that your friend's school—or the school in your community—is your best choice. But you'll be confident that you made your decision the right way.

Vocabulary

- accredited
- faculty
- curriculum
- alumni
- early-admissions policy
- rolling-admissions policy
- waiting list

This is the first of three lessons about applying for college. In this lesson, you'll learn about the *criteria*, or standards, you should think about when choosing a college. You'll learn how to apply these criteria to come up with a list of a half-dozen or so colleges that will best meet your needs. You'll learn a strategy for applying to the colleges you've selected. Lesson 2 will cover college entrance exams and college placement tests. And in Lesson 3, you'll learn how to write your application essay, which is an important entrance requirement. You'll also learn how to prepare for an admissions interview and what to look for during a campus visit.

It's important to get started right away on the college admissions process. As early as September of your junior year you should be taking the first steps.

College Preparation Calendar for High School Students

Here's a simple checklist, season by season, of things you can do in your junior and senior years to prepare for college. For a more detailed list, visit the National Association for College Admission Counseling website at http://www.nacac.com/p&ssenior.html.

Junior Year

Fall

- Register for and take the October Preliminary Scholastic Aptitude Test (PSAT). Junior-year PSAT scores may qualify you for the National Merit Scholarship competition and the National Achievement and the National Hispanic Scholars programs. Many students also consider the PSAT a good practice run. The more times you take standardized tests, the more familiar you will become with the format and the types of questions asked, and the better you'll probably do.
- If you will require financial aid, start looking into options for grants, scholarships, and work-study programs.

Winter

- Begin to make a list of colleges you would like to investigate. Surf the Internet and use the resources in your school guidance office or public library.
- Meet with your guidance counselor to discuss your preliminary list of colleges.
- Register for and take the SAT, the ACT, or any other tests required by the schools you're thinking of applying to.

Spring

- Write, telephone, or use the Web to request admission and financial aid information from the colleges on your list.
- Continue to refine your list. Eliminate schools that no longer interest you and add others as appropriate.
- Look into summer jobs or apply for summer academic or enrichment programs. Students who participate in such activities impress colleges.

Summer

- Visit college campuses, take tours, have interviews, and ask questions. Make visiting colleges a family event.
- Begin preparing for the application process. Draft essays, collect writing samples, and assemble portfolios or audition tapes if appropriate. If you are an athlete and plan to play in college, contact the coaches at the schools you are applying to. Ask them about sports programs and athletic scholarships.

Senior Year

Fall

- Beginning in the fall and throughout most of your senior year, make sure that you get all the application forms required for admission and financial aid at the schools you'll apply to. Mark all deadlines in your calendar. Register for and take the SAT, the ACT, and any other required tests if you haven't done so already. Have the testing agency send the scores to the colleges you apply to.
- Ask people to write your recommendations. Give them at least three weeks' notice to do this, and provide them copies of all the necessary forms. Include a stamped, addressed envelope. Make sure to write a thank-you note to these people afterward.
- Visit any colleges that you did not see over the summer. Schedule interviews with admissions staff.
- Make sure that your guidance counselor has forwarded your transcripts to the schools you'll apply to.
- If you plan to apply for early admissions, send in your application now.

Winter

- File any remaining applications. Make sure these applications, as well as any you've filed earlier, are updated to include your first-semester grades.
- If you'll need financial aid, complete the Free Application for Federal Student Aid form early in the year (see Chapter 4, Lesson 2, "Financing for College"). Have your parents or guardian complete their income tax forms as soon as possible; you'll need this information for the FAFSA.
- Check over your Student Aid Report, which you should receive from FAFSA within four weeks of applying. Make sure the report is correct. If you don't get your report, call the Federal Student Aid Information Center (319-337-5665).
- Complete scholarship applications.
- If you've applied for early admission, you should receive the results by early winter. If you're accepted and you want to enroll in that college, your search is over! Contact the school and move forward with final plans for enrollment. If you're not accepted, continue to pursue other choices.

Spring

- As you hear from the colleges to which you've applied, begin to rank them. Compare the financial aid packages they offer. If you're sure that you don't want to go to one or more of the colleges that have accepted you, write to tell them this. This will let them give your spot to someone else.
- By 1 May, decide on the college you will attend. Send in your tuition deposit. Notify the other colleges that you are enrolling elsewhere.
- If a college puts you on a waiting list, write to the admissions office and emphasize your continued interest.
- Take advanced placement (AP) exams if relevant, and have the results forwarded to your college.
- Notify the college of any scholarships that you've received.
- Find out when final payments for tuition, room, and board are due. If necessary, talk to the financial aid office to see if you can make installment payments.

Summer

- Respond promptly to any correspondence you get from the college. These letters will ask you, for example, about course selection, housing preferences, and roommates.
- Enjoy yourself. Get prepared for a big change in your life. Make plans for keeping in touch with friends—and for meeting a lot of new ones. Set out for campus with confidence and a determination to succeed both academically and personally.

Criteria for Selecting a College

The first step in choosing a college is to decide on your selection criteria. Here are some criteria that every prospective college student should consider.

1. Accreditation

A college that is **accredited** *is one that is approved as meeting certain standards.* These standards cover such matters as the qualifications of the **faculty,** *or teachers*; the content and range of the courses; grading; and the adequacy of a school's libraries and laboratories. An accredited college also has sufficient funds to meet its needs. The US Department of Education oversees the accreditation of colleges by delegating accrediting authority to national or regional organizations.

The size of a campus often determines such things as the size of the library collection.
Courtesy of Corbis Images

A degree from a nonaccredited college is less valuable than a degree from an accredited school. Many employees will not hire graduates of nonaccredited schools because they believe that such students do not have a top-quality education. And if you transfer from a nonaccredited school to an accredited one, you will have to start over. An accredited college will not accept the credits you've earned from courses taken in a nonaccredited school, even if you got good grades.

2. Length of Degree Program

If your goal is a bachelor's degree from a four-year institution, it's usually best to enroll in a four-year college right from the start. You could, of course, earn a two-year associate's degree from a community college and then transfer to a four-year institution. In some cases, this approach makes sense. For example, if you're not sure that you can handle college study, attending a community college might be a good first step. But if possible, you should enroll directly in the school from which you plan to get your four-year degree.

3. Reputation

Ask your parents or guardian, a school guidance counselor, and other adults about schools that interest you. Although reputation doesn't always equal excellence, you'll probably want to consider it. Attending a prestigious institution doesn't guarantee success, but it might make it easier to get a job interview after college.

4. Breadth and Depth of the Curriculum

The main purpose of going to college is to learn. You want to attend a school that has a **curriculum,** *or course of study*, that is broad enough to challenge you and to make you feel sure you've received a solid education, whatever your area of study.

Of course, you can't study everything. At some point you will have to decide on a major, or area of academic focus. If you want to concentrate on history, for example, you should attend a school that has a good program in history. That means it has a variety of general courses in the history of the United States, Europe, Africa, Asia, and other areas of the world. It also has courses in certain eras, such as the Renaissance, or in certain topics, such as women's history. A college with a rich curriculum in your field of interest will give you a variety of courses to choose from. It will have faculty who are experienced and knowledgeable in their areas of specialty. And it will have plenty of graduates who have gone on to good jobs or to graduate education in your field. Employers and graduate school faculty will probably know some of these students. If these students have done well, you may find it easier to get a good job or gain acceptance into a top graduate school. If you know what you want to study, talk to people in the field that interests you and ask them which schools they would recommend.

If you are undecided about your major at this point, don't worry. Pick a school that offers a range of majors and programs. Most colleges offer counseling to help you find a major. By the time you've completed a year or so of general study, you may feel more ready to select one.

5. Size

The size of colleges and universities varies widely. Some private liberal arts colleges have only a few hundred students and a few dozen faculty members. State-supported schools may have tens of thousands of students and hundreds of faculty members.

In addition to the number of faculty and students, the size of the college will determine such things as:

- the number of majors offered
- the range of extracurricular activities
- the amount of personal attention students receive from faculty and advisers
- the size of the library collection
- the availability of computer and science labs
- the diversity and backgrounds of the student body.

Criteria for Selecting a College

1. Accreditation
2. Length of degree program
3. Reputation
4. Breadth and depth of the curriculum
5. Size
6. Academic admission standards
7. Cost
8. Location
9. Special programs and employment opportunities
10. Student body
11. Role of alumni
12. Employment services.

6. Academic Admission Standards

Some colleges have strict admission criteria. They accept less than 10 percent of the students who apply. Other schools accept a greater percentage of applicants. Schools consider many things in evaluating students for admission, including the essays they've written for their applications, references, and interviews. But academic qualifications are probably the first thing they'll explore. They'll look at your grade point average (GPA) and, in most cases, your scores on standardized college entrance tests.

It's never too early to start working to make sure your GPA is as high as possible. Your GPA is important because it represents your cumulative effort. It's also a fair estimate of your performance.

Your scores on standardized tests are important because they let a school see how you rank with all other students who take the tests. Most schools require applicants to take either the SAT or the ACT. You will learn more details about standardized tests and how to prepare for them in Lesson 2, "Navigating the Testing Maze."

If parts of your academic record are weak, you may still have a chance for admission. Colleges want students with good all-around records, not just top grades and test scores. The best thing to do is to aim high but also to be realistic. Applying to college takes time and money. Don't apply to a college unless you are reasonably sure that you meet its academic admission requirements.

7. Cost

College costs, as you learned in an earlier lesson, include much more than tuition. You need to think about costs of housing and meals, and these vary from school to school. Travel expenses between campus and your home could be as cheap as a half-tank of gas or as expensive as a cross-country plane ticket.

Don't forget daily living expenses. And include the costs of entertainment, such as tickets for movies and athletic events. Remember that city living is more expensive than country living. A college in an urban area offers many attractions, but the cost of living will be higher, especially if you live in off-campus housing.

But as you learned in an earlier lesson, there are many ways to finance an education. Schools want to attract different types of students, and they offer a number of types of financial aid. If a school seems perfect, but the cost is on the high side, don't give up. Talk things over with your parents or guardian and your guidance counselor, as well as people in the college's financial aid office.

When it's time for the final decision, however, make sure that you think seriously about cost. If you've narrowed your decision to two schools and one is much less expensive than the other, it's probably better to choose the cheaper school. You want as little debt as possible when you graduate.

8. Location

Do you want to come home frequently while you're a student, or do you see college as a time to experience a new part of the country? Perhaps you like an urban environment with access to museums, ethnic foods, diverse people, or major league ball games. Or maybe you value access to the outdoors or the serenity of a small town.

You'll probably want to find an area where you'll feel comfortable but that is also stimulating. That's because part of a quality college experience is meeting a wide variety of people and enjoying new experiences. College is a place for social and emotional growth as well as intellectual growth.

9. Special Programs and Employment Opportunities

Some colleges offer students from diverse ethnic or cultural backgrounds an opportunity to take advantage of programs designed to meet their unique needs. These include everything from campus social organizations to entire schools geared to a specific ethnic group, such as historically black colleges and universities.

If you want to work part-time while you're a student, you'll need to look into job opportunities on campus and in the community. You may also explore the possibility of internships and work-study programs.

Think about social relationships also when choosing a college—you need to feel comfortable in the campus atmosphere.
Courtesy of Corbis Images

10. Student Body

While you're a student, you'll spend a lot of time in classrooms and labs. The drive for academic excellence will be powerful. The atmosphere will be competitive. For this reason, you probably won't want to attend a school where your academic ability is too far above or too far below that of the average student.

But you need to think about social relationships, too. Would you be comfortable in an atmosphere where everyone had a lot more money than you do? Or a place where you were surrounded by people of different ethnic, religious, or racial backgrounds? How important are political issues to you? You don't want a school where everyone thinks exactly the same way as you do. On the other hand, you don't want to find yourself the only member of a one-person club on campus.

11. Role of Alumni

How loyal are the **alumni**, or *people who have graduated from a certain school*? This is important for a variety of reasons. First, alumni support often translates into money for laboratory equipment, computers, athletic facilities, library materials, and other necessities. Loyal alumni can also mean easier access to jobs for a school's new graduates.

Once you've identified a few colleges that interest you, talk to some of their alumni. Ask them your toughest questions. Such conversations can give you a good indication of whether the school is right for you.

12. Employment Services

Many schools take active roles in helping their graduates find jobs. They have student employment offices. Many companies send recruiters to campus to interview candidates who are about to graduate. Some schools have internship or cooperative (co-op) programs that allow students to gain practical work experience for class credit. Depending on your expectations and needs, these may be important selection criteria for you.

College Admission Standards

A college or university evaluates applications for admission using several factors. These include the following:

Scores on standardized entrance examinations. How well did you do on the SAT or ACT? Some schools seek students with outstanding test scores, while others are open to students with more-modest scores.

Grades. What's your GPA? Many schools believe that a student's grades are more important than scores on standardized tests. This is because the GPA indicates a student's academic abilities over four years.

Extracurricular activities. Which clubs, sports, and volunteer activities have you participated in during high school? Are you active in community groups? A college will be more likely to accept a student who has a 3.8 GPA and who was an athlete, participated in plays, and worked in the community than a student with a 4.0 GPA who did nothing but hit the books. Colleges want well-rounded students.

Interview. An interview is a key part of the admissions process at most schools. If possible, you should schedule an interview with every school you apply to. In some communities, college alumni conduct these interviews. If that's the case for a school that you're interested in, you won't need to travel to the campus.

Admission essay. The essay is a part of the written application for almost every college. An essay helps college admissions staff see how you write, but it also gives them insight into your character. You'll learn about how to write a good essay in Lesson 3, "Essays, Interviews, and Campus Visits."

Recommendations. Every college will ask you for letters of recommendations from teachers, counselors, or other adults. Pick people who know you well. The longer they've known you, the better. Resist the temptation to ask someone who is famous but doesn't know you well. The school won't find such a letter nearly as impressive as one from a person who has known you for a long time and can provide an honest picture of your character, abilities, and interests.

Identifying the Colleges That Will Best Meet Your Needs

Once you've defined your selection criteria, you'll have a good idea of the type of school you'd like to go to. The next step is to make a list with which you can identify the schools that best meet your criteria.

Making a List

Looking at the 12 criteria discussed in the section above, list those that are important to you. Keep the list short: You don't need to write an essay, or even complete sentences. Just capture the essentials. Your list might look like this:

I want to attend a college that:

- ***is accredited***
- ***offers a four-year degree***
- ***has a good reputation***
- ***has a strong engineering program***
- ***is large***
- ***accepts students with a 3.0 GPA***
- ***is moderately priced, with a possibility of scholarships***
- ***is located in a city but within a day's drive from my home***
- ***has students who like to study but also like to have fun***
- ***has supportive alumni***
- ***does everything it can to help its graduates get good jobs.***

Make an appointment with your guidance counselor. Bring your list, and ask him or her to help you find colleges that meet your criteria. Or go to an online database and create a list of possibilities. You can find a good college-matching database at *www.collegeboard.com*. Check out others, too. Just type phrases such as "college matching" or "college choices" into a search engine.

College admissions officers sometimes visit high schools to tell students about their institutions. Take advantage of as many of these visits as you can. Be prepared with a list of questions. The answers can help you decide where to apply.

Begin by creating a fairly long list. Then narrow your list to five to 10 schools. Request information, catalogs, applications, and other necessary forms from these schools. You can do this by US mail or online.

Making the Decision: A Strategic Plan

By now, you have a stack of application forms on your desk. The big moment has arrived. It's time to decide where you'll apply and to start filling out your applications. Your goal should be to apply to enough schools so that you will have a choice—but not to overdo it. You don't want to spend time applying for schools that really don't interest you or where your chances of being accepted are too low.

It's a matter of money, too, although given the importance of this decision, the application fees are not too high. At 87 percent of schools, the fee is under $50. If paying this fee presents a hardship for your family, you may be able to request a fee waiver. You can usually find information on fee waivers in a school's application packet. If you can't find information there, check with the admissions office.

Think strategically at this point. Try to apply for admission to at least three types of schools:

1. *A "safe" school.* This is a school whose qualifications you probably exceed. It's one you have a strong chance of being admitted to. It's a school that you like, although maybe it's not your No. 1 choice. Nevertheless, you'll feel comfortable having it as a fallback if your top choices don't work out.
2. *Two or more "match" schools.* These are schools with standards and requirements that are pretty much in line with your qualifications. You think you have a reasonable chance of being admitted to these schools and you're confident that they will meet your educational needs and other criteria.
3. *Two or more "reach" schools.* Your acceptance at these schools is a long shot. Perhaps your GPA and test scores are below the school's average, or these schools are very expensive. But stretching your limits financially, academically, or otherwise gives you an opportunity to be accepted by a more select program. Many students are surprised to learn about scholarships or other opportunities that help them gain admission to schools they thought were beyond their reach. You never know until you try.

By the end of your junior year you should have taken the SAT or the ACT, or any other required tests. If you haven't already looked into these, ask your guidance counselor right away about application deadlines and procedures and dates of administration. Your test scores are an important part of your application at most schools, and you'll want to make sure they arrive in the college admissions offices on time.

Finally, throughout this process, be sure to talk things over with your family, school counselor, other trusted adults, and friends.

Filing Your Application

Colleges set their own application dates, and it's up to you to learn the deadlines of the colleges to which you will apply. Colleges' customary deadline for informing applicants of their decision is 1 May of the student's senior year.

Some schools, however, have an **early-admissions policy**, *under which they inform you by December whether they have accepted you.* The deadline for early admissions applications will likely be sometime in the fall of your senior year.

Many students like this approach because they want to know where they'll be going to college as soon as possible. But if you choose this route, one disadvantage is that you'll have to make your decision whether to accept the school's offer promptly. If you're sure this is the school for you, you're set. But if you're undecided, you may want to wait until 1 May, by which time you may have more than one college to choose from.

If you've applied for early admission and the school doesn't accept you in December, you may still have a chance to be admitted. This is because the school will put your application with those of students who have applied under its normal schedule. Schools usually make early-admission offers only to their highest-ranking applicants.

In addition, some schools have a **rolling-admissions policy**, *under which they make acceptance decisions as students apply.* If the school you're interested in has a rolling-admissions policy, you should apply as early as you can; otherwise, the school may fill all the positions in its freshman class before it even receives your application.

The Application Process

Photocopy application forms before filling them out, so you can practice perfecting the information before you write on the original. Never mail the completed application without making a photocopy of it. If the application gets lost in the mail or the college misplaces it, you'll have to start over.

It's up to you to learn the application deadlines for applying to the colleges on your list.
Courtesy of Colin Young-Wolff/PhotoEdit

Mark all application deadlines, test dates, and interview times on your calendar. Keep track of which colleges will be sending representatives to your high school, and arrange to meet with people from the schools you are applying to.

Playing the Waiting Game

Throughout the last few months of your senior year, trips to the mailbox will probably be both uplifting and disappointing. If you get a few rejections, don't be discouraged. You'll eventually find the school that's right for you.

If a school doesn't accept you right away, it might place your name on a **waiting list**, or *list of students who will be admitted if others choose not to come*. Take this as a good sign: The school would not put your name on the list if it didn't think you were qualified. Write to the admissions officer to let him or her know how much you would like to attend the school, and emphasize why you are qualified to do so. As you hear back from schools you've applied to, inform your guidance counselor.

What if you aren't accepted into any of the schools you applied to? Don't panic—there are still plenty of other colleges that are looking for someone with your qualifications. Reexamine your list of potential colleges and call the admissions offices of some you did not apply to. They might accept late applications. Even if they do not, they might be able to provide helpful advice.

CHECKPOINTS

Lesson 1 Review

Using complete sentences, answer the following questions on a sheet of paper.

1. List at least five college selection criteria and describe how each one applies to your potential choice of a college.
2. What are the basic factors that colleges use to judge an applicant's suitability for admission?
3. What can you do to improve your chances that the colleges that interest you most will accept you?

Applying College-Selection Skills

4. Using the 12 criteria described in this lesson, write a paragraph describing your ideal college. Then go to the Internet and find five colleges that match your profile. (You've just started your college list!)

LESSON

2

Navigating the Testing Maze

College Entrance Examinations

As you learned in the last lesson, one of the important parts of applying to college is taking an **entrance examination,** *a standardized test that helps admissions officers determine who is qualified to attend their schools.* A **standardized test** *is one that is given and scored under the same conditions for all students.* A standardized test is carefully constructed by a testing agency. The College Board, for example, creates, scores, and oversees the administration of the SAT. As many as 2 million students take the SAT each year. A college to which you've applied can compare your score on such a test with the scores of all its other applicants.

Most schools look both at a student's grade point average (GPA) and at scores on standardized tests when evaluating candidates for admissions. A GPA is a good indication of how well you do in your own school. But standardized test scores show how well you stack up against students your age across the country who are applying for college. Colleges need both types of information to make fair decisions.

Most colleges in the United States require applicants to take at least one entrance exam.
Courtesy of Jack Hollingsworth/Getty Images

Quick Write

Are you a good test taker? If not, why? What difficulties do you usually face? How could you solve them?

Learn About...

- college entrance examinations
- college placement examinations
- conquering test anxiety
- test-taking strategies
- sample SAT questions
- procedures for taking standardized tests

Vocabulary

- entrance examination
- standardized test
- SAT
- aptitude test
- ACT
- achievement test
- placement test
- PSAT

For this reason, most colleges in the United States require applicants to take at least one college entrance exam. You can find information on a school's test requirements in its catalog or on its website. Your guidance counselor should have information about test dates, locations, and registration procedures.

SAT

The **SAT** *is a widely used entrance exam that measures the academic skills and knowledge students most need for success in college.* It is an aptitude test. (In fact, the SAT was originally called the Scholastic Aptitude Test.) You've learned that an aptitude is a talent or skill. An **aptitude test** *is designed to demonstrate a student's talent, skill, or potential for learning, rather than his or her accumulated knowledge.* Both private and public colleges use SAT scores in evaluating students for admission. They also use SAT results as a basis for granting scholarships. Many educators believe that SAT scores are the best predictors of how well a student will perform in college.

The SAT is offered several times a year at locations across the country. It takes three hours and 45 minutes to administer. Students generally take this test late in their junior year. If their scores are not as high as they would like, they can take it again in the fall of their senior year. The College Board submits both scores to the colleges a student has applied to; the college will then generally use the higher score in its evaluation of the student's qualifications.

The SAT gives students three scores—one for reading, one for writing, and one for math. The highest-possible score on each part is 800, meaning that the entire test has a maximum of 2,400 points. The average SAT score is around 1,500.

In addition to a numerical score, students receive percentile rankings on the SAT. Your percentile ranking tells you what percentage of students scored below you. For instance, if you score in the 80th percentile, then you have scored better than 80 out of every 100 students who took the SAT.

SAT *subject tests* are one-hour tests in specific areas such as science, English, or foreign languages. Schools with strict admission standards may require that applicants take two or three subject tests as well as the overall SAT. They use the scores to place students in the most appropriate classes. For example, if you do well on the English SAT, you may be able to take an advanced English course during your freshman year. You'll be able to skip the entry-level course required for freshmen.

To take the SAT, you must register and pay a fee. You can apply for a waiver of the registration fee if you can't afford it. To find out more information, you can visit the SAT website at *www.collegeboard.org.*

ACT

The **ACT** *is a college entrance examination that is an alternative to the SAT.* Like the SAT, it used to have a longer name: the American College Test. Whereas the SAT primarily measures a student's aptitude, or learning potential, the ACT is an **achievement test,** *which tests what a student has actually learned.* Most schools require either the SAT or the ACT.

The ACT has four sections: English, mathematics, reading, and science reasoning. It is two hours and 55 minutes long and is composed entirely of multiple-choice questions. There is an optional 30-minute writing test. (The writing test on the SAT is mandatory.) Scores on each of the four sections range from 1 to 36. These scores are averaged to produce a composite score.

Colleges use ACT scores, just as they use SAT scores, in making decisions regarding admissions and scholarships as well as in placing students in special programs and honors or remedial courses. Like the SAT, the ACT has a waiver of registration fees for students who can demonstrate financial hardship.

Most students take the ACT during the winter or spring of their junior year. If they think they can improve their scores, they take the test again in the fall of their senior year.

If a college gives you the option of taking either the SAT or the ACT, you may want to take both. Then you can decide which score you want to have submitted to the college. You can learn more about the ACT at *www.act.org*.

College Placement Examinations

As you've learned, colleges often use the results of students' performance on college entrance exams such as the SAT or ACT to place them in particular classes. But there are other types of exams. One of the most common is a **placement test,** *which is designed to help schools place, or assign, students in classes where they'll learn most.*

Advanced Placement Examinations

Colleges give advanced placement (AP) exams to students who have taken AP courses in high school. Doing well on these exams gives students the opportunity to earn credit or advanced standing at most colleges and universities. AP exams cover 34 subjects, including history, government, English, music, art, some sciences, and foreign languages.

College-Level Examination Program

The College-Level Examination Program (CLEP) enables new college students to receive college credit without taking a basic or introductory course if they can show they already know the information covered in that course. Around 2,900 colleges grant credit or advanced standing for CLEP exams. Receiving such credit enables a student to move on more quickly to studying advanced topics. Business, industry, government, and professional groups use the CLEP to decide whom to admit to training programs.

ACT ASSET

ACT ASSET is a series of short placement tests designed to measure a student's strengths and needs in language, reading comprehension, mathematics (numerical skills, elementary algebra, and geometry), and study skills. ACT ASSET takes two to three hours to complete. It is used primarily by community and technical colleges. For more information on ACT ASSET, visit *www.act.org/asset.*

ACT COMPASS

The ACT Computerized Adaptive Placement Assessment and Support System (COMPASS) is a series of tests in mathematics, reading, and writing. It also has a component that determines placement levels for students who want to take classes in English as a Second Language. Like ASSET, COMPASS is used primarily by community colleges. You can find out more about COMPASS at *www.act.org/compass.*

Institutional Challenge Examinations

Some colleges allow students to take an *institutional challenge exam* to qualify for course credits. If a student demonstrates proficiency on this exam, he or she receives college credit for the course without having to enroll. For more information on institutional challenge examinations, consult individual colleges and universities.

Helpful Reminders for Reducing Test Anxiety

- Approach the test with an "I can" attitude
- Prepare yourself emotionally for the test, control what you say to yourself, and be positive
- Remind yourself that you studied and that you know the material
- "Overlearn" the material—you can't study too much
- Chew gum or eat hard candy during the test if allowed; it may help you relax
- Go to bed early. Do not pull an all-nighter before the test
- Eat a healthy meal before the test
- Arrive early for the test (at least 15 minutes early)
- Sit back, relax, breathe, and clear your mind if you become nervous
- Come to the test with everything you need: pencils, calculator, and other supplies
- Read over the entire test first; read all the directions; highlight the directions
- Listen to the professor before the test begins

Conquering Test Anxiety

The thought of taking any test fills some students with dread. A major test such as the SAT or ACT—one that has major consequences for a student's future—can produce even greater anxiety. Many students are sure they will not do well. They may fear the test so much that they question their decision to go to college in the first place.

Do these thoughts occur to you? Don't despair. You can't study for entrance exams the way you study for a math quiz, but you can do several things to overcome your fears and make sure you get the highest-possible score.

1. Take the preliminary SAT, or **PSAT**, *a standardized test that covers the same areas the SAT does*. The PSAT measures reading skills, math problem-solving skills, and writing skills. It will help you prepare for the SAT by showing you the kinds of questions you will see on the SAT. Taking the PSAT also gives you a chance to compete in the National Merit Scholarship Program. Students take the PSAT in their junior year.
2. Take a test-preparation course to get ready for specific college entrance exams such as the SAT and ACT. Your school may offer such courses. Commercial courses are also available. To take commercial courses, however, you must pay a tuition fee. Just type a phrase such as "SAT prep" into an Internet search engine to find out some of the possibilities, or talk to your guidance counselor.

- Keep an eye on the clock
- Answer what you know first, the questions that are easiest for you
- Check your answers, but remember, your first response is usually correct
- Find out about the test before it is given; ask the professor what types of questions will be on the test
- Find out exactly what the test will cover ahead of time
- Ask the professor for a study sheet—you may not get one, but it doesn't hurt to ask
- Know the test's rules and the professor's rules
- Attend the review session if the instructor offers one
- Know what grade value the test holds
- Ask about extra credit or bonus questions on the test
- When you get the test, jot down any mnemonic (memory device) you might have developed on the back or at the top of a page
- Never look at another student's test or let anyone see your test.

You can't be sure that test-prep courses will make a major difference in your test performance. They can, however, ease your anxiety. They will introduce you to the test format. They'll give you a chance to apply basic strategies involved in analyzing and answering different types of questions. They'll provide opportunities to practice and increase your speed. And they'll give you a chance to analyze your test-taking strengths and weaknesses.

If nothing else, taking the PSAT or a test-prep course will give you a psychological boost and the assurance that you've done all the preparation you can. You'll feel more in control of the situation.

Test-Taking Strategies

Here are some test-taking tips that other students and the experts have found helpful. You may find them useful for an upcoming quiz or final exam, as well as for a standardized test.

- *Don't jump the gun.* When you first read a question, you may think you know the answer immediately. This is called a *quick-time response.* But take your time. Read the whole question, and then read it again. You may find that the wording is a little tricky, and that the answer is not what you thought.
- *Keep moving.* Suppose you read a question and have no idea what the answer is. You reread it: Nothing comes to mind. When that happens, move to the next question. You don't have to answer the questions in order. An idea may occur to you later—perhaps while you are reading another question. This is called a *lag-time response.*
- *Guess smart.* Sometimes neither quick-time nor lag-time responses work for a question. What if you have no idea what the answer is? Should you guess or leave the item blank? Don't guess unless you know you won't be penalized for wrong answers. For example, the SAT penalizes you for wrong answers, but the ACT does not.

  So if you are taking the ACT or any other test that does not penalize you for wrong answers, go ahead and do some intelligent guessing. For example, if it's a multiple-choice question, do you know that some of the answers are obviously wrong? Then narrow the choices, and make your best guess. You can also try this strategy for multiple-choice questions on the SAT, although you'll be doing it at a greater risk.
- *Relax.* Don't cram the night before the exam. If you're not ready by that time, you never will be. Get a good night's sleep. Take time for breakfast. Get to the exam site a bit early. Do the best you can. If you don't do as well as you think you should, don't be too hard on yourself. Learn from the experience, and you'll do better next time around.

Tips for Answering Multiple-Choice and Essay Questions

Multiple-Choice Questions:

- Try to answer the question before you read the options provided. That will get your mind set in the right direction
- Be aware that answers containing extreme modifiers, such as *always, every,* and *never,* are usually wrong
- Read all the options before selecting your answer
- Cross off answers that you know are incorrect.

Essay Questions:

- Realize that bigger is not always better—be as concise and informative as possible (The person who grades your essay would rather see one or two pages of substance than five pages of fluff)
- Outline your thoughts before you begin writing
- Be careful about spelling, grammar, and punctuation
- Use details, such as times, dates, places, and proper names, where appropriate
- Write neatly
- Proofread your answer.

Sample SAT Questions*

As you have read, questions on the most common entrance exam, the SAT, cover three areas: writing, critical reading, and math. This section describes the types of questions you'll find in each area. It also gives examples from previous tests.

Writing

The questions in the writing section test your skills in the following areas:

> *Improving sentences.* These sentences test correctness and effectiveness of expression. Part of each sentence or the entire sentence is underlined; beneath each sentence are five ways of phrasing the underlined material. Choice A repeats the original phrasing; the other four choices are different. If you think the original phrasing produces a better sentence than any of the alternatives, select choice A; if not, select one of the other choices.

---

*SAT test material selected from the SAT Reasoning Test, the College Board. Reprinted by permission of the College Board, the copyright owner.

In making your selection, follow the requirements of standard written English; that is, pay attention to grammar, choice of words, sentence construction, and punctuation. Your selection should result in the most effective sentence—clear and precise, without awkwardness or ambiguity.

Example: According to the study, as the body ages, the chance that medications will cause harmful side effects are on the increase.

(A) are on the increase

(B) are increasing

(C) has increased

(D) increase

(E) increases

(Correct answer: E, increases)

Identifying sentence errors. This section tests your ability to recognize grammar and usage errors. Each sentence contains either a single error or no error at all. No sentence contains more than one error. The error, if there is one, is underlined and lettered. If the sentence contains an error, select the one underlined part that must be changed to make the sentence correct. If the sentence is correct, select choice E. In choosing answers, follow the requirements of standard written English.

Example: In 1772, four years before/A the Declaration of Independence, Mercy Otis Warren published/B *The Adulateur,* a satiric play that cast the colonial governor to be/C a villain intent on robbing/D the colony. No error/E

(Correct answer: C, to be)

Improving paragraphs. This section has a number of short passages. You read a paragraph and select the best answers for the questions that follow. Some of the questions focus on sentence structure or word choice. Others focus on the organization and development of the passage.

Essay writing. This section tests your ability to develop your ideas in writing; to reason and present evidence; and to use standard written English. The SAT graders know that students must write these essays under time constraints. So they aren't looking for perfection. They just want to see whether you can organize your thoughts and write a good first draft.

Critical Reading

Critical-reading questions test your skills in the following areas:

Sentence completion. For each question in this section, select the best answer from among the choices given and fill in the corresponding circle on the answer sheet.

Example: Having inherited a staff known for _______ resources, the new chairman had no choice but to introduce a number of more efficient practices.

(A) defining

(B) harboring

(C) neglecting

(D) bolstering

(E) squandering

(Correct answer: E, squandering)

Passage-based reading. You read a paragraph and answer questions about it. The purpose of this part of the test is to determine how well you understood what you read.

Mathematics

Items in the math test are of two types: multiple-choice questions and student-produced responses.

Multiple-choice questions

Example: Emily's school offers 3 English classes and 4 History classes for her to choose from. She must choose 3 of these classes to complete her schedule. If exactly one of these must be an English class, how many different combinations of classes are possible for Emily?

A. 7

B. 12

C. 18

D. 21

E. 35

(Correct answer: C, 18)

Student-produced responses. In this section you compute your own answers to math questions. These are not multiple-choice questions.

Example: If x and y are positive integers and if $x^2 - y^2 = 17$, what is the value of xy?

(Correct answer: 72)

Procedures for Taking Standardized Tests

Consult the colleges you are applying to and ask which tests they require. Then talk to your guidance counselor about when and where the test will be given in your area.

If you decide to take a test-prep course, schedule it well before the test date. This will give the studying and test-taking tips you learn time to sink in. You'll be able to apply at least some of them to taking quizzes and class tests in the meantime.

Even if you don't take a course, reading books a half-hour or so per day will help you develop a good sense of English usage. Also, practice working a variety of math problems every day.

As the test day draws near, relax. Remember that the test is only one of the factors that the school will look at in evaluating you. They'll look at your GPA. Your references, essay, and interview are also important, as you'll learn in Lesson 3.

CHECKPOINTS

Lesson 2 Review

Using complete sentences, answer the following questions on a sheet of paper.

1. What is the main purpose of college entrance exams? What are the two basic entrance exams used by colleges in the United States?
2. Why do you think some students have trouble taking tests? What are two tips for reducing test-taking anxiety?
3. Give three strategies named in this lesson for improving your test-taking ability. Can you add any other strategies that have helped you?

Applying Test-Taking Skills

4. Ask your guidance counselor for a sample of SAT questions, or go to **www.collegeboard.com.** The College Board administers the SAT and has sample questions on its website. See how well you can answer them.

Essays, Interviews, and Campus Visits

LESSON 3

The Personal Side of the College Application Process

As you are finding out, applying to college is a multistep process. You must decide which criteria are most important to you and make a list of schools that meet those criteria. Then you must prepare for and take college entrance exams and other tests. Finally, you must deal with the personal side of college applications. That's what this lesson is about.

The personal side of the application process is important because most colleges want to know more about you than just your test results and high school records. They want to get to know you as a person. To do this, they rely on two main things: 1) an essay that you include with your written application; and 2) what they learn about you during an interview. The interview, along with a third element, the campus visit, also provides you an opportunity to learn more about the college.

Quick Write

Write a paragraph about yourself that would be suitable to submit to a college admissions officer. What are your strong points? What are your ambitions? Why do you want to go to college?

Writing a College Entrance Essay

Most colleges require that prospective students submit an essay with their applications. By reading your essay, an **admissions officer,** or *a person who helps decide whom to admit to a college,* can discover how you think and what is important to you. Reading the essay also enables the admissions officer to determine how you organize and express your thoughts. This information helps the admissions officer decide why the college should, or should not, admit you.

Learn About...

- the personal side of the college application process
- writing a college entrance essay
- how to have a successful interview
- campus visits

Vocabulary

- admissions officer
- transcript
- itinerary
- teaching assistant

If you are not a good writer, get some guidance in advance from your English teacher, your parents or guardian, or a tutor when you write your essay. If your English teacher has read and graded several papers you've written, ask him or her for specific tips about how to improve your style.

Write a draft, edit it, let it mellow a day or two, and then look at it again. You might have to do several drafts before you're satisfied. Remember, this is an important piece of work. It's not a routine homework assignment. College admissions staff will examine it carefully for spelling and grammar, as well as for content and style.

If the college specifies a length, stick to it. Even if the college places no limits on length, you should keep the essay as short as possible, while still covering the topic completely. If the reader sees you can make a point clearly and succinctly, it's a definite plus.

Essay Questions

Many colleges have their own application forms, while others use a common form. The essays topics on this common form are good examples of the types of questions colleges ask applicants to write about:

- "Evaluate a significant experience, achievement or risk that you have taken and its impact on you."
- "Discuss some issue of personal, local, or national concern and its importance to you."
- "Indicate a person who has had a significant influence on you, and describe that influence."
- "Describe a character in fiction, a historical figure, or a creative work (as in art, music, science, etc.) that has had an influence on you."

"Notice that the common theme in all these questions is you," writes Madeleine R. Eagon, vice president, strategic communications and financial aid at DePauw University in Indiana. "Regardless of your choice of topic, your essay should provide the reader insight into who you are, how you think and what matters in your life."

Choose your topic with care. Remember that admissions officers and committees have thousands of essays to read through. Try to select a topic that distinguishes you from other students. Some topics, such as "My Family's Trip to Europe," or—a favorite with student athletes—"The Big Game," suffer from overuse. If you can think of a topic quickly, chances are thousands of your peers will have the same idea.

Tips on Writing a Great Essay

The Cambridge Essay Service gives the following general tips for writing any type of essay:

1. *Don't strive for perfection.*

   Writing a college application essay is not like competing in an Olympic diving match. You don't start with a perfect score and then lose points for every error. The admissions officers who read these essays are not tyrants with red pencils. They are smart, busy people who know their colleges well and who want to learn whether you'd be a good fit. They are looking for an impression. That impression is mostly emotional. Their goal is to reach a conclusion about you, not about the intellectual content of your essay. The best conclusion that a reader can reach is, "I really like this kid."

2. *Focus on one great idea.*

   The person who reads your essay will want to get the gist of what you have to say quickly. Focus your essay on one point and express your ideas clearly. If you have more than one point, or if you try to be too complex, the reader might get confused.

3. *Keep it personal.*

   Avoid big topics. This is not the place to set forth your ideas on global warming or peace in the Middle East. Don't introduce heavy-duty moral principles. If you must have a moral, make it fresh and right for you.

4. *Show your best self.*

   On hearing that you have to write an essay, someone may say, "Don't worry—just be yourself." That may sound like good advice, but it's not realistic. Just who is "yourself"? You have several selves—one for your family, one for friends, one for formal occasions, one for when you're alone. Should you tell the admissions officer about yourself alone or as part of a group? Think about this carefully. Then pick the "self" that is honest and that presents you in the best possible light.

Your essay should provide insight into who you are and what matters in your life.
Courtesy of John Henley/Corbis Images

5. *Be upbeat.*

   If you have a choice of topics, select something upbeat. Write about a passion, not a doubt. Teen anxiety and cynicism are tiresome to admissions officers. If you love something or someone and can convey that love with detail and conviction, do it.

6. *Use dialogue.*

   If it's appropriate for your topic, use dialogue instead of a third-person narrative. It's livelier and more direct. Suppose, for example, that you were writing about Ms. Von Crabbe, your beloved childhood piano teacher. Which of the following passages is more effective?

   - Ms. Von Crabbe, my piano teacher, taught me more than just how to play the piano. Her lessons were filled with advice that one could use in life. Even though her English was often just a little off, and her manner seemed odd, she will always be memorable to me.
   - "Alex," Ms. Von Crabbe would say, "the concert is starting even so before you sit down on the bench." She had warned us the first day, "Never call me 'Ms. Von Crabapple,' even with my back in the behind." But how could we? We loved and feared her too much.

   The second essay is rich in quotation and detail. It helps the reader identify with Alex, the writer, and like him. Making the reader like you is an important goal of a college essay. The second essay also demonstrates an important principle of good writing: "Show, don't tell." While the first essay *tells* the reader that Ms. Von Crabbe's English was a little off and her manner odd, the second essay *shows* both mannerisms by quoting Ms. Von Crabbe in her own words.

7. *Use details.*

   Journalists and other good writers know the importance of detail. Details create sharp, memorable images. Which of these sentences is more memorable?

   - I live in a suburb outside a big city where half the property is conservation land, and the other half is large plot houses.
   - I live in Lincoln, Massachusetts, a small town 15 miles west of Boston, where half the property is conservation land and the other is large plot houses.

   The second sentence is better than the first because it is more detailed. The second sentence helps the reader see you in a real place. In the process, you become a real person.

   Notice that these details don't make the sentence significantly longer, even though they do make it much more interesting. Choose each word with care, especially if the number of words you can write is limited.

How to Have a Successful Interview

Your essay shows how you think and how well you express yourself in writing. But it is one-way communication. An essay is not interactive. An interview is your chance to interact with a representative of a college. It's an exchange of information: You learn about the college, and the college learns about you.

Many colleges require interviews. But even if a college doesn't require one, it should be willing to set one up at your request. A face-to-face meeting with an admissions officer benefits both you and the college.

The interview will give you a chance to broach issues regarding your application and background more effectively than you could in writing or on the phone. Some of these may involve your **transcript,** or *official record of your grades.* The interview will also give the college admissions officer a chance to ask an in-depth question on something that you've said in your essay or your application.

Most interviews don't last more than an hour. The interviewer will most likely be an admissions officer but could also be a faculty member, a college *alumnus,* or a student. The interview might even be a group session with admissions staff and current students. If your college requires an interview, and you can't afford a trip to campus, the college may arrange for one of its representatives or alumni to interview you in your hometown.

Alumnus is the singular of the Latin word *alumni,* which you learned in Chapter 5, Lesson 1.

When you phone the school to schedule your interview, ask what materials you should bring. Most of these materials will be in your application packet. Before you end the conversation, ask the college to mail you any other helpful information, such as an activity calendar that will let you know of any special events at the time of your visit.

Before you start your interviews, find a friend or family member with whom you can practice. Doing this with a friend can be especially helpful. Ask each other questions, taking turns playing the roles of student and interviewer. It might even help to have someone sit in on these sessions and then offer feedback.

Also think back about other interviews you've had—perhaps for a summer job or internship. How could you have handled yourself better during that session? What did you do well?

Finally, if you plan to interview at all the colleges on your list, begin with the colleges that are not your top choices. By the time you arrive at the college of your choice, you'll have well-polished interviewing skills.

Interview Day Etiquette

Dress

Wear comfortable clothes, but look neat and well groomed. Guys don't need to wear a suit. Pants with a dress shirt or sweater are fine. Girls should choose a dress, a suit, or a well-coordinated skirt and top. Wear dress shoes instead of sneakers, and leave your baseball cap in the car. Don't wear jeans or denim.

Introductions

Make sure you get to the interview office with plenty of time to spare. Make eye contact as you greet the interviewer. Have a firm handshake. Introduce your parents, guardian, or anyone else who has accompanied you. Let them ask any questions they may have. They should not, however, participate in the actual interview.

Body Language and Demeanor

It's natural to be somewhat nervous during an interview, no matter how well you've prepared. The interviewer won't count that against you. Do your best, however, not to slouch, fidget, or cross your arms tightly. The interviewer might interpret this body language as a lack of confidence. Speak clearly and maintain eye contact. Try to "read" the interviewer's reaction to what you're saying and adjust your remarks accordingly.

The Interview Process

Each interviewer and interview is different. Some interviews are structured. The interviewer will have a list of questions and choose those most relevant to you. But a good interviewer will give you plenty of leeway in the conversation, too. That means you'll have to be prepared to ask questions as well as answer them.

Each interview is different. Some colleges use a group session with admissions staff and current students.
Courtesy of Corbis Images

Asking Questions

Don't interrupt your interviewer or try to take the lead in the conversation. But do take an active role in it. This will help you steer the conversation in the direction you want. You'll be able to get answers to any questions that the materials you've read haven't answered. Your ability to participate in the interview is also an indication of your interest and initiative.

If you want to ask good questions, do your homework. Read the college catalog and website carefully, and don't ask questions that they answer. Instead, use such information sources as a springboard for in-depth questions.

For example, suppose you're thinking about majoring in chemistry. Ask questions such as, "I noticed that Dr. Laura Brown is head of the chemistry department. Where did she train? Is she doing any research, and are students involved in it?" Another good question might be, "Where have some recent chemistry graduates found employment?"

Answering Questions

Although you'll want to have questions to ask, chances are you'll spend most of the time during the interview answering questions. Be prepared to do some hard thinking. The interviewer does not want to grill you or make you feel uncomfortable; he or she does, however, want to see how you think and how you express yourself. The interviewer will want to find out how you respond to predictable questions, as well as how you think on your feet. He or she will want to make sure that you can speak intelligently not only about your grades, career plans, and test scores, but also about a variety of other topics.

Typical interview questions include the following:

- Which courses have you enjoyed most in high school?
- Do you think your grades reflect your potential?
- Other than your studies, which school activities have been important to you and why?
- How did you spend last summer?
- Have you had a mentor? Who is it? How has this person influenced you?
- What has been your toughest challenge in life and how did you overcome it?
- What was your proudest achievement?
- What would you add to campus life at this college?
- Which other colleges are you considering?

The interviewer may even throw in some questions about topics of the day. He or she may ask your opinion on an important world issue. Answer these questions as knowledgeably as you can, but don't express any radical, hotheaded opinions. Support your ideas with facts.

The interviewer might ask you about the best book you've ever read. Don't try to bluff it. Don't pick an impressive title unless you can speak about the book in an intelligent way. Pick a book you know well.

Above all, don't get flustered if you get an unexpected question and find yourself tongue-tied. Simply say you'd like some time to think about the question and ask if you can send in a written answer later. If you don't know something, don't pretend that you do.

College Interview Dos and Don'ts

Interview DOs

1. Do take the interview process seriously
2. Do be prepared for the interview. Research the school prior to arriving on campus—look at its website
3. Do dress appropriately—you never get a second chance to make a first impression
4. Do arrive on time
5. Do bring a résumé of your activities and leadership projects to give to the admissions officer
6. Do bring a list of questions you would like to ask during the interview
7. Do be ready to actively engage in a conversation
8. Do be yourself—the admissions staff is trying to get to know who you are and how you will fit into the school
9. Do enjoy the interview
10. Do say thank you to the interviewer and send a thank-you note.

Follow-Up

Within a day or so of returning home, send a thank-you note to your interviewer. Mention a few highlights of the interview. Stress how much you're interested in the school. Without overdoing it, emphasize why you think you'd be an asset to the campus. If you forgot to mention something about yourself during the interview, say it at this time. If you promised to write an answer to an interview question, include it with the thank-you note.

There is a lot to remember when it comes to college interviews. Figure 5.1 covers some of the main things.

Interview DON'Ts

1. Don't say you came to the interview because your parent(s) made you
2. Don't mumble or speak unclearly—this is your opportunity to convey information that might not be asked again on the application
3. Don't give one-word answers, even if you are shy
4. Don't be afraid to talk about yourself or your accomplishments
5. Don't forget that this is your opportunity to make a great impression
6. Don't be afraid that you might give the wrong answers—there are no wrong answers and the admissions staff is only trying to get to know you and your interests
7. Don't make excuses for poor performance
8. Don't be arrogant or obnoxious, even if you are nervous
9. Don't forget to ask questions—this is your interview with a school, not just the school's interview with you. Get everything out of the interview that you need to make your decision about the school
10. Don't use profanity or inappropriate language
11. Don't chew gum during your interview.

College Interview Checklist

Before

- ☑ Research colleges through brochures, course catalogs, and the Web.
- ☑ Make an appointment.
- ☑ Get directions to the campus and admissions office.
- ☑ Practice answering the following sample questions.

During

Be prepared to answer . . .

- ☑ Why do you want to attend this school?
- ☑ What do you think will be your major? Why?
- ☑ How would you describe yourself to a stranger?
- ☑ What is your greatest accomplishment?
- ☑ What is the most significant contribution you've made to your school or community?
- ☑ What do you see yourself doing in the future? In five years? In 10 years?
- ☑ What is your favorite book? Who's your favorite author?
- ☑ Tell me about your family.
- ☑ What extracurricular activities are important to you?
- ☑ What is your strongest/weakest point?
- ☑ If you could have lunch with one special person (dead or alive) who would it be? What would be your first question?
- ☑ Who are your heroes and why?
- ☑ How would you spend $1 million in 24 hours?

Ask

(Ask at least three questions that can't be answered in the school's brochures.)

- ☑ Why would you recommend this school?
- ☑ How would you describe college life at this school?
- ☑ Do you have any advice for me?

FIGURE 5.1

College Interview Checklist

Campus Visits

Most colleges strongly encourage applicants to visit their campuses during the search process. Nothing beats seeing a college campus for yourself and talking with the faculty and students there. Many colleges will arrange for prospective students to visit overnight.

You should plan to visit colleges before applying, if possible. That way, if you find after visiting that a college doesn't appeal to you, you can cross it off your list. If you wish, you can schedule your interview during your campus visit.

Nothing beats seeing a campus for yourself. If you can, bring your family along and get their input.
Courtesy of Ed Kashi/Corbis Images

Planning the Visit

Once you've finalized your list of possible colleges, start planning an **itinerary,** or *travel schedule,* that leaves time to explore each school, as well as time to get from one to the other.

Set up appointments. Call the admissions office at least three weeks before your planned trip. Try to find a mutually convenient time for an interview. If you have a choice, it's better to have the interview toward the end of your visit rather than at the beginning. By that time, you'll be more familiar with the campus and have better questions to ask. Also, ask about campus tours. If one is occurring during your visit, sign up. Finally, ask whether you need to bring anything with you to the interview.

Plan to bring your family on your trip. Although it's ultimately up to you to select the college that you'll attend, family members' input can help you make the decision. They know you best, and they can help you sort through your choices. Seeing the campus will help them decide what college they think is best for you, and their opinions should factor into this important decision.

What to Do on Campus

Try to begin your visit by taking the official campus tour. Then get a campus map and go off on your own to places that interest you most. Go inside the buildings and look around. Sit in on classes, if allowed. Talk to professors and students.

Classrooms and labs are important, but don't overlook the student union. Talk to students there. Try to see what they think of the school. Ask them what advice they'd give an incoming freshman.

In addition, you might want to:

- Read the bulletin boards. What events are coming up on campus? What kinds of parties are advertised?
- Stop by the bookstore. Are the textbooks exciting? What other items do they have on sale?
- Tour the library and the computer and science labs. Do they look modern and well equipped? Well staffed? Are they busy? Are students actively engaged in learning?
- Spend time in the cafeteria. Eat at least one meal. How is the food? Is it varied? Are there choices for vegetarians?
- Visit entertainment areas, such as the stadium, auditorium, art center, or dance studio. Are they spacious and well maintained?
- Read the student newspaper. Look at accounts of recent activities. Also, read the editorials and letters to the editor. Do you care about the same issues that the students do?

Throughout the visit, take notes. Take photographs, too, if you want. Once you've seen several campuses, you can use the photos to jog your memory.

Questions to Ask

You should prepare for your campus visit as carefully as you do for your interview. While on campus, you should seek answers to the following questions, among others:

- What is the student/faculty ratio? The average class size? The retention rate?
- Are most classes taught by professors or by teaching assistants? (A **teaching assistant** *is a graduate student who is specializing in the course topic.* The college pays teaching assistants to teach introductory courses while they are studying for their graduate degrees.)
- What housing options are available? If you live in a dorm, can you choose your roommate?
- Are there fraternities and sororities on campus? What other student activities are there?
- Are the student facilities, such as the library, health center, and gym adequate for your needs?
- What student employment is available on and off campus?
- Do you need a car? Do many students bring cars? Is adequate parking available?

Options to a Campus Visit

If you can't visit one or all of the colleges on your list, make especially good use of the colleges' websites and written materials. Pick up information at college fairs. Find out from your guidance counselor whether a representative from the college will be making a recruitment visit to your high school. In addition, many colleges produce their own videos, CDs, and DVDs. Ask about such materials in your high school guidance office or school library.

CHECKPOINTS

Lesson 3 Review

Using complete sentences, answer the following questions on a sheet of paper.

1. Give some examples of the types of essay questions colleges will ask on their application forms.
2. List two overall guidelines for writing a good essay.
3. Why is an interview a good idea for both you and the college to which you're applying?
4. What are three things you should definitely do and three things you should not do during a college interview?
5. What are the main things you should look for when visiting a college campus?
6. Why is it a good idea to have your family take part in college visits?

Applying Essay, Interview, and Campus Visit Skills

7. Imagine that a college essay question is, "What are your career goals, and why does this college fit into them?" Outline the main points you will include in the essay. Then draft the essay itself, using the points in this lesson.
8. Practice a college interview with a friend. Take turns being the interviewer and the student. Ask each other some tough questions.

AIR FORCE
JUNIOR
ROTC

CHAPTER

6

Charting Your Course

Chapter Outline

- LESSON 1: **Adjusting to Campus Life**
- LESSON 2: **Choosing a Major**
- LESSON 3: **Planning Your Schedule**

Each of you will experience your education uniquely—charting and ordering and dwelling in the land of your own intellect and sensibility, discovering powers you had only dreamed of and mysteries you had not imagined and reaches you had not thought that thought could reach.

—A. Bartlett Giamatti,
former president,
Yale University

LESSON

1 Adjusting to Campus Life

Quick Write

Write a paragraph on what you think will be the three biggest challenges in adjusting to college.

Learn About...

- aspects of campus life
- what's expected of you as a student
- making healthy lifestyle choices
- personal accountability

Aspects of Campus Life

If you go to college, you'll face some of the biggest challenges you've ever experienced. You may be living away from home for the first time. You will have to make new friends. You'll face greater academic demands than you did in high school. You will be exposed to activities, lifestyles, and temptations that you may not have encountered before.

Perhaps most important, you will have to make many decisions for yourself. This may sound ideal because you've probably wanted more independence for a long time. But there's a catch: You'll also have to face the consequences of your decisions. Your parents, guardian, or a favorite teacher won't be there to cushion the blow if you make mistakes. You'll be on your own. Many college students get into trouble because they love the freedom of college life but don't realize that freedom carries responsibilities.

Autumn at the University of Michigan in Ann Arbor
Courtesy of Andy Sacks/Getty Images

In this lesson you'll learn about some of the decisions you'll have to make in your freshman year and throughout your college career. The more you know about the options, the better prepared you'll be to make good decisions.

Vocabulary

- academic organization
- professional organization
- political organization
- religious organization
- social organization
- fraternity
- sorority
- rush
- hazing
- recreational organization
- intramural athletics
- service organization
- international organization

(continued on next page)

Campus Organizations

Among the decisions you will make in college is what to do other than study. Colleges offer a variety of organizations and activities you can become involved in. Participating in them can broaden your perspective, give you new experiences, and teach you skills that you'll find helpful when you enter the workplace.

Here are some of the organizations and activities typically available on campus. For information on specific groups or activities at the college or colleges you're interested in, check each institution's catalog or website.

Academic Organizations

An **academic organization** *is a group that helps members learn about an academic subject and meet other people with a similar interest.* These organizations are similar to the math club or other groups in high school. College will offer a broader choice of organizations and a wider range of experiences than high school does.

Accounting Society, University of Louisiana at Lafayette

"It is the organization's goal to cultivate an interest in accounting that may lead to a possible career in this field. The organization works with the Business Department to build accounting students. [It aims to improve their] communication skills and problem-solving techniques in order to strengthen [their] marketable talents. The club also works with [corporations], small businesses, and the local community to increase students' participation in the accounting profession. These objectives are to be accomplished through guest speakers, firm tours, social events, [and] other academic and nonacademic activities."

Vocabulary

(cont.)

- academic success center
- academic adviser
- on-campus housing
- residential adviser
- off-campus housing
- plagiarism
- credit
- drop/add
- stress
- burnout

Other academic organizations on your campus may stretch from international groups such as a German club or an Asian studies society, to science groups such as a horticulture club or a women-in-science group, to arts organizations such as an American Literature group. They may invite guest speakers, host educational events for the entire campus, and produce publications you can read and write for. Some even sponsor tours that include travel to other countries. Joining such a club is a great way to deepen an existing interest or explore a new one.

Professional Organizations

A **professional organization** *helps its members learn about careers in a particular field.* These organizations sometimes overlap with academic organizations; for example, accounting is both an academic subject and a profession. The difference is that professional organizations focus exclusively on careers.

Political and Religious Organizations

If you are interested in politics, you will probably find on your campus an appropriate **political organization,** or *group of people with similar political interests.* These may range from traditional groups such as Young Republicans or Young Democrats to activist groups focused on controversial issues such as climate change or immigration.

A **religious organization** *unites students with a similar religious faith or interest.* Such groups might include, for example, a Korean Catholic students' ministry or a Jewish students' association.

Electronic Game Developers Society, University of Texas

"Purpose"

"To allow students opportunities to network with the gaming industry and to provide a forum where they may learn about game development and improve their skills."

"Functions"

"Throughout the year we invite guest speakers from the industry. We also initiate projects within committees so students may gain experience working with others and in leadership."

Social Organizations

A **social organization** *focuses on bringing people together for social activities.* It may be a group with a specific interest, such as ballroom dancing or skiing. Or it might be a **fraternity**, or *social club for men,* or a **sorority,** or *social club for women.*

Unlike other social organizations, which are open to all students, fraternities and sororities choose their members. This happens on a regular basis during **rush,** *which is a drive each semester by sororities or fraternities to recruit new members.* During rush, members get to know you. They then determine, by vote, whether to invite you to join.

Fraternities and sororities offer opportunities to have fun, make friends, and do good things for the college and community. Many have their own "houses" where some of the members live. Fraternities and sororities play major roles in social life on some campuses. Many are national organizations; they establish *chapters* at campuses throughout the country. Some have alumni groups. Joining a national fraternity or sorority can open opportunities to meet your fraternity or sorority "brothers" or "sisters" in other cities throughout your life.

But fraternities and sororities don't always have the best of reputations. Some are known for giving wild parties. Some require their new members to undergo **hazing,** or *persecution and harassment with meaningless, difficult, or humiliating tasks.* Fraternities and sororities also charge annual or monthly fees. Members may have to buy pins, blazers, and other items.

Fraternities and sororities can provide wonderful experiences. But they have pluses and minuses: Consider everything membership entails before you decide to participate in rush.

Recreational Organizations and Intramural Athletics

If you like to be physically active, you'll certainly find a **recreational organization,** or *group focused on a specific activity,* that you can join. Recreational organizations can be based on anything from a sport (fencing, tae kwon do, squash) to the arts (dance and theater companies, comedy groups) to hobbies (photography, cars). If you enjoy competitive athletics but are not skilled enough to join a college varsity team, most schools offer a program in **intramural athletics,** or *sports competition between teams within the college.*

Service Organizations

A **service organization** *performs social or educational services for the community.* Most campus social organizations also perform community service as part of their larger mission. For example, a fraternity may sponsor a car wash, or a sorority may give proceeds from a dance to a charity. A service organization is different from these because, as the name implies, its sole purpose is to serve.

Service organizations can range from groups whose members provide tutoring or recreational opportunities for disadvantaged children to groups such as the campus American Red Cross club, which works with adults and families. Some campus service organizations are local; others have a national affiliation. Being part of such a group can provide some of the most satisfying activities at college.

International Organizations

An **international organization** *is a group composed of people from a certain nation or part of the world or of students who have a special interest in such a place.* Depending on the diversity of the student body at your college, you could find international groups formed around countries from Australia to Zambia. Topics of discussion at these groups' meetings might include anything from international trade to international health to diplomacy.

Campus Resources

Deciding which campus organizations to join might be challenging, simply because of the number of options. But other decisions you'll face at college will be even more difficult because they will affect your future in a big way. College can be a confusing place. Fortunately, most colleges offer resources to help you overcome these difficulties. For new students, these resources can be real lifesavers.

Academic Success Centers

An **academic success center** *provides one-on-one or group study sessions, tutoring, specialized instruction, and self-paced tutorials.* These centers can help if you start to fall behind in a certain subject, want to understand a class better, or need to enhance your study strategies. Although you may receive personalized attention, you will not have to pay a separate fee for these services. The college includes them in its tuition fees. Some of these academic success centers may include:

- computer labs
- writing centers
- math centers
- tutoring centers
- language labs

Colleges encourage students to use these centers, because they want each student to succeed.

Besides the wealth of information they contain, college libraries are great places to study.
Courtesy of Bob Handelman/Getty Images

Libraries

One of the great pleasures of college is access to books. Every college has at least one library. Large universities often have several libraries. The University of Virginia, for example, has 11 libraries. These include a main library and smaller, specialized libraries in fields such as chemistry, mathematics, astronomy, and fine arts.

In these libraries, you'll meet librarians who can help you find books and gain access to online information or other resources. A final advantage: Libraries are great places to study. You won't be disturbed by music, loud talking, or other distractions.

Academic Advisers

Your **academic adviser,** or *person who helps you make academic decisions,* is one of the most important people you'll meet at college. A good adviser can help you choose classes, organize your schedule, find resources, or suggest ways to get the most out of your college experience. Although your adviser may also teach one or more of the courses you take, it's possible that you will see your adviser only when you register for classes each semester.

On most campuses, the college assigns an adviser to each student; a few colleges, however, allow students to select their own advisers. Once you've chosen your college, find out your adviser's name as soon as you can. When you get there, make an appointment, and stop by to get acquainted. Usually these relationships work out well; most advisers are knowledgeable faculty members as well as experienced counselors. But personal compatibility and comfort are also important. If you find that you and your adviser are not compatible, you can go to the dean of students, who holds primary responsibility for student affairs, and request a reassignment. Keep in touch with your adviser throughout your college years. If you need advice during a term, don't wait: Make a date to see your adviser and talk through any academic issues that are troubling you. The closer your relationship, the more you can benefit from your academic adviser.

Support, Health, Career, Safety, and Other Services

College is not just a place for intellectual challenges. Many students face social, personal, physical, career, and spiritual challenges as well. Recognizing that students will sometimes need extra help, colleges provide a number of special services.

Support Services for Special-Needs Students

International students, minority students, disabled students, or others with special needs can usually find sources for help in adjusting to campus life. These might range from individual counseling to group sessions on adapting to college.

Health Services

Your college will be concerned about your physical, mental, and emotional health. Most students receive health services through the campus health center.

Physical and mental health services you receive from the campus center should be confidential. In other words, the center will not share any health-related information with other campus offices or with organizations or individuals off campus, unless you provide consent. If you are particularly concerned about confidentiality, ask about the health center's privacy policies.

Career Services

Most colleges offer career advice to students or help them identify summer jobs or work-study programs, as well as full-time employment following graduation. Staff of these offices sometimes help students set up job interviews. At large universities, corporate interviewers will conduct interviews right at the career center.

Campus Safety and Security Services

All campuses have some type of security or police service. The purpose of these services is to protect students and other members of the campus community. For example, if you are working at the library late at night, the campus police might walk you to your car. They will make sure that drinking doesn't become a problem for drivers, pedestrians, or anyone else. They may oversee crowd control during sports events or concerts.

Other College Resources

- Child care center—offers day care for students' young children
- Registrar—oversees the office where students register for courses
- Student newspaper—source of information about campus events and issues
- Student government—student-elected body that discusses and helps resolve campus issues and serves as a liaison to the college administration
- Student radio station—provides information and entertainment, as well as practice for students who are interested in media careers
- College website—provides up-to-date information on campus news and policies.

What's Expected of You as a Student

A campus is a community. Like all communities, campuses have rules and regulations. Members of the campus community must be aware of these rules and policies and follow them. It's your responsibility as a student to learn about them. Unlike in high school, no parent, guardian, or teacher will be there to make sure you follow all the rules, meet all the deadlines, and fulfill all the requirements you will face as a college student.

Residential Policies

Some colleges require that all their students live on campus; others do not. Some campuses require freshmen or sophomores to live on campus but permit upperclassmen to live off campus. **On-campus housing** *includes dormitories or residence halls owned and operated by the college.* If you live in such a facility, you will be subject to its policies. You'll have a **residential adviser,** or *an adult or older student who lives in your dormitory and helps you solve living problems.* You will probably have one or more roommates.

In your first semester, the school usually assigns you a roommate. After that, you can choose both roommates and rooms. (For tips on how to get along with your roommate, see "Coping With Roommates" later in this lesson.) Many colleges now have co-ed dorms, meaning that men and women live in the same building. In some cases they share the same floor and even share bathrooms. If you do not want to live in a dorm with the opposite sex, find out what options your college offers and request a situation that is comfortable for you. Most colleges also offer "quiet" dorms or floors, in which students agree not to engage in rowdy behavior so that residents can concentrate on studying.

As an entering student, you may have the opportunity to choose a dormitory, or even a room in a dormitory. But you must sign up by a deadline. If you've visited the campus and have your heart set on living in a certain building, don't miss out by forgetting the deadline for registration.

Off-campus housing *includes apartments, houses, or rooms in someone else's home.* Many of these are located next to or near the campus. If you plan to live quite a distance off campus, however, you'll need a car or bike—or public transportation you can easily get to. Although some large colleges and universities offer bus service for some students living off campus, most do not provide such service.

Academic Policies

Every college has written academic policies. It's up to you to become familiar with the policies and procedures of your college. You can find them in the college catalog or on the school's website.

Academic policies cover a wide variety of matters, including how many semesters you have to live on campus to graduate, deadlines for adding or dropping a course, and how many courses you have to take during a semester to be considered a full-time student. They also cover social issues, such as the use of illegal drugs or alcohol. And they cover academic problems such as dishonesty and plagiarism. **Plagiarism** *is passing off someone else's work as your own.*

In order to graduate, you must earn a certain number of credits and fulfill the requirements of your major. A **credit** *is a point that the college assigns to a certain course.* Every student must earn a certain number of credits to graduate. Colleges have different systems of credits. Most systems are based on the number of hours a class meets per week. For example, if your English class meets every Tuesday and Thursday, an hour each time, the class would probably be worth two credits. But this can vary. When you meet with your academic adviser, be sure to clarify the college's credit system. Then each time you register, make sure you are collecting enough credits to graduate on schedule. If not, you may have to remain in college for another term or two to earn the required number of credits.

Colleges will also require that you maintain a minimum grade point average (GPA) to graduate. If you consistently get poor grades, you may not be able to graduate—or at least graduate on time. If your grades are very poor, the college might refuse to let you take any further classes.

A college instructor teaching a class outdoors
Courtesy of Getty Images

Deadlines

To ensure that things run smoothly, colleges set deadlines. They're strict about enforcing them. These deadlines cover both residential and academic policies.

Registration for Classes

While you are still in your first semester, you will have to register for second-semester classes. The school will give a deadline. Don't miss it! If you want to register for a class that has 35 spaces, and 45 people want to take that course, the registrar will accept only the first 35 students who sign up. If that course is required for your major, you may be in trouble. Don't jeopardize your chance of completing all your required courses because you missed a registration deadline. Remember, the school does not offer all courses every semester.

Drop/Add

What if you start a class and then decide that you don't like it? Maybe the course covers material that you're already familiar with. Maybe it's too challenging. Maybe the teacher does not meet your expectations. Or maybe you've got more coursework than you can handle.

To cover these possibilities, a college may have a drop/add option. Under **drop/add,** *a student can attend a course for a week or two before deciding whether to take it or to drop it and substitute another course in its place.* This is a significant opportunity. Colleges offer many courses—far too many for a single student to take in four years. It's a waste of time and money to take a course that's uninteresting, redundant, or over your head. Use the drop/add option if you feel it's appropriate.

Exams

Colleges post final-exam schedules each term. The exam might not be held in the room where your class met; it may also be on a different day of the week or at another time. Get all the information before the exam. Double-check it, and then be there on time. Scheduling makeup exams is difficult.

Making Healthy Lifestyle Choices

In college it's important to maintain physical as well as emotional health. A healthy lifestyle, like a healthy GPA, requires making some choices. You'll need to stay physically fit. You'll also need to learn to deal with interpersonal problems, including, perhaps, getting along with roommates.

Staying Fit

College will put many demands on you—you can't afford the time to be sick! So don't take good health for granted. You can't make the most of your college experience if your body is not functioning well.

Eat Well

Eating a well-balanced diet can be hard once you're on your own. Constant snacking is a temptation for some people, because at college you are always studying or running somewhere. People talk about the "freshman 10," meaning the 10 pounds that the typical freshman puts on because of all the snack food he or she consumes.

Try to eat three well-balanced meals every day. It will help you stay alert and energetic. Don't depend on caffeine from coffee or energy drinks to get through the down times—caffeine is addictive. Keep your intakes of salt, fat, and sugar at moderate levels. For expert information about nutrition and eating right, visit *www.foodpyramid.gov*.

Exercise Regularly

If you're used to working out, keep doing so. Find a regular time to go to the gym, and write it down in your schedule. Working out can also help you keep your weight down. Table 6.1 shows various activities, how many calories they burn, and what kind of *aerobic* (bodily circulation and respiration) benefits they have.

TABLE 6.1

Calories Burned and Aerobic Benefits for a 150-Pound Person

Activity	Number of Calories Consumed per Minute	Aerobic Benefits
Skiing (cross-country, uphill)	18.6	Very good
Running (at 7.5 miles per hour)	13.2	Very good
Squash	14.4	Very good
Basketball	9.4	Very good
Skiing (cross-country)	9.7	Very good
Swimming (at 2 miles per hour)	8.1	Very good
Tennis	7.4	Very good
Skiing (downhill)	7.1	Fair
Aerobic dancing	6.6	Very good
Bicycling (at 9.4 miles per hour)	6.35	Very good
Golf (no cart)	5.8	Poor
Walking (at 3 miles per hour)	3.8	Good

From Starke, M.C. (1996). *Strategies for College Success,* Third Edition. Upper Saddle River, NJ: Prentice-Hall, p. 211.

If you haven't usually worked out in a gym, this might be a good time to start. But you don't need a gym workout to keep physically fit. If you walk to class each day and you're on a large campus, that's probably enough. Bicycling, running, and swimming are great exercise, too.

Tobacco, Alcohol, and Illegal Drugs

Fortunately, smoking is down among teens. If you don't smoke now, don't let the stresses of college be the reason for starting to use tobacco. And although partying and alcohol are part of life on most campuses, don't feel you have to join in the drinking. You can have a great time without it.

Why is drinking alcohol a bad idea? First of all, underage drinking is illegal. Second, excessive drinking is a health risk. And finally, getting drunk can cause you, at best, to do things that will embarrass you the next day. At worst, it can cause you to do things that put your life at risk. Alcohol use is a major factor in campus sexual assaults and rapes. At least 1,400 college student deaths a year are linked to alcohol.

And what about illegal drugs? The answer is simple: Don't use them. Ever. If you think you need drugs to get through college, you don't belong at college right now. Get your life straightened out first, then return.

Relationship Problems: Coping With Roommates

One of the biggest challenges for college students is relationships, and one of the biggest relationship challenges involves roommates. Think about it: For many years you have probably lived with the same people—your family. They might not be perfect, but you know their quirks. You've adjusted to them, and they've adjusted to you.

Suddenly, you have to live with a stranger whose habits, likes, and dislikes may be quite different from your own. A roommate may want to listen to music when you want to sleep, entertain visitors when you want to study, or sleep when you finally have a chance to relax and talk.

As noted above, your college will select your first roommate. It will make this decision based on information you provide regarding your likes and dislikes. So the first step in finding a compatible roommate is to give this information frankly. Don't try to be cool—just be honest. If, hoping to sound impressive, you say you are a bodybuilder because you lifted weights once a year ago, you might end up with someone who seems to live in the gym.

If the college sends you your roommate's name ahead of time, make contact and get to know him or her in person or over the phone. If you don't seem compatible, ask for a change. It's better than waiting until school starts, when the pressures of college life will be on top of you. You don't want to have to pack up and move to another room once classes have started.

Here are some other tips for good roommate relations:

1. Wait until all your roommates arrive before dividing up space. Claiming space because you were there first is not a good way to start a relationship.
2. Respect pet peeves. If a roommate hates to see toothpaste in the sink, be careful about your messes. Little things can strengthen or destroy relationships.
3. Air grievances politely. If your roommate does something that annoys you, bring it up in a nice way. He or she may not even be aware of what's bothering you.
4. Don't buy things jointly. If you need a toaster oven for your room, one of you should buy and own it. Don't split the cost. This will make it easier to divide possessions at the end of the year.
5. Be careful about rooming with friends from high school, unless you know your lifestyles are compatible. You could ruin a perfectly good friendship.
6. Divide housekeeping tasks fairly. Develop and agree on a schedule for cleaning, cooking, and other chores.
7. Work out a study and sleeping schedule that everyone in the room can live with. If necessary, do your studying in a quiet place such as a library rather than in your room.

Managing Stress and Preventing Burnout

Adjusting to college life is exciting, but it can also be difficult—no doubt about it. You need to take steps to protect your mental as well as physical health. Here are some ideas on how to prevent two common, related threats to a college student's well-being: stress and burnout.

Tips for Managing Stress and Preventing Burnout

1. Maintain a balance among family, work, and play
2. Find satisfying activities that take your mind off your schoolwork for a while—for example, help children in the community, play a sport, create art or play a musical instrument, or pursue a hobby
3. Explore religion as a source of spiritual strength
4. Don't be reluctant to seek help—go to family members or trusted friends first. If that isn't effective, seek professional help from your campus health center or counseling center

Stress

Stress *is a mentally or an emotionally upsetting condition that occurs in response to outside influences.* Stress can have both physical and psychological effects.

For many college students, the greatest source of physical stress is fatigue. You will have a lot to do at college. You might stay up all night several times a term to study for an exam or to write a paper. You may also stay up late for parties or other social events. You may travel home some weekends. You may not eat as well as you should, and this reduces your energy level.

Psychological stress comes from being away from home, feeling pressured to accomplish a lot in a little time, preparing for exams and writing papers, and dealing with social pressures. Other sources of stress might include family emergencies, financial problems, problems with a boyfriend or girlfriend, or problems with a job. They're not related to school, but they can complicate your college life.

The first step in dealing with stress is to identify exactly what's causing it. Be as specific as you can. For example, if relationship problems are causing the stress, what is the real source? Is it your roommate? Or is your boyfriend or girlfriend making you irritable, and you're just taking it out on your roommate? Is the source of stress an overly demanding professor? Or is it your own poor study habits?

Burnout

One common result of stress in college is **burnout,** or *the feeling of being worn out and unable to carry on usual activities.* A person with burnout often forces himself or herself to keep going, to the point of physical and emotional exhaustion. Symptoms of burnout include irritability, anxiety, feelings of hopelessness, and lack of motivation and enthusiasm. You may feel burnout if you believe that you've put more into something than you have received in return, whether it is a course, a job, or a relationship. In its most severe forms, burnout can lead to depression and suicide.

---

5. Ask yourself these questions each day:
   - Have I had fun? This could be something as simple as enjoying a good meal or a great joke
   - Have I done something hard but worthwhile? If you haven't, you may be letting the hard things pile up—if you have to do all the hard things at once, your stress level will grow
   - Have I helped someone? Doing something for someone else will give you a feeling of satisfaction
   - Have I done something physically strenuous? Get some exercise every day—on a busy day, a quick walk around the block will do it
   - Have I been close with someone? Spend time with someone you care about, even if it's only a short phone call
   - Have I been in touch with nature? Don't just glance at the sunset or notice the wind—stop a few moments to appreciate the beauty they represent.

You can reduce your risk of burnout by taking preventive measures. For example, it might not be wise to be a full-time student while holding a full-time job. That's a big load for anyone to carry. And don't take more courses, or harder courses, than you can handle. Set high expectations for yourself, but be realistic.

A small amount of anxiety is normal. It's even beneficial. For example, if you are totally relaxed before a test, you may not perform as well as you otherwise would. But too much anxiety is disruptive. It interferes with your concentration. To learn more about how to deal with stress, depression, and burnout, visit your campus health center or go online to *www.nimh.nih.gov/publicat/students.cfm.*

Fight stress and burnout by planning to spend time with people you care about.
Courtesy of John Giustina/Getty Images

Personal Accountability

When it comes to meeting deadlines, following campus policies, being academically honest, or maintaining a healthy lifestyle, personal accountability is key. Being *accountable* means being answerable for the outcomes of your words and actions. No one expects small children to be accountable; they're too young. Adolescence involves a growing sense of accountability. Being an adult, however, means being fully accountable.

The importance of being accountable is a hard lesson for many students to learn. It means accepting responsibility for consequences. If you sign up for a course and then skip classes or don't study enough, you'll do poorly on exams. You might even fail. You are responsible for that failure. Don't expect your professor to be sympathetic to your excuses. You may have been able to talk your way out of trouble in high school, but that strategy won't work in college.

Other adults in positions of authority on campus will also expect you to be accountable. For example, your academic adviser will expect you to prepare for meetings. You'll need to become familiar with the course offerings for the next term, know the requirements for graduation, and come to your appointment with a list of courses you want to take. Your residential adviser will expect you to be accountable for your actions in the dorm. If you have a scholarship, the organization giving you the scholarship will hold you accountable for any requirements connected with it, such as maintaining a certain GPA.

Think about all the decisions you will make at college regarding courses you'll take, friends you'll make, organizations you'll join, and how you'll spend your free time and study time. All these decisions will have consequences. Make mature decisions, and enjoy the good results.

CHECKPOINTS

Lesson 1 Review

Using complete sentences, answer the following questions on a sheet of paper.

1. What are three types of campus organizations? What are their functions?
2. List three types of resources on campus available to help and protect students.
3. What residential options can you expect to have at college?
4. Why should you have a good relationship with your academic adviser?
5. List some of the deadlines you must be aware of at college.
6. Explain ways to maintain your physical and mental health in college.
7. Name five things you should do to have a good relationship with your college roommate.
8. What are some questions that you should ask yourself every day to make sure you are not becoming a victim of stress or burnout?

Applying Campus-Living Skills

9. Reread the paragraph you wrote under Quick Write on what you think will be the biggest challenges in adjusting to college. Now that you've studied this lesson, would you change any of the challenges you listed? If so, which ones?
10. Go to the website of a college that you think you will apply to. Find a list of campus organizations. Which ones do you think sound interesting?

LESSON

2

Choosing a Major

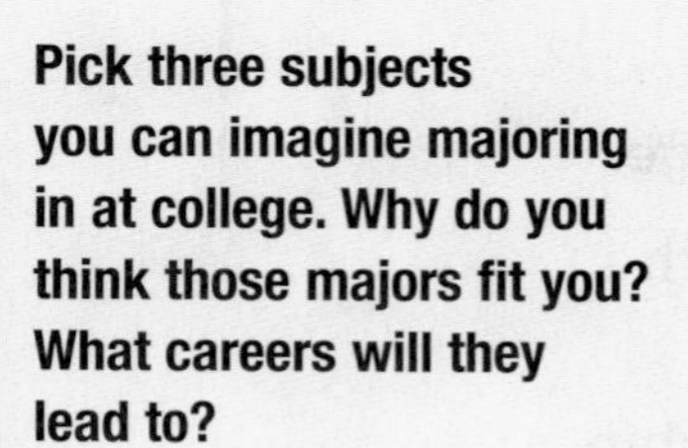

Pick three subjects you can imagine majoring in at college. Why do you think those majors fit you? What careers will they lead to?

- how college majors relate to personal interests and desires
- basic areas of college study
- careers associated with specific majors
- a six-step process for selecting a college major

How College Majors Relate to Personal Interests and Desires

At some point early in your college years, you will have to choose a major—your primary subject of study and academic specialty. You won't need to make this important decision right away. At most schools, students can wait until their sophomore year to declare a major. That gives them time to get used to college course work and to think more about their career interests and preferences.

Selecting the right major is an important decision—almost as important as selecting the right college. So it's a good idea to start weighing the options as early as possible. Your major should be a subject that interests you so much that you want to learn more and more about it—not only while you're in college but throughout your life.

Maybe you had a high school course that opened your eyes to the fascinating complexities of physics. Or perhaps a relative who's an actor has turned you on to the arts. Your favorite book, a biography of a US president, might have sparked an interest in political science. Or perhaps Wall Street and the world of high finance fascinate you, and you want to study business and economics.

But it's also possible that you don't know where your career interests lie. You haven't taken time to think about it. Or you may have so many interests that you're not ready to narrow them down to one or two. As college approaches, how do you choose?

A good place to start is to listen to people who know you well. Your parents, guardian, or other relatives will probably have some ideas on what you should major in. Your high school guidance counselor may also be able to guide you. And when you get to college, you'll have a faculty adviser who will help you choose the right major. You won't have to do it alone.

Vocabulary

- minor
- elective
- core requirements
- prerequisites

Listen to all these people, and ask them lots of questions. But remember also: This is your decision. You're the one who has to live your life.

That's why, when it's time to choose a major, you need to think seriously about what kind of person you are. You need to know yourself. You can approach this task in several ways. For example, in the lesson on Aptitudes and Orientations (Chapter 2, Lesson 1) you learned about the Myers-Briggs Type Indicator (MBTI), which helps people determine their personality types. You learned that where you direct your energy, how you process information, how you make decisions, and how you organize your life help determine your personality. You also learned that certain personality types are often associated with specific careers.

If, for example, you are an ISTJ (Introverted, Sensing, Thinking, Judging) person, you would probably do well in a career in business, medicine, or the armed forces. A major in business or economics, the sciences, aerospace, or perhaps in history or a foreign language would prepare you for these careers. If you're an ISFP (Introverted, Sensing, Feeling, Perceptive) person, you may lean toward a career in the arts or teaching. An ISFP might major in art, education, English, or music.

An interest in chemistry and lab work can lead you to careers in a variety of fields.
Courtesy of Corbis Images

You can also approach the decision about a major based on your personal interests. Do you love working on cars? Maybe you should major in mechanical engineering. Do you love to draw? If so, a major in architecture or art history might be right. If you are an athlete and want to coach or play professionally, you will probably want to major in physical education.

Don't be too narrow in your approach to choosing a major. What if you love art but want to work in business? There's no reason why you can't study both business and art. It just might take a little longer. For a great career in business, you could decide to get a master's degree after you've earned your undergraduate degree. This would require enrolling in business school. If you do this, you won't need to take a full load of heavy-duty business courses as an undergraduate—that's what you'll focus on in business school. You could earn an undergraduate degree in art. As an art major, you will acquire knowledge and skills that you can enjoy and use throughout your life. You will have a broad-based education. That will serve you well as a businessperson, because you'll be able to talk knowledgeably with all kinds of people. You may even find unusual ways to combine business and art—for example, by becoming an art dealer or the head of an art studio.

Choosing a Minor

So how would you prepare for graduate work in business while majoring in art? By choosing a **minor,** or *a secondary focus for your academic career,* in business. A minor in business does not require as many courses as a major does, but it will give you a good understanding of marketing, finance, and other subjects essential for business.

Your college minor allows you to focus on a second area that interests you.
Courtesy of Jose Luis Pelaez, Inc./Corbis Images

A minor can also help prepare you for a second career. For example, you may major in physical education because you're aiming for a career as a coach. But what if you want to switch careers after working in the sports field for 10 years or so? A minor in social work, business, religious studies, or any number of other subjects could help you prepare for a second career after your coaching days are over.

When you major in a subject, you will need to complete a certain number of required courses in your field. For example, as a studio art major, you might have to take courses in such topics as art history, drawing, graphic design, illustration, and digital media. Someone majoring in business might be required to take courses in accounting, economics, statistics, and leadership, as well as finance and marketing.

Together, these required courses may account for more than half the courses you'll take during your four years of college. This is why you need to declare a major at least by your sophomore year. If you wait longer, you might not have time to complete all the required courses by the time you graduate.

A course that is not required is called an **elective,** *a course you choose, or elect, to take.* Electives round out, or complement, your major. For example, if you're majoring in French, you might want to minor in Spanish. If you're majoring in US history, you might want to minor in political science. Or you might want to major in political science and minor in French; this would ensure you have language skills that could help you in a career in international affairs.

As you ponder these options, don't forget the main point: You want to be excited about learning. Your major and your minor should be subjects that you love.

Basic Areas of College Study

Every college offers a different selection of majors. The number of choices depends primarily on the size of the college. A large university may offer more than 150 majors; a small college may offer only a few dozen.

Whatever size school you choose, your choice of majors will fall into one of four basic categories: technical and engineering; arts and humanities; social sciences and human sciences; and science. These categories are listed in Table 6.2. Under each category are possible majors and examples of the typical interests of students who major in these fields. (Some majors fall into more than one category.)

These lists are far from complete. They simply give you an idea of the kinds of majors, interests, and skills that fall under the four basic categories of study.

Careers Associated With Specific Majors

Every major prepares students for one or more careers. A major in architecture would naturally lead to a career as an architect, and a major in fashion design could lead to a career as a fashion designer.

But don't take these associations too literally. A major in architecture could also lead you to a career in city planning, landscape design, or business (for example, managing an architecture firm). Or you could teach architecture. If you majored in fashion design, you might find employment with a New York design house, be a buyer for a retail clothing chain, become a model, or help women in a developing country learn how to design clothes for export. You could even start your own clothing-design business. It all depends on where your interests and abilities lie.

Table 6.3 lists careers that fall under each of the four categories of majors. This list, like the lists above, is not complete. You and your guidance counselor may be able to think of more.

TABLE 6.2

Basic Areas of College Study

Category	Sample Majors	Examples of Interests or Skills of Students Majoring in this Area
Technical and Engineering	• agricultural technology • architecture • aviation • engineering • computer science • medical technology	• repairing electrical appliances or electronic equipment • building houses • developing computer hardware • working on cars • preserving the environment • solving mechanical problems
Arts and Humanities	• advertising • art history • classics • English or foreign languages • history • music • religious studies	• playing in an orchestra or band • drawing • writing poetry or short stories • acting • taking photographs • learning languages
Social Sciences and Human Services	• anthropology • business • child development • communication • criminology • economics • family relations • journalism	• working in parks or recreation facilities • tutoring or mentoring • helping people solve their personal problems • working in a religious setting • helping people who have disabilities • supervising a project or team
Science	• astronomy • biology • computer science • forestry • geology • nutrition • statistics	• doing lab experiments • designing models • programming computers • solving mathematical problems • playing chess

TABLE 6.3

Occupations by Area of College Major

Technical and Engineering

- agricultural educator
- animal breeder or trainer
- aviator
- computer software engineer
- computer data systems analyst
- construction engineer
- dental technologist
- electrical engineer
- electronics technician
- environmental designer
- fish and wildlife manager
- fitness trainer
- forest ranger
- geologist
- industrial arts teacher
- industrial engineer
- mechanical engineer
- oceanographer
- scientific photographer

Arts and Humanities

- actor
- architect
- art teacher
- artist
- cartoonist
- dance therapist
- digital graphic designer
- editor
- English teacher
- film editor
- graphic designer
- historian
- interior designer
- interpreter
- musician
- orchestra conductor
- writer

Social Sciences and Human Services

- athletic director or coach
- athletic trainer
- chef
- clergy member
- clinical psychologist
- criminologist
- dental hygienist
- detective
- dietitian
- family counselor
- geographer
- historian
- librarian
- motion picture director
- nurse
- park naturalist
- police officer
- social worker
- speech or hearing pathologist
- teacher or professor

Science

- aeronautical engineer
- airplane pilot
- astronomer
- biochemist
- biomedical engineer
- chemist
- city and regional planner
- computer scientist
- dentist
- geologist
- horticulturist
- marine biologist
- mathematician
- metallurgist
- optometrist
- pharmacist
- physician or surgeon
- sociologist
- statistician
- veterinarian

From Gordon, Virginia N. and Susan J. Sears. (2003). *Selecting a College Major: Exploration and Decision Making,* Fifth Edition. Upper Saddle River, NJ: Prentice-Hall, p. 58.

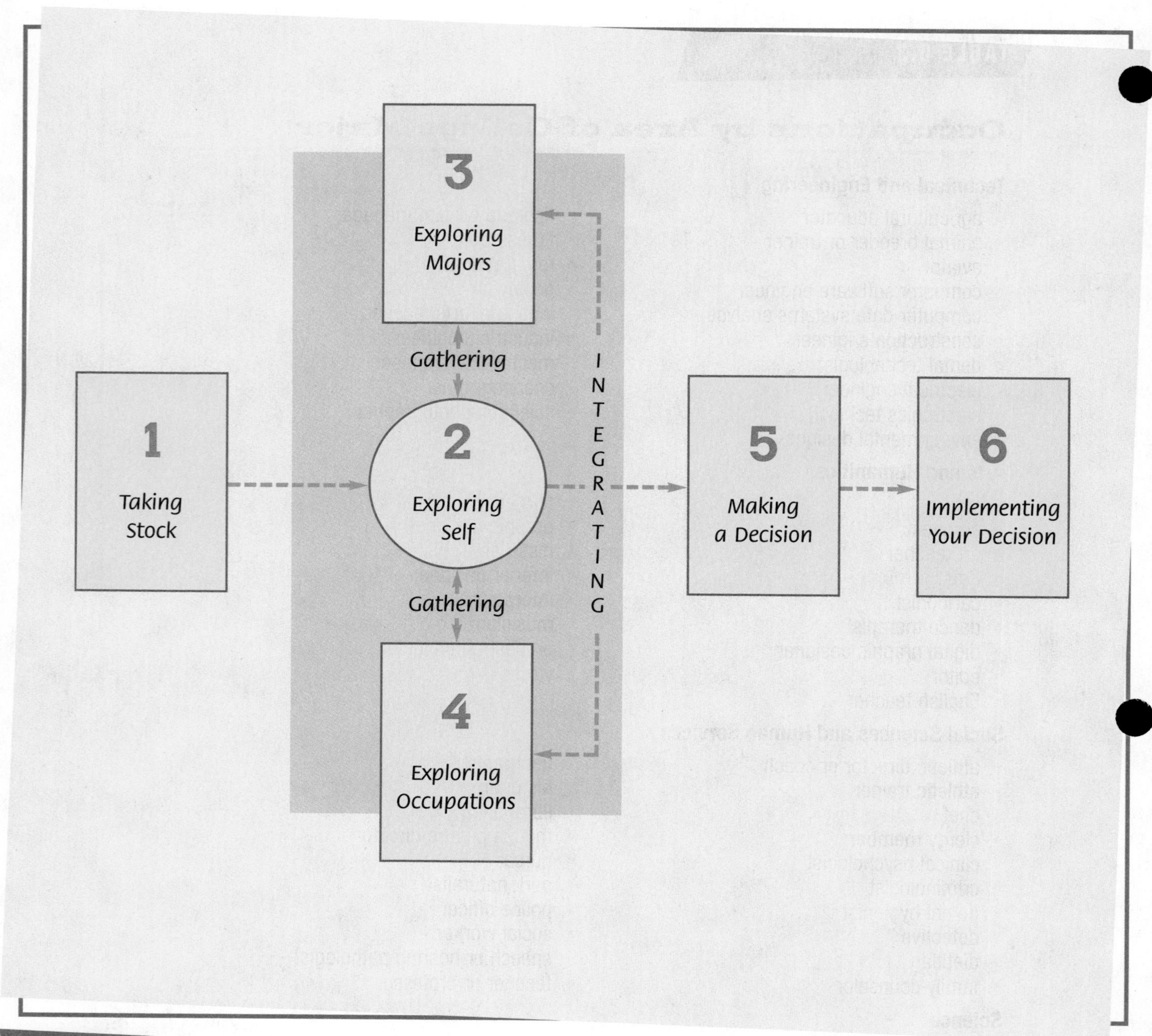

FIGURE 6.1

A Model for Choosing a College Major

From Gordon, Virginia N. and Susan J. Sears. (2003). *Selecting a College Major: Exploration and Decision Making,* Fifth Edition. Upper Saddle River, NJ: Prentice-Hall, p. xvi.

A Six-Step Process for Selecting a College Major

Figure 6.1 illustrates the six steps involved in choosing a college major. It provides a handy way of organizing your thoughts about some of the issues and decisions covered in this lesson and in previous lessons about college and careers. Following these steps should help you come up with a major that's right for you. You might also be able to adapt this six-step approach for use when you face other major life decisions.

1. Taking Stock

Start the decision-making process by figuring out what you know, what you don't, and what further knowledge you need. Ask yourself questions such as:

- Do I know which career I want to pursue?
- Do I know which major will best prepare me for that career, or do I need to do some research?
- Am I undecided about my career but sure of where my interests lie and which major I will enjoy?
- Am I unsure about everything at this point?

Remember, if you responded "yes" to the last question, don't worry. Few high school students are sure about their college majors.

2. Exploring Self

Here is where you consider your interests, skills, and personality. You should also think about your values. What kind of life do you want to lead? Do you want a life of service to others? Do you want to be an entrepreneur? Is money your top priority? If not, what is? Think, too, about the type of work environment you prefer. Do you like to work alone or with others? Indoors or outdoors? In a rural area or a city? Are you a leader or a follower?

3. Exploring Majors

Look at the majors offered by the colleges you're considering. Then narrow your choices to one or two majors. Consider not only your interests and goals but also matters such as:

- *Courses.* Are there plenty of courses in the major that interest you? Can you see yourself spending many hours a day reading, talking, thinking, and writing about topics covered by these courses?
- *Faculty.* Are the faculty in this major good teachers? Are they knowledgeable? Where did they train? Have they published in their areas of expertise? Do the professors teach most of the classes, or do they rely on teaching assistants? Do faculty spend time advising and mentoring students?
- *Students.* Are the students in this major interesting? Are they people you feel at ease with?
- *Class size.* How big are classes? Are there enough students in this major so that you will feel comfortable, but not so many that you'll find it difficult to get individualized attention?
- *Graduates.* Have recent graduates who've majored in this area gone on to interesting careers? Will it be easy to find a job, or to get into a good graduate school, after graduation?
- *Requirements.* What are the **core requirements,** or *basic demands,* of majoring in this area? For example, what kind of grade point average does this major require? What **prerequisites,** or *courses required to enter a certain field of study,* do you need? Can you meet them? How heavy is the course load? Will you be able to juggle the required courses with electives and any job or family responsibilities you might have?

It's not possible to answer all these questions fully in advance. But they're things you should think about. When you're talking with your guidance counselor, interviewing with college admissions officers, making campus visits, and doing your research, ask questions about topics such as these.

4. Exploring Careers

Once you've narrowed your choice of majors, examine the careers that these majors might lead to. You might select a major directly related to a career that you have already decided to pursue. Such majors include, for example, physical therapy, electrical engineering, or elementary education. Or you can choose a major that provides a general background that will prepare you to enter a variety of professions. Such majors include history, literature, or philosophy.

5. Making a Decision

By this point, you should be ready to commit yourself to one of your alternatives.

As you do so, remember that there is no perfect choice. Every decision will require trade-offs. A business major may be more academically demanding than some other majors, but it may give you greater possibilities for earnings upon graduation as well as more opportunities for advancement. A physical education major may be easier, but the chances for earning lots of money, as well as the variety of job choices and opportunities for growth, may be limited.

If you prefer being outdoors to working in an office, take that into account when choosing your major.
Courtesy of Gaetano/Corbis Images

Once you've identified your probable major, test it against the following questions. If you can answer "yes" to these questions, this major may be the one for you:

- **Does this major match my skills and interests?**
- **Are the courses interesting?**
- **Are careers related to this major interesting and within my reach?**
- **Am I comfortable in the work environments of careers associated with this major?**
- **Are the careers associated with this major consistent with my values?**
- **Do I meet the academic and other prerequisites for this major?**
- **Do I think I can do the work?**
- **Do I have the time to fulfill all the requirements?**
- **Do I feel good about my choice?**

6. Implementing Your Decision

Once you've decided on a major, contact your faculty adviser and start the formal process of committing to the major. This will involve registering in the department of your major (for example, chemistry department, philosophy department, education department), meeting with an adviser in that department, and signing up for courses.

But remember, your decision isn't set in stone. You can change it, assuming you still have time to complete the requirements for another major. And even if switching majors means you have to stay in school an extra term or year, it might be worth it in the long run.

After you make and implement your decision, continue to think about it. Does it feel right? As you take more and more courses, are you still excited about this major? Are your grades as good as you thought they'd be? Can you still see yourself in a career that this major will prepare you for?

If so, you are on your way. If not, start over. Reexamine your interests and ambitions. If, after careful thought and consultation with adults, you find a better fit, don't be afraid to make a change. Base each new decision on the self-knowledge and experience you have already gained.

CHECKPOINTS

Lesson 2 Review

Using complete sentences, answer the following questions on a sheet of paper.

1. Write down the four letters that you believe correspond with your Myers-Briggs personality type. Based on your personality type, list three majors that should fit you well.
2. Write down three of your main interests. Then list a college major that would fit each of those interests.
3. Write down three careers that you might like to pursue. List three possible majors that would prepare you for each of those careers. Now compare this list with the lists you made in response to Questions 1 and 2. Are majors you chose the same or at least similar? Why or why not?
4. What are six steps in the process of choosing a college major?

Applying Choosing a Major Skills

5. List the three majors that are the most interesting to you at this point. Then go to the websites of five colleges on your priority list. Do they offer the majors you're considering? If so, find out the prerequisites for a major in those areas, what kinds of courses the college offers in your major areas, the size of the departments offering the majors, the backgrounds of the faculty (for example, which schools they attended and when, what have they published), and where alumni who've majored in that field are employed. This information will help you select a college as well as a major.

LESSON 3

Planning Your Schedule

The Importance of Time Management

When you get to college, you'll enter a whole new world. One aspect of this new experience is that you will have more control of your time than ever before. This will require you to exercise your skills at **time management**, or *keeping control of your time*. Think about this for a minute: Do you make the best use of every minute? Do you meet your deadlines? Or do you postpone some tasks until it's almost too late, then work in a frenzy to get them done? Have you ever asked a teacher for an extension on a deadline for a major assignment?

Time-management skills are important for everyone—not just college students. You can learn and practice time management while you're still in high school. Some of the concepts of time management are setting priorities, planning, eliminating distractions, and eliminating activities that don't help you meet your goals.

When you manage your time well, you get things done; you maintain order in your life; you create time for things you want to do as well as things you have to do; and you reduce stress. When you don't manage your time well, you constantly feel stressed and under pressure; you bounce from activity to activity feeling unprepared and constantly trying to catch up; you don't accomplish tasks as well as you could; and you waste time. Using time-management skills can make your life a lot easier.

Quick Write

Do you sometimes have trouble getting things done on time? Do you put off certain tasks? Make a list of the kinds of work you tend to put off, and the reasons you put it off.

Learn About...

- the importance of time management
- procrastination and how to beat it
- managing your college schedule

Setting Priorities

- time management
- priority
- procrastination
- multitasking
- distraction

You may think people succeed because they're rich, talented, or just lucky. Those things do help. But one of the most significant reasons for many people's success is much simpler: They know how to make good use of their time. They know how to set priorities. A **priority** *is something that you give attention to before you think about other things*. You can't do everything. There's just not enough time. So you have to make choices about what to do, or what to do first. Successful people know their priorities, and they manage their time with an eye toward achieving them.

Your priorities should reflect your goals—the things that are most important to you. For example, getting good grades is a goal for most college students, but meeting people and enjoying new experiences are important, too. This means making choices about how to spend your time. To be a successful college student, you'll need to manage your time in a way that reflects your priorities and helps you meet your goals.

In college you'll spend far less time in class than you do in high school. The average undergraduate student takes four to five courses per semester. Each course meets for an average of two to three hours a week. So instead of heading off to school five days a week at 7:00 a.m. and staying there until around 3:00 p.m., you'll spend only a few hours in class each day.

At first, you may feel as though you have lots of time on your hands. But don't think you're in for the easy life. Some experts advise college students to spend at least two hours studying for every hour spent in easy classes, three hours for every class hour for average classes, and four hours for the toughest classes. That study will require self-discipline. There are no study halls in college, and you won't have your parents or guardian around to ask whether you've done your homework.

Suppose you sign up for one easy course, two average courses, and two hard courses during the first term of your freshman year. Each course meets two hours a week. That would mean you'd need to spend at least 32 hours a week studying.

Managing your time, however, doesn't mean giving up fun. A well-balanced schedule includes time for play as well as for work. Too much of one and not enough of the other can make for a boring life.

Time management isn't just for college students, however. It's a skill you can use in high school and throughout life. This lesson provides some well-tested hints on how to use your time well.

Procrastination and How to Beat It

One of the most significant obstacles to good time management is **procrastination,** *the tendency to delay, or to put things off.* Did you ever wait until the last minute to write a paper and then work on it all night? And did you swear that the next time you'd start earlier? Did it work?

If you're like most people, you didn't learn from that unhappy experience. You repeated your mistake—if not the next time, then soon thereafter. Like many other people, you may have a habit of procrastinating.

Many people think that using time well means working all the time. But what do you really mean by "working"? Are you watching TV while reading your history assignment? If so, you're not concentrating fully on your assignment. You're not learning effectively. What's more, you're probably not enjoying the TV show as much as you would if you didn't have a book on your lap. You're wasting time.

Or you might be working well, but working on the wrong thing. For example, if you're working on your art project, which is due next week, rather than your English paper, which is due tomorrow, you are not setting proper priorities or managing your time well.

Why People Procrastinate

Why do people procrastinate? There are many reasons, including:

- *Superhuman expectations.* You put more on your calendar than you could possibly accomplish, hoping that by sheer willpower you'll get it all done. When you discover that you can't do it all, you eliminate the things that are the hardest.
- *Whining.* You come up with all kinds of reasons why you just aren't good enough. For example, you tell yourself that smart people don't have to study, and everybody is smart but you—so why even try? But everyone has to study. No one is born with calculus formulas in their heads. People seem smart because they are disciplined. They know how to use their time well.
- *Fear of failing.* Perhaps you've done poorly in a difficult subject in the past. You're scared that's going to happen again, so you give up without trying.
- *Emotional blocks.* You know that it's already past time to start working on your science project, but you don't know how to start. You feel guilty because you have wasted so much time. You feel defeated before you even begin. "I might as well just play some video games for an hour or so," you say. "They will get me relaxed, and then I can start." Soon other distractions come along. Before you know it, you are really behind. It's a vicious cycle: Delay leads to greater delay.

It might be helpful to think of time management not as a way to get more work done but as a way to make more time for fun. If you get your work done on time, you will have more "free time" that really is free. You won't be thinking in the back of your mind, "Man, I have to get that paper done." That's no fun.

How to Beat Procrastination

Procrastination is such a widespread problem that many experts have made entire careers advising people how to beat this dangerous habit. These experts agree that the first step in using your time better is to *become aware of how you use it now.* They recommend that you keep track of your time in 15-minute blocks over an entire week. This lets you know how much time you really spend watching TV, playing games, instant messaging, or talking on the phone. You may be surprised at how much time you waste.

To fight procrastination, try these strategies:

- *Look at each task in terms of your long-range goals.* Will getting an A on this test help raise your grade point average (GPA) and increase the chances you'll get into the college at the top on your list? If you keep your long-term goals in mind, you'll be more likely to focus on short-term tasks.
- *Think positive thoughts.* When you're ready to study, push negative thoughts out of your mind. Tell yourself that you are growing and becoming more competent. Look your fears in the face. If you procrastinate because you're afraid you'll fail, be honest about it. Make up your mind you are going to overcome this fear by studying and preparing every day.
- *Set a regular time for study.* Work when you're most alert. That's when you'll be most productive. Some people work better in the mornings; others work better in the evenings. Determine your personal best time to study, and build your schedule around it.

  Once you've done this, tell your friends about your schedule. Give them a certain time when they can call—say, between 8 p.m. and 9 p.m. You'll be able to enjoy phone conversations without being distracted from your studies.
- *Set a regular place for study.* Having a suitable place to study is essential. It might be the library or your room. It might be a coffee house, provided you find a quiet place in the corner and resist the temptation to join some friends that drop in. Don't kid yourself—unless you are very unusual, you can't study best in front of the TV or while instant messaging friends.

- *Allow time for having fun, for downtime, and even for sleeping.* Don't get involved in too many outside activities, but don't turn into a bookworm. You'll have a lot of options on campus. Think seriously before you decide to join a club, a music group, or a team. Each choice will have pros and cons. How much time will it take? Will it help you grow and learn? Does it fit with your goals?

  "No" is a powerful word. Use it. But at the same time, give yourself time to explore new activities. If something ends up taking too much time, find a way to bow out gracefully.

  Don't over-program your life. Spend some time every day doing what you want to do. This includes exercise: Physical fitness is essential. Set aside time for friends and family. Don't overlook time for spiritual development. And don't manage your schedule to the point that you lose sight of the important things in life.

  Give yourself time to sleep, too. You can't get into a habit of staying up all night—whether to party or to study—and expect to do your best.

- *Break up big tasks into small ones, and set a time limit for each task.* If you have to write a paper, can you work on one segment tonight and another one tomorrow? If you finish a small segment each day, a term paper becomes nothing more than a series of small tasks.

  Next, decide how much time it should take to do each part. Push yourself to complete each part of the job in that time limit. Try to work more efficiently.

- *Jump in.* Sit down in your study area, take a deep breath, and plunge in. You might not work at 100 percent efficiency from the beginning, but you will have made a start. Good students have a lot in common with athletes: Both need a warm-up period before they can function at their best.

- *Juggle tasks.* Your overall goal should be to organize your time so that you don't miss a deadline and are well prepared for the next. But you do have some leeway. Be creative in your approach to studying, and choose the method that best fits you.

  Some students, for example, have a "do it now" policy. They do simple tasks as they receive them. They get them out of the way and off their "to-do" lists. Other students like to do the hardest task first. They find that gives them a psychological boost.

  Another strategy is to practice **multitasking,** or *doing more than one thing at a time.* What things can you do simultaneously? For example, can you read a chapter in your biology text while you're waiting to use the printer in the library or riding on the bus? (As noted before, multitasking does not include studying and watching TV at the same time.)

- *Be good to yourself.* Promise yourself small and large rewards for your accomplishments. Perhaps you've just spent two hours looking for articles on the Internet. You found what you need. Before you plunge into writing your paper, reward yourself. Watch a TV program. Talk to a friend for a few minutes. Answer your e-mail.

  And think about the rewards you will get when you finally complete a difficult task. You can go to a movie or hang out with friends guilt-free, because you've finished your work.

Try out these new study habits for 21 days. Focus on the ones that you think will be most helpful to you. By then, you'll be on the way to overcoming the habit of procrastination. If you're still having trouble, talk to your adviser or a professor about it. Show him or her what you have done, and ask if you're on the right track.

Most colleges realize that time management is a problem for new college students, so they give freshmen help. Some colleges include information on time management in required orientation classes for freshmen. George Mason University in Fairfax, Virginia, offers tips to students online at *www.gmu.edu/gmu/personal/time.html.* You can find more information online, including time-management tips from other colleges, by typing "time management in college" into a search engine.

Some Common Distractions

Eliminating **distractions,** *things that draw your attention or interest away from what you are doing,* is an important part of managing your time. Some common distractions for students are:

- telephone calls
- socializing
- watching television
- spending too much time on the computer sending e-mails and instant messages
- playing video or computer games.

If you avoid these activities when you are supposed to be studying, you can complete your assignments, feel less pressured, and still make time to have fun.

Managing Your College Schedule

College presents many challenges for students. The first few months of freshman year can be particularly difficult—many students find it hard to manage their time. They become stressed out or even depressed. Their grades suffer.

Managing your time in college begins with setting up your class schedule, and then fitting your other activities around it.
Courtesy of Corbis Images

Managing your time while in college begins with setting up your class schedule. You do this when you register for classes for the following semester. Among other things, you must consider which days each class meets, which building it meets in, where you will be immediately before the class, and how long it will take you to get there. If you're a student at a small college, that may not be such a problem. But if you're at a large university, it can take 30 minutes or more to get from one location to another. You may have to take a bus, ride a bike, or even drive. And if you're living off campus, it can take even longer.

For example, say you schedule yourself for an English class that meets in the southwest corner of campus. You want to take an anthropology course that meets at the other end of campus 10 minutes after your English class ends. But after considering the distance and checking the campus bus schedule, you realize you won't be able to make that class. So you find another section of the course that meets at another time that's more convenient for you. Or, you decide to schedule the anthropology course and find another section of the English class.

Another factor is the time of day classes meet: If you're an early riser, you may want to schedule your classes in the mornings. But if you're a night owl, it might not be wise to schedule yourself into 8:00 a.m. classes that you won't be able to get up for. Some students also like to group their courses so they have a day or two off per week for studying or working a part-time job.

You should also think about the number of credits and the balance of difficult versus easy courses you take each semester. Don't schedule all your hard courses in the same semester if you can help it—try to spread them out over several semesters. Remember that those difficult courses will require more study time.

Once you've got your class schedule worked out, you need to think about fitting in your other activities. To manage your time wisely, make out a schedule in advance, using the following five tips.

Five Tips for Managing Your College Schedule

1. *Set specific academic and personal goals.* If you know where you're going, it's a lot easier to determine what you need to do to get there. So write down your goals. For example, goals for your freshman year might be to:

    - earn at least a 3.25 GPA
    - make the college volleyball team
    - have an active social life
    - write for the school newspaper
    - decide on a major
    - get a summer internship.

    Look at your list at least weekly. Add or change goals as appropriate, but make sure they're realistic. Determine whether your activities are helping you meet your goals or interfering with meeting your goals.

2. *Create a term calendar that lists major campus events.* Important things can fall through the cracks when you're focused on everyday demands. Don't forget the big picture. Get a term calendar and write down one-time things such as orientation week, homecoming and parents' weekends, vacations and term breaks, visits by guest speakers, and recruitment visits by employers. Keep the calendar handy and refer to it often.

3. *Create a weekly schedule of your classes, labs, meetings, and other activities.* In addition to a term calendar, get a weekly calendar that lets you enter activities by the hour. Write in all your classes and other regular activities, such as science and language labs, review sessions, or workouts. If you have a part-time job, put those hours in. Don't forget to set aside time to do your laundry and clean your room. Schedule regular time to relax—to go to a party or a movie. Also write in one-time activities as they come up. These might include a special meeting of your chemistry study group, a session with your faculty adviser, or coffee with a friend. Carry your weekly schedule with you all the time.

4. *Decide on specific times to work on each course.* Block out regular times for study, and don't let other things on your agenda get in their way. Specify which courses you will study for at which time. For example, if you have sociology and art history classes on Tuesdays and Thursdays, plan to study for them on Mondays and Wednesdays. But don't forget: If you also do a little each day on those courses, you won't have to cram it all into two days.

5. *Make a to-do list for each day.* Write down on it the things you must accomplish that day, followed by the things you'd like to get done if you can. Use a piece of paper, a 3 by 5 card, or whatever will be most convenient for you. Take it out several times a day and look at it—especially when you're thinking about what you should do next.

   No matter how well you plan your week in advance, you'll always have last-minute things to do—for example, making a quick trip to the store, stopping by your professor's office to ask a question, or meeting a friend from home who's in town for a day or two. These spur-of-the-moment activities can eat up your time. Set aside a few minutes every evening to enter these activities on your calendar and to-do list.

Making a Sample Weekly College Schedule

Figure 6.2 shows a sample weekly calendar for a college student. It will give you an idea of the kinds of activities you'll need to include in your own schedule.

Using your time well in college might be harder than it is in high school for several reasons. The course work will be more challenging, your life will have less structure, and you'll have greater independence. At first, you may have trouble adjusting. But if you learn to use your time well in high school, you'll have taken a big step toward using it well in college.

So don't procrastinate—start managing your time right now!

Week of: ____________________

	Mon	Tues	Wed	Thur	Fri	Sat	Sun
6–7 AM							
7–8 AM		Study		Study			
8–9 AM	Eng 101	Study	Eng 101	Study	Eng 101	Work	Study
9–10 AM	Eng 101	Study	Eng 101	Study	Eng 101	Work	Study
10–11 AM	Mgt 210	Exercise	Mgt 210	Exercise	Mgt 210	Work	
11–12 AM	Mgt 210	Exercise	Mgt 210	Exercise	Mgt 210	Work	
12 (noon)–1 PM	Study	Math 110	Study	Math 110	Study	Work	Exercise
1–2 PM	Chem group	Math 110	Chem group	Math 110	Chem group	Work	Exercise
2–3 PM	Chem group	Study	Chem group	Study	Chem group	Work	
3–4 PM	Exercise	Phil 101	Exercise	Phil 101	Exercise	Work	
4–5 PM	Exercise	Phil 101	Exercise	Phil 101	Exercise	Work	
5–6 PM		Work		Work	Work	Free Time	
6–7 PM	Dinner	Work	Dinner	Work	Work	Free Time	
7–8 PM		Work		Work	Work	Free Time	
8–9 PM	Study	Work	Study	Work	Work	Free Time	
9–10 PM	Study	Work	Study	Work	Work	Free Time	
10–11 PM	Study	Work	Study	Work	Work	Free Time	
11 PM–12 (midnight)							

FIGURE 6.2

A Weekly College Calendar

From Sherfield, R.M., Rhonda J. Montgomery, and Patricia G. Moody. (2005). *Cornerstone: Building on Your Best*, Concise Fourth Edition. Upper Saddle River, NJ: Prentice-Hall, p. 95.

CHECKPOINTS

Lesson 3 Review

Using complete sentences, answer the following questions on a sheet of paper.

1. List some concepts of time management.
2. What are some benefits of managing your time well? What are some consequences of poor time management?
3. Is working all the time the same as managing time well? Why or why not?
4. Give two reasons why people procrastinate. Do they apply to you?
5. Give five strategies for preventing procrastination that you think could work for you. Why do you think they might be successful?
6. List three activities in a college schedule.
7. What are some challenges in scheduling your college courses?

Applying Scheduling Skills

8. Think about how you'll plan your schedule when you get to college. Get a blank calendar for one week. Imagine five courses you will take in your first semester. Sketch out a possible schedule.

UNIT 4

Pursuing a Career

Unit Chapters

In Your Home and Community

BEGINNING TO NETWORK

Talk to five adults you know who hold various jobs and play different roles in your local community. Tell them about your career aspirations and plans. Ask each one to suggest someone you could talk to who could give you more information about careers you are interested in, the education and qualifications required, and ways to search for jobs in those careers.

Cadet Technical Sergeant Joseph Foley
ET ATTIRE
006

CHAPTER

7

Applying for Jobs

Chapter Outline

- LESSON 1: The Job Search Process
- LESSON 2: Preparing Your Résumé
- LESSON 3: Building Interviewing Skills

I don't think there is anyone [who] hasn't blown an interview or two. If it happens, look at it like it just wasn't meant to be, learn from your mistakes, and move on to the next opportunity.

—Alison Doyle,
job-search expert

LESSON

1 The Job Search Process

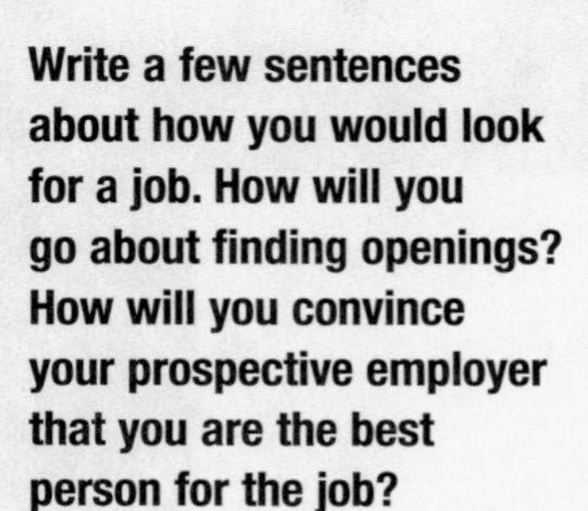

Quick Write

Write a few sentences about how you would look for a job. How will you go about finding openings? How will you convince your prospective employer that you are the best person for the job?

Learn About...

- identifying your personal job preferences
- selling your skills to an employer
- how to organize a job search

Identifying Your Personal Job Preferences

Finding a job isn't just a matter of searching the **want ads**, or *advertisements for job openings and items for sale*. It's not a matter of making a few phone calls, or having a successful interview. Getting a good job requires more than a great résumé. Important as job ads, interviews, and résumés are, one thing is even more important—knowing your own personal job preferences. To get the job that's right for you, you need to know yourself well.

That's why, as you learned in Chapter 1, Lesson 1, finding a good job begins with appraising who you are, what is important to you, and where you are going. Self-analysis doesn't come easily. Most people resist looking long and hard at themselves. They give little thought to questions such as, "What kind of person am I?" "What kind of people do I best interact with?" and "Based on my values, what are the most important things I want in a job?"

Finding a good job begins with appraising who you are, what's important to you, and where you are going.
Courtesy of Kayte M. Deioma/PhotoEdit

But to find the job that's best for you, you need to know the answers to these questions. One way to find these answers is to do an inventory of your personal job preferences. In this context, an **inventory** *is an evaluation or survey*. Doing a personal job-preferences inventory involves analyzing and recording several things about yourself. These include your interests, needs, and wants; your abilities and skills; your values; and your goals.

Vocabulary

- want ads
- inventory
- need
- want
- skill
- benchmark
- benefit statement
- informational interview
- entry-level
- network

Interests, Needs, and Wants

You should base your inventory on an understanding of what you are interested in, what you need, and what you want in a job.

Interests

To identify your interests, ask yourself some probing questions. Write down the answers.

- What do I do really well? In what areas am I most competent? Don't focus just on classes—take into account all your activities
- What things do I find most enjoyable or rewarding? Again, draw on ideas from any area of your life
- What do people often compliment me on?
- What's been my greatest accomplishment? What unique abilities (for example, playing the piano, repairing a car, organizing an event) and personal traits (for example, honesty, compassion, and intelligence) made those accomplishments possible?

The answers to these questions won't lead to a particular job. For example, people may compliment you on your fashion sense, but this doesn't necessarily mean you should become a model or fashion designer. Your answers to these questions will, however, reveal what you're best at. And chances are you're good at something because it interests you. By helping you identify your interests, these questions will give you a start toward knowing where to focus your job-search effort.

Needs

A **need** *is something that you must have in order to survive or to be happy.* Food and shelter are the two most important ones. Your job-related needs may not be a matter of life and death; they are, however, things that you need to be satisfied and content.

Ask yourself about your needs in the following areas:

- *Salary*: How much money will you need to pay your bills, have a decent lifestyle, and add to your savings? Using the skills you developed in Chapter 3, Lesson 1, Creating a Budget, figure out how much you'll need to earn.
- *Benefits*: Do you need a job that offers health insurance and a paid vacation as well as holidays?
- *Work environment*: Some people need a quiet work environment. Others would fall asleep in such an environment; they need one that is more active.
- *Schedule*: Some people are able to work only during the days. Others don't mind, or even prefer, the night shift. Some people can travel and some cannot.
- *Challenge*: Some people need a job that is continually challenging. Others find their challenges elsewhere. They'd rather focus their creativity on such things as family or hobbies.
- *Opportunity for advancement*: Are you ambitious? Or, are you happy just to do a job well, without worrying about advancement?

Wants

A **want** *is a thing that you'd like to have, but that is not necessary.* For example, most people want the highest possible salary, but some people could be happy with less money. For them, a high salary is not a need. Filling wants is not essential, but it can make a job more appealing.

Go through the list above. Ask yourself if you have some wants in those areas. Consider, for example, any wants that might fit under the "Schedule" category. Maybe you enjoy tutoring children after school. You don't *need* to do this—but you enjoy it and find it rewarding. If a job offers the possibility of flexible hours, you might be able to continue your tutoring. You wouldn't make flexible hours a job requirement, but if a job offered this possibility, you'd consider it a plus.

Everybody is different: One person's need, such as health insurance, may be another person's want. To a third person, health insurance may not matter—for example, a married man who has coverage under his wife's policy.

Look at each item on Table 7.1: Is it a need, a want, or is it irrelevant? Keep these factors in mind as your job search gets under way. You'll probably never find a job that offers you everything you want. But understanding what's most important for you can help you weigh your options.

Using this list, write down your 10 most important needs and your five most important wants. Keep the list handy as you search for jobs.

TABLE 7.1

Needs or Wants?

Personal preferences	• popularity and fame • wealth • respect • time with family • time to pursue private interests
Job/career preferences	• status and recognition • top salary • friendly coworkers • fair boss • pleasant work environment • responsibility and challenge • opportunity to advance • good benefits
Leisure-time preferences	• watch TV • participate in sports • write poetry or stories • do yard work • do crafts and artwork • read • go to movies, plays, or sports events • travel
Long-range wants and needs	• more education and training • new activities and interests • reaching a top position • marriage and children • a home • a great car • continued good health

Abilities and Skills

A **skill** *is the ability to do something that you have acquired through training or experience.* Abilities are inborn; skills are developed.

For most people, abilities and skills are linked. If you have an ability to do something, you're likely to want to become skilled in it. For example, you could have good hand-eye coordination, which would give you the ability to hit a moving ball with a piece of wood. But you will not be a good baseball player until you get the training and experience to turn that ability into a skill—people will be able to count on you to hit a baseball out of the park.

Similarly, you may have been born with an ability to draw or to take apart machines and put them back together easily. Those abilities, however, will not be enough to earn a living. You would need art or engineering training before you get a job. And once you had the job, you'd need ongoing training to turn those abilities into skills that could make a career.

As you begin the job-search process, you must have a clear idea of your abilities and skills. The ones that are the most developed are those you will sell to employers. List specific work-related skills that you have gained on any past jobs or in other activities. Examples could be operating a computer or teaching. Also list abilities that you could turn into skills with education and training. These might be an ability to write interesting stories, to persuade people to do things, or to do math quickly in your head.

Values

The organization you work for—its leaders, its goals and accomplishments, and its employees—should reflect your values and beliefs. Otherwise, you'll be unhappy. For example, if you believe that nicotine is a major threat to health and that people shouldn't smoke, would you be happy working for a tobacco company? A workplace where people believe in the product or service they offer is more productive than a workplace where workers do not share company values.

Identifying your values is a personal matter. Friends and family are not the authorities on who you are or what you should believe. You are the authority on you! When it comes to deciding on values that relate to jobs and careers, you might find it helpful to think of them in three broad categories: *things and processes; intrapersonal values,* and *interpersonal values.*

Things and Processes

These refer to your values at work in terms of what you have and what you do. Some choices of work-related values in this category are:

- a clean, quiet workplace or a crowded, bustling workplace
- strict regulations or flexible regulations
- top money and benefits versus average compensation
- casual or traditional dress
- a slow-paced or a fast-paced work environment.

Intrapersonal Values

These values refer to things inside you. Examples of things you might value or not value are:

- respect and honesty from boss and peers
- working with details
- varied assignments
- a sense of achievement
- power and status
- education and training opportunities.

Interpersonal Values

These refer to values among people. Choices that relate to this value include:

- working in teams or working independently
- interacting with customers versus interacting only with coworkers
- communicating face-to-face or via letters or e-mail
- leading a group or working independently.

Think of two or three other values that you could add to each of these lists. Now take five values from each category and list them in order of priority. If you decide that *money* and *compensation* are the most important things you want from a job, list those first. If *respect* is also important, but not quite as important as *money*, list that second. On the other hand, if you value *honesty* above all, even above *money*, then put *respect and honesty from boss and peers* first.

Goals

Now that you've defined your needs, wants, and values, you're ready to set some job or career goals. Your goals will help you focus your job-search process. They'll also be your **benchmark,** or *standard by which to judge your progress*. They will help you decide whether your job search is on track.

You learned in an earlier lesson that time-management skills are an important ingredient of success. The ability to set goals is equally important. For example, researchers at Yale University asked seniors, "Have you set goals? Have you written them down? Do you have a plan to accomplish them?" Only 3 percent of the class answered "yes." When the researchers surveyed these alumni 20 years later, they found some interesting results: The 3 percent of graduates who said that they had set goals were more likely to be happily married, successful, have satisfying family lives, and be in better health than their classmates who had not set goals.

So take out a pen or pencil, or sit down at your computer, and make a goal statement. Writing down the statement is essential, because if your goals are only in your head, they're likely to stay there. You can stay focused and organized only by writing out your goals, keeping them handy, and reviewing them regularly.

Elements of a Goal Statement

A goal statement should answer three questions:

1. What is going to happen?
2. When is it going to happen?
3. How is it going to happen?

Suppose you've decided you want to be the chief software engineer for a computer company. That's the first question, and you've answered it: You now know what is going to happen, at least (you hope) eventually.

The second question, When will it happen? is harder. You obviously can't become a chief software engineer tomorrow. You need to take steps to get there. The key is setting short-term and long-term goals. *Short-term goals* are things that you hope to accomplish within six months. *Long-term goals* are things you want to accomplish within six months to five years, or even longer. You'll need to set both types of goals.

Setting short- and long-term goals will not only tell you when you will reach certain stages of progress but also tell you *how*. In other words, it will answer the third question. For example, your long-term goal may be to be a chief software engineer, but that doesn't tell you how you'll get there. It doesn't tell you what you need to do to accomplish that goal.

That's where short-term goals come in. If you want to be a chief software engineer, you may want to get a summer internship with a computer company. By the end of the summer (*when*) you will have taken one more step (*how*) toward your long-term goal. Another short-term goal might be to read at least one computer magazine a month (*how*), starting next month (*when*). A third short-term goal might be to join the high school computer club tomorrow. Building on these short-term goals, you might then decide that getting into a college with a top-flight computer program is a good goal. Many short-term goals feed into a long-term goal.

Seven Steps for Writing a Goal Statement

Here are seven steps that will help you write a good goal statement:

1. *State your goal specifically and completely.* The more detailed your goal, the better you will be able to do what needs to be done to reach it.
2. *Set dates.* Setting dates will help you avoid procrastination.
3. *Make your goals realistic but challenging.* Use goals as an opportunity to test your limits. A goal must motivate you. If you have low goals, you'll have low achievements.

4. *Make your goals measurable.* Use each short-term goal as a benchmark. If your long-term goal is to get into a top college, define five things you need to do to reach that goal. Then track your progress. Celebrate your successes. Analyze the reasons for your failures and learn from them.
5. *Base your goals on your values.* If a goal is not yours, you won't be committed to it. Listen to what your parents or guardian, teachers, and advisers have to say. But write your goals to please yourself, not them.
6. *Identify internal roadblocks.* You'll come up against many barriers on the road to a successful career. Make sure that none of them is self-imposed. The most damaging internal roadblock is your attitude—perhaps the belief that you're not good or smart enough. Keep positive. There's great truth in the old saying, "Attitude is everything."
7. *Have fun!* Keep a sense of humor. If reaching your goals is all work and no play, you may feel overwhelmed and give up.

Summing It Up

Once you've listed your interests, needs, and wants, your skills and abilities, your values, and your goals, you have the raw material needed to launch a job search. Now it's time to bring all these things together and to organize them in a way that will help you present yourself to employers in the best light.

Drawing on your notes and everything you've learned about yourself so far, make a list that contains the following four sections:

1. Personal qualities and characteristics that can be useful in a job, such as dependability, enthusiasm, honesty, a high energy level, tact, cooperativeness, punctuality, or a sense of humor
2. Skills that you've developed in a job or another activity outside school, such as computer maintenance and repair, accounting, or the ability to work with children—don't forget abstract skills such as leadership, the ability to learn quickly, organizational ability, and problem-solving skills
3. Work-related skills and abilities that you have been trained or educated for, but haven't necessarily performed in a job, such as operating a cash register, building a cabinet, or writing a news article
4. Personal, educational, and job accomplishments—examples might be a high grade point average, a scholarship, a sports honor, or an award for community service.

Sample Benefit Statements

Skill: I am a detail-oriented person.

Proof: When I was working for United Aviation and the Marine Corps, I followed step-by-step procedures, schematics, drawings, and prints. I troubleshot and pinpointed problems on systems using schematics. I fabricated parts to the customer's drawings.

Benefit to an employer: I will follow instructions to the detail, thereby saving time by doing things correctly the first time. This is a benefit to any employer, as not following instructions and having to do things over is costly in terms of profit and time.

Skill: I have excellent time-management skills.

Proof: While attending college to obtain my degree and working 50 hours a week for Commnet Cellular as a senior systems engineer, I still carried a 4.0 GPA in school.

Benefit to an employer: This ability will allow me to complete more projects in a timely manner, thereby offering you a more productive workforce and an increase in profits due to your not having to pay overtime.

Selling Your Skills to an Employer

If you've ever tried to sell something, you know that to be successful you need two things: You need to know everything about the product you're selling, and you need to know what your customer is looking for. When you're looking for a job, your task is to sell yourself to your prospective employer. And the same principles apply: Know your product (that is, yourself) and know your customer (the employer).

To sell yourself to an employer, it's not enough to make general statements about how good you are or how much you want the job. You must back up your statements with evidence. An effective way to present yourself is to prepare a **benefit statement,** or *a well-thought-out statement of your skills and abilities, with examples that illustrate them.* You'll need a slightly different benefit statement for each job you apply for—but you can base each individual statement on a single, comprehensive statement.

Skill: Leadership is one of my strongest qualities.

Proof: One of my responsibilities at Commnet Cellular was to implement digital technology as an overlay to our analog system. This required coordinating and managing multiple departments to ensure that everything was done. The project was completed one and a half months ahead of schedule.

Benefit to an employer: All progressive companies need leadership, and employers want to be satisfied that when they delegate responsibility for a project to someone, that person will be able to coordinate all departments, stimulate cooperative teamwork, and complete the project on time. I can do this.

Skill: One of my greatest strengths is excellent communication skills. I can express myself clearly, both orally and in writing.

Proof: At Quality Insurance, where I worked for five years, I was responsible for dealing directly with customers who were filing claims. I was able to assist them, over the phone and in person, in an effective manner by listening carefully and then transcribing the information correctly for the claims adjustors. This saved time and kept the customers happy because the company quickly identified and handled their claims.

Benefit to an employer: I believe you would find this skill very useful in your business because listening to the customer and identifying what he or she needs is critical to good business and repeat business.

A benefit statement has three parts:

1. A statement of your skills, abilities, and knowledge
2. Examples of when and where you demonstrated or learned those skills, abilities, and knowledge
3. How and why your skills, abilities, and knowledge will benefit the employer.

The more specific your benefit statement is, the better. Give facts, figures, and evidence of your knowledge or experience in the relevant area. Remember, the bottom line for all organizations is to save money and time. Organizations that operate for a profit, such as corporations, also want to make money. How can you convince your prospective employer that you can help the organization do those things?

To construct a benefit statement, you should know your "buyer." This means you need to research the position you are applying for and the company that's offering it. Read the job description carefully; study the company's website. What skills does the job demand? What kind of education and experience should the successful applicant have?

Once you know these things, put together your own benefit statement for this job. Make sure it shows how you meet all or most of the requirements.

How to Organize a Job Search

As your job search gets under way, you'll need to discover where the best jobs are and determine the company's requirements for the job you're going after.

Begin by putting together a list of employers you would like to work for. These can be not only companies, but also government and nonprofit organizations such as charities, schools, or environmental organizations. You might start at a local library or in your school guidance office. You can find books on organizations classified by industry, size, and location. The Internet can be a good source, as can local newspapers and magazines.

Informational Interview

Build a list of names and contact information for every organization you think could be a possibility. Once you have compiled the list, you are ready for the next step in organizing your search: the **informational interview,** or *a conversation with someone working in the field you are interested in.*

One great way to find out if your skills and abilities match those of your targeted job is to talk to people working in your field. This will help you learn more about the requirements of the position. You'll also learn about trends in the field. An informational interview can eliminate surprises in an actual job interview. It can help you learn to ask questions, as well as to answer them intelligently. Moreover, informational interviews can help you develop employment leads. An informational interview may also lead to a job offer.

Here are several tips for conducting an informational interview:

1. Choose the top five organizations from your list of potential employers. Not all organizations will have someone available to talk with you, so start with the top five and work your way down.
2. Try to talk with the person in charge of the department that does the type of work you want to do. The person who answers the phone will often be a receptionist or secretary. Part of that person's job is to screen callers, so you need to get past that person. Be firm but polite. Say that this is not an employment call, but an information call. Stress that you are not looking for work at this time. You simply want to learn more about the field and would appreciate speaking with someone who has that information.
3. When you reach the person you want to speak with, state your name and the purpose of your call. Emphasize that you need his or her expertise. Ask for 15 to 20 minutes of time. If possible, arrange a personal interview; don't settle for a phone conversation.

4. *Prepare your questions.* Your objective is to find out all you can about the requirements and characteristics of the job you are looking for as well as the industry. Write down questions you want to ask. Below are a few examples. If answers to some of these questions appear in the company's website, build on that information to ask an in-depth question of your own.
   - What is unique about this company? How is it different from others in its field?
   - Who are the company's competitors? (This could give you clues as to other places to go for job possibilities.)
   - What skills, abilities, and personal qualities are you looking for in **entry-level,** or *beginning,* workers?
   - What are the main duties and responsibilities of entry-level positions?
   - What are the opportunities for training in the job?
   - What is the salary range for entry-level positions? What are the advancement opportunities?
   - Could the interviewer suggest any other people to talk to? Could you use the interviewer's name as a reference?
5. Treat this interview as seriously as you would a job interview. Dress professionally and be on time. Listen carefully and make eye contact. Keep to the allotted time unless the person you're interviewing offers more. When the interview is over, thank the person.
6. Write a thank-you note after the interview. Let the person know that you appreciate the time he or she took from a busy day and how much it has helped you. If other people helped you arrange the interview, send notes to them as well.

Your Objective

Once you have conducted your informational interviews, you should be clearer than ever about your objective in your job search. In the next lesson you will learn how to write a job objective. It is an important part of your résumé, and will help to keep you focused in your job search.

Networking

Of all the resources available to you in your search for employment, *human resources* will provide the greatest return. Human resources are the people you already know and those you meet in the course of a job search. Human resources can also make your job search more enjoyable.

As you learned in Chapter 1, Lesson 1, meeting people and making contacts in your job search is called *networking. The group of people you meet and contact is called a* **network.** A resourceful job hunter spends a good deal of time networking, because people who provide advice and information often offer the quickest and surest means of obtaining leads that result in employment. Experts who study the job market say that a majority of people get their jobs through networking.

Creating Your Network

The following types of people should be in your network:

- *Family, friends, and acquaintances.* This group includes not only people you know directly but also friends of your parents, friends of neighbors, and friends of friends. As employers and employees themselves, these people know which jobs are open and whom you should talk to about the openings. They might be able to tell you about a job before it's advertised.

  Family members, friends, and acquaintances may answer your questions directly or put you in touch with someone who can. This can open the door to a meeting with someone who can provide information on a specific career or company. This is also a good way to learn about the training necessary for a certain position, the prospects for advancement, and what the person likes and dislikes about the work.

- *People working in your field.* People working in your field can offer information about their jobs as well as other jobs available in their companies. Talking with them can enable you to clarify and reaffirm your interest in a particular type of work.

  You can find these individuals through the organizations they work for. As an example, maybe you want to be a computer programmer. You could call almost any bank, insurance company, brokerage firm, or other business likely to have computer systems and ask for the systems department or the computer department. The person who answers will probably be not only knowledgeable about the position you want, but also able to recommend the name of someone you might talk to. You won't always get a positive response—sometimes people are just too busy to talk—but if you are persistent, you will likely find someone who is willing to help you. If you would prefer to have the name of an individual to talk to before speaking to the department itself, ask the switchboard operator. Explain what you are doing, and he or she may recommend a particular individual to talk with.

  In either case, the person you talk to is likely to feel flattered that you have asked for help. Most people are willing to share thoughts and ideas. Just be well prepared, let them know that you won't take a lot of their time, and thank them before closing.

- *Other job hunters.* In your search for employment, you'll meet many other job hunters. You may meet them at the companies you are interviewing with, at employment agencies, or at other locations.

  Introduce yourself and share your experiences with them. Although your career interests might be quite different from theirs, they may be able to provide you with information relevant to your job search and give you the names of individuals you might contact. Other job hunters may also be able to suggest job-hunting techniques you haven't considered.

Once you're serious about your job search, virtually anyone can turn into a member of your network. For example, you may get some names during your informational interviews. Put them on your networking list. Don't forget former employers with whom you had a good experience. They can provide names of employers they know. Your teachers are also good sources.

Letters of Introduction

Besides giving you leads, some members of your network may be willing to write letters of introduction or serve as references for you. A reference would give you an opportunity to arrange an interview with a potential employer who might not otherwise be willing to talk with you.

Maintaining Your Network

Once you develop a contact network, you'll need to devote time to maintaining it. Keep in touch with everyone on your list. This doesn't mean bugging them until they want you to go away. It means keeping them informed of your progress, asking for their help, and giving them help when they need it.

Your contact network will expand many times over with each new person you meet. You'll see a ripple effect. The more people you know, the more people you'll meet who may be able to help you in your job search.

Finding Lists of Job Openings

The most likely places to find lists of job openings are in *classified ads* and on the Internet.

Classified Ads

Classified ads is another name for want ads. These appear in your local newspaper and in magazines published by trade and professional organizations. They're simple to find. Because so many people use the ads, however, employers receive many responses. Hundreds of people may apply for just one job. In this case, the employer can be choosy. You might not get an interview—in some cases, the employer might not even respond to your application. Nevertheless, you should use the classified ads. Just don't rely on them as your only source for job leads.

Always read the ads thoroughly. Follow the exact directions written in the ad. If the ad says "No phone calls," don't call.

Classified ads are an important place to find job leads—just don't rely on them as your only source.
Courtesy of Frank Siteman/PhotoEdit

The Internet

More and more job listings are appearing online. If you want to work for a specific organization, go to its website. Find the link titled "Jobs," "Careers," or "Employment" and click there. If you don't see these categories, enter those words in the website's search engine. If you still don't find the information you want, call the main number (usually listed under "Contact Us") and ask the person who answers how you can get a list of job openings.

Popular online job sites include:

- America's Job Bank: *www.ajb.dni.us*
- CareerBuilder: *www.careerbuilder.com*
- Hotjobs.com: *www.hotjobs.yahoo.com*
- Monster.com: *www.monster.com*

For US government jobs, visit the free website *www.usajobs.gov*.

The Internet also has a number of job databases. Some of them are supported by ads and are free to job hunters; others charge a fee. On a job website, you might find thousands of openings. Narrow your search by defining specifically what you want. For example, if you are looking for an office assistant job, you can specify "office assistant" and then "entry-level." You will get a list of jobs matching those criteria. You can also specify locations in the country, size of organization, or other preferences.

Most job databases offer you the opportunity to post information. The information you provide is compiled to form a *job profile*. A job profile posted by someone looking for a job might include:

- name
- e-mail address
- type of job sought
- experience
- training and education you have achieved
- other wants or needs (such as where in the country you want to work, the type of organization you want to work for, and the salary you are seeking).

Internet job databases list thousands of job openings, and most allow you to post information about yourself.
Courtesy of Colin Young-Wolff/PhotoEdit

Millions of people use online job sites, so your chances of landing one of the jobs listed are not high. Still, if you feel your qualifications match the needs of the job, you should apply.

But remember: Networking is the single best source of job information. Talking directly to people will always yield better information than a website or want ads will.

CHECKPOINTS

Lesson 1 Review

Using complete sentences, answer the following questions on a sheet of paper.

1. What are the four elements of a personal job-preference inventory?
2. What is the difference between an interest, a need, and a want? Why should you know each of those things about yourself?
3. Why are your skills and abilities important to your job search?
4. Name five of your values when it comes to work and describe why each one is important to you.
5. What are five steps you should follow when writing a goal statement? What are your goals?
6. Why is an information interview a valuable tool for a job seeker? How can you prepare for such an interview?
7. How can you start to build a job network? List three people you can contact today.
8. Name three job websites.
9. Name three organizations that you would like to work for. How will you find out what jobs they have open? How will you apply?

Applying Job-Search Skills

10. Choose a job that you would like to get and an organization that you would like to work for. Construct a benefit statement that you could use to sell yourself to that employer.
11. Select an online job database or several organizations you want to work for. Go online and find five openings for the kind of job you would like to get.

LESSON

2 Preparing Your Résumé

Quick Write

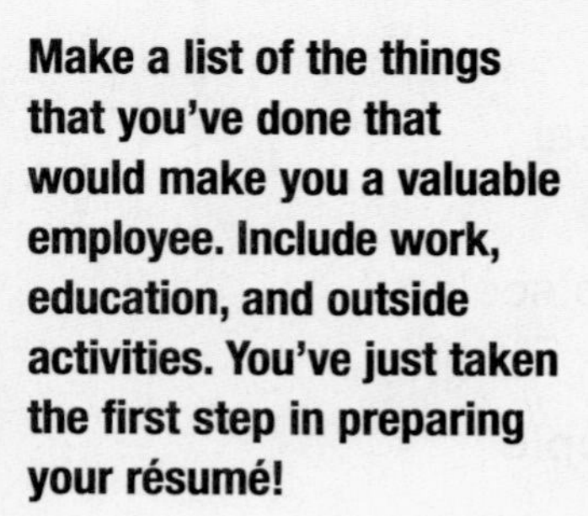

Make a list of the things that you've done that would make you a valuable employee. Include work, education, and outside activities. You've just taken the first step in preparing your résumé!

- the purpose of a résumé
- types of résumés
- six tips for writing a great résumé
- preparing a personal résumé
- cover letters

The Purpose of a Résumé

When you apply for a job, the person in charge of hiring will probably not know much about you. To make a good hiring decision, he or she will have to learn a lot about you very quickly. What is your background? What are your skills? What experience do you have? How are you different from other people applying for the job?

How will the employer find out these important things quickly and efficiently? His or her first step will usually be to look at your **résumé,** or *brief summary of your work experience and qualifications*. (When the word *résumé* refers to a job document, it is pronounced "REZ-oo-may.") Everyone who applies for a job should have a résumé.

Your résumé gives a potential employer a lot of information about you quickly and efficiently.
Courtesy of Jeff Greenberg/PhotoEdit

The main purpose of a résumé is to get a job interview with the company you submit it to. But a good résumé has a life far beyond that original purpose. For example, employers sometimes forward résumés they've received to their counterparts at other companies who are hiring. If you have impressed a company with your résumé, but it can't use you at this time, the person who reviews the résumés might send it on to someone else.

And between interviews, you may post your résumé on career websites. As you found out in the previous lesson, job searching can be a long process. So it never hurts to have as many irons in the fire as possible.

A good résumé has other purposes. For example, you might want to do some volunteer work in the community. The organization for which you want to do this work may ask for a résumé so it can review your qualifications. Or you might decide to apply for an internship or other job-related experience that has a tight deadline. If you've got your résumé ready, you're a step ahead of the game.

Vocabulary

- résumé
- chronological résumé
- functional résumé
- hybrid résumé
- targeted résumé
- electronic résumé
- job objective
- summary of qualifications
- keyword
- cover letter

Types of Résumés

There are five basic résumé styles:

1. A **chronological résumé** *lists your jobs, education, and other relevant accomplishments in* reverse *chronological order* (Figure 7.1). It begins with your current or most recent job and schooling, and works backward. This is the most common résumé type and is the easiest to write. Use it if you have followed a clear progression of jobs and education and if there are no big gaps in your record that this approach would reveal.
2. A **functional résumé** *arranges your information under skill headings, without focusing on dates* (Figure 7.2). The headings will depend on your particular experience and skills. Examples of such headings might be "Administration," "Sales," or "Computer." You might want to use a functional résumé if there are gaps in your chronological record. When they look at a chronological résumé, some interviewers question gaps of time during which you've been unemployed. Even though you had a valid reason for this—perhaps you had to care for a sick relative—you should not put this personal information on your résumé. In such a case, a functional résumé that does not give dates may be more effective.
3. A **hybrid résumé** *is a combination of the chronological and functional formats* (Figure 7.3). As in the functional résumé, you list skills you can offer an employer, and as in the chronological résumé, you list your work experience in reverse chronological order. In a hybrid résumé, however, you list the number of years that you worked in a particular job rather than the dates.

JOHN E. JONES
11567 East 17th Street, Spokane, Washington 01435
(609) 555-4587 (Please leave message)
johnjones95@aol.com

SUMMARY OF QUALIFICATIONS

Eight years' experience as a Surveyor. Proficiency, knowledge, and strengths in the following areas: Surveying, Field Engineering, Mapping, Drafting, Blueprinting, Supervision, Training, Customer Relations. Roads/Bridges: Commercial & Residential.

SUMMARY OF EXPERIENCE

Currently work as an independent contractor doing surveying and drafting for some firms in the Spokane area. Contracts include boundaries, commercial, heavy construction, and topographic jobs.

2003–2005 **Avery Structures, Inc.**, Spokane, WA
Party Chief on large construction jobs. Responsible for surveying and drafting.

2000–2002 **Centennial Engineering**, Seattle, WA
Party Chief for survey team in the construction of bridges and roads. Responsible for calculations and drafting on all phases of the jobs.

1998–2000 **J.R. Developers**, Tacoma, WA
Party Chief completing all survey work on the subdivisions.

1994–1998 **Al Messahaq/ARAMCO**, Saudi Arabia
Party Chief on all project work in Geodetic Control, roads and highways, in addition to plant layout.

EDUCATION

ITT Technical Institute, Spokane, Washington, 2000
2000 Hours in Map Drafting

Spokane School of Surveying and Mapping, Seattle, Washington, 1994
Certificate for 1600-hour program in Surveying and Mapping.

REFERENCES

Will be provided upon request.

FIGURE 7.1

Chronological Résumé

From Robbins, Carolyn R. (2006). *The Job Searcher's Handbook*. Upper Saddle River, NJ: Prentice-Hall, p. 68.

JOHN E. JONES
11567 East 17th Street, Spokane, Washington 01435
(609) 555-4587 (Please leave message)
johnjones95@aol.com

OBJECTIVE
A position in Computer Operations with progressively expanding responsibilities leading to an appointment to Systems Analyst.

EDUCATION
Spokane Technical Institute, Spokane, Washington
672-hour course in Computer Programming & Operations. State Certified. Graduated with honors. GPA: 3.67

Washington State University, Seattle, Washington
Completed 15 semester hours in Computer Science, including mastering Fortran.

Seattle School of Surveying and Mapping, Seattle, Washington
Certificate, 1600-hour program in Surveying and Mapping.

ITT Technical Institute, Spokane, Washington
Map Drafting (2000 hours).

PROFESSIONAL EXPERIENCE
Computer Computations/Data Processing
Involved in all aspects of data retrieval from computations to design to the finished product in the land surveying industry.

Mathematical
Performed daily algebraic and trigonometric calculations.

Teamwork
Worked cooperatively and effectively in fast-paced, demanding environment with all members of surveying crew, and interacted with various executive key personnel.

EMPLOYMENT HISTORY
Party Chief for the following companies:
- Avery Structures, Inc., Spokane, Washington
- Centennial Engineering, Seattle, Washington
- J.R. Developers, Tacoma, Washington
- Al Messahaq/ARAMCO, Saudi Arabia

FIGURE 7.2

Functional Résumé
From Robbins, Carolyn R. (2006). *The Job Searcher's Handbook.* Upper Saddle River, NJ: Prentice-Hall, p. 69.

JOHN E. JONES
11567 East 17th Street, Spokane, Washington 01435
(609) 555-4587 (Please leave message)
johnjones95@aol.com

OBJECTIVE

A position in Data Processing, preferably in Computer Operations or Programming.
Five-Year Career Goal: Systems Analysis Management

SUMMARY OF QUALIFICATIONS

COMPUTER SCIENCE, OPERATIONS & PROGRAMMING—Two years Computer Programming with emphasis in the following languages, software and operating systems: BASIC, FORTRAN, COBOL, MS-DOS, EXCEL, DBASE III, SPF/PC, IBM, OS/VS, JCL and CICS.

COMPUTER COMPUTATIONS/DATA PROCESSING—*Eight Years*. Involved in all aspects of data retrieval from computations to design.

MATHEMATICAL—*Five Years*. Performed daily algebraic and trigonometric calculations.

TEAMWORK—*Eight Years*. Effectively and cooperatively worked in a fast-paced, demanding environment with all members of a surveying crew, and interacted with various executive key personnel.

ADDITIONAL QUALIFICATIONS—Demonstrated ability to "debug" programs written by others. Developed training and instructional materials for software packages. Designed, set up and operated PC-based database for record-keeping.

EDUCATION

SPOKANE TECHNICAL INSTITUTE, Spokane, Washington, 2005
672-hour course in Computer Programming & Operations. State certified. Graduated with Honors. GPA: 3.67

WASHINGTON STATE UNIVERSITY, Seattle, Washington, 2004
Completed 15 semester hours in Computer Science which included courses in Computer Networking.

SEATTLE SCHOOL OF SURVEYING & MAPPING, Seattle, Washington, 2001
Certificate for 1600-hour program.

EMPLOYMENT BACKGROUND

Party Chief for the following companies:
Avery Structures, Inc., Spokane, Washington, 2002–2005
Centennial Engineering, Seattle, Washington, 2000–2002
J.R. Developers, Tacoma, Washington, 1998–2000
Al Messahaq/ARAMCO, Saudi Arabia, 1994–1998

REFERENCES

Professional references will be provided upon request.

FIGURE 7.3

Hybrid Résumé

From Robbins, Carolyn R. (2006). *The Job Searcher's Handbook.* Upper Saddle River, NJ: Prentice-Hall, p. 70.

4. A **targeted résumé** *includes the title of the actual job or career you are seeking.* You can write such a résumé in the same form as you would write a chronological, functional, or hybrid résumé. A targeted résumé, however, presents your qualifications in terms of the specific job you are applying for. This format is especially effective when you are interested in a particular job and need a separate résumé for it.
5. An **electronic résumé** *is one prepared specifically for online use.* It includes certain words that computers can recognize, and you write it in plain text format. You can write an electronic résumé as a chronological, functional, hybrid, or targeted résumé.

Six Tips for Writing a Great Résumé

Your résumé is an advertisement for you. In it, you tell prospective employers who you are, what you've done, and what you can do. Your résumé's appearance is very important. You want to deliver your message in a clear, concise, and readable form, free of grammar and spelling errors.

So you should put a good deal of thought into your résumé. Before you start writing, read over these tips. Then keep them in mind as you do your first draft.

1. *Use action verbs.* Your résumé should be lively. It should portray you as a dynamic person who has done many good things and can bring lots of value to an organization. For this reason, you should use action verbs when describing your accomplishments in a print résumé. (You'll have to use nouns in an electronic résumé because of technical requirements, as explained below.) Table 7.2 contains two summaries of accomplishments related to the same job, an office assistant. Both these people are seeking to move up to an office manager job. Which candidate does a better job of summarizing his or her qualifications?

TABLE 7.2

Using Action Verbs in Résumés

Résumé 1	• Telephone answering • Picking out office supplies and buying them • Advising new employees.
Résumé 2	• Responded to calls from customers and suppliers and assisted them in finding information • Selected and purchased office supplies • Advised new employees on office policies, computer installation, and security procedures.

An employer would be more likely to see the person who wrote Résumé 2 as able to respond to demands, make important decisions, and advise people. This person would clearly be a valuable employee.

2. *Give facts, figures, results, and numbers.* You'll never impress an employer with vague phrases such as, "I am a great problem solver and a hard worker"—*unless* you follow up with proof to support them. Tell the prospective employer where and when you obtained your skills, and where and how long you used them. If you say you're "detail oriented," give an example of a situation in which you used that talent and describe its outcome. Numbers work well on résumés. For example, if you made a financial difference for a previous employer—you may have found a way to save $500 on office supplies—say so. Employers love it when employees find new ways to save or earn money.

3. *Give your résumé a personality.* Make your résumé reflect the things that are unique about you. Don't be afraid to deviate from the norm or to be innovative, but do it carefully. If you are applying for a job in the arts field, creativity might be acceptable; it might even be expected. But a job in the computer field might demand something more traditional. Always use good taste. If you're striving for originality and are unsure about whether a certain strategy works, have a friend—or better yet an adult working in the field—review it.

4. *Be honest.* Preparing a résumé is not an exercise in fiction writing. It's now easier than ever to verify facts, and more and more employers are checking résumés for accuracy.

5. *Keep it positive.* Don't put anything that could be interpreted as criticism, conflict, or hostility on your résumé—especially criticism of a previous employer. Also, be careful not to include any information that could stereotype you. For example, if you're interested in guns, don't say it. It might alarm some employers.

6. *Keep it concise.* A résumé for a high school student should usually be just one page long. As you grow older and get more experience, you can expand it as needed.

Preparing a Personal Résumé

Preparing a résumé is not difficult. It just takes time and organization. Like any other piece of writing, it's easier when you follow a process to plan and organize. Here are the basic steps:

Gather Your Information

You begin by gathering your background information. List everything you think could interest an employer. This might include information on:

- full-time or part-time jobs
- education, including relevant courses you have taken and your grade point average (GPA) if it is above 3.0
- volunteer work
- hobbies and free-time activities
- awards and honors
- anything else that might be interesting to an employer, such as places you have traveled or languages that you speak besides English.

Here is where you can use the *benefits statement* that you prepared in the last lesson. It will provide the basic information you need to draft your résumé.

Organize Your Information

Next, you organize your information, based on the type of job you are going to apply for. Keep in mind that your résumé is not your life history. Employers may discard a résumé if it is too long or contains irrelevant information. For example, if you are applying for a job in a computer company, the fact that you got an A in a computer-programming course would be relevant, and you should include it on your résumé. But if you're applying to be an assistant to an animal trainer, a programming course is probably irrelevant, regardless of your grade.

Writing the First Draft

Once you've compiled your information and decided on the résumé style that best suits your job objective, you're ready to write the first draft.

Here are the basic parts of a résumé and what to include in each of them. Most résumés will have all these sections, usually in the order presented. You do have some leeway, however. For example, if you're just entering the job market and have little work experience, the education section should precede the work-experience section. Once you're an experienced worker, your job experience is probably more important than your formal training, so you could move back the education section.

Job Objective

The **job objective** *is a brief statement that describes the type of position you are seeking*. It always appears at the beginning of the résumé, immediately after your name and address. This section is very important—it's the employer's first opportunity to get to know you. If it appears that you didn't take the time to construct a coherent job objective or, worse yet, that you don't know what you want to do, the employer may read no farther.

As you write your objective, keep one idea in mind: "What is my career goal?" The objective should consist of one or two short sentences and should mention your long-term employment goals. You can use the goal statement that you prepared in the last lesson to help you decide what to say. But be careful about making your objective too specific. For example, don't say you are seeking a specific job title or that you want to work only for a specific company. A general title, such as "editor," is fine. A title such as "associate editor for community news" is too specific. You never know where your résumé will end up, and you don't want to rule out any possibilities.

> **Sample Job Objectives**
>
> - Banquet Manager with responsibilities in food preparation, purchasing, staff development, and menu planning. Long-term goal: General Manager of Hotel Operations
> - Editor, preferably within the textbook department of a publishing company. Long-term-goal: Director of Publications
> - Communications Specialist, with responsibility for preparing news releases; designing and editing brochures, displays, and posters; and executing advertising strategies. Long-term goal: Director of Public Relations.

Summary of Qualifications

The **summary of qualifications** *is a brief overview of your skills, experience, and knowledge*. For the reader's convenience, place the summary near the top of the first page. The order in which you present your qualifications is important. Put the ones that are most relevant to the job first.

Education

The education section includes all the relevant training and education you have received—whether it was formal education in a school or college, on-the-job training, or training you received elsewhere. Include any education that is relevant to the skills or knowledge needed for the job you're seeking. But don't forget education that gave you broader skills, such as ability to communicate, handle conflict and stress, take initiative, and think strategically. These are essential in today's workplace.

List the names of the institutions you attended, starting with the most recent one, along with the city and state they are located in. If you have a high school education, list relevant courses. Include your GPA if it's above 3.0. (If you go to college, you'll include your major and any other relevant courses.) Unless you're doing a functional résumé, give the dates when you attended high school or college.

Employment History

The employment history section lists all the jobs you've had—full-time, part-time, student, and co-op jobs, as well as internships. On a chronological résumé, you'll list these jobs in order, starting with your current or most recent job. Include dates of employment, expressed in months and years. Give the name of the organization and the city and state. You do not need to provide the address and phone number.

For each job, briefly describe the duties you performed and the responsibilities you held. Tell what you accomplished in the job, in measurable terms if possible. For example, if you painted houses one summer, say how many houses you painted, especially if the number is impressive. Give the outcomes of your work: If you worked in sales, for example, say how much money you made for your employer. If it isn't clear from the name, say in a few words what the company does. Do not include reasons for leaving a job or your salary there.

Related Professional Experience

Include this section if you have done volunteer work that pertains to the job. For example, if you led a Boy or Girl Scout troop on a camping expedition and the job you are applying for requires leadership skills or working with youth, tell prospective employers about your Scouting experience.

Other

This is the place for information on such topics as fluency in a second language, awards, and travel.

References and Letters of Recommendation

You don't need to include references on a résumé. If an interviewer decides that you are a serious candidate, at that point he or she will ask for references. The people who serve as references should be former employers, teachers, counselors, or others who know you well.

Some people have letters of reference or commendation from former employers or teachers, testifying to their skill level or good character. If you have such letters, you could include them with your résumé. An option is to bring copies of the letters to the job interview and to give them to the interviewer at that time.

What to Omit

Do not include *personal information* on your résumé. This includes, for example, your age, marital status, any children you might have, religion, race, or state of health. Antidiscrimination laws prohibit employers from asking about these issues.

Do not put your Social Security number on your résumé or give it when applying for a job. Give it only if you are hired.

Revising and Proofreading

You'll need to do several drafts before your résumé really starts to shape up. If possible, let some time pass between each draft. You'll probably think of things to add or other ways to improve it.

This is time well spent. Employers may receive dozens of résumés in response to a single job ad. They will throw out any that are messy or confusing, or have grammar errors and misspellings. Remember, your résumé is your first introduction to the employer. You must present your qualifications in a professional manner. If your résumé is not well prepared, you will probably not have a chance even to land an interview, much less get the job.

Proofread your résumé carefully. Scrutinize every word for spelling and grammar mistakes. Then, when you're satisfied, have at least three other people read your résumé for content as well as accuracy.

Preparing the Final Copy

You've already given great thought to what your résumé says. Now it's time to focus on how it looks.

- *Use an appealing format and layout.* The résumé should look neat, balanced, and uncrowded. Single-space the text; use double or triple spaces between sections. The font size should be 11 point or 12 point; and margins should be between 1 and 1.5 inches. You may vary fonts to make the résumé attractive, but don't overdo it. Use no more than three fonts, and make sure they are readable. Highlight important points by CAPITALIZING, **bolding**, or underscoring them.
- *Number and identify pages.* If your résumé is more than one page long, place a heading in the top left corner of all following pages that includes your name and the page number.
- *Forget the title.* A title such as "Résumé" is unnecessary. Your reader knows what the document is.
- Use standard 8.5-by-11-inch white, ivory, or light-gray paper.
- Print your résumé using a letter-quality printer with dark ink. If you make photocopies, make sure they are bright and clear.
- If you mail your résumé, put it in a 9-by-12-inch or 10-by-13-inch envelope. If you fold it to fit in a smaller envelope, the résumé will not look neat and crisp.

Whether you're preparing a paper résumé or an electronic one, review and proofread it carefully. Remember, this is your first introduction to a potential employer.

Completing an Electronic Résumé

Most of the guidelines for a print résumé also apply to an electronic résumé. An electronic résumé, however, has some unique requirements that affect its content and format.

Content

The most important element of an electronic résumé is the use of keywords. A **keyword** *is a specific word that a computer looks for when searching a database.* In the case of résumés, the employer's computer will look for words that correspond to the job requirements. Keywords are usually noun forms. For example, on your paper résumé you may write, "Answered telephones for busy office." On your electronic résumé, write "Telephone receptionist."

Format

You must usually save an electronic résumé as a text-only file. This means that your résumé can contain virtually no formatting. You can't use boldface, underlined, or italic type; document borders; or document headers or footers that may help to make a print résumé look attractive. Moreover, don't center your headings; use only flush-left text instead. If you must emphasize something, use all caps.

Put your name at the top, along with the title of the job you are seeking (if you're sending the résumé in response to a specific job). Put your address, e-mail address, and phone number at the bottom of the last page.

Cover Letters

Once your résumé is complete, you must take a final step—writing a cover letter. A **cover letter** *gives prospective employers further information about you that is not in your résumé.* It points out items in your résumé that show why you could be of value to the organization. It helps generate interest in you and gives you an opportunity to sell yourself. For these reasons, you must draft your cover letter thoughtfully.

A cover letter is attached to your résumé. It identifies the position you're applying for and explains why you're suitable for it. You should always include a cover letter to your résumé, including electronic résumés.

You should structure your cover letter along the following lines:

The opening. Address this to a specific person. If you don't have a name, address the letter to the head of the department who would be in charge of the position you're applying for.

The first paragraph. Begin by explaining why you're writing. State the position you're applying for or the position you qualify for. If someone referred you to the employer, tell the reader who that was. Explain in one sentence why the company or organization is attractive to you.

The second and third paragraphs. State your qualifications for the position in these paragraphs. Remember that your purpose is to prompt the reader to select you for an interview. So relate your qualifications to the organization's needs. This means you must do some research into the company or organization before you apply for the job.

The closing paragraph. Thank the reader for taking the time to review your qualifications, but not for anything he or she hasn't done yet, such as granting you an appointment. *Always ask for an interview,* and explain how the reader may contact you.

Don't send a generic cover letter. You should carefully adapt and personalize each cover letter for each prospective employer. Figure 7.4 gives an example of a good cover letter.

7854 East Martin Luther King Blvd.
Aurora, Colorado 80010

October 15, 2005

Mr. Dennis Kelly
MAC Tools Corporation
1757 Hoyt Street
Lakewoord, Colorado 80215

Dear Mr. Kelly:

I have recently earned my Associate's degree in Occupation Sciences of Automotive Technology from the Westwood College of Technology (formerly Denver Institute of Technology) graduating with a GPA of 4.0. This accelerated education, in addition to years of great interest in the field of automotive technology, makes me eager to be placed in a position with your company.

The attached résumé summarizes my experience and education for you. Westwood College offers, to all graduates, the opportunity to receive lifetime training, so I can keep current with new material and procedures. This benefit will be an asset to your company because I will have ongoing retraining in my field at no cost to you.

As for my other qualifications, I have completed EDGE training that has taught me diagnostic procedures for automotive repair. I am ASE certified and have a clean, no-ticket driving record. I have most of the tools needed to begin my career and am in the process of purchasing more diagnostic equipment.

I believe you will consider me for a position with MAC Tools Corporation when you review the enclosed résumé and see that I match the qualifications that you ask of your automotive technicians. I look forward to meeting with you and becoming part of your team. You can contact me at the number below between 5 and 10 p.m. weekdays and all day on the weekends. I have voice messaging and pick up my messages regularly. Please do not contact my present employer as he is not aware of my decision to leave, and I want to give two weeks' notice at the appropriate time.

Sincerely,

Harold Blake

Harold Blake
(303) 555-1221
blake56@yahoo.com

Enclosed: Résumé

FIGURE 7.4

Sample Cover Letter

From Robbins, Carolyn R. (2006). *The Job Searcher's Handbook*. Upper Saddle River, NJ: Prentice-Hall, p. 89.

CHECKPOINTS

Lesson 2 Review

Using complete sentences, answer the following questions on a sheet of paper.

1. Why is it important to have a good résumé?
2. What are the basic résumé styles? What are the main differences among them?
3. Why is it important to use active verbs on a print résumé? Why should you not emphasize verbs on an electronic résumé?
4. Explain the purpose and importance of a job objective.
5. List some additional pointers that will make your printed résumé effective.
6. What is different about the electronic résumé?

Applying Résumé-Preparation Skills

7. Prepare a résumé for yourself in two different styles.
8. Pick a job with a company you think you might be interested in working for some day, and write a draft cover letter to go along with the résumés you have prepared.

LESSON

3

Building Interviewing Skills

The Interview Process

Of all the phases of job searching, most people find the interview the most difficult and stressful. And no wonder: The impression you make during that brief period is the most critical part of your job search. It will determine whether you are hired.

What can you do to minimize the anxiety and the sweaty palms? With a job interview, as with almost any other part of life, preparation makes all the difference. Knowing how the interview process works, and understanding what to do and not to do, will make you feel more secure. Knowing how employers evaluate interviews can also help.

The interview process is not complicated. You see a job that appeals to you, decide to apply, and submit your résumé along with the company application form or any other required paperwork. Then you wait. Meanwhile, the company reviews all the résumés it has received and selects those that look most promising. This process generally takes a few weeks, but it may take longer, depending on the size of the company and the number of résumés it receives.

If your résumé is among those selected, someone from the organization will call or e-mail you to schedule an interview. In some cases, you may interview with someone in the **human resources department,** *the department that handles hiring, benefits, and other issues concerning employees.* In other cases, you may have an interview with the person who would be your boss or your boss's boss. Sometimes you'll talk with a combination of these people. And if the company decides after the first interview that it likes you, it may ask you to come back another day for more interviews.

Quick Write

Imagine you are an employer. Make a list of the qualities you would look for in a job applicant.

Learn About...

- the interview process
- interview dos and don'ts
- types of interviews
- basic interview questions
- how employers evaluate interviewees

Vocabulary

- human resources department
- industry sector
- body language
- group interview
- peer
- rapport
- unstructured interview
- structured interview
- stress interview
- behavioral interview

Interview Dos and Don'ts

As noted before, a successful interview takes preparation. You must do your research, dress and act appropriately, and know how to answer and ask questions well.

How to Prepare

The first step in preparation is to research the company and its **industry sector,** or *general field in which it is working.* If your interview is with a computer company, find out as much as you can about what is happening in the computer industry today. This will help you ask good questions.

Become as familiar as you can with what the company does—its history, its goals, and its people. Go to the organization's website. It should contain most of what you need to know. You can also enter the organization's name into a search engine and find out what people are writing about it.

Discover as much as you can about the people you will speak with during your interview. Some company websites give a short biography of each of the company's top executives. Or you can ask the person who schedules your interview to send you bios of the people you'll meet.

Know the job requirements well. The interviewer won't be impressed if you don't even understand the position you're applying for. Practice for the interview by role-playing. Get together with a friend or relative and have him or her pretend to be your interviewer. Tell these people to ask tough questions about your background, goals, and knowledge of the company and industry. Chances are your role-play interviewer will be harder on you than the real one. But if you practice, the questions that arise during the actual interview will be less likely to throw you off balance.

Know how to get to the interview site. If you arrive late at your interview, you'll be in big trouble. Being late to the interview tells the employer just one thing: You'll probably be late to work, too. So be sure you know how to get to the interview, where to park, and any rules for visitors, such as getting a security badge to enter the building. Take a dry run beforehand if you think it will help. Be sure to account for variations in traffic, especially during rush hours.

Try to find out the salary range. If you can't, don't bring up salary in the interview. It will seem like you are more interested in money than the job. But do come to the interview knowing the lowest salary you can afford to accept and how much others with your background earn. You can get this information from friends, your counselor, or on websites such as *www.salary.com.*

Bring along a copy of your résumé, a list of your references, transcripts, or extra copies of any other material the interviewer might need.

How to Dress

First impressions count. During the interview, you want to give the message that you expect to be taken seriously. Your clothes can help convey that message. Your interviewer will notice the amount of care you take in your dress. He or she will assume you'll take the same amount of care with your work. Don't let anyone think you'll be a sloppy employee.

Look neat and clean. Other than that, the exact type of clothing you'll wear depends on the job you're seeking. If you're applying for an office job or a job in which you'll meet the public, formal dress (suit and tie for guys, suit or dress for girls) is best. If you're applying for a job in a repair shop, by contrast, you can dress more casually.

Dress conservatively. Don't try to make a fashion statement. Wear a neutral color—for example, dark blue is better than black or white. If you do choose black, wear a bright scarf or tie to offset it. Studies have shown that business executives like greens and yellows least of all colors.

Watch out for the style of your clothing as well as for color. If you're a girl, don't wear a low-cut top or one that exposes your midsection. Guys should avoid casual sportswear and wear socks that are the same color as their pants. Whether you're a guy or girl, don't wear sandals, flip-flops, or sneakers.

Be careful with the extras. If you wear jewelry, avoid anything that dangles or glitters excessively. If you're a guy who usually wears an earring, leave it at home unless you are sure the interviewer will like it.

Go easy on makeup and cologne. This is an interview, not a party!

Dressing carefully conveys the message that you want a potential employer to take you seriously.
Courtesy of Corbis Images

In your interview, be clear about your career direction and goals. Sell yourself.
Courtesy of P. Winbladh/zefa/Corbis Images

During the Interview

Your behavior during the interview also conveys a lasting impression about you. Follow these tips to present yourself at your best:

- Arrive early. Get to the site at least 15 minutes ahead of time. Go to the restroom for a final check of your clothes, hair, and makeup.
- Don't take notes unless the interviewer asks you to.
- Remember the interviewer's name, make sure you know how to pronounce it correctly, and use it during the interview. Refer to the person as "Mr." or "Ms." unless the interviewer invites you to use his or her first name or another title.
- Shake hands firmly, whether the interviewer is male or female. If your hands tend to perspire, run them under cold water for a few minutes before the interview.
- Do not smoke, chew gum, or drink anything during the interview. If you are offered something to drink, politely turn it down. Even handling a cup or glass can be distracting, and spilling something could really disrupt the image you want to create.
- Wait for the interviewer to offer you a chair before you sit down.
- Answer all questions truthfully and appropriately. Put your best foot forward. Talk about things that put you in the best light possible, but don't lie—don't even exaggerate.
- Keep positive. Don't badmouth your school or teachers. Never criticize a past employer.
- Be enthusiastic and confident, but don't boast.
- Be aware of your body language.
- Be clear about your career direction and goals. Have in mind the points you want to make about how well you can do this job and be sure you make them. Sell yourself.

Body Language—the Silent Communication That Comes Through Loud and Clear

Body language *is the nonverbal messages that your facial expressions, physical stance, and gestures convey to a listener.* Experts estimate that as much as 65 percent of communication is nonverbal. During your interview, pay particular attention to the following:

1. **Facial expressions.** Eye contact is important. If you avert your eyes, the interviewer may interpret this as a lack of self-confidence or even dishonesty. Avoid touching your face or hair during the interview. It can indicate nervousness. Your mouth is a major silent communicator. Smiling appropriately is great. But if you constantly smile or purse your lips, the interviewer may interpret this negatively. A good rule of thumb: If in doubt, do what your interviewer is doing.
2. **Body gestures.** Crossed arms can indicate defensiveness or dissatisfaction. Keep your hands in your lap. If you tilt your head too far up, people think you feel superior. If you tilt it too far down, you give a message of inferiority. Sitting too straight can make you seem inflexible, but slouching makes you appear lazy. Don't lean on the desk or get too close to the interviewer.
3. **Hand gestures.** Gesture naturally. Avoid clenched hands, as this can reveal anxiety. Never put your hands in your pockets. Avoid straightening your clothing, because the interviewer may view this as a sign you're unsure of yourself.

Your body language and your dress leave a lasting impression about you.
Courtesy of Dana White/PhotoEdit

Interview Day Checklist

- [x] I have prepared a list of appropriate questions to ask the interviewer.
- [x] I have brought a list of references.
- [x] I have reviewed my benefit statements and am prepared to sell myself to get the job.
- [x] I have done research on the company.
- [x] I am well groomed and appropriately dressed:
  My hair is cut, washed, and combed.
  I have bathed and used deodorant.
  My makeup, jewelry, and perfume or after-shave lotion are not excessive.
  My fingernails are trimmed and clean and I have brushed my teeth.
  My shoes are clean, neat, and unscuffed.
- [x] I will be myself, whatever the circumstances of the interview.
- [x] I will take extra copies of my résumé, transcript, and any other print materials that the interviewer may request.
- [x] I have a pen or pencil to fill out the company application form, should this be necessary.
- [x] I will smile, be positive, and present myself in the best possible light.

FIGURE 7.5

Interview Day Checklist

From Robbins, Carolyn R. (2006). *The Job Searcher's Handbook.* Upper Saddle River, NJ: Prentice-Hall, p. 139.

Ending the Interview

You will know the interview is ending when the interviewer asks if you have any questions. Ask your questions. Then reiterate the main points that make you a strong candidate. Ask the interviewer when he or she thinks the company will make its decision. Emphasize how much you would like the job, and thank the interviewer for spending time with you.

Follow-Up

As soon as you get home, make notes about your impressions. List any points you forgot to mention or questions you forgot to ask. Within two days of the interview, send a follow-up letter or note (by US mail preferably, but e-mail is acceptable). Mention the points or questions that have come up since the interview ended. Stress again that you want the job and explain why you are qualified. Send separate notes to everyone who interviewed you.

Types of Interviews

Interviews can take many formats, from a face-to face interview to a videotaped session to a lunch or telephone interview. Here are the most common types of interviews you will experience:

Group or Committee Interviews

In a **group interview,** *several people will ask you questions.* These interviewers may include a potential **peer,** or *coworker at your level.* In some cases, you may be one of several applicants interviewed simultaneously. In that case, you may find yourself interacting with other applicants as well as with your interviewer(s). The objective of this interview approach is to determine how well you function in a group. Another variety of the group interview is a *committee* or *panel* interview, in which several people will interview you alone at once.

In any of these situations, you should:

- Make eye contact with, and speak to, each individual
- Try to establish **rapport,** or *a relationship,* with everyone in the group
- Never interrupt anyone
- Think before you reply to a question, but don't pause too long
- Keep your answers short and direct.

Unstructured Interviews

The **unstructured interview** *is an informal session during which the interviewer will expect you to do most of the talking.* He or she will ask broad questions that you could answer in any number of ways. Employers like these kinds of interviews because they yield information about a candidate's opinions and reactions.

An unstructured interview can give you a great opportunity to sell yourself. You can bring up what you want to, as long as it relates to the question. The risk is that you might talk yourself right out of the job if you stray from the subject or say anything controversial. Stay focused: Talk about your ability to fill the position, your qualifications, and what you can do for the company. Don't get sidetracked into talking about irrelevant topics or personal trivia.

Structured Interviews

The **structured interview** *is a set of questions that the employer asks all candidates.* The questions are usually based on the job description. The drawback to this type of interview is that it does not allow you full opportunity to exhibit your personality, communication skills, or other attributes. You must stick to the canned questions the interviewer asks.

Stress Interviews

The **stress interview** *deliberately creates an environment that puts you under pressure so that the employer can see how you behave in tense situations.* This kind of interview is relatively rare. If you're applying for a job that may have a lot of stress, however, the employer may use it.

If you find yourself in a stress interview, stay calm. The interviewer may deliberately and frequently interrupt you, remain silent for long periods, or ask intimidating questions. Don't take the questions personally. Answer them as well as you can, and remember that the interviewer is testing you to see if you can handle stress.

Behavioral Interviews

A **behavioral interview** *is an interview during which the interviewer asks you to give examples of situations in which you demonstrated particular behaviors or skills.* Employers are using behavioral interviews more and more because they find they can often predict a potential employee's future conduct based on his or her past behavior.

During a behavioral interview, someone will ask you to describe in detail a particular event, project, or experience; how you dealt with it; and what the outcome was. Some questions might be:

- Describe a time when you faced a problem that tested your coping skills. What did you do?
- Give an example of a situation in which you had to make a quick decision
- What is one of your important goals? How are you doing in meeting it?
- Describe the most creative work-related project you have completed
- Give me an example of when you had to show good leadership.

The key to answering these questions is to be specific and honest. Don't describe how you should have behaved; describe how you *did* behave. If you later decided you should have behaved differently, explain why. The employer will be impressed to see that you learned from the experience.

In preparing for this type of interview, it's helpful to review your experience and have a few stories ready to tell. That way you don't hesitate or draw a blank when the interviewer asks you to relate one.

Other Types of Interviews

If you are applying for a job in another city, a prospective employer may ask you to do a *videotaped interview.* If you face a camera instead of a person, speak slowly and clearly and show enthusiasm. Body language is especially important on camera—the camera sees you somewhat differently than the human eye does.

A prospective employer may need to interview you by phone. Don't worry: Preparing for a *telephone interview* is just like preparing for a face-to-face interview.

During a *lunch interview,* you may be tempted to relax too much. Remember, this is still an interview. Order something that you can handle and eat easily, without too much mess. This probably isn't the time for lobster or spaghetti with tomato sauce!

Basic Interview Questions

Some standard questions pop up during virtually any interview, regardless of type. You'll also want to have a set of questions to ask at any interview. Here are some questions you'll probably have to answer at one point or other and some questions you may want to ask.

Questions Interviewers Ask

Tell me about yourself. The interviewer does not want to know about your hobbies, your boyfriend or girlfriend, or your favorite TV show. He or she wants to know what you think is important about yourself with respect to the job you've applied for. Take this opportunity to present your best qualities and to explain how much you are interested in the company. Focus on the company's needs, not yours.

What do you see yourself doing in five years? The interviewer wants to see if you plan or live day-to-day. To answer this question impressively, your career goals should relate to those of the company. This is also a good opportunity to ask about the career path for the position you are interviewing for.

What is your greatest weakness (or strength)? The question is about your work behavior. The interviewer wants to find out how well you know yourself. If you need to talk about a weakness, focus on one that you are correcting, and tell the interviewer how you are doing that. This will show that you are mature. Everyone has weaknesses, but not everyone admits them or is working to correct them.

Why should we hire you? Think about this question beforehand and have a few good reasons ready. Make your reasons specific: Match your skills with those of the job.

What salary do you expect? Many employers want to know if your salary expectations match what they are willing to pay. If possible, avoid salary negotiations until you actually have a job offer. If the interviewer presses you, give a salary range rather than a specific figure. For example, say, "I understand that positions of this type generally pay between $21,000 and $25,000. That range would be acceptable."

Why do you want to work for us? Do your research, and then give an honest answer about why you like the organization.

Questions You May Want to Ask

- What would a typical workday be like if I had this position?
- What is the expected career path in your organization for a person in this position?
- Do you have a formal training program? Can you describe it?
- How do you evaluate your employees? How often?
- From your experience, what would you say are the organization's greatest strengths?

Questions You Should Not Ask

- *What happened to the person who had this job before?* Answering this question could make the interviewer uncomfortable. Perhaps the employee moved on to a competing company. Or maybe the company asked the employee to leave because of poor performance. Frame this question in a positive way: Ask if the position is vacant because the person received a promotion.
- *Will I have to work overtime?* This might make the interviewer think that you don't want to work too hard.
- *How much job security do you offer?* Today's job market doesn't offer a great deal of security. Asking this question will only make you seem insecure.
- *When will I get my first raise?* This question is inappropriate until you have been hired.
- *What benefits does the company offer?* This question is not appropriate for the first interview, but you will want to find out the benefits of the job before you accept an offer.

How Employers Evaluate Interviewees

During and after the interview, your potential employer will be evaluating you. What is he or she looking for? There is no standard evaluation or rating form that all employers use. Each company evaluates applicants differently. How you dress and speak, your mannerisms, and the validity and content of your answers to questions will all influence the evaluation. The employer will probably evaluate you in three basic areas: *character, commitment,* and *competence.*

Character

Employers want to be sure you are a person with a positive personality and good habits. In evaluating your character, they will look at your:

- attitude
- appearance
- ability to communicate orally and in writing
- ability to work collaboratively
- self-confidence and poise
- school or work absenteeism record
- community or extracurricular activities
- leadership potential.

Commitment

Employers also want to be sure you really want to work for them, will show up for work, and won't leave them in a few months—after they've invested time and effort in training you for the job. When employers look for commitment, they are looking for:

- enthusiasm for the job and the company
- goals and self-motivation
- willingness to do what your employer asks.

Competence

Finally, potential employers need to be sure you can do the work and do it well. In evaluating your competence, they'll look at your:

- job-related skills and ability to perform the job
- grades on courses and tests
- educational qualifications for the job.

It's important to understand that the person who gets the job is not always the person with the best skills, education, and experience. An employer wants someone who fits with the organization and its culture. Your interpersonal skills are very important, and that's one thing the interviewer will look for. Can you take criticism? Are you a good team player? Are you flexible? Can you communicate well?

Your personality is also important—especially qualities such as creativity, warmth, diplomacy, and self-confidence. In the end, people hire people they like. After all, they have to work with you every day.

CHECKPOINTS

Lesson 3 Review

Using complete sentences, answer the following questions on a sheet of paper.

1. What are several things you should do to make sure your interview goes well?
2. Imagine that you have an interview next week at a major bank in your city. Describe what you will wear to the interview. List some types of clothing you should not wear.
3. List some body language you should avoid during an interview.
4. List and explain the different types of interview.
5. Why are more and more employers using behavioral interviews?
6. Give one question you are afraid an employer might ask you. Decide how you would respond to the question. Write down your answer.
7. List some questions you should ask during an interview.
8. List some questions you should not ask during an interview.
9. What are the three basic areas that an employer will evaluate you on? Give examples of each area and explain its importance.

Applying Interviewing Skills

10. Imagine that you've been asked to interview for a job you have your heart set on. Ask a friend or relative to do a role-play. Dress as if you were going to a real interview. Tell your interviewer to ask you the hardest questions he or she can. If you have a video camera, tape the interview. Play it back and analyze how you answered the questions. Pay attention to your body language.

RMA
RMA
MSgt.
JUST THINK OF M
GUIDANCE CO

CHAPTER

8

Developing Your Career Skills

Chapter Outline

Don't be afraid to give your best to what seemingly are small jobs. Every time you conquer one it makes you that much stronger. If you do the little jobs well, the big ones tend to take care of themselves.

—Dale Carnegie, self-improvement expert

LESSON 1

Planning Your Professional Development

Quick Write

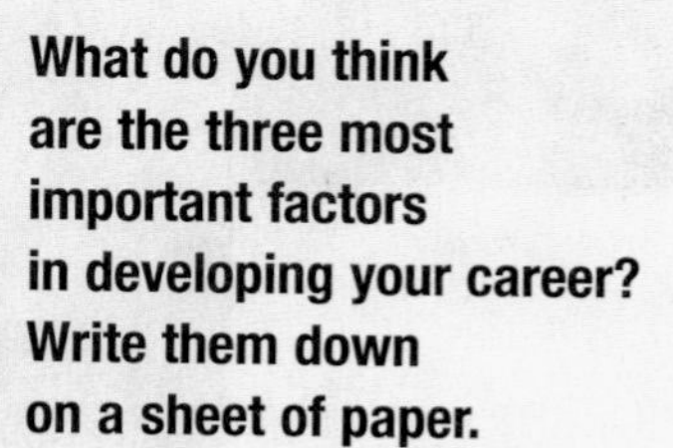

What do you think are the three most important factors in developing your career? Write them down on a sheet of paper.

Learn About...

- how to plan your professional development
- preparing a career portfolio
- organizational and personal values that contribute to success

How to Plan Your Professional Development

Your career is one of the most important parts of your life. Unless you are independently wealthy, you'll depend on it to earn a living. If you choose the right career, it will also give you great personal and professional satisfaction. It's one of the things that will help you eventually say, "I've lived a worthwhile life."

Professional development *includes all the activities necessary to have a successful career.* Professional development is a personal activity. No one can set your goals or plan your career for you.

Planning your career development means answering the following questions: What field do I want to work in? How high in that career do I want to advance? What steps must I take to qualify for the promotions I will need to achieve my goals?

For example, you may want a career in sales. Some sales representatives enjoy their work so much that they prefer to remain in that role. Others aspire to become sales managers, supervising the work of several sales representatives. Or, if they work for a large organization, they may want to become zone sales managers, regional sales managers, or sales vice presidents.

Your employer may offer training programs that will enable you to acquire new skills that you need in your current job and for future advancement. The company may provide opportunities to move on to higher-level jobs. Ultimately, however, you are in charge of your professional development. Why? Because the workplace has changed in recent decades. In your grandparents' day, an employee often spent his or her whole working life with one organization. That organization took care of professional development for its employees. Today, most people work for several organizations over the course of a lifetime. They can't depend on their employers to help them grow.

So most of your professional development will come from your own efforts. Just as you will have to do some research and other work to find a good job, you'll have to work to find good opportunities for professional development.

Vocabulary

- professional development
- career ladder
- career portfolio
- courtesy
- compassion
- dependability
- perseverance
- work ethics
- honesty

(continued on next page)

Knowledge, Skills, and Attitudes for Your Career

Planning your professional development includes two activities:

1. *identifying* the knowledge, skills, and attitudes you need for success in your career
2. *developing* that knowledge and those skills and attitudes.

Suppose your goal is to be a corporate executive. First, you have to identify the knowledge, skills, and attitudes you will need to do well in that career. Some of these might be:

Knowledge
- how to sell things
- how to manage money
- how to manage people
- how to manage a company.

Skills
- sales and marketing
- financial planning
- management and leadership
- organizational ability.

Attitudes
- concern for pleasing customers
- conscientious approach to handling money
- commitment to helping your subordinates grow professionally
- desire to promote the company's welfare.

Planning your professional development includes identifying the knowledge, skills, and attitudes you need for success.
Courtesy of Getty Images

To rise to the top in business, you'll eventually need to know more, acquire more skills, and cultivate other attitudes. But this list is a good starting point. You can make a similar list for any other career that you want to pursue.

Vocabulary

(cont.)

- integrity
- loyalty
- mutual trust
- competitiveness
- organizational values
- equity
- risk taking
- teamwork
- visionary leadership

You will need to develop new knowledge and skills throughout your career.
Courtesy of Davis Barber/PhotoEdit

How do you develop the knowledge, skills, and attitudes you need? You begin by getting an education. You complete high school with a strong grade point average. You learn as much as you can about the basics—subjects such as history, English, math, and science. These will help you in any job.

If you go to college, you will extend your education. You will major in a subject that coincides with your career ambitions. Graduate school could enable you to deepen your knowledge, skills, and attitudes.

If your career goal is to be a journalist, for example, you will study subjects that will give you the *knowledge* necessary to write about many subjects. In your classes, you will perform exercises and write articles that will help you acquire the *skills* to write news stories the way a professional journalist does. You might do an internship to get on-the-job experience. You will also bring certain *attitudes* with you to college that will help make you a good journalist. These attitudes include curiosity, objectivity, and a love for language. College will also help you refine those attitudes to the point where they become second nature. You'll be able to express them all the time in your work.

But high school, college, and graduate school are only the start of your professional development. You will need to continue to develop new knowledge, skills, and attitudes throughout your career. The organization you work for may give you the opportunity to enroll in a training program to improve your skills. It may pay tuition fees that will enable you to attend an adult education program in a community college or even enroll in classes at a university. It may offer you a chance to take part in career-testing programs to identify attitudes that you must develop to be successful. Some organizations may offer a **career ladder**, *a series of jobs that, over time, will take you higher and higher in the organization.*

You'll want to take advantage of as many of these opportunities as possible. Self-learning, however, is as important as taking courses. You'll find self-education opportunities everywhere, once you start looking.

Improve Your Knowledge

Be on the lookout for ways to improve your *knowledge* by reading books, magazines, and journals—even by watching quality television programs. Attend lectures by well-known people in your field. Take advantage of opportunities to travel and meet "as many different kinds of people as you can. You can also write articles for professional journals. Writing is one of the best ways to learn about a subject, because in order to explain it to others you have to know it well yourself.

Expand Your Skills

Practice and expand your *skills* by doing volunteer work. For example, if you're in the computer field, volunteer to help a community nonprofit organization maintain its computers. Teach computer skills at a local senior citizens' home. You'll have the satisfaction of helping others. At the same time, you'll improve your skills.

Develop Good Attitudes

Attitudes may seem more abstract than skills. But you can develop good attitudes if you work at them all day, every day. Whether you're on the job, in a volunteer program, out with your friends, or at home with your family, making a conscientious effort to develop a positive, "can do" attitude will help you become a better person—and a better professional. Look for the opportunity behind every challenge. Treat setbacks as learning experiences and move beyond them. Strive to see the glass as half full, instead of half empty.

Preparing a Career Portfolio

As you move forward with your professional development, people will often ask you about your background and accomplishments. The request might come from your boss if he or she is writing your annual evaluation. Or it might come when you are interviewing for a new job. You can provide this information orally if the person making the request has the time. But a more effective strategy is to do it in writing.

As you have learned, a résumé can be one tool for doing this. Another, more detailed tool is a career portfolio. A **career portfolio** *is a folder or notebook that contains information on you and your achievements over time.* It provides examples of your work and evidence of your accomplishments, your educational development, and your career growth.

Reasons for a Career Portfolio

Creating and maintaining a career portfolio has many advantages. A portfolio will:

- serve as an ongoing record of your completed work
- allow you to track your improvement and growth over time and to identify your strengths and career-growth needs
- make it easier to apply to schools and for jobs
- document your accomplishments as you move from one school or one job to another
- keep your family updated on your progress.

You may think you have little to put in a career portfolio at this time. Don't sell yourself short. If you've been participating in school and community activities, you'll have plenty to include. Start now, and review and expand your portfolio regularly. Soon it will be impressively strong.

Elements of a Career Portfolio

A career portfolio contains different elements, depending on its purpose. A college-application portfolio contains different materials than a job-application portfolio does. If you are applying for a scholarship based on academic accomplishment, your portfolio should contain information on grades and other evidence of academic success. If you are applying for a scholarship based on community activity, the portfolio should contain evidence of your work with neighborhood organizations. Although most portfolios are in print, sometimes your file will need to be electronic (for example, if you are applying for a job as a webmaster or web content developer).

Regardless of their purpose, most portfolios have these common elements:

- a cover page
- a cover letter (addressed and tailored to the person you're submitting it to)
- a table of contents
- a personal statement (a one-page summary of goals that relate to the job you are seeking or the school you're applying to)
- your résumé
- letters of reference
- transcripts, diplomas, and certificates
- a list of awards you've received
- samples of your schoolwork and job accomplishments
- names and contact information of people who have agreed to serve as your references.

Assembling Your Portfolio

Assemble all the materials listed above. Then select those that are most appropriate for the purpose at hand. You'll need a slightly different combination of materials for each portfolio, and you'll tailor the cover letter and table of contents accordingly.

Don't let your portfolio get too bulky. You don't want to overwhelm the reader. But do make sure that you include any needed support materials. If you received an award, for example, you should briefly explain its purpose. Also include explanations of the circumstances under which you wrote or produced any work samples.

Put your materials in logical order. If you're responding to a scholarship application, for example, put your materials in the order they appear on the application.

Make your portfolio as neat and professional looking as possible. Organize the contents so that they're easy to find. For example, if you include a great deal of information, consider including tabs or stapled sections.

Start a file folder for storing work you have accomplished and other material for your portfolio. Keep the original and copies. Mark the original in some way so you don't inadvertently put it in the portfolio and send it away.

In a separate section of your portfolio, keep contact information on people in your professional network, such as fellow AFJROTC cadets, other classmates, teammates, parents' friends, and people you meet at camp, at church, in business, or while traveling. Keep this information separate, because it is for your own use only. You should not share it with others.

Once you've assembled your portfolio, give it to a few friends or adults. Ask them for feedback and change the portfolio accordingly.

Updating Your Portfolio

Review the information in your portfolio at least three times a year. Remove anything that is outdated, such as phone numbers or e-mail addresses. Add anything new, such as a reference from the supervisor of an internship you've just completed.

Questions to Ask When Preparing a Portfolio

- **Purpose:** Why am I creating this portfolio? Is it for a particular school or academic program? A job? A scholarship? A promotion?
- **Audience:** Who will read this portfolio? My boss? A prospective employer? A scholarship committee? Community members?
- **Format:** How should I present this information? In a notebook? A folder? Electronically?
- **Required materials:** Have I included all the required documents?
- **Other information:** Do I need multiple copies of the portfolio? Whom should I contact if I have questions?

Keep your portfolio growing. To do this, look for opportunities to participate in activities you excel in, and then document your experiences. Get references from teachers when you've done well in their classes. The same goes for bosses. But go beyond this. For example, participate in an internship or join a school or community organization that is in line with your career goals. Do a good job for them; volunteer to do things, and take a leadership role if possible. Then ask the head of the group to write you a letter of reference. Creating a portfolio will keep you organized and ready for any opportunity that comes your way.

Organizational and Personal Values That Contribute to Success

In previous lessons you learned about the importance of personal values. Your values are a big part of who you are. They help determine how you handle difficult situations, how you make decisions, and how you relate to others. Good personal values are a key to your success in life.

Personal Values in the Workplace

The values of a workplace start with each individual's personal values. How do you measure up in these areas?

A Positive Attitude

Attitudes are of fundamental importance in any work setting—on an assembly line, in a classroom, at a construction site, or in an office. If you want to succeed, you must keep a positive attitude toward yourself, your coworkers, your boss, and even your boss's boss. This isn't always easy. It can be especially hard when you feel your coworker isn't pulling his or her share of the load, or when you think your boss is unfair. But don't be a complainer. Keep positive; look on the bright side.

The most popular and productive people in any work environment are usually those with the best attitudes. These people inject humor into work. They bolster team spirit. This makes everyone happier and more productive. An upbeat attitude is contagious. Continual negativism, on the other hand, will turn people off. It will eventually affect your success on the job.

Courtesy and Enthusiasm

Being courteous is more than saying "Please" and "Thank you." It's more than being polite. **Courtesy** *is consideration and cooperation in dealing with others*. Being courteous means always being helpful to other people—customers, coworkers, subordinates, supervisors, and anyone else you deal with.

Enthusiasm ties in both with a positive attitude and with courtesy. Each of these traits can spell success or failure for an organization. Can you remember a time when a worker in a store, a bank, or another business was not courteous to you or seemed bored? Did you feel like going back? Courtesy and enthusiasm, like a positive attitude, are contagious. Practice them wherever you are, and you will build a successful career.

Your organization and coworkers will judge you based on how you treat people.
Courtesy of Getty Images

Compassion and Caring

Compassion *is a feeling for and understanding of another person's situation.* To show compassion, put yourself in the other person's shoes. How does this person feel? Your organization and your coworkers will judge you based on how you treat people. When employees treat one another poorly, they create poor morale. Poor morale leads to poor performance.

Dependability and Reliability

Dependability *is the quality of being dependable or reliable.* It means showing up on time, to be sure, but it's more than that. A dependable person is one whom others can trust. Employers can count on people who are dependable and reliable to get the job done well and to get it done on time—even in tough times. Whether you are a boss or an employee, you always want to be dependable and reliable.

Perseverance and Diligence

Perseverance *is the quality of sticking to something until you achieve it.* It's persistence. A person who perseveres learns from mistakes. Perseverance is one of the most important factors in personal success. Don't be a quitter. No one becomes successful without a lot of hard work. And no organization gets to the top without employees who keep working hard until they reach their goals.

Personal and Organizational Values

Successful individuals and successful organizations share many of the same values. Among them are the following:

Work Ethics

Ethics are the basic values or standards that govern people and organizations. Showing good **work ethics** *means taking into consideration the effects of your decisions and actions on all people connected with your organization—employees, customers, owners, suppliers, and competitors.* The golden rule is a good basis for work ethics: "Do unto others as you would have them do unto you."

Ethics come into play when you have to make a difficult decision. When you face a decision at work, ask yourself three questions:

1. Is it legal? Will I be violating either civil law or company policy?
2. Is it balanced? Is my decision fair to all concerned in the short term as well as the long term? Does it promote win-win relationships?
3. How will it make me feel about myself? Will this decision make me proud? Would I feel good if a newspaper published my decision? Would I feel good if my family knew about it?

Making the decision, although challenging, is just the first step. The most difficult part of being ethical is *doing* what is right, not simply deciding what is right. It's usually easy to decide what you should do in a hypothetical situation. But would you actually do it?

Honesty and Integrity

Honesty *is the practice of being truthful, trustworthy, and sincere; it is refraining from lying, cheating, or stealing.* Honesty strengthens an organization. Even when the truth hurts, it is best in the long run to be open and honest. **Integrity** *is commitment to a code of values or beliefs that results in a unified, positive attitude and approach to life.* It is a sense of wholeness in your actions and beliefs. A person with integrity "walks the talk."

Honesty and integrity in making business decisions have significant long-term effects. A lack of honesty and of integrity, by contrast, eventually drives away customers and demoralizes employees.

Loyalty

Loyalty *is being faithful to someone or something.* Loyalty is a two-way street. If you tell an organization you will do something, you must follow through and do it. If you do not, you are being disloyal. Likewise, if an organization makes you a promise, it must follow through on that promise.

In today's work environment, where people change jobs more often they sometimes did in the past, loyalty is often in short supply. Be loyal: It helps make personal and organizational relationships successful.

Mutual Trust and Respect

Mutual trust *develops when people and organizations know that they can rely on one another to do the right thing.* Trusting someone does not mean that you necessarily agree with that person. It simply means that you know where he or she stands. You know that such people mean what they say. As a result, you respect them.

Trust and respect don't happen overnight: You must earn them over time. Personal and organizational trust are based on dependability, faith, and ongoing communication.

Competitiveness

Have you competed in a sports event, a spelling bee, a debate, or any other type of contest? If so, you know what competitiveness means. **Competitiveness** *is striving against others to achieve an objective.* In sports, the objective is simple: winning the game. In the workplace, the objective is sometimes more complex, but the purpose for competition is the same. Competitiveness is essential in a business environment. Your employer will value you if you can help the organization do well against the competition.

Patience

In a work environment, you may often be under pressure to get things done as quickly as possible. That won't always happen. Delays and problems will come up, despite your efforts. When they do, you'll have to be patient. *Patience* is the ability to bear difficulty, delay, frustration, or pain without complaint. People who are patient have a calming effect on those around them. Once people calm down, everyone can focus on getting the task done.

Patient people have a calming effect on those around them.
Courtesy of Getty Images

Organizational Values

From a career perspective, some values apply more to organizations as a whole than to their individual employees. **Organizational values** *include the combined personal values of the people in an organization and the values of the organization itself.* Strong organizational values such as the following can make the difference between a good organization and a great one.

Equity

Equity *is justice or fairness.* Equity is essential in human relationships. People want to work for an organization that has equity. For example, an equitable organization pays its employees fairly. It promotes people according to accepted practices that it sets forth in writing. Leaders of an equitable organization don't play favorites.

Risk Taking

Risk taking *is taking chances.* An organization usually needs to take risks if it wants to get ahead—otherwise it can get stuck in a rut or in outdated ways of doing things. It should not, however, take foolish risks. An organization that is a healthy risk taker is an exciting place to work. Its employees are stimulating people because they, too, have adventurous spirits.

Teamwork and Cooperation

Teamwork *is working together to identify and solve group-related problems and to achieve goals.* A spirit of cooperation pervades organizations whose employees excel at teamwork. Teamwork is as important in the workplace as it is on the basketball court or football field.

Visionary Leadership

Visionary leadership *is leadership exercised by people who have a clear sense of where they are guiding their organizations and who can persuade others to follow them.* Visionary leaders see into the future. Most people find it satisfying to work for an organization with visionary leaders because they feel they are participating in an important effort.

Teamwork is as important in the workplace as it is on the basketball court or football field.

CHECKPOINTS

Lesson 1 Review

Using complete sentences, answer the following questions on a sheet of paper.

1. What are the three basic areas of your life that you must identify and develop to have a successful career?
2. What are three reasons to have a career portfolio?
3. Name five things to include in a career portfolio.
4. What are three personal values that will help you be successful in the workplace? Do you have those values? If not, how can you develop them?
5. What are three values that are common to successful people and to successful organizations?
6. What are three organizational values that any successful organization should have?

Applying Professional Development Skills

7. Pick a career you would like to pursue. Make a list of the knowledge, skills, and attitudes you will need to succeed in that career. Then list ways that you will develop them.
8. Prepare your own career portfolio.

LESSON 2

Learning to Work With Others

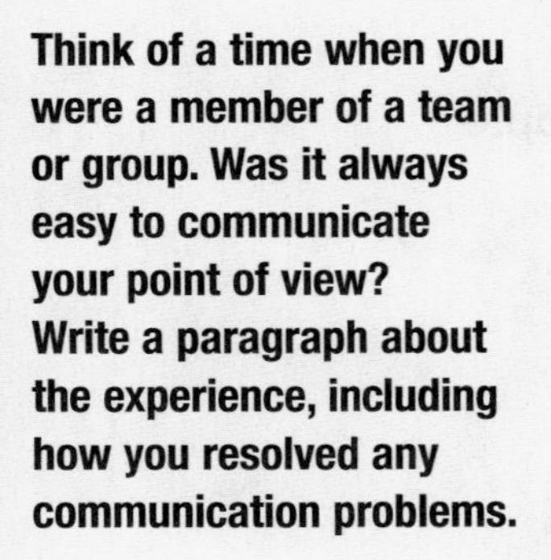

Quick Write

Think of a time when you were a member of a team or group. Was it always easy to communicate your point of view? Write a paragraph about the experience, including how you resolved any communication problems.

Learn About...

- the communication process
- barriers to effective communication
- communicating in organizations
- collaboration and teamwork

The Communication Process

Whenever you work with other people—at school, at work, or anywhere else—you have to communicate. *Communication* is the creation or sending of information, thoughts, and feelings from one person to another.

Communication has two sides. It includes *sending* messages, in speech, writing, or another medium, such as music or video. It also includes *receiving* messages through listening, reading, or watching, and, most important, understanding. The ultimate test of successful communication is understanding. If your listener understands your message, you have succeeded. If not, you have failed to communicate.

Words are a primary vehicle for communication. So when two people speak the same language and use the same vocabulary, communication should be easy, right? Well, not always. Words can have different meanings for different people. That's because people base the meanings of words not only on dictionary definitions but also on personal experience. For example, if you say to Brad and Cyndi, "I'll meet you at the club tonight," Brad might be happy, because he enjoys clubs. He's spent many happy evenings with friends in clubs. But Cyndi might be afraid because she was once in a club when there was a fire. The word *club* has a different **subjective meaning,** or *personal significance,* to each of your friends.

Subjective meanings vary even more for abstract words such as *democracy* and *freedom*. To the average American, *democracy* has a positive subjective meaning. It refers to a form of government in which the people elect their rulers. To someone from a country ruled by a dictator, however, *democracy* may imply chaos and lack of leadership. This is because he or she has never seen a democracy in action.

To discover if your listener has understood you, or to let a speaker know that you don't understand what he or she is saying, you either ask for or provide *feedback*. Feedback is the receiver's response to the sender's message. If you express ideas well and the person listens well but doesn't give you any feedback, you still have no idea whether you communicated successfully. Feedback closes the communication loop.

Recall that feedback is not always oral. Body language can be one of the most effective forms of feedback. A nod of the head signifies agreement and understanding; a frown might indicate confusion. Eye contact usually means the listener is with you; if a listener averts the eyes, you might be having a communication problem. Finally, one of the most effective forms of feedback is silence. Silence can speak volumes—it often indicates a failure of communication.

Vocabulary

- **subjective meaning**
- **distortion**
- **filtering**
- **semantics**
- **defensiveness**
- **informal communication**
- **grapevine**
- **formal communication**
- **horizontal communication**
- **vertical communication**
- **collaboration**

Verbal and Nonverbal Communication

There are two types of communication: *verbal* and *nonverbal*. The word *verbal* can refer to written as well as spoken, or oral, words. In this lesson, however, verbal communication refers to spoken words. Verbal communication consists of two actions: *speaking* and *listening*.

Speaking

When speaking, you must pay particular attention to three things: the tone of your voice, your emotions, and self-disclosure. For example, when you shout, your *tone of voice* makes you sound angry or upset, even if you are not. But a whisper can convey anger, too.

Because voice tone can be misleading, you also must be careful of your *emotions*. Your emotions convey silent messages that you may not be aware of. For example, if you don't trust a person, your verbal communication will usually convey that mistrust, whether you whisper, shout, or speak in a normal tone. If you are afraid of someone, your verbal communication will reflect that fear.

Be aware also of the power of *self-disclosure*. To communicate well, you must disclose yourself to others. You must let the other person see your fears, likes and dislikes, beliefs, and perceptions. But too much disclosure can be risky, especially in the workplace, where competitors as well as friends surround you. While some people will appreciate your honesty, others might take advantage of what they learn and use it against you. Think about who your listener is, and use self-disclosure accordingly.

Listening

Contrary to what many people think, listening is an active, not a passive, activity. *Active listening* is genuine, two-way communication. It's giving undivided attention to a speaker in a genuine effort to understand the speaker's point of view. Listening consists of four actions:

1. *hearing*—receiving the physical sound through your ears
2. *understanding*—interpreting and comprehending the message
3. *remembering*—retaining what you've heard
4. *acting*—responding by action or inaction.

It is not enough to hear. You must also understand, remember, and act.

Some people think they are communicating when all they're doing is talking. To communicate, however, you must have an active listener. If you tend to talk a lot, ask yourself whether people are actively listening or tuning you out. If they don't volunteer feedback, seek it out. Test their understanding. It will let you know how well you are communicating.

Truly listening is a form of paying attention. When you pay attention to someone, you focus on what he or she is saying and block out distractions such as background noise and competing thoughts. This isn't always easy—in fact, studies show that people often only really listen to about 25 percent of what others say. If you tend to dominate a conversation, force yourself to talk less and listen more. Then structure your response based on what you've heard.

One barrier to active listening is the fact that most people can understand information much more quickly than a speaker can provide it. As a result, a listener's mind might wander, return to the speaker, and then wander again many times during an average conversation. Think about the last time you listened to someone. Did your mind wander? Was it because the person wasn't speaking fast enough? If not, what was the reason?

Finally, fear and anger create barriers to good listening. If people are upset before they even begin to listen, or get angry soon after someone begins to talk, they won't hear much. Communication will suffer.

Nonverbal Communication

Nonverbal communication is communication without words. It's more common than you might think. Studies show that 70 percent of all communication is nonverbal.

Body language is the primary means of nonverbal communication. As you learned in the lesson on interviewing, body language includes things such as posture, eye contact, gestures, and distance from the other person. Keep aware of what you are doing with your body when you are communicating.

When in doubt about body language, mirror the other person. If the other person is folding his or her arms, do the same. It may help the other person feel more comfortable with you, too.

Six Rules for Effective Listening

1. **Don't evaluate what you're hearing.** Suspend judgment. Take it all in. Evaluate the speaker's ideas later.
2. **Don't anticipate.** Sometimes you may think you know what someone is going to say before he or she even says it. You might be right, but more often than not, you'll be wrong. Don't try to second-guess the speaker.
3. **Take notes to boost your recall, but don't go overboard.** People forget one-third to one-half of what they hear within eight hours. For this reason, taking notes can be helpful. If you focus too much on note taking, however, your listening suffers. Find the right balance.
4. **Listen for themes and facts.** Listen for the speaker's major themes as well as for important facts. Remember, the person is communicating ideas, not just words. Listen for the ideas.
5. **Really pay attention.** Pay attention; don't fake it. It's not that hard. In fact, concentrating takes less work than pretending does. Acting is difficult!
6. **Review.** If you're listening to a speech, periodically review in your mind the main points you've heard so far. Pretend you're going to summarize the speech to a friend later in the day. What key points would you mention?

Barriers to Effective Communication

Communication experts call the barriers to communication *noise*. Some of the most common forms of noise are *distortion, semantics, defensiveness, external noise,* and *mistrust*.

Distortion

Distortion *is a distraction that interferes with communication.* For example, you may try your best to listen to your history teacher, but you're distracted because you're worrying about your upcoming math exam. One experiment showed that at any given time in a college classroom, only 20 percent of the students are paying attention. Other types of distortion include *stereotyping,* or holding a concept that is based on oversimplified assumptions or opinions, rather than on facts, and **filtering,** or *hearing only what you want to hear.*

Semantics

Semantics *refers to the meaning of a word.* Consider, for example, the many dictionary meanings of an ordinary word such as *love*. Add to these the subjective meanings that a word such as this has, and you can see how communication barriers might arise. If you want to talk about love, make sure your listener understands the word in the same way you do. If you're not sure, define it up front and even ask for feedback if you think it's needed. Make sure the listener understands how you intend to use the word.

Defensiveness

When people feel threatened by communication, they may become defensive. **Defensiveness** *is an effort to justify oneself.* For example, if you feel a person is judging you wrongly, you may feel threatened. You become less likely to trust, or understand, what he or she says. You may become defensive if you think someone is trying to control or manipulate you, or if you think the other person has no concern for your welfare or feelings.

Just as you want other people to be supportive in their communication with you, you should support them. People are supportive when they judge fairly, do not try to control, are concerned about others' feelings, and listen to others' points of view.

External Noise

External noise in the environment is a barrier to communication. Noise doesn't have to be loud: While a jackhammer outside your window may certainly be a distraction, whispering can also be. External noise affects people differently—some people study best when music is playing; others find any kind of music a distraction.

Mistrust

Mistrust between two people or among group members can also create a barrier to communication. If you don't trust your boss, for example, he or she will have a hard time communicating instructions to you in a way you will understand and respond to. In an organization, trust comes from openness, constant feedback, freedom to act with integrity, and shared goals and values. One moment of dishonesty or lack of support for another person can ruin weeks, or even years, of efforts to build trust.

Communicating in Organizations

When you interact with others in an organization, you use many types of communication. The type of communication you use depends on the situation in which communication takes place, the positions of the people participating in the communication, and the nature of the information to be shared.

Informal and Formal Communication

Informal communication *refers to social interactions among people who work together or are associated with one another in some other way.* Informal communication happens when people gossip, tell stories, spread information, and participate in the **grapevine,** or *the informal channel of communication among people in an organization.* The grapevine can include both personal information—who just had a baby or who got fired—and business-related information, such as rumors about a new company product. Its reliability isn't guaranteed; it can have positive or negative effects on the organization.

Formal communication *is a structured, stable method of communication among people.* Speeches, memos, written instructions, e-mail, and Web communications are examples of formal communication. All official communication in an organization flows through this channel.

Horizontal and Vertical Communication

You can also define communication within an organization based on the direction in which it moves. For example, **horizontal communication** *is communication among people at the same level in an organization, no matter what department they are in.* If you are an entry-level worker in the finance department of a bank and you communicate with an entry-level worker in the marketing department, you are conducting horizontal communication. This kind of communication increases the organization's flexibility, helps with problem solving, and allows information sharing among the organization's various parts. Its primary drawback can be simply that there is too much of it.

Vertical communication *takes place between people at different levels within the same department.* The communication between you and your boss is vertical communication. The communication between your boss and his or her boss is also vertical communication. In most organizations, information flows fairly well from top to bottom; the challenge is usually to increase the amount of information that flows from bottom to top.

Written Versus Oral Communication

Written communication is essential in the workplace. If the leaders of an organization want to put into place new policy, for example, they should always communicate it in writing. The written document will ensure that everyone gets the same message. The company may later supplement the written message by oral communication. For example, it may schedule informal sessions during which employees may ask questions about the new policy.

Sometimes you must express one-on-one business communications in writing. For example, if your boss tells you that you will get a 10 percent raise next month, ask him or her to put it in writing. This should ensure that both of you remember the oral commitment.

Written communication, especially e-mail, is more likely to cause misunderstanding than oral communication. Be especially careful about communicating anything negative in e-mails. If you're like most people, you write e-mail messages and send them off quickly. Haste alone increases the possibility of miscommunication. The main problem with e-mail messages, however, is that the receiver can easily share them with others. To save yourself potential trouble and embarrassment, follow this basic rule of e-mail protocol: *Never* say something in an e-mail that you would not want the whole world to read.

In some cases, communicating verbally is much better than communicating in writing. Some issues or topics are so sensitive that it is best not to write them down. For example, if you must criticize a fellow employee, always do so face-to-face. This lets you use body language that conveys your support of the person. It also lets you read the other person's body language and adjust your words accordingly.

Ethics in Organizational Communication

Ethics plays a central role in the communication process, especially in an organization. You cannot collaborate with others and work as a team if you cannot trust one another to tell the truth and do what is right.

You may have read about ethical breakdowns in a few large US corporations in the past few years. Executives were dishonest in their communication with employees, stockholders, the public, and the government. As a result, stockholders and employees lost billions of dollars, companies failed, and the guilty parties often paid huge fines or went to jail. Ethical behavior—especially ethical communication—is essential on the job, at school, and in all other areas of your life.

Three Benchmarks for Ethical Communication

To ensure that you are being ethical in your communication, ask yourself three questions:

1. Is my message truthful, honest, and fair?
2. Am I communicating as clearly as I can? Misunderstanding can be an inadvertent source of unethical actions. Be sure everything is clear from the start.
3. If I am saying something negative (for example, if I'm a supervisor who must reprimand an employee), am I communicating in a way that protects the other person's dignity and sustains the relationship? A good rule of thumb when communicating something negative is to condemn the action but never the person.

Collaboration and Teamwork

Collaboration *is working with others in a team or group.* Effective collaboration leads to innovation, quality improvement, and the sharing of knowledge.

People must communicate to collaborate. To communicate effectively, you must understand people's different communication styles.

You've probably realized by now that people can't collaborate if they can't communicate. But different people have different communication styles. These styles quickly become evident when a team or group begins to collaborate on a project. How should team members overcome differences in communication and work styles?

The Myers-Briggs Type Indicator (MBTI), which you read about in an earlier lesson, can come in handy at this point, because communication style relates closely to personality type. You may recall that according to the MBTI, everyone fits into one of two choices in four categories: extraversion and introversion; sensing and intuition; thinking and feeling; and judgment and perception.

Table 8.1 shows some of the basic preferred methods of communication for each MBTI personality type.

TABLE 8.1

Personality Type and Communication Preferences

Extraversion	Introversion
Communicate energy and enthusiasm	Keep energy and enthusiasm inside
Respond quickly	Think before responding
Focus on people and things	Focus on ideas and thoughts
Like to communicate in groups.	Prefer one-to-one communication.
Sensing	**Intuition**
Like to talk about evidence (facts, details) first	Like to talk about broad issues first
Like to use an orderly, step-by-step approach	Like to use a roundabout approach
Like specific examples	Like general concepts
Like to follow an agenda.	Prefer open-ended agendas.
Thinking	**Feeling**
Prefer to be brief and concise	Prefer to be sociable and friendly
Can be critical and objective	Can be appreciative
Convinced by reasoning	Convinced by enthusiastic, personal information
Value logic.	Value emotions and feelings.
Judgment	**Perception**
Like deadlines	Don't like deadlines
Dislike surprises and want advance warning	Enjoy surprises and last-minute changes
State positions and decisions clearly	Willing to change views when needed
Focus on the task.	Focus on the process.

Now imagine what happens when two or more people of different MBTI types try to communicate and collaborate. For example, if you are a "Thinking" personality, you probably prefer to be brief and concise. You like to state your opinions directly. You probably like to work with people who are the same as you. If a colleague on your team is a "Feeling" personality, however, he or she may prefer not to be so direct. That person might like a more relaxed, indirect style of communication. In fact, the other person may take offense at your forthright approach.

So what do you do? This is where your communication skills come in. Pay attention to what you are communicating verbally and nonverbally. Choose your words and tone carefully. Practice active listening. Get feedback. Pay attention to your body language as well as the other person's. Can you see why communication is one of the most important aspects of working in an organization?

Teamwork and Communication

The opportunity to be a member of a team is one of the most rewarding parts of working in an organization. A four-person team can usually accomplish much more than those same four people could accomplish working individually. This is because a good team gives every member a chance to contribute his or her unique skills to a project.

Think of a doctor. Doctors are highly trained professionals, yet they can't do it all alone. For this reason, they work in teams that consist of nurses, anesthesiologists, paramedics, midwives, interns, pharmacists, and others. Teamwork is essential not only in health care, but also in business, education, and the military—just about everywhere.

When a group shares a goal and is able to think and act as one, it's a satisfying and productive experience for the individuals and the organization. But working in teams can also be frustrating. When you have to work with people who are not your personality type, who have a different cultural background, or who have different ideas about how to attain the team's goals, you have to be careful about what you say and how you say it.

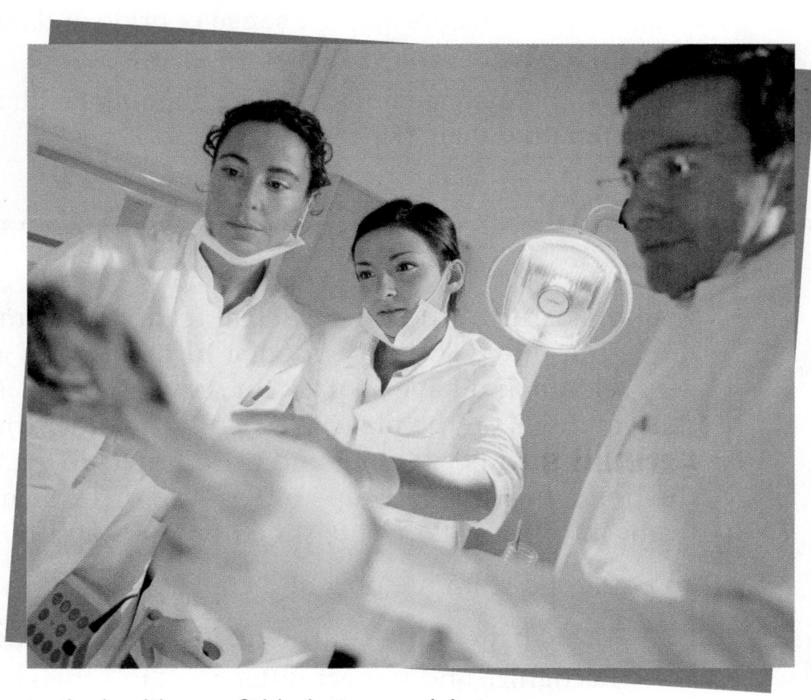

In the health-care field, doctors work in teams that consist of nurses, anesthesiologists, pharmacists, and many others.
Courtesy of Peter Wattendorff/zefa/Corbis Images

Some people think that good team members have to be good friends. That's not necessarily true. Good team members do, however, have to be good communicators. Good collaborators know how to take personality, cultural, and philosophical differences among team members and make those differences work for the team's benefit.

Characteristics of an Effective Team

- **Purpose:** Members share an understanding of why the team exists—they are invested in accomplishing its mission and goals
- **Priorities:** Members know what needs doing, when, and who should do it
- **Roles:** Members know their roles—the team leader assigns tasks to the people best qualified to do them
- **Decisions:** Team members understand who holds authority and decision-making responsibility
- **Conflict:** Team members deal with disagreements openly—they understand that overcoming conflict is essential to team effectiveness and personal growth
- **Personal Traits:** Members feel their personalities are appreciated and that they contribute to the welfare of the group
- **Norms:** The group sets and adheres to well-defined performance standards
- **Effectiveness:** Team meetings are efficient and productive—members enjoy working together
- **Success:** Members share a sense of pride and accomplishment when the team achieves its goals
- **Training:** Team members receive ongoing feedback and opportunities for updating their skills.

Take the batting order of a baseball team, for example. Not everyone is a slugging home-run hitter. Some are good at hitting singles and doubles. Others strike out very seldom and have a knack for drawing walks. The manager takes these various skills and sets up the players to bat in the order that will best benefit the team. He wants the first, second, and third hitters to get on base so the fourth batter—the home-run or "clean-up" hitter—can drive them in and score more runs. Successful teams in other walks of life similarly find ways to best use each team member.

To be a good team member and collaborator, you should do the following:

- Participate fully—contribute ideas and solutions
- Recognize and respect differences in others
- Value the ideas and contributions of others
- Listen and share information
- Ask questions and get clarification
- Keep your commitments
- Be flexible and respect the partnership created by the team
- Have fun and care about the team and the outcomes
- Work for a climate of trust and open, honest communication.

Different Approaches to Life and Work

Remember that different people at the workplace will have different approaches to life and work. These approaches aren't necessarily wrong—they're just different. Some have their origin in personality; others are based on an individual's personal philosophy. People in different circumstances will also balance different priorities, such as spouse, work, family, education, and religious faith, in different ways. Others will complete a task quite differently from you.

The key point is not to ignore these differences or get upset by them. It's to figure out how to make the most of what each individual brings to the workplace.

CHECKPOINTS

Lesson 2 Review

Using complete sentences, answer the following questions on a sheet of paper.

1. What are three barriers to communication? What can you do to overcome each of them?
2. Explain the importance of ethical communication.
3. What is active listening? Why is it important?
4. What is your Myers-Briggs personality type? What challenges would you expect when communicating and collaborating with someone whose Myers-Briggs type was exactly the opposite of your own? What would you do to solve these challenges?
5. Suppose you work with someone who grew up in another country, but who speaks English well. How would you go about learning to communicate and collaborate better with that person?

Applying Collaboration Skills

6. Think about a time when you disagreed with someone—a friend, family member, or teammate. Write a one-page paper on the communication and collaboration difficulties you faced, and how you might better overcome such difficulties in the future.

LESSON 3

Seeking Feedback and Promotions

Quick Write

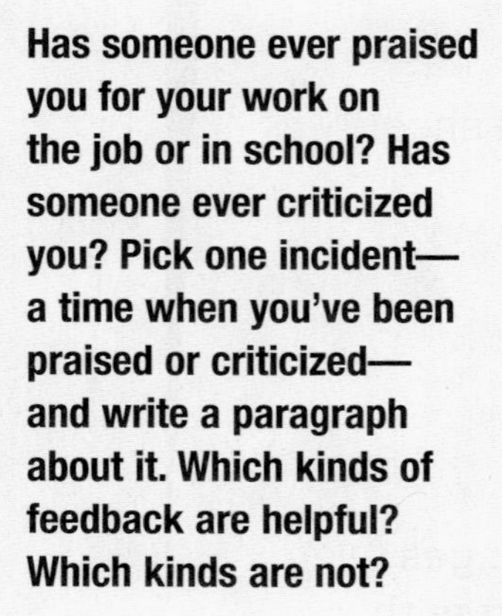

Has someone ever praised you for your work on the job or in school? Has someone ever criticized you? Pick one incident—a time when you've been praised or criticized—and write a paragraph about it. Which kinds of feedback are helpful? Which kinds are not?

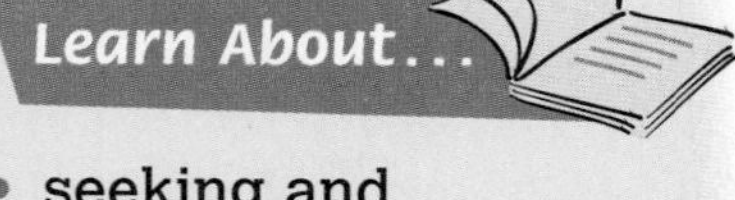

Learn About...

- seeking and receiving feedback in the workplace
- earning a promotion
- developing a career-path strategy

Seeking and Receiving Feedback in the Workplace

You've learned that giving and receiving feedback is part of the communication process. Feedback may involve asking a question, repeating information for understanding, or providing other input in response to someone else's words or actions. It can be verbal or nonverbal.

Although feedback is important in any communication, it is essential in the workplace. Feedback can come from your boss or your coworkers. In some jobs, it comes from customers.

Feedback is a good source of motivation. It lets you know whether you're doing good work. It can reassure you. It can also provide suggestions for improvement. You need other people's feedback, and they need yours. If well used, feedback leads to improvements that can benefit individuals and organizations.

Feedback can come from your boss, coworkers, or customers.
Courtesy of Digital Vision/Getty Images

Feedback can be informal or formal. Informal feedback occurs daily in the course of business operations. If you don't get the feedback you think you need to do your job well, you should seek it out—from your boss or others. In many workplaces, formal feedback occurs on a scheduled basis. It's often tied to a supervisor's evaluation of an employee's work.

Vocabulary

- performance appraisal
- 360-degree feedback
- halo effect
- promotion
- benefits
- merit promotion
- ability promotion
- career-path strategy

Seeking Feedback

Suppose you labored hard on a project at work. You spent several days doing research and writing a draft. You polished the draft to make sure it was the best you could do. You presented it to your boss, and all he or she said was "Thanks." That's the last you heard about it. The boss didn't give you any feedback. As a result, you don't know for sure whether your work was good or bad. You don't have any tips for how to do it better the next time.

Unfortunately, lack of feedback is common in the workplace. It's usually not intentional. Sometimes bosses and others are so busy that they just forget. Or they may assume that as long as they don't criticize your work, you automatically understand that they approve of it.

What's the solution to this communication gap? It's simple: If your boss doesn't give feedback, ask for it. As you hand in a report, say to your boss, "Could you please let me know if this is what you need? And how I could I make it better?" Such questions will show your boss that you want to improve. That alone will be impressive. And when you ask the question, it helps your boss remember that you value feedback. You may soon start to receive it.

Feedback can come from just about anyone in an organization. For example, if you are new to a job, seek out experienced people whom you can trust to evaluate your performance. Their feedback can be just as helpful as your supervisor's remarks.

Also be aware that feedback isn't only a vertical, top-down activity. Feedback should flow horizontally as well. Team members should evaluate each other as well as the team itself. You should ask for feedback from your colleagues, coworkers, and fellow team members. Ask them to be honest about your strengths and weaknesses. Give them feedback, too.

Finally, if you deal with customers, always ask them how you and the company are doing. People appreciate requests for their opinions. It shows them that you care about doing a good job.

Receiving Feedback

Informal feedback helps organizations and their employees improve continually. It allows supervisors, employees, and team members to be aware of their day-to-day performance. But organizations also need a more regular, structured means of providing feedback. They do this through a variety of evaluation processes.

The Performance Appraisal

One means of formal feedback in an organization is a **performance appraisal,** or *a systematic review of how well an individual employee has performed during a specified period.* Some companies refer to this as a *performance review* or a *performance evaluation.* A performance appraisal is often based on written standards or expectations that the employee and supervisor have discussed in advance. If you're a new employee, you may receive a copy of these standards at the time the organization hires you. A performance appraisal is a tool for growth. It is often part of a long-range plan for an employee's professional development.

If your organization gives performance appraisals, your boss will probably schedule one with you once or twice a year. It will be a one-on-one session—just you and your boss will take part. Your supervisor may use the results of your appraisal to decide whether to give you a salary increase or a promotion. If necessary, a boss can also use the appraisal to initiate disciplinary action.

You should look forward to these private sessions with your boss. They'll give both of you a chance to review your progress, your problems, and your contribution to your group's work. They'll let you know whether your work is meeting the company's standards, values, and goals. They'll identify your strengths as well as your weaknesses. A good appraisal will also offer specific suggestions on how to overcome your weaknesses. If your organization doesn't give formal performance appraisals, you should ask your boss for an informal one at least yearly.

To get the most out of a performance appraisal, prepare for it. Think about what you've accomplished since your last appraisal or since you joined the organization. Think about what strengths you've shown, what weaknesses you have uncovered, or even what mistakes you have made. (Some supervisors will ask you to write a memo highlighting what you think are your accomplishments during the evaluation period.) Make notes and bring them to the meeting. If you've identified weaknesses and mistakes, show what you are doing to correct them. Most organizations will tolerate mistakes, at least the first time, if you show that you understand the error and have taken steps to ensure it won't happen again.

360-Degree Feedback

Another type of formal feedback in organizations is **360-degree feedback,** *which is a performance appraisal that comes from all levels around the employee—from a boss, coworkers, and subordinates, as well as the employee himself or herself.* The "360 degrees" refers to the degrees in a circle, and like a circle, this appraisal is complete. It gives everyone an opportunity to provide input. Such 360-degree feedback lets you learn how people see you from many angles. It can be even more helpful than a performance appraisal, which evaluates you from only one perspective—your supervisor's.

Getting feedback—both formal and informal—is important in just about every situation in life. In school, you get feedback from teachers. You might meet with them periodically and ask them how you are doing and how you can improve. The school also provides a formal feedback system—grading and report cards. Outside the classroom, you may ask friends or family to read your papers and give you comments. If you're an athlete, your ultimate feedback is winning or losing a game or receiving a trophy. You even face feedback in dating. If someone likes you, you know you are doing well!

Getting feedback—whether a formal award or an informal comment—is important in almost every facet of life.
Courtesy of Yellow Dog Productions/The Image Bank/Getty Images

If you aren't getting feedback, seek it out. It can make the difference between doing only a fair job and achieving real success.

Responding to Feedback

Responding to feedback can be difficult. If the feedback is positive, you'll naturally be proud. But don't become arrogant. Instead, ask the person what you could do to improve your work even more. And never let a positive appraisal be an excuse for coasting. The workplace is competitive. You need to continue to do your best every day.

If the feedback is negative, don't get defensive. Don't respond with a sentence that begins with the words, "But I . . . ." That's a sure indication that a defensive statement is about to emerge. Learn from what the person giving the feedback tells you. Ask polite questions that help you understand the remarks and see things from the other person's point of view. Above all, don't reply to the reviewer in anger. Go away and think about what the reviewer has said so you can come up with a calm and useful response.

When assessing whether you've received fair feedback, watch out for the halo effect. The **halo effect** *is a reviewer's or boss's tendency to assume that if an employee is above (or below) average in one area of performance, he or she is above (or below) average is all areas.* The halo effect can also stem from a reviewer's tendency to rate someone based on experience rather than on recent observations. For example, if you've always received great appraisals but have begun to get lazy recently, the reviewer may give you a good rating solely based on past performance. On the other hand, if you've done only fair work in the past but have recently made a real commitment to do well, the reviewer may give you a mediocre rating because he or she is basing the review on your previous efforts.

Whether feedback is positive or negative, remember that people sometimes do have biases that can interfere with an objective appraisal of someone else's work. It's a fact of life that people will not always judge you fairly. The bottom line: Always be aware of your strengths and weaknesses, no matter what others say. In the light of this self-knowledge, listen carefully to others. And always give and receive feedback graciously.

Earning a Promotion

If you've worked for an organization for a while and done a good job, you may be eligible for a **promotion,** or *a new job at a higher level.* This new position will enable you to use the skills and knowledge you've developed in your current job and give you opportunities to develop new ones. A promotion will usually give you a higher salary and more impressive title.

A promotion may also increase your **benefits,** or *compensation you receive from your employer in addition to your salary.* Benefits can include a number of things: health insurance, more paid vacation days, participation in a company retirement-savings plan, life insurance, or a company car, just to name some of the most common. Many employers offer these kinds of benefits as a way of building good employer-employee relations. These employers value their employees and want them to stay loyal to the company or organization. For some employees, such benefits—especially health insurance—can be the single determining factor in deciding whether to stay with one organization or to accept a job with another.

But promotions have disadvantages as well as advantages. A promotion will mean more responsibility and higher expectations. You might have to work longer hours. You may have to supervise people for the first time, or your supervisory responsibilities may increase. If you think management isn't one of your strengths, you may initially be uncomfortable in that role.

Some people turn down promotions if they think the disadvantages outweigh the advantages. For example, if you value your free time and feel that a new job will require you to give up too many personal activities, think twice about accepting a promotion. But if the new job is an important step in reaching your career goal, you'll probably jump at the opportunity to grow and to learn.

Types of Promotions

There are two kinds of promotions: merit promotions and ability promotions.

A **merit promotion** *is based on your performance in your current job.* Merit promotions are like rewards. You get more money and a higher position because you've done well in your present post.

An **ability promotion** *is based on your potential to do a new job, rather than how you did in your old one.* You might think of an ability promotion as a challenge. It rests on someone's belief that you are able to handle broader responsibilities.

Both types of promotions result from someone else's estimation of your abilities. Ultimately, however, you are the person who will do the job, and you need to be comfortable in it. Before accepting a promotion, be sure you understand what you are getting into and that you can do what the new job requires. You don't want to be a victim of the "Peter principle." This principle, popularized by Dr. Laurence J. Peter, states that employees of an organization are eventually promoted to their highest level of competence. After this point, further promotions raise them to a level at which they are no longer competent. When this happens, the organization, as well as its employees, may suffer. The person is not comfortable in the job because he or she can't do it well.

If you like challenges and feel ready to move to a higher level, however, ability promotions are usually exciting. The key is self-knowledge. You must be aware of your strengths and weaknesses. You must have the self-confidence to accept new opportunities, but you should not try to exceed your limits.

One more thing to keep in mind about promotions: If you receive a promotion, you might find that your coworkers resent your success. Some may feel that they, not you, deserved the promotion. Deal with this through your attitude. Be sensitive to other people's feelings. Never brag or boast.

How to Get a Promotion: Some Tips

As you've seen, promotions have pluses and minuses. As a result, some people have mixed feelings about promotions. They are happy to receive an offer of a promotion, but they don't necessarily seek it out. Other people seek promotions.

If you decide it's time for a promotion, you should do several things:

If you've developed good relationships with many people in your organization, they'll be likely to recommend you for recognition and promotion.
Courtesy of the US Air Force

1. *Seek more responsibility in your current job.* You will have to prove that you deserve a promotion. Pave the way by taking on more responsibility whenever you can. Volunteer to tackle new and difficult projects, and complete them successfully.
2. *Document the good things you've done in your current job.* Keep a list of projects you've successfully completed, money you have saved or earned for the company, suggestions you've made that increase productivity, and any other accomplishments or attitudes that make you a valuable employee. Share this list with your boss during your performance appraisals and at other times as appropriate. Convince your boss that if you've done this much in a lower position, you could do much more in a higher one.
3. *Understand the responsibilities of the new job and do the needed preparation.* Many jobs look enticing from the outside. But when you find out what they involve, you may realize you are not prepared. For example, if you are a beginning journalist, you might ask your editor for the city hall beat. You want to write about the mayor and other city officials.

   But think about the knowledge and experience that this assignment would entail. Do you understand how city government works? Are you confident enough to ask the important questions that the public wants to know? Can you write on a tight deadline without making mistakes? Make sure you're ready for the job. Otherwise, your boss will not take your request seriously. Even worse, you might get the job and fail.

4. *Be prepared to explain why you are a good match for the new position.* Why should your boss promote you, and not someone else, to this position? In a competitive situation, you must convince your boss that you are the best one to fill it. Outline your strengths and explain how they meet the requirements of the job you're seeking.
5. *Be able to explain why promoting you will help the organization.* Your boss is not going to promote you just because you want more money or a more impressive title. You'll get a promotion if the organization believes you will be more valuable in your new position than you are in your current one. Be able to persuade your boss that this is true.
6. *Know where you want to go with your career and how a promotion fits with your ambitions.* If you're sure of your career goal and can help your boss understand how this new position is in line with that goal, your boss will be likely to promote you. If you're uncertain about your career goal, your boss may question your ability to advance. An organization wants strong, confident leaders who know where they're headed.
7. *Develop a good relationship with your employer.* Employee-employer relationships are essential to achieving promotions. This means establishing good relations not only with your boss, but also with other high-ranking people in the organization—your boss's boss, people in the human resources department, and other managers. If your boss is considering you for promotion, he or she may ask such people what they think of you. If you've developed good relationships with many people in the organization, they'll be likely to recommend you for promotion. Don't become so immersed in your work that you forget to build relationships.

Developing a Career-Path Strategy

A *career path* is the route a person follows in pursuing his or her career goals.

Suppose, for example, that you want to become the branch manager of a bank. Figure 8.1 shows several career paths that you might pursue to get to reach this position. The diagram shows many bank positions, and the arrows indicate where each position could lead. The positions shown in the diagram don't have to be in the same organization. You could be a teller in one bank, then move on to be a loan analyst and assistant branch manager in another, and then gain a position as the branch manager at a third bank.

To achieve your career goal, you must have a **career-path strategy**, or *a plan for how you will make progress in your career.* A career-path strategy will help ensure that you reach your goal as quickly and efficiently as possible.

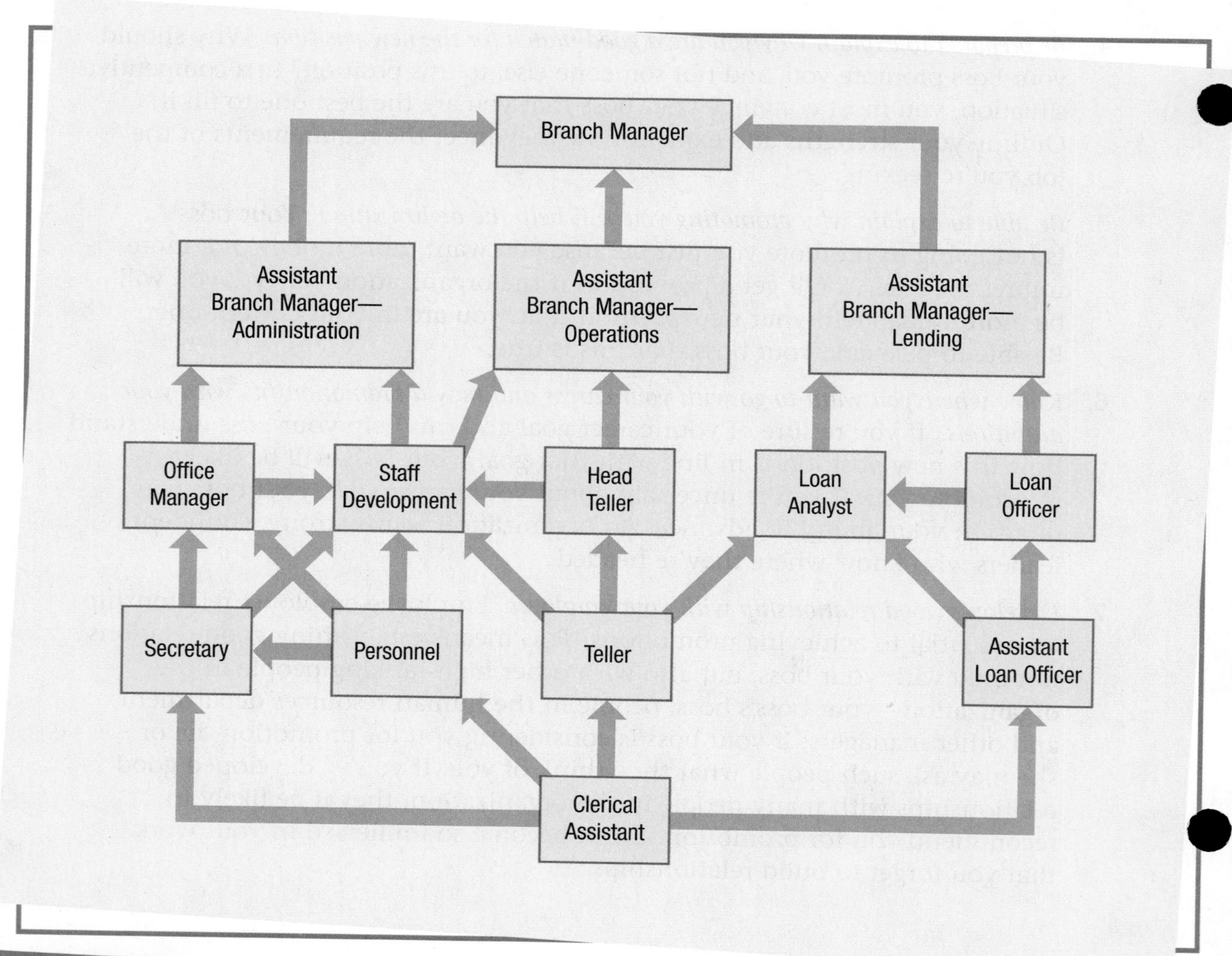

FIGURE 8.1

Potential Career Paths in a Bank Branch Office

From Tucker, Mary L., Anne M. McCarthy, and Douglas A. Benton. (2002). *The Human Challenge: Managing Yourself and Others in Organizations.* Upper Saddle River, NJ: Prentice-Hall, p. 75.

A career-path strategy is a written document that sets forth everything you'll need to do to gain the knowledge, skills, and competence to function well in the career you've selected. Your school or employer can help, but it's ultimately up to you to develop your career-path strategy. You must take the initiative in planning your career. If you know what career path you want to pursue, you can start to outline a strategy now. You can also do this during college or when you begin working. But the sooner you start, the better.

Begin your career-path strategy by writing down your ultimate goal: for example, to be the manager of a branch bank. Then outline the types of positions you want to hold and the organizations (by name or by type) that you want to work for as you progress toward your goal. Set a time frame for your short-term goals. For example, you may want to be a bank teller for two years and then become a head teller.

But what if a head teller position isn't available in your bank at the time you feel you're ready to move up to that job? You could wait until a position became open at your bank, but that might take a long time. To keep your career path on track, you'll have to be aware of opportunities at other banks that you would like to work for. Then when you're ready for a promotion, investigate openings at these banks. In the meantime, look for opportunities to get to know important people in other banks, so they won't feel you're a stranger when you apply for a job. In fact, if you network successfully, one of these people might even call you and ask if you're interested in a new job. It's a good idea to look five, 10, and even 20 years down the road when developing your career-path strategy.

When you write your career-path strategy, include the educational qualifications you'll need—such as degrees—and the training each job requires. What are the best schools in your field? If your goal is to be a branch manager, choose a college that has a good program in business and finance. You may want to go to graduate business school as soon as you get your bachelor's degree. Another option is to work in your field for a few years between college and graduate school. In that case, you could work as a teller after college, move on to a head teller position, and then go to graduate school. After graduate school, you could apply to be an assistant branch manager, which is the next step on your career path. As soon as you enter the workplace, be sure also to take advantage of any training programs your employer offers.

Think about informal, as well as formal, opportunities for learning. Ask yourself, "What other experience do I need to reach my career goals?" To be a branch bank manager, you may want to write articles for publications in the banking field. You may want to learn about the newest software in the banking field. For other career goals, you might need to learn another language or travel to certain countries or regions of the world. It also might be helpful to become active in professional associations and to attend their local and national meetings. This kind of networking is essential throughout your professional life.

Ultimately, you want to become an authority in your field—someone to whom others look for answers and expertise. A career-path strategy is an excellent way to ensure you'll achieve your professional goals.

Steps in Career Advancement

1. Learn how to learn
2. Learn from your job
3. Perform your job well
4. Know your potential next jobs
5. Try to understand your next job
6. Find a mentor and develop a network
7. Keep track of your career accomplishments
8. Make clear career choices.

From Tucker, Mary L., Anne M. McCarthy, and Douglas A. Benton. (2002). *The Human Challenge: Managing Yourself and Others in Organizations.* Upper Saddle River, NJ: Prentice-Hall, p. 75.

CHECKPOINTS

Lesson 3 Review

Using complete sentences, answer the following questions on a sheet of paper.

1. Why is feedback so important in workplace communication?
2. Is it a good idea to ask your boss for feedback? Why or why not?
3. Name one of the two formal appraisal systems described in this lesson and explain how it works.
4. What do you need to watch out for when receiving feedback?
5. What are four things that you should do when seeking a promotion?
6. Explain why many employers offer additional benefits to employees.

Applying Feedback and Promotion Skills

7. At this point in your life, what career do you think you will pursue? Outline a career-path strategy that would enable you to reach that goal.

McREL Standards

UNIT 1 Mapping Your Future

Correlated to McREL Standards for Life Work, Self-Regulation, Thinking and Reasoning, Working With Others, Behavioral Studies, and Language Arts

McREL Standards	Unit 1: Mapping Your Future
Life Work (LW)	
LW 1. Makes effective use of basic tools	Researching and Choosing Careers, 6–23 Military Careers, 24–44 Careers in Aerospace, 45–61 Aptitudes and Orientations, 64–78 Career Paths, 79–92 Educational Paths, 93–107
LW 2. Uses various information sources, including those of a technical nature, to accomplish specific tasks	Learning from Others' Experience, 3 Researching and Choosing Careers, 6–23 Applying Career Skills, 44, 61, 92 Applying Personality Skills, 78 Applying Education Skills, 107
LW 4. Studies or pursues specific job interests	Learning from Others' Experience, 3 Applying Career-Choosing Skills, 23 Military Careers, 24–44 Careers in Aerospace, 45–61 Career Paths Based on Your MBTI Personality Type, 73–77
LW 5. Makes general preparation for entering the work force	Researching and Choosing Careers, 6–23 Military Careers, 24–44 Careers in Aerospace, 45–61

Copyright © 2003 McREL: Mid-Continent Research for Education and Learning, 2550 S. Parker Road, Suite 500, Aurora, CO 80014, Telephone: 303-337-0990, www.mcrel.org/standards-benchmarks

Standard	Lesson
LW 6. Makes effective use of basic life skills	Researching and Choosing Careers, 6–23 Military Careers, 24–44 Careers in Aerospace, 45–61 Aptitudes and Orientations, 64–78 Career Paths, 79–92 Educational Paths, 93–107
Self-Regulation (SR)	
SR 1. Sets and manages goals	Researching and Choosing Careers, 6–23 Military Careers, 24–44 Careers in Aerospace, 45–61 Aptitudes and Orientations, 64–78
SR 2. Performs self-appraisal	Career Direction—Getting to Know Yourself, 8–9 Aptitudes and Orientations, 64–78
SR 3. Considers risks	Researching and Choosing Careers, 6–23 Military Careers, 24–44 Careers in Aerospace, 45–61 Career Paths, 79–92 Educational Paths, 93–107
SR 4. Demonstrates perseverance	Researching and Choosing Careers, 6–23 Military Careers, 24–44 Careers in Aerospace, 45–61 Career Paths, 79–92 Educational Paths, 93–107
SR 5. Maintains a healthy self-concept	Career Direction—Getting to Know Yourself, 8–9 Aptitudes and Orientations, 64–78
Thinking and Reasoning (TR)	
TR 1. Understands and applies the basic principles of presenting an argument	Applying Career Skills, 44
TR 2. Understands and applies basic principles of logic and reasoning	Applying Career-Choosing Skills, 23 Applying Career Skills, 44 Applying Personality Skills, 78 Applying Education Skills, 107
TR 3. Effectively uses mental processes that are based on identifying similarities and differences	Learning from Others' Experience, 3 Applying Career-Choosing Skills, 23 Applying Personality Skills, 78 Applying Education Skills, 107
TR 6. Applies decision-making techniques	Applying Career-Choosing Skills, 23 Applying Career Skills, 44 Applying Education Skills, 107

Working With Others (WO)	
WO 3. Works well with diverse individuals and in diverse situations	Aptitudes and Orientations, 64–78
WO 4. Displays effective interpersonal communication skills	Applying Career Skills, 44 Applying Personality Skills, 78
WO 5. Demonstrates leadership skills	Applying Personality Skills, 78
Behavioral Studies (BS)	
BS 1. Understands that group and cultural influences contribute to human development, identity, and behavior	Aptitudes and Orientations, 64–78
BS 2. Understands various meanings of social group, general implications of group membership, and different ways that groups function	Aptitudes and Orientations, 64–78
BS 3. Understands that interactions among learning, inheritance, and physical development affect human behavior	Aptitudes and Orientations, 64–78
BS 4. Understands conflict, cooperation, and interdependence among individuals, groups, and institutions	Aptitudes and Orientations, 64–78
Language Arts (LA)	
Writing	
LA 1. Uses the general skills and strategies of the writing process	Quick Write, 6, 24, 45, 64, 79, 93 Applying Career-Choosing Skills, 23 Applying Career Skills, 44, 61 Applying Education Skills, 107
LA 3. Uses grammatical and mechanical conventions in written compositions	Quick Write, 6, 24, 45, 64, 79, 93 Applying Career-Choosing Skills, 23 Applying Career Skills, 44, 61 Applying Education Skills, 107
LA 4. Gathers and uses information for research purposes	Learning from Others' Experience, 3 Researching and Choosing Careers, 6–23 Applying Career Skills, 44, 61, 92 Applying Personality Skills, 78 Applying Education Skills, 107
Reading	
LA 5. Uses the general skills and strategies of the reading process	Checkpoints, 23, 44, 61, 78, 92, 107
LA 7. Uses reading skills and strategies to understand and interpret a variety of informational texts	Checkpoints, 23, 44, 61, 78, 92, 107

Listening and Speaking	
LA 8. Uses listening and speaking strategies for different purposes	Checkpoints, 23, 44, 61, 78, 92, 107
Viewing	
LA 9. Uses viewing skills and strategies to understand and interpret visual media	Figure, 10, 11, 12 Table, 30, 31, 34, 36, 37, 47, 53, 54, 69, 70, 71, 72, 74, 75, 76, 77, 80, 81, 82, 86, 87, 88, 98, 99, 100, 101, 102, 104, 105, 106

UNIT 2 Charting Your Financial Course

Correlated to McREL Standards for Life Work, Self-Regulation, Thinking and Reasoning, Language Arts, Mathematics, and Economics

McREL Standards	Unit 2: Charting Your Financial Course
Life Work (LW)	
LW 1. Makes effective use of basic tools	Creating a Budget, 112–121 Savings and Bank Accounts, 122–133 Real-Life Issues in Buying and Selling, 134–149 Avoiding the Credit Trap, 152–169 Financing for College, 170–179 Insurance for Protecting Your Resources, 180–193
LW 2. Uses various information sources, including those of a technical nature, to accomplish specific tasks	Creating a Budget, 112–121 How to Choose a Bank, 127 How to Conduct Banking Business, 128–132 Real-Life Issues in Buying and Selling, 134–149
LW 3. Manages money effectively	Creating a Budget, 112–121 Savings and Bank Accounts, 122–133 Real-Life Issues in Buying and Selling, 134–149 Avoiding the Credit Trap, 152–169 Financing for College, 170–179 Insurance for Protecting Your Resources, 180–193
LW 5. Makes general preparation for entering the work force	Savings and Bank Accounts, 122–133 Real-Life Issues in Buying and Selling, 134–149
LW 6. Makes effective use of basic life skills	Creating a Budget, 112–121 Savings and Bank Accounts, 122–133 Real-Life Issues in Buying and Selling, 134–149 Avoiding the Credit Trap, 152–169 Financing for College, 170–179 Insurance for Protecting Your Resources, 180–193

Self-Regulation (SR)

SR 1. Sets and manages goals	The Steps for Developing a Financial Plan, 117–119 Applying Budgeting Skills, 121
SR 2. Performs self-appraisal	Creating a Budget, 112–121 How to Choose a Bank, 127 Real-Life Issues in Buying and Selling, 134–149 When It Comes Time to Apply for a Credit Card, 160 Applying Financial-Aid Skills, 179 Applying Insurance Skills, 193
SR 3. Considers risks	Real-Life Issues in Buying and Selling, 134–149 Avoiding the Credit Trap, 152–169 Financing for College, 170–179 Insurance for Protecting Your Resources, 180–193
SR 6. Restrains impulsivity	Real-Life Issues in Buying and Selling, 134–149 Avoiding the Credit Trap, 152–169

Thinking and Reasoning (TR)

TR 2. Understands and applies basic principles of logic and reasoning	How to Choose a Bank, 127 Real-Life Issues in Buying and Selling, 134–149
TR 3. Effectively uses mental processes that are based on identifying similarities and differences	Comparing Rates and Prices, 109 Applying Buying and Selling Skills, 149 Applying Financial-Aid Skills, 179 Comparison of Private Health Insurance Plans, 187 Applying Insurance Skills, 193
TR 6. Applies decision-making techniques	Applying Budgeting Skills, 121 How to Choose a Bank, 127 Real-Life Issues in Buying and Selling, 134–149

Language Arts (LA)

Writing	
LA 1. Uses the general skills and strategies of the writing process	Quick Write, 112, 122, 134, 152, 170, 180
LA 3. Uses grammatical and mechanical conventions in written compositions	Quick Write, 112, 122, 134, 152, 170, 180
LA 4. Gathers and uses information for research purposes	Applying Budgeting Skills, 121 Applying Banking Skills, 133 Applying Buying and Selling Skills, 149 Applying Credit Skills, 169 Applying Financial-Aid Skills, 179 Applying Insurance Skills, 193

Reading	
LA 5. Uses the general skills and strategies of the reading process	Checkpoints, 121, 133, 149, 169, 179, 193
LA 7. Uses reading skills and strategies to understand and interpret a variety of informational texts	Checkpoints, 121, 133, 149, 169, 179, 193
Listening and Speaking	
LA 8. Uses listening and speaking strategies for different purposes	Checkpoints, 121, 133, 149, 169, 179, 193
Viewing	
LA 9. Uses viewing skills and strategies to understand and interpret visual media	Table, 120, 182, 187 Figure, 129, 130, 148, 158, 167, 168
Mathematics (M)	
M 1. Uses a variety of strategies in the problem-solving process	Applying Budgeting Skills, 121 Applying Banking Skills, 133 Applying Financial-Aid Skills, 179
M 2. Uses basic and advanced procedures while performing the processes of computation	Applying Budgeting Skills, 121 Applying Banking Skills, 133 Applying Financial-Aid Skills, 179
Economics (E)	
E 1. Understands savings, investment, and interest rates	Savings and Bank Accounts, 122–133

UNIT 3 Aiming Toward a College Degree

Correlated to McREL Standards for Life Work, Self-Regulation, Thinking and Reasoning, Working With Others, Behavioral Studies, Language Arts, Arts and Communication, and Health

McREL Standards	Unit 3: Aiming Toward a College Degree
Life Work (LW)	
LW 1. Makes effective use of basic tools	Selecting a College, 198–210 Navigating the Testing Maze, 211–220 Essays, Interviews, and Campus Visits, 221–233 Adjusting to Campus Life, 236–251 Choosing a Major, 252–262 Planning Your Schedule, 263–273

LW 2. Uses various information sources, including those of a technical nature, to accomplish specific tasks	Selecting a College, 198–210 Navigating the Testing Maze, 211–220 Essays, Interviews, and Campus Visits, 221–233 Adjusting to Campus Life, 236–251 Choosing a Major, 252–262 Planning Your Schedule, 263–273
LW 4. Studies or pursues specific job interests	Choosing a Major, 252–262
LW 5. Makes general preparation for entering the work force	Choosing a Major, 252–262
LW 6. Makes effective use of basic life skills	Selecting a College, 198–210 Navigating the Testing Maze, 211–220 Essays, Interviews, and Campus Visits, 221–233 Adjusting to Campus Life, 236–251 Choosing a Major, 252–262 Planning Your Schedule, 263–273
LW 7. Displays reliability and a basic work ethic	The Importance of Time Management, 263–264 Procrastination and How to Beat It, 265–268 Managing Your College Schedule, 269–272
LW 8. Operates effectively within organizations	Aspects of Campus Life, 236–242

Self-Regulation (SR)

SR 1. Sets and manages goals	Selecting a College, 198–210 Navigating the Testing Maze, 211–220 Essays, Interviews, and Campus Visits, 221–233 Choosing a Major, 252–262 Planning Your Schedule, 263–273
SR 2. Performs self-appraisal	Selecting a College, 198–210 Helpful Reminders for Reducing Test Anxiety, 214 Conquering Test Anxiety, 215 Choosing a Major, 252–262 Planning Your Schedule, 263–273
SR 3. Considers risks	Selecting a College, 198–210 Navigating the Testing Maze, 211–220 Essays, Interviews, and Campus Visits, 221–233 Adjusting to Campus Life, 236–251 Choosing a Major, 252–262 Planning Your Schedule, 263–273
SR 4. Demonstrates perseverance	Selecting a College, 198–210 Navigating the Testing Maze, 211–220 Essays, Interviews, and Campus Visits, 221–233 Choosing a Major, 252–262 Planning Your Schedule, 263–273

SR 5. Maintains a healthy self-concept	Selecting a College, 198–210 Adjusting to Campus Life, 236–251 Choosing a Major, 252–262 Planning Your Schedule, 263–273
SR 6. Restrains impulsivity	Selecting a College, 198–210 Navigating the Testing Maze, 211–220 Essays, Interviews, and Campus Visits, 221–233 Adjusting to Campus Life, 236–251 Choosing a Major, 252–262 Planning Your Schedule, 263–273

Thinking and Reasoning (TR)

TR 1. Understands and applies the basic principles of presenting an argument	Selecting a College, 198–210
TR 2. Understands and applies basic principles of logic and reasoning	Navigating the Testing Maze, 211–220 Essays, Interviews, and Campus Visits, 221–233
TR 3. Effectively uses mental processes that are based on identifying similarities and differences	Navigating the Testing Maze, 211–220 Essays, Interviews, and Campus Visits, 221–233
TR 5. Applies basic trouble-shooting and problem-solving techniques	Selecting a College, 198–210 Navigating the Testing Maze, 211–220 Essays, Interviews, and Campus Visits, 221–233 Choosing a Major, 252–262 Planning Your Schedule, 263–273
TR 6. Applies decision-making techniques	Selecting a College, 198–210 Navigating the Testing Maze, 211–220 Essays, Interviews, and Campus Visits, 221–233 Choosing a Major, 252–262 Planning Your Schedule, 263–273

Working With Others (WO)

WO 1. Contributes to the overall effort of a group	Adjusting to Campus Life, 236–251
WO 2. Uses conflict-resolution techniques	Relationship Problems: Coping With Roommates, 247–248
WO 3. Works well with diverse individuals and in diverse situations	Adjusting to Campus Life, 236–251
WO 4. Displays effective interpersonal communication skills	How to Have a Successful Interview, 225–230 Relationship Problems: Coping With Roommates, 247–248
WO 5. Demonstrates leadership skills	Adjusting to Campus Life, 236–251

Behavioral Studies (BS)	
BS 1. Understands that group and cultural influences contribute to human development, identity, and behavior	Adjusting to Campus Life, 236–251
BS 2. Understands various meanings of social group, general implications of group membership, and different ways that groups function	Adjusting to Campus Life, 236–251
BS 4. Understands conflict, cooperation, and interdependence among individuals, groups, and institutions	How to Have a Successful Interview, 225–230 Relationship Problems: Coping With Roommates, 247–248
Language Arts (LA)	
Writing	
LA 1. Uses the general skills and strategies of the writing process	Writing a College Entrance Essay, 221–225 Quick Write, 198, 211, 221, 236, 252, 263 Applying College-Selection Skills, 210 Applying Test-Taking Skills, 220 Applying Essay, Interview, and Campus Visit Skills, 233 Applying Campus-Living Skills, 251 Applying Choosing a Major Skills, 262 Applying Scheduling Skills, 273
LA 2. Uses the stylistic and rhetorical aspects of writing	Writing a College Entrance Essay, 221–225
LA 3. Uses grammatical and mechanical conventions in written compositions	Writing a College Entrance Essay, 221–225 Quick Write, 198, 211, 221, 236, 252, 263 Applying College-Selection Skills, 210 Applying Test-Taking Skills, 220 Applying Essay, Interview, and Campus Visit Skills, 233 Applying Campus-Living Skills, 251 Applying Choosing a Major Skills, 262 Applying Scheduling Skills, 273
LA 4. Gathers and uses information for research purposes	Research a College, 195 Applying College-Selection Skills, 210 Applying Campus-Living Skills, 251 Applying Choosing a Major Skills, 262
Reading	
LA 5. Uses the general skills and strategies of the reading process	Navigating the Testing Maze, 211–220 Checkpoints, 210, 220, 233, 251, 262, 273
LA 7. Uses reading skills and strategies to understand and interpret a variety of informational texts	Navigating the Testing Maze, 211–220 Checkpoints, 210, 220, 233, 251, 262, 273

Listening and Speaking	
LA 8. Uses listening and speaking strategies for different purposes	How to Have a Successful Interview, 225–230 Checkpoints, 210, 220, 233, 251, 262, 273
Viewing	
LA 9. Uses viewing skills and strategies to understand and interpret visual media	Figure, 230, 258, 272 Table, 246, 256, 257 Applying Scheduling Skills, 273
Arts and Communication (AC)	
Practice Creativity	
AC 3. Uses critical and creative thinking in various arts and communication settings	Navigating the Testing Maze, 211–220 Essays, Interviews, and Campus Visits, 221–233 Checkpoints, 210, 220, 233, 251, 262, 273
Health (H)	
H 2. Knows environmental and external factors that affect individual and community health	Adjusting to Campus Life, 236–251
H 4. Knows how to maintain mental and emotional health	Helpful Reminders for Reducing Test Anxiety, 214 Conquering Test Anxiety, 215 Making Healthy Lifestyle Choices, 245–250 Relationship Problems: Coping With Roommates, 247–248 Managing Stress and Preventing Burnout, 248–250 Personal Accountability, 250 The Importance of Time Management, 263–264 Procrastination and How to Beat It, 265–268
H 6. Understands essential concepts about nutrition and diet	Making Healthy Lifestyle Choices, 245–250
H 7. Knows how to maintain and promote personal health	Making Healthy Lifestyle Choices, 245–250
H 8. Knows essential concepts about the prevention and control of disease	Making Healthy Lifestyle Choices, 245–250
H 9. Understands aspects of substance use and abuse	Making Healthy Lifestyle Choices, 245–250
H 10. Understands the fundamental concepts of growth and development	Helpful Reminders for Reducing Test Anxiety, 214 Conquering Test Anxiety, 215 Making Healthy Lifestyle Choices, 245–250 Relationship Problems: Coping With Roommates, 247–248 Managing Stress and Preventing Burnout, 248–250 Personal Accountability, 250 The Importance of Time Management, 263–264 Procrastination and How to Beat It, 265–268

UNIT 4 Pursuing a Career

Correlated to McREL Standards for Life Work, Self-Regulation, Thinking and Reasoning, Working With Others, Behavioral Studies, Language Arts, Arts and Communication, and Health

McREL Standards	Unit 4: Pursuing a Career
Life Work (LW)	
LW 1. Makes effective use of basic tools	The Job Search Process, 278–293 Preparing Your Résumé, 294–308 Building Interview Skills, 309–321 Planning Your Professional Development, 324–335 Learning to Work With Others, 336–347 Seeking Feedback and Promotions, 348–358
LW 2. Uses various information sources, including those of a technical nature, to accomplish specific tasks	The Job Search Process, 278–293 Preparing Your Résumé, 294–308 Planning Your Professional Development, 324–335 Seeking Feedback and Promotions, 348–358
LW 4. Studies or pursues specific job interests	The Job Search Process, 278–293 Preparing Your Résumé, 294–308 Planning Your Professional Development, 324–335 Seeking Feedback and Promotions, 348–358
LW 5. Makes general preparation for entering the work force	The Job Search Process, 278–293 Preparing Your Résumé, 294–308 Building Interview Skills, 309–321 Planning Your Professional Development, 324–335 Learning to Work With Others, 336–347 Seeking Feedback and Promotions, 348–358
LW 6. Makes effective use of basic life skills	The Job Search Process, 278–293 Preparing Your Résumé, 294–308 Building Interview Skills, 309–321 Planning Your Professional Development, 324–335 Learning to Work With Others, 336–347 Seeking Feedback and Promotions, 348–358
LW 7. Displays reliability and a basic work ethic	The Job Search Process, 278–293 Preparing Your Résumé, 294–308 Building Interview Skills, 309–321 Planning Your Professional Development, 324–335 Learning to Work With Others, 336–347 Seeking Feedback and Promotions, 348–358
LW 8. Operates effectively within organizations	Learning to Work With Others, 336–347 Seeking Feedback and Promotions, 348–358

Self-Regulation (SR)	
SR 1. Sets and manages goals	Identifying Your Personal Job Preferences, 278–286
SR 2. Performs self-appraisal	Identifying Your Personal Job Preferences, 278–286
SR 3. Considers risks	Identifying Your Personal Job Preferences, 278–286 How to Organize a Job Search, 288–292 Six Steps for Writing a Great Résumé, 299–300 Preparing a Personal Résumé, 301–305 Building Interview Skills, 309–321 Learning to Work With Others, 336–347 Seeking Feedback and Promotions, 348–358
SR 5. Maintains a healthy self-concept	Identifying Your Personal Job Preferences, 278–286 Interviews Dos and Don'ts, 310–314 Body Language—the Silent Communication, 313 Barriers to Effective Communication, 339–340 Communicating to Others, 341–342 Collaboration and Teamwork, 343–347 Seeking and Receiving Feedback in the Workplace, 348–351
SR 6. Restrains impulsivity	Identifying Your Personal Job Preferences, 278–286 Interviews Dos and Don'ts, 310–314 Body Language—the Silent Communication, 313 Barriers to Effective Communication, 339–340 Communicating to Others, 341–342 Collaboration and Teamwork, 343–347

Thinking and Reasoning (TR)	
TR 1. Understands and applies the basic principles of presenting an argument	Communicating to Others, 341–342 Collaboration and Teamwork, 343–347
TR 2. Understands and applies basic principles of logic and reasoning	Checkpoints, 293, 308, 321, 335, 347, 358
TR 5. Applies basic trouble-shooting and problem-solving techniques	Identifying Your Personal Job Preferences, 278–286 How to Organize a Job Search, 288–292 Six Steps for Writing a Great Résumé, 299–300 Preparing a Personal Résumé, 301–305 Building Interview Skills, 309–321 Learning to Work With Others, 336–347 Seeking Feedback and Promotions, 348–358
TR 6. Applies decision-making techniques	Identifying Your Personal Job Preferences, 278–286 How to Organize a Job Search, 288–292 Six Steps for Writing a Great Résumé, 299–300 Preparing a Personal Résumé, 301–305 Building Interview Skills, 309–321 Learning to Work With Others, 336–347 Seeking Feedback and Promotions, 348–358

Working With Others (WO)	
WO 1. Contributes to the overall effort of a group	Learning to Work With Others, 336–347
WO 2. Uses conflict-resolution techniques	Learning to Work With Others, 336–347
WO 3. Works well with diverse individuals and in diverse situations	Learning to Work With Others, 336–347
WO 4. Displays effective interpersonal communication skills	Building Interview Skills, 309–321 Learning to Work With Others, 336–347 Seeking Feedback and Promotions, 348–358
WO 5. Demonstrates leadership skills	Learning to Work With Others, 336–347
Behavioral Studies (BS)	
BS 1. Understands that group and cultural influences contribute to human development, identity, and behavior	Body Language—the Silent Communication, 313 Learning to Work With Others, 336–347 Seeking Feedback and Promotions, 348–358
BS 2. Understands various meanings of social group, general implications of group membership, and different ways that groups function	Learning to Work With Others, 336–347 Seeking Feedback and Promotions, 348–358
BS 4. Understands conflict, cooperation, and interdependence among individuals, groups, and institutions	Learning to Work With Others, 336–347 Seeking Feedback and Promotions, 348–358
Language Arts (LA)	
Writing	
LA 1. Uses the general skills and strategies of the writing process	Preparing Your Résumé, 294–308 Applying Job-Search Skills, 293 Applying Professional Development Skills, 335 Applying Collaboration Skills, 347 Applying Feedback and Promotion Skills, 358 Quick Write, 278, 294, 309, 324, 336, 348
LA 2. Uses the stylistic and rhetorical aspects of writing	Preparing Your Résumé, 294–308
LA 3. Uses grammatical and mechanical conventions in written compositions	Preparing Your Résumé, 294–308 Applying Job-Search Skills, 293 Applying Professional Development Skills, 335 Applying Collaboration Skills, 347 Applying Feedback and Promotion Skills, 358 Quick Write, 278, 294, 309, 324, 336, 348

Standard	Pages
LA 4. Gathers and uses information for research purposes	Beginning to Network, 275 The Job Search Process, 278–293 Applying Job-Search Skills, 293 Applying Professional Development Skills, 335 Applying Collaboration Skills, 347 Applying Feedback and Promotion Skills, 358
Reading	
LA 5. Uses the general skills and strategies of the reading process	Checkpoints, 293, 308, 321, 335, 347, 358
LA 7. Uses reading skills and strategies to understand and interpret a variety of informational texts	Checkpoints, 293, 308, 321, 335, 347, 358
Listening and Speaking	
LA 8. Uses listening and speaking strategies for different purposes	Building Interview Skills, 309–321 Checkpoints, 293, 308, 335, 347, 358
Viewing	
LA 9. Uses viewing skills and strategies to understand and interpret visual media	Figure, 296, 297, 298, 307, 314, 356 Table, 281, 299, 344
Arts and Communication (AC)	
Practice Creativity	
AC 3. Uses critical and creative thinking in various arts and communication settings	Identifying Your Personal Job Preferences, 278–286 Selling Your Skills to an Employer, 286–287 Building Interview Skills, 309–321 Checkpoints, 293, 308, 321, 335, 347, 358
Health (H)	
H 4. Knows how to maintain mental and emotional health	Needs or Wants, 281 Body Language—the Silent Communication, 313
H 10. Understands the fundamental concepts of growth and development	Needs or Wants, 281 Body Language—the Silent Communication, 313

References

UNIT 1

Chapter 1

Lesson 1—Researching and Choosing Careers

Foundations for Success in Life, Career, Health and Wellness. (2005). Boston, MA: Pearson Custom Publishing.

Mitchell, N. (Ed.). (1999). *Leadership Education III: Life Skills.* Maxwell Air Force Base, AL: US Air Force Reserve Officer Training Program, Junior Program Branch.

Occupational Outlook Handbook, 2006–07 Edition. Washington, DC: Bureau of Labor Statistics. Retrieved 19 December 2005 from http://www.bls.gov/oco/

Office of Personnel Management website. (n.d.). Student Educational Employment Program. Retrieved 20 January 2006 from http://www.opm.gov/employ/students/intro.asp

Robbins, C. R. (2006). *The Job Searcher's Handbook.* Upper Saddle River, N.J.: Pearson Education, Inc.

Lesson 2—Military Careers

Air Force Link. (5 December 2005). Brothers meet at 25,000 feet. *Air Force Print News.* Retrieved 30 January 2006 from http://www.af.mil/news/story.asp?storyID=123013323

Battle, C. (11 January 2005). Commissioning program available for active-duty Airmen. *Air Force Link.* Retrieved 2 May 2006 from http://www.af.mil/news/story.asp?storyID=123009581

Community College of the Air Force. (n.d.). Retrieved 1 January 2006 from http://www.au.af.mil/au/ccaf/

Lopez, T. (21 April 2004). ASVAB changes will not mean lower standards. *Air Force Print News.* Retrieved 28 January 2006 from http://www.af.mil/news/story.asp?storyID=123007527

Mitchell, N. (Ed.). (1999). *Leadership Education III: Life Skills.* Maxwell Air Force Base, AL: US Air Force Reserve Officer Training Program, Junior Program Branch.

Learn More Indiana. (n.d.). Retrieved 1 January 2006 from http://www.learnmoreindiana.org/@default/

The Black Collegian Online. (n.d.). Retrieved 30 December 2005 from http://www.black-collegian.com/career/career-reports/military2002-2nd.shtml
US Air Force. (n.d.). Air and Space Expeditionary Force. Unpublished paper.
US Air Force Academy Admissions website. Retrieved 30 January 2006 from http://www.academyadmissions.com/
US Air Force ROTC. (2006). Scholarships. Retrieved 2 May 2006 from http://www.afrotc.com/scholarships/index.php
US Department of Defense. (2001). *Military Careers*. Washington, DC: Government Printing Office.
US Department of Defense Instruction 1304.26, *Qualification Standards for Enlistment, Appointment, and Induction*. 20 September 2005. Retrieved 2 May 2006 from http://www.dtic.mil/whs/directives/corres/pdf/i130426_092005/i130426p.pdf

Lesson 3—Careers in Aerospace

AvJobs.com website. (n.d.). Retrieved 3 January 2006 from http://www.avjobs.com/table/airsalry.asp and http://www.avjobs.com/careers
Employment Spot website. (n.d.). Aerospace and Aviation Employment Resources. Retrieved 3 January 2006 from http://www.employmentspot.com/vocations/aerospace/
Federal Aviation Administration. (n.d.). FAA Career Opportunities: Destination FAA. Retrieved 3 January 2006 from http://jobs.faa.gov/
Michigan Department of Civil Service. (2000). Job Description: Aviation Specialist. Retrieved 30 January 2006 from http://www.michigan.gov/documents/AviationSpecialist_12110_7.pdf
Mitchell, N. (Ed.). (1999). *Leadership Education III: Life Skills*. Maxwell Air Force Base, AL: US Air Force Reserve Officer Training Program, Junior Program Branch.
National Aeronautics and Space Administration. (17 October 2005). What Does NASA Do? Retrieved 3 January 2006 from http://www.nasa.gov/about/highlights/what_does_nasa_do.html

Chapter 2

Lesson 1—Aptitudes and Orientations

Hirsh, S. K. & Kummerow, J. M. (1990). *Introduction to Type in Organizations*. Palo Alto, CA: Consulting Psychologists Press, Inc.
Know Your Type. (2004). Myers-Briggs® for All Now Available. Retrieved 14 January 2006 from http://www.knowyourtype.com
TeamTechnology. (2005). MBTI Personality Type Descriptions. Retrieved 14 January 2006 from http://www.teamtechnology.co.uk/mb-types/mb-types.htm
US Department of the Interior. (2000). Connecting Personality Type with Careers and Jobs. Retrieved 14 January 2006 from http://www.doi.gov/octc/typescar.html

Lesson 2—Career Paths

America's Career Resource Network website. (n.d.). Students. Retrieved 13 February 2006 from http://www.acrnetwork.org/students.aspx

Association for Career and Technical Education. (2006). ACTE Online. Frequently Asked Questions. Retrieved 24 January 2006 from http://www.acteonline.org/career_tech/faq.cfm

Construction Craft Training Center website. (2005). Retrieved 28 January 2006 from http://www.cctc.edu

Electricians. (2004). Occupational Outlook Handbook Survey. Retrieved 28 January 2006 from http://www.bls.gov/oco/ocos206.htm

Foundations for Success in Life, Career, Health and Wellness. (2005). Boston, MA: Pearson Custom Publishing.

High School Career and Technical Education. (2006). Career Prospects in Virginia. Retrieved 28 January 2006 from http://www3.ccps.virginia.edu/career_prospects/Trends/education/highschool.html

Crosby, O. (2002). Apprenticeships: Career Training, Credentials—and a Paycheck in Your Pocket. *Occupational Outlook Quarterly, Summer 2002*. Washington, DC: US Department of Labor. Retrieved 24 January 2006 from http://www.pueblo.gsa.gov/cic_text/employ/apprentice/apprentice.htm

Universal Technical Institute, Inc., website. (2006). Retrieved 28 January 2006 from http://www.uticorp.com/

US Department of Labor and US Department of Education. (n.d.). Career Voyages. Retrieved 13 February 2006 from www.careervoyages.gov/

Vocational Information Center. (2005). Career and Technical Education Web Resources. Retrieved 24 January 2006 from http://www.khake.com/index.html

Lesson 3—Educational Paths

Cheeseman-Day, J., & Newburger, E. C. (July 2002). The Big Payoff: Educational Attainment and Synthetic Estimates of Work-Life Earnings. *Current Population Reports, Special Studies*. Washington, DC: US Department of Commerce, Economics and Statistics Administration, US Census Bureau. Retrieved 17 January 2006 from http://www.census.gov/prod/2002pubs/p23-210.pdf

College Board (2006). Find the Right Colleges for You. Retrieved 26 January 2006 from http://apps.collegeboard.com/search/index.jsp

Colorado Department of Labor and Employment. (n.d.). Jobs in Colorado Requiring Higher Education: Looking Ahead to 2012. Retrieved 11 January 2006 from http://www.coworkforce.com/lmi/WRA/COHigherEd2012.pdf

Hill, C., and Silva, E. (19 April 2005). Public Perceptions of the Pay Gap. American Association of University Women Educational Foundation. Retrieved 11 January 2006 from http://www.aauw.org/research/paygapperceptions_April05.pdf

Merisotis, J. P. (1998). Who Benefits from Higher Education? An American Perspective. Boston College, Center for International Higher Education. Retrieved 11 January 2006 from http://www.bc.edu/bc_org/avp/soe/cihe/newsletter/News12/text1.html

The Ohio State University website. (n.d.). Retrieved 11 January 2006 from http://www-afa.adm.ohio-state.edu/undergrad/academics/majors.asp
US Department of Education. (2000). Why attend college? *Preparing Your Child for College*. Retrieved 25 January 2006 from http://www.ed.gov/pubs/Prepare/pt1.html
US Department of Labor, Bureau of Labor Statistics. (2006). *Occupational Outlook Handbook,* 2006–07 Edition. Retrieved 11 January 2006 from http://www.bls.gov/oco/
US Department of Labor, Bureau of Labor Statistics. (2005). Median usual weekly earnings of employed full-time wage and salary workers 25 years and over by educational attainment and sex, 2004 annual averages. *Women in the Labor Force: A Databook*. Retrieved 5 May 2006 from http://www.bls.gov/cps/wlf-table17-2005.pdf

UNIT 2

Chapter 3

Lesson 1—Creating a Budget

Madura, J. (2004). *Personal Finance.* Boston, MA: Pearson Education, Inc.

Lesson 2—Savings and Bank Accounts

Madura, J. (2004). *Personal Finance.* Boston, MA: Pearson Education, Inc.
Mitchell, N. L. (1999). *Leadership Education III: Life Skills.* Maxwell Air Force Base, AL: Air Force Reserve Officer Training Corps.
National Credit Union Administration website. Retrieved 9 February 2006 from http://www.ncua.gov/index.html

Lesson 3—Issues in Buying and Selling

Automotive.com website. (n.d.). Car Loan Tips. Retrieved 14 February 2006 from http://www.automotive.com/auto-loans/36/loan-tips/car-loan-tips.html
Consumer Reports website. (April 2005). The big push in lending. Retrieved 14 February 2006 from http://www.consumerreports.org/cro/personal-finance/the-lowdown-on-car-leasing-405.htm
Kelly Blue Book website. (n.d.). Retrieved 14 February from http://www.kbb.com/
Madura, J. (2004). *Personal Finance.* Boston, MA: Pearson Education, Inc.
Mitchell, N. (Ed.). (1999). *Leadership Education III: Life Skills.* Maxwell Air Force Base, AL: US Air Force Reserve Officer Training Program, Junior Program Branch.

Chapter 4

Lesson 1—Avoiding the Credit Trap

Choosing a Credit Card. (2004). Washington, DC: Board of Governors of the Federal Reserve System. Retrieved 7 March 2006 from http://www.federalreserve.gov/pubs/shop/

Highlight Investments Group. (2006). Market Trader Glossary. Retrieved 16 February 2006 from http://www.trading-glossary.com/p0136.asp

Madura, J. (2004). *Personal Finance*. Boston, MA: Pearson Education, Inc.

Mitchell, N. (Ed.). (1999). *Leadership Education III: Life Skills*. Maxwell Air Force Base, AL: US Air Force Reserve Officer Training Program, Junior Program Branch.

The Motley Fool website. (n.d.). Credit Center. Scary debt stats. Retrieved 13 February 2006 from http://www.fool.com/ccc/secrets/secrets.htm

Sahadi, J. (17 October 2005). The new bankruptcy law and you. *CNNMoney.com*. Retrieved 14 February 2006 from http://money.cnn.com/2005/10/17/pf/debt/bankruptcy_law/index.htm

Weston, L. P. (n.d.). How to blitz your college debts. *MSN Money*. Retrieved 14 February 2006 from http://moneycentral.msn.com/content/CollegeandFamily/Moneyinyour20s/P36953.asp

Weston, L. P. (n.d.). The truth about credit card debt. *MSN Money*. Retrieved 14 February 2006 from http://moneycentral.msn.com/content/Banking/creditcardsmarts/P74808.asp

Lesson 2—Financing for College

American Association of Community Colleges. (2004). Student Costs and College Finance. Retrieved 15 February 2006 from http://www.aacc.nche.edu/Content/NavigationMenu/AboutCommunityColleges/Trends_and_Statistics/CostAndFinancialInfo/Cost_And_Financial_Info.htm

College Board. (n.d.). What Exactly Is a Pell Grant? Retrieved 17 February 2006 from http://www.collegeboard.com/article/0,3868,6-30-0-36318,00.html

College Board. (n.d.). 2005-06 College Costs. Retrieved 20 February 2006 from http://www.collegeboard.com/article/0,3868,4-21-0-4494,00.html

Griffith, M. (April 2005). Issues in Community College Funding. Denver, CO: Education Commission of the States. Retrieved 15 February 2006 from http://www.ecs.org/clearinghouse/60/67/6067.htm

FinAid.com. (n.d.). Number of Scholarships. Retrieved 17 February 2006 from http://www.finaid.org/scholarships/awardcount.phtml

FinAid.com. (n.d.). Scholarships. Retrieved 17 February 2006 from http://www.finaid.org/scholarships/

FinAid.com (n.d.). Scholarship Scams. Retrieved 17 February 2006 from http://www.finaid.org/scholarships/scams.phtml

FinAid.com. (n.d.). Student Loans. Retrieved 17 February 2006 from http://www.finaid.org/loans/

FinAid.com. (n.d.). US State Government Aid. Retrieved 17 February 2006 from http://www.finaid.org/otheraid/state.phtml

Mitchell, N. (Ed.). (1999). *Leadership Education III: Life Skills*. Maxwell Air Force Base, AL: US Air Force Reserve Officer Training Program, Junior Program Branch.

Sallie Mae website. (n.d.). Interest Rates and Annual Percentage Rates (APR). Retrieved 21 February 2006 from http://www.salliemae.com/apply/borrowing/interest.html

US Department of Education. (2003–2004). Types of Federal Student Aid: Federal Work Study. Retrieved 17 February 2006 from http://studentaid.ed.gov/students/publications/student_guide/2003_2004/english/types-fed-workstudy.htm

US Department of Education. (2003–2004). Types of Federal Student Aid: Federal Supplemental Educational Opportunity Grant. Retrieved 17 February 2006 fromhttp://studentaid.ed.gov/students/publications/student_guide/2003_2004/english/types-campus-fseog.htm

Washington State University, Grays Harbor and Pacific Learning Center. (n.d.). Frequently Asked Questions. Retrieved 17 February 2006 from http://learningcenters.wsu.edu/ghp/FAQ/#q10

Lesson 3—Insurance for Protecting Your Resources

Core Competence, Inc. (n.d.). Phishing and Fraud Prevention Resources. Retrieved 27 February 2006 from http://hhi.corecom.com/phishing.htm

Esurance.com website. (n.d.). FAQ: Demystifying Auto Insurance Definitions. Retrieved 22 February 2006 from http://www.esurance.com/FAQ/auto_insurance_policy_definitions.asp#4

Federal Emergency Management Agency. (2006). Flood Insurance. Retrieved 3 March 2006 from http://www.fema.gov/nfip/whonfip.shtm

Federal Trade Commission. (n.d.). Welcome to the Federal Trade Commission, Your National Resource About Identity Theft. Retrieved 27 February 2006 from http://www.consumer.gov/idtheft/

Fowles, D. (2006). When Bad Things Happen in Your Good Name. Retrieved 27 February 2006 from http://financialplan.about.com/od/fraudandfinancialscams/a/IdentityTheft.htm

Insure.com. (2004). Minimum levels of required auto insurance. Retrieved 22 February 2006 from http://info.insure.com/auto/minimum.html

Madura, J. (2004). *Personal Finance*. Boston, MA: Pearson Education, Inc.

Mitchell, N. (Ed.). (1999). *Leadership Education III: Life Skills*. Maxwell Air Force Base, AL: US Air Force Reserve Officer Training Program, Junior Program Branch.

National Education Association. (n.d.). Long-Term Care vs. Long-Term Disability vs. Critical Injury Insurance. Retrieved 1 March 2006 from http://www.nea.org/money/pf020923.html

Reed, P. (n.d.). Auto Insurance Tips: Car Insurance for Teenage Drivers. Retrieved 24 February 2006 from http://www.edmunds.com/apps/vdpcontainers/do/vdp/articleId=97806/pageNumber=1

UNIT 3

Chapter 5

Lesson 1—Selecting a College

College Board. (n.d.). Tips for Finding Your College Match: Characteristics You Should Consider. Retrieved 27 February 2006 from http://www.collegeboard.com/article/0,,4-21-0-52,00.html

CollegeData website. (n.d.). Getting Application Fees Waived. Retrieved 28 February 2006 from http://www.collegedata.com/cs/content/content_getinarticle_tmpl.jhtml?articleId=10050

Information Please Database. (2005). Number of U.S. Colleges and Universities and Degrees Awarded. Retrieved 24 February 2006 from http://www.infoplease.com/ipa/A0908742.html

Mitchell, N. (Ed.). (1999). *Leadership Education III: Life Skills.* Maxwell Air Force Base, AL: US Air Force Reserve Officer Training Program, Junior Program Branch.

National Association for College Admission Counseling. (Revised March 2005). NACAC Pact Guide. Preparation for College Calendar—Junior Year. Retrieved 3 March 2006 from http://www.nacac.com/p&sjunior.html

WorldWideLearn. (n.d.). Accreditation Answers: U.S. Regional Accrediting Associations. Retrieved 24 February 2006 from http://www.worldwidelearn.com/accreditation/accreditation-associations.htm

Lesson 2—Navigating the Testing Maze

ACT.org. (n.d.). What Is the Difference Between the ACT and SAT? Retrieved 3 March 2006 from http://www.actstudent.org/faq/answers/actsat.html

College Board. (2004). SAT Reasoning Test—Materials Available for License.

College Board. (n.d.). About CLEP. Retrieved 28 February 2006 from http://www.collegeboard.com/student/testing/clep/about.html

Mitchell, N. (Ed.). (1999). *Leadership Education III: Life Skills.* Maxwell Air Force Base, AL: US Air Force Reserve Officer Training Program, Junior Program Branch.

National University Online. (n.d.). General Information for Undergraduate Degrees/ACT PEP. Retrieved 28 February 2006 from http://natu.redirect2.ecollege.com/index.real?action=academic&subaction=D2_Ugrad_degree&subsubaction=page9

Nova Press. (2006). About the New SAT Test. Retrieved 16 March 2006 from http://novapress.net/sat/index.html

Ross, R. (2003). The History of the SAT. Whimsplace.com. Retrieved 3 March 2006 from http://www.whimsplace.com/011504/technosociety.htm

Sherfield, R. M. (2005). *Cornerstone: Building on Your Best.* Upper Saddle River, NJ: Pearson Education, Inc.

Lesson 3—Essays, Interviews, and Campus Visits

American University. (n.d.). College Interview Tips. Retrieved 19 April 2006 from http://admissions.american.edu/public/contentPage/contentPage.asp?catID=4&navID=0&docID=1677&textOnly=True

Cambridge Essay Service (n.d.). Seven Great and Unexpected Tips about College Entrance Essays. Retrieved 6 March 2006 from http://world.std.com/~edit/tips3.htm

College Planning Center. (2003). Suggested ?s to Ask During Your Campus Visit. Retrieved 19 April 2006 from http://www.collegeplanning.org/ChooseCollege/QuestionsToAsk1.htm

Eagon, M. (n.d.). Writing the College Admission Essay. DePauw University. Retrieved 19 April 2006 from http://www.depauw.edu/admission/applying/tips/essay/

Mitchell, N. (Ed.). (1999). *Leadership Education III: Life Skills*. Maxwell Air Force Base, AL: US Air Force Reserve Officer Training Program, Junior Program Branch.

Sallie Mae website. (2004). School Interview Checklist. Retrieved 19 April 2006 from http://www.collegeanswer.com/global/checklists/InterviewChecklist.pdf

Chapter 6

Lesson 1—Adjusting to Campus Life

CollegeSafe.com. (2004). Guide to Dealing with Your College Roommate. Retrieved 23 April 2006 from http://www.collegesafe.com/pdf/roommate_guide.pdf

National Institute on Alcohol Abuse and Alcoholism. (2005). College Drinking—Changing the Culture. Retrieved 27 April 2006 from http://www.collegedrinkingprevention.gov/NIAAACollegeMaterials/TaskForce/Intro_00.aspx

National Institute of Mental Health. (2006). What do these students have in common? Retrieved 27 April 2006 from http://www.nimh.nih.gov/publicat/students.cfm

Sherfield, R. M. (2005). *Cornerstone: Building on Your Best*. Upper Saddle River, NJ: Pearson Education, Inc.

Starke, M. C. (1996). *Strategies for College Success*. Upper Saddle River, NJ: Pearson Education, Inc.

University of Louisiana at Lafayette. (n.d.). Accounting Society. Retrieved 23 April 2006 from http://www.louisiana.edu/Student/Organizations/AccountingSociety/

University of Texas at Austin. (n.d.). Electronic Game Developers Society. Retrieved 23 April 2006 from http://utdirect.utexas.edu/dsorg/detail.wb?code=02428

University of Virginia. (2006). University of Virginia Library. Retrieved 23 April 2006 from http://www.virginia.edu/lib.html

US Department of Agriculture. (n.d.). Steps to a Healthier You. Retrieved 27 April 2006 from http://www.foodpyramid.gov/

Lesson 2—Choosing a Major

Gordon, V. N. (2004). *Selecting a College Major: Exploration and Decision Making.* Upper Saddle River, NJ: Pearson Education, Inc.

Sherfield, R. M. (2005). *Cornerstone: Building on Your Best.* Upper Saddle River, NJ: Pearson Education, Inc.

Lesson 3—Planning Your Schedule

Dartmouth College Academic Skills Center. (2001). Five Steps to Successful Time Management. Retrieved 21 March 2006 from http://www.dartmouth.edu/~acskills/docs/planning_well.doc

George Mason University. (n.d.). Time Management Tips. Retrieved 27 March 2006 from http://www.gmu.edu/gmu/personal/time.html

Sherfield, R. M. (2005). *Cornerstone: Building on Your Best.* Upper Saddle River, NJ: Pearson Education, Inc.

UNIT 4

Chapter 7

Lesson 1—The Job Search Process

Mitchell, N. (Ed.). (1999). *Leadership Education III: Life Skills.* Maxwell Air Force Base, AL: US Air Force Reserve Officer Training Program, Junior Program Branch.

Robbins, C. R. (2006). *The Job Searcher's Handbook.* Upper Saddle River, NJ: Pearson Education, Inc.

Lesson 2—Preparing Your Résumé

Mitchell, N. (Ed.). (1999). *Leadership Education III: Life Skills.* Maxwell Air Force Base, AL: US Air Force Reserve Officer Training Program, Junior Program Branch.

Robbins, C.R. (2006). *The Job Searcher's Handbook.* Upper Saddle River, NJ: Pearson Education, Inc.

Lesson 3—Building Interviewing Skills

Robbins, C. R. (2006). *The Job Searcher's Handbook.* Upper Saddle River, NJ: Pearson Education, Inc.

Virginia Polytechnic Institute and State University website. (February 2006). Behavioral interviewing. Retrieved 31 March 2006 from http://www.career.vt.edu/JOBSEARC/interview/Behavioral.htm.

Chapter 8

Lesson 1—Planning Your Professional Development

Blanchard, K., & Peale, N. V. (1988). *The Power of Ethical Management.* New York: William Morrow Co.

Pruitt B. E., Carter, C., & Sukiennik, D. (2005). *Foundations for Success in Life, Career, Health and Wellness.* Boston, MA: Pearson Custom Publishing.

Tucker, M. L. (2002). *The Human Challenge: Managing Yourself and Others in Organizations.* Upper Saddle River, NJ: Pearson Education, Inc.

Lesson 2—Learning to Work With Others

Hirsh, S. K. & Kummerow, J. M. (1990). *Introduction to Type in Organizations.* Palo Alto, CA: Consulting Psychologists Press, Inc.

National School Boards Association. (n.d.). Leadership Teams. Retrieved 15 April 2006 from http://www.nsba.org/sbot/toolkit/LeadTeams.html

Tucker, M. L. (2002). *The Human Challenge: Managing Yourself and Others in Organizations.* Upper Saddle River, NJ: Pearson Education, Inc.

Lesson 3—Seeking Feedback and Promotions

Aschaiek, S. (2006). Preparing for a Promotion. CanadianLiving.com. Retrieved 18 April 2006 from http://www.canadianliving.com/canadianliving/client/en/Family/DetailNews.asp?idNews=230214&idSM=428

Peter, L., & Hull, R. (1993). *The Peter Principle: Why Things Always Go Wrong.* Cutchogue, NY: Buccaneer Books.

Tucker, M. L. (2002). *The Human Challenge: Managing Yourself and Others in Organizations.* Upper Saddle River, NJ: Pearson Education, Inc.

Glossary

360-degree feedback—a performance appraisal that comes from all levels around the employee—from a boss, coworkers, and subordinates, as well as the employee himself or herself. (p. 351)

abilities—powers you were born with. (p. 8)

ability promotion—a promotion based on your potential to do a new job, rather than how you did in your old one. (p. 353)

academic adviser—a person who helps you make academic decisions. (p. 241)

academic organization—a group that helps members learn about an academic subject and meet other people with a similar interest. (p. 237)

academic success center—a center that provides one-on-one or group study sessions, tutoring, specialized instruction, and self-paced tutorials. (p. 240)

account statement—a list of transactions in your checking or other account over the month. (p. 125)

accredited—approved as meeting certain standards. (p. 202)

achievement test—an exam that tests what a student has actually learned. (p. 213)

ACT—a college entrance examination that is an alternative to the SAT. (p. 213)

admissions officer—a person who helps decide whom to admit to a college. (p. 221)

aerospace—combines "aero," from aeronautics, describing flight within earth's atmosphere, and "space," describing flight beyond the atmosphere. (p. 45)

Airman—an individual who enters the Air Force at the beginning level and who focuses exclusively on learning skills (note that when used generically can refer to any member of the Air Force). (p. 28)

alumni—people who have graduated from a certain school. (p. 206)

annual fee—a yearly fee that some companies charge in addition to the interest charge. (p. 156)

annual percentage rate (APR)—the yearly interest rate. (p. 152)

apprenticeship—an opportunity to learn a trade on the job while also learning in class. (p. 85)

aptitude test—an exam designed to demonstrate a student's talent, skill, or potential for learning, rather than his or her accumulated knowledge. (p. 212)

aptitudes—talents or skills you possess or that you believe you can develop with practice or training. (p. 8)

asset—something of value that you own. (p. 115)

attitude—your typical mood and activity levels. (p. 9)

bank account—a formal relationship between you and a bank, where the bank keeps your money for you until you need it. (p. 123)

bankruptcy—a situation in which a court rules that a person is not able to pay his or her bills. (p. 156)

basic training—the period during which an enlistee enters the service and learns basic military skills. (p. 33)

behavioral interview—an interview during which the interviewer asks you to give examples of situations in which you demonstrated particular behaviors or skills. (p. 316)

benchmark—a standard by which to judge your progress. (p. 283)

beneficiary—a person who will receive your life insurance benefits when you die. (p. 190)

benefit statement—a well-thought-out statement of your skills and abilities, with examples that illustrate them. (p. 286)

benefits—compensation you receive from your employer in addition to your salary. (p. 352)

blue-collar job—a job that often involves manual labor and for which people may need to wear a uniform or protective clothing. (p. 94)

board—the cost of food. (p. 170)

body language—the nonverbal messages that your facial expressions, physical stance, and gestures convey to a listener. (p. 313)

brand—the distinctive name identifying a product or manufacturer. (p. 136)

budget—a detailed summary of expected expenses and income for a given period. (p. 114)

burnout—the feeling of being worn out and unable to carry on usual activities. (p. 249)

cadet—an ROTC candidate. (p. 38)

capitalizing—adding interest payments to a loan balance. (p. 175)

career—something that defines a person's working life and provides opportunities for continuous advancement and learning. (p. 7)

career ladder—a series of jobs that, over time, will take you higher and higher in the organization. (p. 326)

career-path strategy—a plan for how you will make progress in your career. (p. 355)

career portfolio—a folder or notebook that contains information on you and your achievements over time. (p. 327)

cash advance—borrowed cash. (p. 156)

certificates of deposit—a bank certificate that pays higher rates of interest than savings accounts, on the condition that you agree not to withdraw your money for a certain amount of time. (p. 126)

check—a written order that directs a bank to pay money. (p. 124)

checkbook register—a form on which you keep track of the money you deposit or withdraw. (p. 124)

checking account—a bank account into which you deposit money and from which you can withdraw money by writing checks. (p. 124)

chronological résumé—a résumé that lists your jobs, education, and other relevant accomplishments in reverse chronological order. (p. 295)

civilian—a person who is not on active duty in the armed forces. (p. 25)

civilian equivalents—jobs that are the same or similar to those in civilian life. (p. 27)

claim—a demand for payment in accordance with an insurance policy. (p. 181)

collaboration—working with others in a team or group. (p. 343)

collateral—possessions such as a home, car, or savings that a borrower pledges in return for a loan. (p. 157)

commissioned officers—personnel who enter the armed forces with a four-year college degree or better, and who compete to enter and earn a commission from the president after confirmation by Congress. (p. 35)

comparison shopping—comparing the prices and quality of different items to see which one is a better deal. (p. 135)

compassion—a feeling for and understanding of another person's situation. (p. 331)

competitiveness—striving against others to achieve an objective. (p. 333)

complementary—aspects that support and round each other out. (p. 65)

conceptual—focused on concepts and ideas rather than things. (p. 66)

continuing and adult education—evening or weekend courses designed for working adults who are not able to enroll in college full-time. (p. 95)

cooperative education (co-op) programs—programs that allow you to work part-time in a career field you are interested in, while taking job-related courses at school. (p. 83)

copayment—money you must pay for a doctor's visit or other health service. (p. 188)

core requirements—basic demands. (p. 260)

cosigner—a person with a good credit rating who signs a loan note along with a borrower. (p. 162)

courtesy—consideration and cooperation in dealing with others. (p. 330)

cover letter—a letter that gives prospective employers further information about you that is not in your résumé (p. 306)

credit—an offer to loan you money (p. 126); a point that the college assigns to a certain course. (p. 244)

credit bureau—a public or private agency that gathers credit information on people. (p. 162)

credit cards—cards that represent a promise that the bank will give you credit to buy things. (p. 126)

credit history—your record of paying your bills. (p. 159)

credit rating—an assessment of how trustworthy you are in paying your bills. (p. 153)

credit union—a not-for-profit cooperative that is owned by its members. (p. 127)

creditor—a bank or a financing company that loans money. (p. 152)

curriculum—a course of study. (p. 203)

debit card—a card for which, when you use it, the bank automatically withdraws the amount of your request from your checking account. (p. 125)

deductible—the amount that you must pay before the insurance company pays anything. (p. 181)

default—to fail to pay your bill on time. (p. 161)

defensiveness—an effort to justify oneself. (p. 340)

delinquent—overdue. (p. 164)

dependability—the quality of being dependable or reliable. (p. 331)

dependent—a member of your immediate family who relies on you for financial support. (p. 186)

distortion—a distraction that interferes with communication. (p. 339)

distractions—things that draw your attention or interest away from what you are doing. (p. 268)

down payment—a partial payment that you make when purchasing something. (p. 147)

drop/add—an option by which student can attend a course for a week or two before deciding whether to take it or to drop it and substitute another course in its place. (p. 245)

early-admissions policy—a policy under which colleges inform you by December whether they have accepted you. (p. 209)

education—broad-based learning. (p. 51)

elective—a course you choose, or elect, to take. (p. 255)

electronic résumé—one prepared specifically for online use. (p. 299)

engineers—people who design products, systems, and structures. (p. 46)

enlisted personnel—generally young men and women who enter the armed forces with a high school diploma or equivalent. (p. 28)

entrance examination—standardized test that helps admissions officers determine who is qualified to attend their schools. (p. 211)

entry-level—beginning. (p. 289)

equity—ownership value. (p. 147); justice or fairness. (p. 334)

expense—money you spend. (p. 119)

extraverted (E)—preferring to direct your energy to people, things, activities, or the "outer world." (p. 65)

faculty—teachers. (p. 202)

Federal Aviation Administration (FAA)—the government agency responsible for the safety of civil aviation. (p. 50)

feeling (F)—preferring make decisions on the basis of values and your own personal beliefs. (p. 67)

filtering—hearing only what you want to hear. (p. 339)

finance charge—another term for interest and the annual percentage rate (APR). (p. 152)

financial plan—a document that outlines your financial goals and how you plan to reach them. (p. 113)

financing—obtaining or providing money for a specific purpose. (p. 115)

formal communication—a structured, stable method of communication among people. (p. 341)

fraternity—college social club for men. (p. 239)

functional résumé—one that arranges your information under skill headings, without focusing on dates. (p. 295)

grace period—the time during which you can pay a credit card bill on new purchases without being charged interest. (p. 160)

graduate school—formal education after you graduate from college, which will give you in-depth knowledge about your specific career area. (p. 96)

grants—types of student financial aid that you do not have to repay. (p. 172)

grapevine—the informal channel of communication among people in an organization. (p. 341)

gross income—income before taxes and other deductions. (p. 143)

group interview—an interview in which several people will ask you questions. (p. 315)

halo effect—a reviewer's or boss's tendency to assume that if an employee is above (or below) average in one area of performance, he or she is above (or below) average is all areas. (p. 352)

hazing—persecution and harassment with meaningless, difficult, or humiliating tasks. (p. 239)

hierarchy—established levels of authority. (p. 69)

higher education—study at a college or university—perhaps starting at a community or junior college. (p. 93)

honesty—the practice of being truthful, trustworthy, and sincere; refraining from lying, cheating, or stealing. (p. 332)

horizontal communication—communication among people at the same level in an organization, no matter which department they are in. (p. 341)

human resources department—the department that handles hiring, benefits, and other issues concerning employees. (p. 309)

hybrid résumé—a combination of the chronological and functional formats. (p. 295)

in-state resident—a resident of the state in which a college is located. (p. 171)

income—money that you receive regularly. (p. 119)

indemnity plan—a health-insurance plan that enables you to go to any health provider to receive care. (p. 187)

industry sector—the general field in which a business is working. (p. 310)

informal communication—social interactions among people who work together or are associated with one another in some other way. (p. 341)

informational interview—a conversation with someone working in the field you are interested in. (p. 288)

installment—a monthly payment. (p. 156)

instinctive—behavior that is unconscious and happens naturally. (p. 65)

insurance—an agreement between two parties under which one party—usually an insurance company—guarantees the other that if an asset is lost or destroyed, the insurance company will pay for it. (p. 116)

insurance agent—a person who sells insurance. (p. 185)

integrity—commitment to a code of values or beliefs that results in a unified, positive attitude and approach to life. (p. 332)

interest—a charge on borrowed money. (p. 115)

interests—a person's likes, dislikes, hopes, or wishes. (p. 9)

international organization—a college group composed of people from a certain nation or part of the world or of students who have a special interest in such a place. (p. 240)

internship—a low-paying or volunteer job in a field that interests you. (p. 84)

intramural athletics—sports competition between teams within a college. (p. 239)

introverted (I)—preferring to direct your energy to ideas, information, explanations, and imagination, or the "inner world." (p. 65)

intuition (N)—the personality preference for dealing with ideas, looking into the unknown, generating possibilities, or anticipating what isn't obvious (p. 66)

inventory—list of your property and its value (p. 185); an evaluation or survey. (p. 279)

investment—something you own that you expect to increase in value over time. (p. 116)

itinerary—travel schedule. (p. 231)

job—work that a person does to make a living. (p. 7)

job objective—a brief statement that describes the type of position you are seeking. (p. 302)

judgment (J)—the personality preference for your life to be planned, stable, and organized. (p. 67)

junior and community colleges—colleges offering courses and programs that lead to associate degrees and training certificates. (p. 95)

keyword—a specific word that a computer looks for when searching a database. (p. 305)

landlord—an apartment owner. (p. 142)

lease—an agreement to pay rent and fulfill other obligations for a certain length of time. (p. 144)

liability—legal responsibility. (p. 180)

liquidity—access to funds to cover a short-term cash need. (p. 115)

loyalty—being faithful to someone or something. (p. 333)

major—subject area on which you want to focus in college. (p. 103)

managed-care plan—a health-care plan that requires that you consult a primary physician when you need medical care. (p. 187)

maturity date—the date by which you must repay money you borrowed. (p. 152)

mentor—a life coach who guides, advises, and advocates for you in your individual life path. (p. 85)

merit promotion—a promotion based on your performance in your current job. (p. 353)

minimum payment—the smallest amount due to keep your credit in good standing. (p. 156)

minor—a secondary focus for your academic career. (p. 254)

multitasking—doing more than one thing at a time. (p. 267)

mutual trust—confidence that develops when people and organizations know that they can rely on each other to do the right thing. (p. 333)

National Aeronautics and Space Administration (NASA)—the government agency responsible for the US space program and general aerospace research. (p. 48)

need—something that you must have in order survive or to be happy. (p. 280)

need based—a type of aid given to students who have a serious financial need. (p. 174)

net income—income after taxes and other deductions. (p. 146)

network—the group of people you meet and contact . (p. 289)

networking—meeting people and making contacts. (p. 22)

noncommissioned officer (NCO)—a person who has developed advanced technical skills and is qualified to serve in some leadership positions. (p. 28)

occupation—activity that defines a person's working life and provides opportunities for continuous advancement and learning. (p. 7)

off-campus housing—apartments, houses, or rooms in someone else's home, located off the college campus. (p. 243)

on-campus housing—dormitories or residence halls owned and operated by the college. (p. 243)

open-admissions policy—a policy that permits enrollment of a student who has a high school diploma or equivalent, or in some cases, regardless of academic qualifications. (p. 95)

organizational values—the combined personal values of the people in an organization and the values of the organization itself. (p. 334)

out-of-state students—students who do not live in the state in which the college is located. (p. 171)

peer—coworker at your level. (p. 315)

perception (P)—the personality preference of preferring to be flexible and to take the outside world as it comes. (p. 67)

performance appraisal—a systematic review of how well an individual employee has performed during a specified period. (p. 350)

periodic rate—monthly rate. (p. 159)

perseverance—the quality of sticking to something until you achieve it. (p. 331)

personal finance—managing your money and other things of financial value. (p. 113)

personality preferences—the ways you like to think and behave. (p. 64)

phishing—creating a replica of a Web page in order to trick a user into submitting personal, financial, or password data online. (p. 192)

placement test—an exam designed to help schools place, or assign, students in classes where they'll learn most. (p. 213)

plagiarism—passing off someone else's work as your own. (p. 244)

policy—in insurance, a contract that promises to pay for any losses. (p. 180)

political organization—group of people with similar political interests. (p. 238)

premium—the fee for insurance protection. (p. 180)

prerequisites—courses required to enter a certain field of study. (p. 260)

principal—the money you borrow. (p. 152)

priority—something that you give attention to before you think about other things. (p. 264)

private university—an institution of higher learning that is operated by a private organization. (p. 171)

procrastination—the tendency to delay, or to put things off. (p. 265)

produce—fresh fruits and vegetables. (p. 136)

product expiration date—the date after which the item will be stale or no longer be at its finest quality. (p. 136)

profession—activity that defines a person's working life and provides opportunities for continuous advancement and learning. (p. 7)

professional development—the activities necessary to have a successful career. (p. 324)

professional organization—a group that helps its members learn about careers in a particular field. (p. 238)

promotion—a new job at a higher level. (p. 352)

PSAT—standardized pre-SAT test that covers the same areas the SAT does. (p. 215)

public university—an institution of higher learning that is operated and funded by the state in which it is located. (p. 171)

rapport—a relationship. (p. 315)

real estate agent—a professional who helps people buy, sell, or rent homes and apartments. (p. 143)

recreational organization—a group focused on a specific leisure activity. (p. 239)

reference—a person whom future employers can contact to ask about what kind of worker you are. (p. 85)

religious organization—a group that unites students with a similar religious faith or interest. (p. 238)

residential adviser—an adult or older student who lives in your dormitory and helps you solve living problems. (p. 243)

résumé—a brief summary of your work experience and qualifications. (p. 294)

retirement—the period of life during which you no longer work at a job. (p. 116)

risk—uncertainty as to the outcome of an investment. (p. 118)

risk taking—taking chances. (p. 334)

rolling-admissions policy—the policy under which colleges make acceptance decisions as students apply. (p. 209)

room—the cost of a place to live. (p. 170)

rush—a drive each semester by sororities or fraternities to recruit new members. (p. 239)

SAT—a widely used entrance exam that measures the academic skills and knowledge students most need for success in college. (p. 212)

savings account—an account for depositing money that you want to keep. (p. 123)

scholarships—types of student financial aid that you do not have to repay. (p. 172)

scientists—knowledge seekers. (p. 46)

security deposit—a payment to make sure you meet your obligations as a tenant. (p. 144)

security investigation—a background check that involves providing information on any past arrests or questioning by law enforcement officers. (p. 29)

semantics—the meaning of a word. (p. 340)

senior NCO—a member of the armed forces who is highly skilled and serves among the top enlisted leaders and managers. (p. 28)

sensing (S)—the personality preference for dealing with facts, certainty, and clarity. (p. 66)

service organization—a group that performs social or educational services for the community. (p. 240)

skill—the ability to do something that you have acquired through training or experience. (p. 282)

social organization—a group that focuses on bringing people together for social activities. (p. 239)

sorority—a college social club for women. (p. 239)

spending limits—the amount above which you should not spend if you are to meet your financial goals. (p. 120)

standardized test—one that is given and scored under the same conditions for all students. (p. 211)

stress—a mentally or an emotionally upsetting condition that occurs in response to outside influences. (p. 249)

stress interview—an interview in which the employer deliberately creates an environment that puts you under pressure so that the employer can see how you behave in tense situations. (p. 316)

structured interview—a set of questions that the employer asks all candidates. (p. 316)

Student Educational Employment Program—a program offering on-the-job experience that could lead to a full-time career with the government after you finish your schooling. (p. 19)

subjective meaning—personal significance. (p. 336)

subsidized—a loan for which the government pays the interest while you're in school. (p. 175)

summary of qualifications—a brief overview of your skills, experience, and knowledge. (p. 302)

targeted résumé—one that includes the title of the actual job or career you are seeking. (p. 299)

teaching assistant—a graduate student who is specializing in the course topic. (p. 232)

teamwork—working together to identify and solve group-related problems and to achieve goals. (p. 334)

technical training program—a learning experience that will give you the knowledge and skills you need to start a technically oriented career. (p. 83)

technically oriented career path—a career path focused on mastering technical skills that do not require a college or university education. (p. 79)

technician—someone who translates the technical plans created by engineers into useful products and services. (p. 47)

technologist—a person who does work similar to that of a technician, but at a higher level. Technologists are graduates of four-year engineering-technology programs. (p. 47)

tenant—a person who rents an apartment. (p. 142)

term life insurance—a policy that you buy for a certain period. (p. 190)

term of enlistment—the number of years you agree to remain in the military before having the option to leave or sign up for another term. (p. 32)

thinking (T)—a personality type that prefers to make decisions on the basis of logic, using an analytic and detached approach. (p. 67)

time management—keeping control of your time. (p. 263)

training—learning that prepares you to perform a function that requires a specific set of skills. (p. 51)

transcript—an official record of your grades. (p. 225)

tuition—the fee for instruction. (p. 170)

undergraduate education—basic college education. (p. 103)

unit price—cost per serving. (p. 136)

universal life insurance—insurance for a specific period that accumulates savings for policyholders during this period. (p. 190)

unsecured loan—a loan that does not require collateral. (p. 161)

unstructured interview—an informal session during which the interviewer will expect you to do most of the talking. (p. 316)

unsubsidized—a type of loan for which you pay all the interest. (p. 175)

utilities—electricity, heat, gas, and water. (p. 145)

values—standards that give your life meaning; the inner goals you strive for in an effort to be a better person. (p. 9)

variable rate—an interest rate that changes over time. (p. 159)

vertical communication—communication between people at different levels within the same department. (p. 341)

visionary leadership—leadership exercised by people who have a clear sense of where they are guiding their organizations and who can persuade others to follow them. (p. 334)

vocational school—a school that gives courses to prepare students for a technically oriented career. (p. 83)

volunteer—an unpaid worker. (p. 84)

waiting list—a list of students who will be admitted to a college if others choose not to come. (p. 210)

want—a thing that you'd like to have, but that is not necessary. (p. 280)

want ads—advertisements for job openings and items for sale. (p. 278)

white-collar job—a job that does not involve manual labor and for which people generally do not have to wear uniforms or protective clothing. (p. 94)

whole life insurance—insurance that provides coverage for your entire lifetime. (p. 190)

work ethics—the effects of your decisions and actions on all people connected with your organization—employees, customers, owners, suppliers, and competitors. (p. 332)

Index

A

B

C

F

G

H

I

J

K

L

M

N

O

P

R

S

T

U

V

W

Y